Sports Illustrated

COLLEGE SPORTS ALMANAC

Soccer

Basketball

Hockey

Wrestling

Swimming

Lacrosse

Golf

Tennis

Track and Field

Baseball

Sports Illustrated

COLLEGE

SPORTS

ALMANAC

TIME INC. HOME ENTERTAINMENT
President ....Rob Gursha
Vice President, Branded Businesses ....David Arfine
Vice President, New Product Development ....Richard Fraiman
Executive Director, Marketing Services ....Carol Pittard
Director, Retail & Special Sales..Tom Mifsud
Director of Finance..Tricia Griffin
Brand Manager ....Niki Whelan
Prepress Manager ....Emily Rabin
Associate Book Production Manager ....Suzanne Janso
Associate Product Manager...Victoria Alfonso

Special thanks: Bozena Bannett, Robert Dente, Gina Di Meglio, Anne-Michelle Gallero, Peter
Harper, Robert Marasco, Natalie McCrea, Jonathan Polsky, Mary Jane Rigoroso, Steven Sandonato

SPORTS ILLUSTRATED Executive Editor ....Rob Fleder
SPORTS ILLUSTRATED Director, New Product Development.........................Bruce Kaufman

SPORTS ILLUSTRATED COLLEGE SPORTS ALMANAC was prepared by
BISHOP BOOKS, NEW YORK, NY
Editorial Director ....Morin Bishop
Project editor ....John Bolster
Managing editor ....Ward Calhoun
Designer...Barbara Chilenskas

Published by
Sports Illustrated Books

Time Inc.
1271 Avenue of the Americas
New York, New York 10020

ISBN: 1-931933-62-6

Sports Illustrated Books is a trademark of Time Inc.

Cover photography credits: Icon SMI (all)
Title Page: David Bergman

We welcome your comments and suggestions about Sports Illustrated Books. Please write to us at:
Sports Illustrated Books
Attention: Book Editors
PO Box 11016
Des Moines, IA 50336-1016

If you would like to order any of our hardcover Collector's Edition books,
please call us at 1-800-327-6388.
(Monday through Friday, 7:00 a.m.- 8:00 p.m. or Saturday, 7:00 a.m.- 6:00 p.m. Central Time).

CONTENTS

GREAT
Expectations

Ohio State fans hope to see their team become college football's first repeat national champion since 1995

EVERY SPRING in Columbus, Ohio, a young man's fancy lightly turns to ... college football. And in the spring of 2003, it wasn't only the young men: Ohio State's annual Scarlet and Gray game in late April attracted 57,200 fans of every age and gender. The spring game!

Yes, it's safe to say that following Ohio State's Fiesta Bowl victory in January 2003, which brought the school its first national championship since 1967, anticipation—and expectations—are running high in Columbus, where the Buckeyes will vie for national supremacy against a slew of talented contenders in 2003.

THE FAVORITES
The excitement in Columbus is by no means unwarranted: Every single offensive starter from **Ohio State**'s undefeated 2002 team will be back in 2003, including senior quarterback Craig Krenzel, and running back Maurice Clarett, who begins 2003 as a front-runner for the Heisman Trophy after rushing for 1,237 yards and 16 touchdowns in his freshman season. Krenzel will again throw to receivers Michael Jenkins and Chris Gamble, who may battle for playing time with Santonio Holmes, a redshirt freshman blessed with breakaway speed. Holmes broke off touchdown receptions of 92 and 68 yards in OSU's first spring scrimmage, finishing the game with five catches for 213 yards.

The Buckeyes lost linebacker Matt Wilhelm and defensive back Mike Doss—All-Americas both—to graduation, but coach Jim Tressel has solid understudies at the ready, particularly in sophomore linebackers A.J. Hawk and Mike D'Andrea, and with their

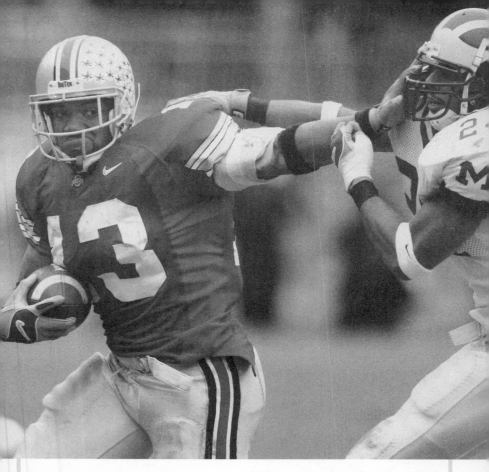

If Clarett can top his dazzling freshman season, when he rushed for 1,237 yards and scored 16 touchdowns, the Heisman Trophy may be within reach at season's end.

more experienced offense, the Buckeyes may not have to rely on their defense as much as they did in 2002. Indeed, the biggest obstacle Ohio State faces could be the pressure of expectations in Columbus.

Last year, Ohio State reinforced the adage that defense wins championships, and **Oklahoma** hopes to buttress that maxim yet again in 2003. The Sooners D,

which was touted on the cover of SI's college football preview issue last season, may be even better this year. Its linebacker corps of Pasha Jackson, Teddy Lehman and Lance Mitchell is arguably the best in the nation, and junior college transfer Donte Nicholson should make a seamless transition to the Sooner defensive backfield. Coach Bob Stoops has no reservations about baptizing Nicholson in the Big 12 fires: "[He's] awfully impressive. He's probably our most natural safety that we've ever coached. He's got great ability, great size and speed, but also has great

Texas overhauled its offense with the departure of Chris Simms, but left one crucial element unchanged: The speedy, 6′5″, 210-pound Williams will remain the No. I option on passing plays.

understanding and picked everything up really quite easily."

On the other side of the ball, though, the Sooners are not world-beaters. For the third straight year, they will kick off the season without a clear-cut starter at quarterback. Senior Jason White, who has battled knee injuries each of the past two years, and sophomore Brent Rawls, whose 2002 season ended when he fell out of the back of a pickup truck and suffered a concussion, will vie for the position.

The quarterback position at **Texas** will undergo a radical transformation in 2003, from the pro-set style of Chris Simms, now with the Tampa Bay Buc-caneers, to a more wide-open look with mobile new QB Chance Mock. Mock's primary target will be receiver Roy Williams, who could emerge as a Heisman contender. Linebacker Der-rick Johnson and cornerback Nathan Vasher will lead the Texas defense. As usual, the Longhorns will be loaded with talent; whether or not they can hook a national title depends on the performance of players like Williams, oft-injured running back Cedric Benson, and of course, Chance.

Perennial powerhouse **Miami** should land in the Top 5 again in 2003. After spring practice, it looked as though the unenviable task of following former quarterback Ken Dorsey (38–2 as a starter) would fall to Florida transfer Brock Berlin, a junior, though senior Derrick Crudup could challenge for the job as well. But the 2003 Hurricanes will probably bank on their defense, anchored by fearsome linebackers Jonathan Vilma, D.J. Williams and Roger McIntosh.

DARKHORSES

North Carolina State has a Heisman candidate (Philip Rivers) at quarter-back, and a 6′7″ true freshman (Mario Williams) at defensive end. The Wolf-pack's sophomore running back, T.A. McClendon, ranks with the nation's elite, and it has a corps of speedy, athletic receivers in Jerricho Cotchery, Sterling Hicks and Tramain Hall. So what prevents North Carolina State from being cast as a favorite? Well, the Wolfpack lost six of its front seven starters on defense, and though the team is studded with promising replacements, they are just that—promising, not proven.

They began last season at 8–0, and they have a quarterback with the surname Vick, so it seems odd to discuss the **Virginia Tech** Hokies as a darkhorse. On the other hand, that 8–0 start degenerated into a 9–4 finish, and that Vick's first name is Marcus, not Michael. He is Michael's younger brother, but he's a redshirt freshman who will probably not begin the season as the starter (that job should fall to Bryan Randall). But worry not for coach Frank Beamer—his defense returns nine starters, including fleet-footed cornerback DeAngelo Hall, who will also play wide receiver in 2003.

North Carolina State is coming off its best season in years, and with Heisman hopeful Rivers returning to lead the offense, the Wolfpack could be on the prowl for a national title in January.

Rounding out SI's spring Top 10 are **Auburn**, which will start two NFL-caliber linebackers, Dontarrious Thomas and Karlos Dansby; **Kansas State**, whose offense should sparkle with versatile quarterback Ell Roberson and running back Darren Sproles, a potential Heisman candidate; **Michigan**, which will rely on sturdy running back Chris Perry and cornerback Marlin Jackson; and **Washington**, whose quarterback, Cody Pickett, and receiver Reggie Williams—both of whom are Heisman candidates—hope to return the Huskies to the national elite.

Not to be overlooked as potential darkhorses are **Georgia**, which must

It was a difficult spring for Bowden and Florida State, which finished 9–5 last season. Four Seminoles players faced legal troubles during the offseason.

replace five starters from the offensive line that helped the team to a 13–1 record and a third-place finish in the national polls last season, and **Pittsburgh**, whose quarterback, Rod Rutherford is being touted for the Heisman.

SIDELINES

For most of the 1990s, the state of Florida could lay claim to the best college football in the nation. Florida, Florida State and Miami routinely finished in the Top 25 during the decade, and in 1991, '92 and '94, all three teams cracked the Top 10. Miami won the national title in 1989 and '91, Florida won it in 1996, and Florida State in '93 and '99. But with the dawn of the 21st century, the sun seems to have set on the Florida football empire. True, Miami has rebounded from NCAA sanctions in the late '90s to rebuild itself into a national power,

winning the title in 2001, but its Sunshine State rivals appear to be on the decline.

Both Florida and Florida State lost five games in 2002, disastrous seasons by their standards, but the sting of losses to the likes of Louisville were the least of FSU coach Bobby Bowden's worries this offseason. No fewer than four FSU players have had recent brushes with the law. Defensive lineman Travis Johnson was charged with sexual assault; Darnell Dockett allegedly received illegal discounts on merchandise; and former receiver Talman Gardner was busted for marijuana possession and concealing a loaded handgun. Then there was the saga of starting quarterback Adrian McPherson, which dwarfed FSU's other legal troubles on the publicity scale. McPherson faced felony theft charges, a misdemeanor gambling charge, and the accusation that he bet on games in which he played. He was dismissed from the team in November 2002. Bowden, along with FSU athletic director Dave Hart and quarterbacks coach Daryl Dickey, has been called to testify at McPherson's trial. Florida State still has elite talent in its ranks, but one wonders how it will handle the distractions as the 2003 season gets under way. One might also wonder, considering the circumstances, how coach Bowden has managed to hold on to his job.

As for Florida, its troubles began, coincidentally or not, when coach Steve Spurrier left for the NFL. Under new coach Ron Zook, the team stumbled to an 8–5 record in 2002, failing to make the final AP Top 25. Zook has recruited two extremely talented classes, but in addition to returning only three starters on defense for the 2003 season, his program has had off-field troubles. In April, Steve Harris and Channing Crowder were arrested on felony aggravated battery charges after they allegedly kicked and punched a man until he was unconscious outside a Gainesville nightspot; and in June, Zook suspended linemen Mo Mitchell and Jonathan Colon from the team for unspecified rules violations.

While its unlikely that these erstwhile powerhouses will be down for long, the Florida weather was just a little less sunny than usual last spring.

A redshirt freshman who will battle for the Hokies' starting quarterback job, Vick hopes to follow in the fleet footsteps of his famous older brother.

FINAL POLLS

ASSOCIATED PRESS

TEAM	RECORD	POINTS	HEAD COACH	SI PRESEASON RANK
1. Ohio St (71)	14–0	1775	Jim Tressel	12
2. Miami [FL]	12–1	1693	Larry Coker	2
3. Georgia	13–1	1598	Mark Richt	10
4. Southern Cal	11–2	1590	Pete Carroll	21
5. Oklahoma	12–2	1476	Bob Stoops	1
6. Texas	11–2	1363	Mack Brown	4
7. Kansas St	11–2	1356	Bill Snyder	32
8. Iowa	11–2	1334	Kirk Ferentz	40
9. Michigan	10–3	1182	Lloyd Carr	20
10. Washington St	10–3	1085	Mike Price	7
11. Alabama	10–3	988	Dennis Franchione	31
12. N Carolina St	11–3	943	Chuck Amato	26
13. Maryland	11–3	844	Ralph Friedgen	16
14. Auburn	9–4	821	Tommy Tuberville	23
15. Boise St	12–1	692	Dan Hawkins	46
16. Penn St	9–4	675	Joe Paterno	25
17. Notre Dame	10–3	657	Tyrone Willingham	39
18. Virginia Tech	10–4	544	Frank Beamer	15
19. Pittsburgh	9–4	520	Walt Harris	45
20. Colorado	9–5	307	Gary Barnett	6
21. Florida St	9–5	291	Bobby Bowden	5
22. Virginia	9–5	250	Al Groh	51
23. Texas Christian	10–2	231	Gary Patterson	75
24. Marshall	11–2	201	Bob Pruett	17
25. W Virginia	9–4	195	Rich Rodriguez	67

Note: As voted by a panel of sportswriters and broadcasters following bowl games.
(1st-place votes in parentheses).

USA TODAY/ESPN

TEAM	RECORD	POINTS	HEAD COACH	SI PRESEASON RANK
1. Ohio St (61)	14–0	1525	Jim Tressel	12
2. Miami [FL]	12–1	1451	Larry Coker	2
3. Georgia	13–1	1378	Mark Richt	10
4. Southern Cal	11–2	1362	Pete Carroll	21
5. Oklahoma	12–2	1244	Bob Stoops	1
6. Kansas St	11–2	1230	Bill Snyder	32
7. Texas	11–2	1140	Mack Brown	4
8. Iowa	11–2	1105	Kirk Ferentz	40
9. Michigan	10–3	1011	Lloyd Carr	20
10. Washington St	10–3	932	Mike Price	7
11. N Carolina St	11–3	876	Chuck Amato	26
12. Boise St	12–1	808	Dan Hawkins	46
13. Maryland	11–3	803	Ralph Friedgen	16
14. Virginia Tech	10–4	644	Frank Beamer	15
15. Penn St	9–4	619	Joe Paterno	25
16. Auburn	9–4	579	Tommy Tuberville	23
17. Notre Dame	10–3	525	Tyrone Willingham	39
18. Pittsburgh	9–4	486	Walt Harris	45
19. Marshall	11–2	333	Bob Pruett	17
20. W Virginia	9–4	297	Rich Rodriguez	67
21. Colorado	9–5	291	Gary Barnett	6
22. Texas Christian	10–2	274	Gary Patterson	75
23. Florida St	9–5	219	Bobby Bowden	5
24. Florida	8–5	145	Ron Zook	8
25. Virginia	9–5	141	Al Groh	51

Note: As voted by a panel of 61 Division I-A head coaches; 25 points for 1st, 24 for 2nd, etc. (1st-place votes in parentheses).

BOWLS

NCAA DIVISION I-A BOWL RESULTS

DATE	BOWL	RESULT	PAYOUT/TEAM ($)	ATTENDANCE
12-17-02	New Orleans	N Texas 24, Cincinnati 19	750,000	19,024
12-18-02	GMAC	Marshall 38, Louisville 15	750,000	40,646
12-23-02	Tangerine	Texas Tech 55, Clemson 15	750,000	21,689
12-25-02	Las Vegas	UCLA 27, New Mexico 13	800,000	30,324
12-25-02	Hawaii	Tulane 36, Hawaii 28	750,000	35,513
12-26-02	Motor City	Boston College 51, Toledo 25	780,000	51,872
12-26-02	Insight	Pittsburgh 38, Oregon St 13	750,000	40,533
12-27-02	Houston	Oklahoma St 33, Southern Miss 23	750,000	44,687
12-27-02	Independence`	Mississippi 27, Nebraska 23	1.2 million	46,096
12-27-02	Holiday	Kansas St 34, Arizona St 27	2 million	58,717
12-28-02	Alamo	Wisconsin 31, Colorado 28 (OT)	1.35 million	50,690
12-28-02	Contintental Tire	Virginia 48, W Virginia 22	750,000	73,535
12-30-02	Music City	Minnesota 29, Arkansas 14	750,000	39,183
12-30-02	Seattle	Wake Forest 38, Oregon 17	1 million	38,241
12-31-02	Humanitarian	Boise St 34, Iowa St 16	750,000	30,446
12-31-02	Sun	Purdue 34, Washington 24	1.35 million	48,917
12-31-02	Silicon Valley	Fresno St 30, Georgia Tech 21	750,000`	10,142
12-31-02	Liberty	Texas Christian 17, Colorado St 3	1.3 million	55,207
12-31-02	Peach	Maryland 30, Tennessee 3	2 million	68,330
12-31-02	San Francisco	Virginia Tech 20, Air Force 13	800,000	25,966
1-1-03	Cotton	Texas 35, Louisiana St 20	3 million	70,817
1-1-03	Outback	Michigan 38, Florida 30	2.55 million	65,101
1-1-03	Gator	N Carolina St 28, Notre Dame 6	1.6 million	73,491
1-1-03	Capital One	Auburn 13, Penn St 9	5.125 million	66,334
1-1-03	Rose	Oklahoma 34, Washington St 14	13.5 million	86,848
1-1-03	Sugar	Georgia 26, Florida St 13	13.5 million	74,269
1-2-03	Orange	Southern Cal 38, Iowa 17	13.5 million	75,971
1-3-03	Fiesta	Ohio St 31, Miami (FL) 24 [2 OT]	13.5 million	77,502

NCAA DIVISION I-AA CHAMPIONSHIP BOXSCORE

Western KY	7	10	7	10	—34
McNeese St	0	6	8	0	—14

FIRST QUARTER
WK: Johnson 16 pass from Michael (Martinez kick), 9:36

SECOND QUARTER
WK: Frazier 55 run (Martinez kick), 14:51
M: FG Marino 30, 7:32.
WK: FG Martinez 40, 4:55.
M: FG Marino 24, :07.

THIRD QUARTER
WK: Frazier 14 run (Martinez kick), 11:03.
M: Lawton 15 pass from Pendarvis (Hamilton pass for two-pt conversion), 3:49.

FOURTH QUARTER
WK: Michael 2 run (Martinez kick), 13:49.
WK: FG Martinez 23, 2:51.

	WESTERN KENTUCKY	MCNEESE ST
First downs	13	26
Rushed–yards	50–235	34–149
Passing yards	185	268
Sacked–yards lost	1–8	3–18
Return yards	103	105
Passes	6-10-0	25-48-3
Punts	6–37.3	6–35.5
Fumbles-lost	1–1	2–0
Penalties-yards	7–38	6–35
Time of possession	30:18	29:42

Att: 12,360.

SMALL COLLEGE CHAMPIONSHIP SUMMARIES

NCAA DIVISION II

First round: Valdosta St 24, Catawba 7; Carson-Newman 40, Fayetteville St 27; UC-Davis 24, Central Washington 6; TX A&M-Kingsville 58, Nebraska Kearney 40; Grand Valley St 62, C.W. Post 13; Indiana (PA) 27, Saginaw Valley St 23; NW MO St 45, Minnesota Duluth 41; Northern CO 49, Central Missouri St 28.
Quarterfinals: Valdosta St 31, Carson-Newman 28; TX A&M-Kingsville 27, UC-Davis 20 [OT]; Grand Valley St 62, Indiana (PA) 21; Northern CO 23, NW MO St 12;
Semifinals: Valdosta St 21, TX A&M-Kingsville 12; Grand Valley St 44, Northern CO 7.

Championship: 12-14-02 Florence, AL

Valdosta St	3	3	7	11—24
Grand Valley St	14	3	7	7—31

NCAA DIVISION III

First round: Wheaton (IL) 42, Alma 14; Wittenberg 34, Hanover 33; Wabash 42, MacMurray 7; Brockport St 16, Springfield 0; John Carroll 21, Hobart 7; Muhlenberg 56, UMass-Dartmouth 6; Wartburg 45, Lake Forest 0; Coe 21, WI-La Crosse 18; St. John's (MN) 31, Redlands 24; King's (PA) 28, Salisbury 0; Washington and Jefferson 24, Christopher Newport 10; Trinity (TX) 48, Mary Hardin-Baylor 38.

SMALL COLLEGE CHAMPIONSHIP SUMMARIES

NCAA DIVISION III (CONT.)

Second Round: Mount Union 42, Wheaton 21; Wabash 25, Wittenberg 14; Brockport St 15, Rowan 12; John Carroll 21, Muhlenberg 10; Linfield 52, Wartburg 15; St. John's 45, Coe 14; Bridgewater (VA) 19, King's 17; Trinity 45, Washington and Jefferson 10.
Quarterfinals: Mount Union 45, Wabash 16; John Carroll 16, Brockport St 10 [OT]; St. John's 21, Linfield 14; Trinity 38, Bridgewater 32.
Semifinals: Mount Union 57, John Carroll 19; Trinity 41, St. John's 34.
Championship: 12-21-02 Salem, VA

Mount Union	7	21	7	13—48
Trinity	0	0	7	0—7

NAIA CHAMPIONSHIP

12-21-02 Hardin County, TN

Carrolll	7	14	0	7—28
Georgetown (KY)	7	0	0	0—7

AWARDS

HEISMAN MEMORIAL TROPHY

PLAYER/SCHOOL	CLASS	POS	1ST	2ND	3RD	TOTAL
Carson Palmer, Southern Cal	Sr	QB	242	224	154	1328
Brad Banks, Iowa	Sr	QB	199	173	152	1095
Larry Johnson, Penn St	Sr	RB	108	130	142	726
Willis McGahee, Miami (FL)	So	RB	101	118	121	660
Ken Dorsey, Miami (FL)	Sr	QB	122	89	99	643

Note: Former Heisman winners and the media vote, with ballots allowing for three names (three points for 1st, two for 2nd, one for 3rd).

OTHER AWARDS

Davey O'Brien Award (QB) ....Brad Banks, Iowa, QB
Doak Walker Award (RB)..Larry Johnson, Penn St, RB
Biletnikoff Award (WR) ....Charles Rogers, Michigan St WR
Vince Lombardi/Rotary Award (Lineman/Linebacker).....................................Terrell Suggs, Arizona St, DL
Outland Trophy (Interior Lineman) ....Rien Long, Washington St, DL
Butkus Award (Linebacker) ....E.J. Henderson, Maryland, LB
Jim Thorpe Award (Defensive Back) ....Terence Newman, Kansas St, DB

COACHES' AWARDS

Walter Camp Award...Kirk Ferentz, Iowa
Eddie Robinson Award (Div I-AA) ....Tommy Tate, McNeese St
Bobby Dodd Award ....Jim Tressel, Ohio St

AFCA COACHES OF THE YEAR

Division I-A..Jim Tressel, Ohio St
Division I-AA ....Jack Harbaugh, Western Kentucky
Division II...Brian Kelly, Grand Valley St
Division III..Larry Kehres, Mount Union

AWARDS (CONT.)

FOOTBALL WRITERS ASSOCIATION OF AMERICA ALL-AMERICA TEAM

OFFENSE

Carson Palmer	Southern Cal	Sr	Quarterback
Larry Johnson	Penn St	Sr	Running Back
Willis McGahee	Miami	So	Running Back
Charles Rogers	Michigan St	Jr	Wide Receiver
Reggie Williams	Washington	So	Wide Receiver
Dallas Clark	Iowa	Jr	Tight End
Shawn Andrews	Arkansas	So	Lineman
Derrick Dockery	Texas	Sr	Lineman
Jordan Gross	Utah	Sr	Lineman
Bruce Nelson	Iowa	Sr	Lineman
Brett Romberg	Miami	Sr	Lineman
Nate Kaeding	Iowa	Jr	Place Kicker
Derek Abney	Kentucky	Jr	Kick Returner

DEFENSE

Michael Haynes	Penn St	Sr	Lineman
Rien Long	Washington St	Jr	Lineman
David Pollack	Georgia	So	Lineman
Terrell Suggs	Arizona St	Jr	Lineman
E.J. Henderson	Maryland	Sr	Linebacker
Teddy Lehman	Oklahoma	Jr	Linebacker
Matt Wilhelm	Ohio St	Sr	Linebacker
Mike Doss	Ohio St	Sr	Defensive Back
Terence Newman	Kansas St	Sr	Defensive Back
Troy Polamalu	Southern Cal	Sr	Defensive Back
Shane Walton	Notre Dame	Sr	Defensive Back
Andy Groom	Ohio St	Sr	Punter

OFFENSIVE PLAYERS OF THE YEAR

Maxwell Award (Player)	Larry Johnson, Penn St, RB
Associated Press Player of the Year	Brad Banks, Iowa, QB
Walter Camp Player of the Year	Larry Johnson, Penn St, RB

2002 NCAA CONFERENCE STANDINGS

DIVISION I-A

ATLANTIC COAST CONFERENCE	CONFERENCE		FULL SEASON		
	W	L	W	L	PCT
Florida St	7	1	9	5	.643
Maryland	6	2	11	3	.786
Virginia	6	2	9	5	.643
N Carolina St	5	3	11	3	.786
Clemson	4	4	7	6	.538
Georgia Tech	4	4	7	6	.538
Wake Forest	3	5	7	6	.538
N Carolina	1	7	3	9	.250
Duke	0	8	2	10	.167

BIG EAST CONFERENCE	CONFERENCE		FULL SEASON		
	W	L	W	L	PCT
Miami (FL)	7	0	12	1	.923
W Virginia	6	1	9	4	.692
Pittsburgh	5	2	9	4	.692
Boston College	3	4	9	4	.692
Virginia Tech	3	4	10	4	.714
Syracuse	2	5	4	8	.333
Temple	2	5	4	8	.333
Rutgers	0	7	1	11	.083

2002 NCAA CONFERENCE STANDINGS (CONT.)

DIVISION I-A (CONT.)

BIG TEN CONFERENCE

	CONFERENCE		FULL SEASON		
	W	L	W	L	PCT
Iowa	8	0	11	2	.846
Ohio St	8	0	14	0	1.000
Michigan	6	2	10	3	.769
Penn St	5	3	9	4	.692
Illinois	4	4	5	7	.417
Purdue	4	4	7	6	.538
Minnesota	3	5	8	5	.615
Michigan St	2	6	4	8	.333
Wisconsin	2	6	8	6	.571
Indiana	1	7	3	9	.250
Northwestern	1	7	3	9	.250

BIG 12 CONFERENCE

	CONFERENCE		FULL SEASON		
NORTH	W	L	W	L	PCT
*Colorado	7	1	9	5	.643
Kansas St	6	2	11	2	.846
Iowa St	4	4	7	7	.500
Nebraska	3	5	7	7	.500
Missouri	2	6	5	7	.417
Kansas	0	8	2	10	.167
SOUTH					
*Oklahoma	6	2	12	2	.857
Texas	6	2	11	2	.846
Oklahoma St	5	3	8	5	.615
Texas Tech	5	3	9	5	.643
Texas A&M	3	5	6	6	.500
Baylor	1	7	3	9	.250

*Full season record includes Big 12 Championship Game in which Oklahoma defeated Colorado 29–7 on Dec. 7.

CONFERENCE USA

	CONFERENCE		FULL SEASON		
	W	L	W	L	PCT
Cincinnati	6	2	7	7	.500
Texas Christian	6	2	10	2	.833
Louisville	5	3	7	6	.538
Southern Mississippi	5	3	7	6	.538
E Carolina	4	4	4	8	.333
Tulane	4	4	8	5	.615
Alabama-Birmingham	4	4	5	7	.417
Houston	3	5	5	7	.417
Memphis	2	6	3	9	.250
Army	1	7	1	11	.083

MID-AMERICAN ATHLETIC CONFERENCE

	CONFERENCE		FULL SEASON		
EAST	W	L	W	L	PCT
*Marshall	7	1	11	2	.846
Central Florida	6	2	7	5	.583
Miami (OH)	5	3	7	5	.583
Ohio University	4	4	4	8	.333
Akron	3	5	4	8	.333
Kent St	1	7	3	9	.250
Buffalo	0	8	1	11	.083
WEST					
*Toledo	7	1	9	5	.643
Northern Illinois	7	1	8	4	.667
Bowling Green	6	2	9	3	.750
Ball St	4	4	6	6	.500
Western Michigan	3	5	4	8	.333
Central Michigan	2	6	4	8	.333
Eastern Michigan	1	7	3	9	.250

*Full season record includes MAC Championship Game in which Marshall defeated Toledo 49–45, on Dec 7.

DIVISION I-A (CONT.)

MOUNTAIN WEST CONFERENCE

	CONFERENCE		FULL SEASON		
	W	L	W	L	PCT
Colorado St	6	1	10	4	.714
New Mexico	5	2	7	7	.500
Air Force	4	3	8	5	.615
San Diego St	4	3	4	9	.308
Nevada–Las Vegas	3	4	5	7	.417
Utah	3	4	5	6	.455
Brigham Young	2	5	5	7	.417
Wyoming	1	6	2	10	.167

PACIFIC 10 CONFERENCE

	CONFERENCE		FULL SEASON		
	W	L	W	L	PCT
Southern California	7	1	11	2	.846
Washington St	7	1	10	3	.769
Arizona St	5	3	8	6	.571
California	4	4	7	5	.583
Oregon St	4	4	8	5	.615
UCLA	4	4	8	5	.615
Washington	4	4	7	6	.538
Oregon	3	5	7	6	.538
Arizona	1	7	4	8	.333
Stanford	1	7	2	9	.182

SOUTHEASTERN CONFERENCE

	CONFERENCE		FULL SEASON		
EAST	W	L	W	L	PCT
*Georgia	7	1	13	1	.929
Florida	6	2	8	5	.615
Tennessee	5	3	8	5	.615
Kentucky	3	5	7	5	.583
S Carolina	3	5	5	7	.417
Vanderbilt	0	8	2	10	.167
WEST					
*Alabama	6	2	10	3	.769
Arkansas	5	3	9	5	.643
Auburn	5	3	9	4	.692
Louisiana St	5	3	8	5	.615
Mississippi	3	5	7	6	.538
Mississippi St	0	8	3	9	.250

*Full season record includes SEC Championship Game in which Georgia defeated Arkansas 30–3, on Dec. 7.

SUN BELT CONFERENCE

	CONFERENCE		FULL SEASON		
	W	L	W	L	PCT
N Texas	6	0	8	5	.615
New Mexico St	5	1	7	5	.583
Arkansas St	3	3	6	7	.462
Middle Tennessee St	2	4	4	8	.333
Louisiana-Lafayette	2	4	3	9	.250
Louisiana-Monroe	2	4	3	9	.250
Idaho	1	5	2	10	.167

2002 NCAA CONFERENCE STANDINGS (CONT.)

DIVISION I-A (CONT.)

WESTERN ATHLETIC CONFERENCE

EAST	CONFERENCE		FULL SEASON		
	W	L	W	L	PCT
Boise St	8	0	12	1	.923
Hawaii	7	1	10	4	.714
Fresno St	6	2	9	5	.643
Nevada	4	4	5	7	.417
San Jose St	4	4	6	7	.462
Louisiana Tech	3	5	4	8	.333
Rice	3	5	4	7	.364
Southern Methodist	3	5	3	9	.250
Texas–El Paso	1	7	2	10	.167
Tulsa	1	7	1	11	.083

INDEPENDENTS

	FULL SEASON		
	W	L	PCT
S Florida	9	2	.818
Notre Dame	10	3	.769
Connecticut	6	6	.500
Utah St	4	7	.364
Troy St	4	8	.333
Navy	2	10	.167

DIVISION I-AA

ATLANTIC 10 CONFERENCE

	CONFERENCE		FULL SEASON		
	W	L	W	L	PCT
Maine	7	2	11	3	.786
Northeastern	7	2	10	3	.769
Villanova	6	3	11	4	.733
Massachusetts	6	3	8	4	.667
William & Mary	5	4	6	5	.545
Delaware	4	5	6	6	.500
Hofstra	4	5	6	6	.500
Richmond	4	5	4	7	.364
James Madison	3	6	5	7	.417
New Hampshire	2	7	3	8	.273
Rhode Island	1	8	3	9	.250

BIG SOUTH CONFERENCE

	CONFERENCE		FULL SEASON		
	W	L	W	L	PCT
Gardner-Webb	3	0	9	1	.900
Elon	2	1	4	7	.364
Liberty	1	2	2	9	.182
Charleston Southern	0	3	4	8	.333

BIG SKY CONFERENCE

	CONFERENCE		FULL SEASON		
	W	L	W	L	PCT
Idaho St	5	2	8	3	.727
Montana	5	2	11	3	.786
Montana St	5	2	7	6	.538
Eastern Washington	3	4	6	5	.545
Northern Arizona	3	4	6	5	.545
Portland St	3	4	6	5	.545
Sacramento St	3	4	5	7	.417
Weber St	1	6	3	8	.273

2002 NCAA CONFERENCE STANDINGS (CONT.)

DIVISION I-AA (CONT.)

GATEWAY COLLEGIATE ATHLETIC CONFERENCE

	CONFERENCE		FULL SEASON		
	W	L	W	L	PCT
Western Kentucky	7	1	12	3	.800
Western Illinois	6	2	11	2	.846
Illinois St	4	3	6	5	.545
Youngstown St	4	3	7	4	.636
Indiana St	3	4	5	7	.417
Northern Iowa	2	5	5	6	.455
Southern Illinois	2	5	4	8	.333
SW Missouri St	1	6	4	7	.364

IVY LEAGUE

	CONFERENCE		FULL SEASON		
	W	L	W	L	PCT
Pennsylvania	7	0	9	1	.900
Harvard	6	1	7	3	.700
Princeton	4	3	6	4	.600
Yale	4	3	6	4	.600
Cornell	3	4	4	6	.400
Brown	2	5	2	8	.200
Dartmouth	2	5	3	7	.300
Columbia	0	7	1	9	.100

METRO ATLANTIC ATHLETIC CONFERENCE

	CONFERENCE		FULL SEASON		
	W	L	W	L	PCT
Duquesne	8	0	11	1	.917
Fairfield	5	3	5	6	.455
Marist	5	3	7	4	.636
St. Peters	5	3	6	5	.545
Iona	4	4	5	6	.455
Siena	3	5	3	7	.300
Canisius	2	6	2	9	.182
La Salle	2	6	2	9	.182
St. John's	2	6	2	8	.200

MID-EASTERN ATHLETIC CONFERENCE

	CONFERENCE		FULL SEASON		
	W	L	W	L	PCT
Bethune-Cookman	7	1	11	2	.846
Florida A&M	5	3	7	5	.583
Hampton	5	3	7	5	.583
Morgan St	5	3	7	5	.583
Howard	4	4	6	5	.545
S Carolina St	4	4	7	5	.583
Delaware St	2	6	4	8	.333
N Carolina A&T	2	6	4	8	.333
Norfolk St	2	6	5	6	.455

NORTHEAST CONFERENCE

	CONFERENCE		FULL SEASON		
	W	L	W	L	PCT
Albany	6	1	8	4	.667
Sacred Heart	5	2	7	3	.700
Stony Brook	5	2	8	2	.800
Wagner	4	3	7	4	.636
Central Connecticut St	3	4	5	6	.455
Monmouth	2	5	2	8	.200
Robert Morris	2	5	3	7	.300
St. Francis (PA)	1	6	2	8	.200

2002 NCAA CONFERENCE STANDINGS (CONT.)

DIVISION I-AA (CONT.)

OHIO VALLEY CONFERENCE

	CONFERENCE		FULL SEASON		
	W	L	W	L	PCT
Eastern Illinois	5	1	8	4	.667
Murray St	5	1	7	5	.583
Eastern Kentucky	4	2	8	4	.667
SE Missouri St	4	2	8	4	.667
Tennessee Tech	2	4	5	7	.417
Tennessee St	1	5	2	10	.167
Tennessee-Martin	0	6	2	10	.167

PATRIOT LEAGUE

	CONFERENCE		FULL SEASON		
	W	L	W	L	PCT
Fordham	6	1	10	3	.769
Colgate	6	1	9	3	.750
Lafayette	5	2	7	5	.583
Lehigh	4	3	8	4	.667
Towson	3	4	6	5	.545
Georgetown	2	5	5	6	.455
Holy Cross	2	5	4	8	.333
Bucknell	0	7	2	9	.182

PIONEER CONFERENCE

	CONFERENCE		FULL SEASON		
NORTH	W	L	W	L	PCT
*Dayton	4	0	11	1	.917
San Diego	3	1	5	5	.500
Butler	2	2	4	6	.400
Drake	1	3	5	6	.455
Valparaiso	0	4	1	10	.091
SOUTH					
*Morehead St	3	0	9	3	.750
Davidson	2	1	7	3	.700
Austin Peay	1	2	7	5	.583
Jacksonville	0	3	3	7	.300

*Full season record includes Pioneer Conference Championship in which Dayton def.Morehead St 28–0, on Nov. 25.

SOUTHERN CONFERENCE

	CONFERENCE		FULL SEASON		
EAST PCT	W	L	W	L	
Georgia Southern	7	1	11	3	.786
Appalachian St	6	2	8	4	.667
Furman	6	2	8	4	.667
Wofford	6	2	9	3	.750
Virginia Military	3	5	6	6	.500
Western Carolina	3	5	5	6	.455
E Tennessee St	2	6	4	8	.333
Chattanooga	2	6	2	10	.167
The Citadel	1	7	3	9	.250

SOUTHLAND CONFERENCE

	CONFERENCE		FULL SEASON		
EAST PCT	W	L	W	L	
McNeese St	6	0	13	2	.867
Northwestern St	4	2	9	4	.692
Nicholls St	3	3	7	4	.636
Stephen F. Austin	3	3	6	5	.545
Jacksonville St	2	4	5	6	.455
Sam Houston St	2	4	4	7	.364
SW Texas St	1	5	4	7	.364

DIVISION I-AA (CONT.)

SOUTHWESTERN ATHLETIC CONFERENCE

EASTERN	CONFERENCE		FULL SEASON		
	W	L	W	L	PCT
*Alabama A&M	6	1	8	4	.667
Jackson St	5	2	7	4	.636
Alcorn St	3	4	6	5	.545
Mississippi Valley St	3	4	5	6	.455
Alabama St	2	5	6	6	.500
WESTERN					
*Grambling	6	1	11	2	.846
Southern	5	2	6	6	.500
Texas Southern	3	4	4	7	.364
Arkansas–Pine Bluff	2	5	3	8	.273
Prairie View A&M	0	7	1	10	.091

*Full season record includes SWAC Championship Game in which Grambling defeated Alabama A&M 31–19, on Dec. 14.

INDEPENDENTS

INDEPENDENTS	FULL SEASON		
	W	L	PCT
St. Mary's (CA)	6	6	.500
Florida International	5	6	.455
Samford	4	7	.364
Cal Poly	3	8	.273
Florida Atlantic	2	9	.182
Savannah St	1	9	.100
Southern Utah	1	10	.091
Morris Brown	1	11	.083

GO FIGURE

4 Career victories at the top of the alltime coaching list separating Penn State's Joe Paterno (336) and Florida State's Bobby Bowden (332) entering the 2003-04 season. With nine wins in 2002-03, Bowden passed Bear Bryant and moved into second place.

24 Consecutive seasons in which at least one of the three major Florida football schools, Miami, Florida State and Florida, has finished among the final AP Top 20. Before 2002, when only No. 2 Miami cracked the Top 20, at least two of those schools had finished in the Top 20 for 15 consecutive seasons.

30 Years since a Pac-10 school won a unanimous national championship. In 1991, Washington finished atop the coaches' poll, but the writers selected Miami No. 1. And in both '74 and '78, USC was the coaches' selection, but the writers selected Oklahoma and Alabama, respectively. USC was the unanimous selection in 1972. Since then, each major conference (except the Pac-10) has had at least one consensus national champ.

2,015 Rushing yards by Penn State senior running back Larry Johnson in 2002, a total that led the nation, and made Johnson the 10th player in Division I history to rush for over 2,000 yards in a season. Oklahoma State's Barry Sanders holds the record for most yards in a season with 2,628 yards in 1988.

96 Wins in the last 97 games played by Division III Mount Union (Ohio) College. The Purple Raiders won an NCAA-record 54 straight games from 1996 to 1999, when they lost the final game of their season to Rowan College. Entering the 2003-04 season, Mt. Union had won another 42 straight games.

2002 NCAA INDIVIDUAL LEADERS (DIVISION I-A)

SCORING

	CLASS	GP	TD	XP	FG	PTS	PTS/GAME
Brock Forsey, Boise St	Sr	12	29	0	0	174	14.50
Willis McGahee, Miami	So	12	27	0	0	162	13.50
Larry Johnson, Penn St	Sr	12	23	0	0	140	11.67
Josh Harris, Bowling Green	Jr	12	22	1	0	134	11.17
Chance Harridge, Air Force	Jr	12	22	0	0	132	11.00
Nick Calaycay, Boise St	Sr	9	0	59	11	92	10.22
Art Brown, E Carolina	Jr	10	17	0	0	102	10.20
Lee Suggs, Virginia Tech	Sr	13	22	0	0	132	10.15
Michael Turner, Northern Illinois	Jr	12	20	0	0	120	10.00
Maurice Clarett, Ohio St	Fr	10	16	0	0	96	9.60
Terry Caulley, Connecticut	Fr	10	16	0	0	96	9.60

FIELD GOALS

	CLASS	GP	FGA	FG	PCT	FG/GAME
Nick Browne, Texas Christian	Jr	11	28	22	.786	2.00
Mike Nugent, Ohio St	So	13	26	24	.923	1.85
Drew Dunning, Washington St	Jr	12	32	22	.688	1.83
Jeff Babcock, Colorado St	So	13	31	23	.742	1.77
John Anderson, Washington	Sr	12	30	21	.700	1.75
Billy Bennett, Georgia	Jr	13	28	22	.786	1.69
Sandro Sciortino, Boston College	Jr	12	29	20	.690	1.67
Nate Kaeding, Iowa	Jr	12	22	20	.909	1.67
Nick Novak, Maryland	So	13	25	21	.840	1.62
Mike Barth, Arizona St	Sr	13	30	21	.700	1.62

TOTAL OFFENSE

			RUSHING		PASSING			TOTAL OFFENSE	
	CLASS	GP	CAR	NET	ATT	YDS	YDS	YDS/PLAY	YDS/GAME
Rex Grossman, Florida	So	11	34	8	395	3896	3904	9.10	354.9
Byron Leftwich, Marshall	Jr	12	64	92	470	4132	4224	7.91	352.0
David Carr, Fresno St	Sr	13	88	97	476	4299	4396	7.79	338.2
Nick Rolovich, Hawaii	Sr	10	49	4	405	3361	3365	7.41	336.5
Luke McCown, Louisiana Tech	So	11	87	144	470	3337	3481	6.25	316.5
Kliff Kingsbury, Texas Tech	Jr	11	66	-48	528	3502	3454	5.81	314.0
Brandon Doman, BYU	Sr	13	142	456	408	3542	3998	7.27	307.5
Woodrow Dantzler, Clemson	Sr	11	206	1004	311	2360	3364	6.51	305.8
Zak Kustok, Northwestern	Sr	11	175	580	404	2692	3272	5.65	297.5
Ryan Dinwiddie, Boise St	So	11	71	97	322	3043	3140	7.99	285.5

RUSHING

	CLASS	GP	CAR	YDS	AVG	TD	YDS/GAME
Larry Johnson, Penn St	Sr	12	251	2015	8.03	20	167.92
Michael Turner, Northern Illinois	Jr	12	338	1915	5.67	19	159.58
Chris Brown, Colorado	Jr	12	275	1744	6.34	18	145.33
Willis McGahee, Miami	So	12	262	1686	6.44	27	140.50
Steven Jackson, Oregon St	So	12	300	1657	5.52	15	138.00
Marcus Merriweather, Ball St	Sr	12	332	1618	4.87	12	134.83
Quentin Griffin, Oklahoma	Sr	13	257	1740	6.77	14	133.85
Avon Cobourne, W Virginia	Sr	12	310	1593	5.14	15	132.75
Joffrey Reynolds, Houston	Sr	12	316	1545	4.89	11	128.75
Brock Forsey, Boise St	Sr	12	271	1533	5.66	23	127.75

2002 NCAA INDIVIDUAL LEADERS (DIVISION I-A) (CONT.)

PASSING EFFICIENCY

	CLASS	GP	ATT	COMP	PCT COMP	YDS	YDS/ATT	TD	INT	RATING PTS
Brad Banks, Iowa	Sr	12	258	155	60.08	2369	9.18	25	4	166.1
Byron Leftwich, Marshall	Sr	11	447	309	69.13	4019	8.99	26	9	159.8
Brian Jones, Toledo	Sr	13	382	270	70.68	3115	8.16	21	7	153.7
Ryan Schneider, Central Florida	Jr	12	430	265	61.63	3770	8.77	31	16	151.6
Jason Gesser, Washington St	Sr	12	368	219	59.51	3169	8.61	27	11	150.1
Carson Palmer, Southern Cal	Sr	12	458	288	62.88	3639	7.95	32	10	148.3
Craig Krenzel, Ohio St	Sr	13	228	141	61.84	1988	8.72	12	5	148.1
Ken Dorsey, Miami	Sr	12	350	194	55.43	3073	8.78	26	10	148.0
Matt Schaub, Virginia	Jr	13	396	272	68.69	2794	7.06	27	7	146.9
Scott McBrien, Maryland	Jr	13	265	151	56.98	2377	8.97	15	10	143.5

Note:Minimum 15 attempts per game.

RECEPTIONS PER GAME

	CLASS	GP	NO.	YDS	TD	R/ GAME
Nate Burleson, Nevada	Sr	12	138	1629	12	11.50
J.R. Tolver, San Diego St	Sr	13	128	1785	13	9.85
Kassim Osgood, San Diego St	Sr	13	108	1552	8	8.31
Rashaun Woods, Oklahoma St	Jr	12	98	1531	16	8.17
Taylor Stubblefield, Purdue	So	9	70	697	0	7.78

RECEIVING YARDS PER GAME

	CLASS	GP	NO.	YDS	TD	YDS/ GAME
J.R. Tolver, San Diego St	Sr	13	128	1785	13	137.31
Nate Burleson, Nevada	Sr	12	138	1629	12	135.75
Rashaun Woods, Oklahoma St	Jr	12	98	1531	16	127.58
Kassim Osgood, San Diego St	Sr	13	108	1552	8	119.38
Reggie Williams, Washington	So	12	89	1390	11	115.83

ALL-PURPOSE RUNNERS

	CLASS	GP	RUSH	REC	PR	KOR	YDS	AVG
Levron Williams, Indiana	Sr	11	1401	289	0	511	2201	200.09
Bernard Berrian, Fresno St	Jr	13	101	1270	552	668	2591	199.31
Mewelde Moore, Tulane	So	12	1421	756	0	82	2259	188.25
Luke Staley, Brigham Young	Jr	11	1582	334	0	102	2018	183.45
Emmett White, Utah St	Sr	11	1361	408	125	120	2014	183.09

INTERCEPTIONS

	CLASS	GP	NO.	INT /GAME
Edward Reed, Miami (FL)	Sr	11	9	.82
Lamont Thompson, WSU	Sr	11	8	.73
Derek Ross, Ohio St	Sr	11	7	.64
Kevin Thomas, UNLV	Sr	11	7	.64
Nathan Vasher, Texas	So	12	7	.58

PUNT RETURNS

	CLASS	NO.	YDS	TD	AVG
Roman Hollowell, Colorado	Sr	29	522	2	18.00
Luke Powell, Stanford	Jr	19	304	0	16.00
DeAndrew Rubin, S Florida	Jr	26	406	1	15.62
Ronnie Hamilton, Duke	Sr	20	311	1	15.55
Dexter Wynn, Colorado St	So	14	214	0	15.29

Note: Minimum 1.2 per game.

PUNTING

	CLASS	NO.	AVG
Travis Dorsch, Purdue	Sr	49	48.37
Dave Zastudil, Ohio	Sr	50	45.60
Andy Groom, Ohio St	Sr	44	45.02
Steve Mullins, Utah St	Jr	50	44.82
John Skaggs, Navy	So	48	44.81

Note: Minimum of 3.6 per game.

KICKOFF RETURNS

	CLASS	NO.	YDS	TD	AVG
Chris Massey, Oklahoma St	Jr	15	522	1	34.80
Chad Owens, Hawaii	Fr	24	807	3	33.63
Derrick Hamilton, Clemson	Fr	15	476	1	31.73
Tom Pace, Arizona St	Sr	17	537	1	31.59
Corey Parchman, Ball St	Sr	15	465	2	31.00

Note: Minimum of 1.2 per game.

2002 NCAA INDIVIDUAL LEADERS (CONT.)

DIVISION I-A TEAM SINGLE-GAME HIGHS

RUSHING AND PASSING

Rushing and passing yards	508, Andrew Walter, Arizona St, QB	Oct 19 (vs. Oregon)
Rushing and passing plays	78, Kliff Kingsbury, Texas Tech, QB	Oct 19 (vs. Missouri)
Rushing plays	48, Tanardo Sharps, Temple, RB	Nov 16 (vs. Rutgers)
Net rushing yards	377, Robbie Mixon, Central Mich., RB	Nov 2 (vs. Eastern Mich.)
Passes attempted	70, Kliff Kingsbury, Texas Tech, QB	Oct 19 (vs. Missouri)
Passes completed	49, Kliff Kingsbury, Texas Tech, QB	Oct 19 (vs. Missouri)
	49, Kliff Kingsbury, Texas Tech, QB	Oct 5 (vs. Texas A&M)
Passing yards	536, Andrew Walter, Arizona St, QB	Oct 19 (vs. Oregon)

RECEIVING AND RETURNS

Passes caught	19, Nate Burleson, Nevada, WR	Nov 9 (vs. Texas–El Paso)
Receiving yards	296, J.R. Tolver, San Diego St, WR	Sep 14 (vs. Arizona St)
Punt return yards	169, Cody Cardwell, SMU, WR	Nov 16 (vs. Texas–El Paso)
Kickoff return yards	243, Kwane Doster, Vanderbilt, TB	Sep 21 (vs. Mississippi)

Note: statistics do not include bowl games.

DIVISION I-AA
SCORING

	CLASS	GP	TD	XP	FG	PTS	PTS/GAME
T.J. Stallings, Morgan St	Sr	12	23	0	0	144	12.00
Dale Jennings, Butler	Sr	10	20	0	0	120	12.00
Chaz Williams, Georgia Southern	So	14	27	0	0	162	11.57
Gary Jones, Albany (NY)	Jr	12	23	0	0	138	11.50
J.R. Taylor, Eastern Illinois	Sr	12	18	0	0	112	9.33

FIELD GOALS

	CLASS	GP	FGA	FG	PCT	FG/GAME
M. Hoambrecker, Northern Iowa	Sr	11	28	25	.893	2.27
Justin Langan, Western Illinois	So	13	27	20	.741	1.54
Jesse Obert, Dayton	Sr	12	23	17	.739	1.42
Matt Fordyce, Fordham	Sr	13	26	18	.692	1.38
Chris Snyder, Montana	Jr	14	32	19	.594	1.36

TOTAL OFFENSE

	CLASS	GP	RUSHING		PASSING			TOTAL OFFENSE	
			CAR	NET	ATT	YDS	YDS	YDS/PLAY	YDS/GAME
Bruce Eugene, Grambling	So	13	137	535	543	4483	5018	7.38	386.0
Ira Vandever, Drake	Sr	11	127	415	361	3239	3654	7.49	332.2
Brian Mann, Dartmouth	Sr	10	118	393	423	2913	3306	6.11	330.6
Robert Kent, Jackson St	Jr	11	118	179	395	3386	3565	6.95	324.1
David Macchi, Valparaiso	Jr	11	132	223	390	3326	3549	6.80	322.6

RUSHING

	CLASS	GP	CAR	YDS	AVG	TD	YDS/GAME
Jay Bailey, Austin Peay	Sr	12	319	1687	5.29	18	140.58
J.R. Taylor, Eastern Illinois	Sr	12	254	1522	5.99	18	126.83
Gary Jones, Albany	Jr	12	231	1509	6.53	22	125.75
Verondre Barnes, Liberty	So	11	221	1304	5.90	5	118.55
P.J. Mays, Youngstown St	Sr	11	255	1284	5.04	11	116.73

PASSING EFFICIENCY

	CLASS	GP	ATT	COMP	PCT COMP	YDS	YDS/ATT	TD	INT	RATING PTS
Eric Rasmussen, San Diego	Jr	10	279	170	60.93	2473	8.86	25	1	164.2
Billy Napier, Furman	Sr	12	276	189	68.48	2475	8.97	16	8	157.1
Ira Vandever, Drake	Sr	11	361	205	56.79	3239	8.97	32	11	155.3
Russ Michna, Western Illinois	Jr	13	330	189	57.27	3037	9.20	23	5	154.5
Jack Tomco, SE Missouri St	Jr	12	372	242	65.05	3132	8.42	29	16	152.9

Note: Minimum 15 attempts per game.

DIVISION I-AA (CONT.)

RECEPTIONS PER GAME

	CLASS	GP	NO.	YDS	TD	R/G
Chas Gessner, Brown	Sr	10	114	1166	11	11.40
Carl Morris, Harvard	Sr	10	90	1288	8	9.00
Rob Milanese, Penn	Sr	10	85	1112	8	8.50
Aryvia Holmes, Samford	Sr	10	84	1158	9	8.40
Jay Barnard, Dartmouth	Jr	10	83	899	8	8.30

RECEIVING YARDS PER GAME

	CLASS	GP	NO.	YDS	TD	YDS/G
T. Douglas, Grambling	Jr	12	92	1704	18	142.0
Carl Morris, Harvard	Sr	10	90	1288	8	128.8
Willie Ponder, SE MO St.	Sr	12	87	1453	15	121.1
Chas Gessner, Brown	Sr	10	114	1166	11	116.6
Aryvia Holmes, Samford	Sr	10	84	1158	9	115.8

INTERCEPTIONS

	CLASS	GP	NO.	YDS	TD	INT/G
R. Mathis, B-Cookman	Sr	13	14	455	3	1.1
Mark Kasmer, Dayton	Sr	12	11	157	2	.92
Antwan Hill, Alabama St	So	12	10	199	1	.83
Corey Oaks, Robert Morris	Sr	10	7	130	2	.70
Chris Blackshear, C Conn St	So	10	7	204	1	.70
Chad King, Stony Brook	Jr	10	7	109	1	.70
Mike Devore, St John's (NY)	Jr	10	7	45	0	.70

PUNTING

	CLASS	NO.	AVG
Mark Gould, Northern Arizona	Jr	62	48.18
Mike Scifres, Western Illinois	Sr	53	48.02
Brent Barth, Virginia Military	Sr	64	47.38
Eddie Johnson, Idaho St	Sr	51	46.22
David Beckford, Alabama St	Sr	57	43.95

ALL-PURPOSE RUNNERS

	CLASS	GP	RUSH	REC	PR	KOR	YDS	YDS/GAME
Stephan Lewis, New Hampshire	Sr	11	1152	419	13	645	2229	202.64
Andre Raymond, Eastern Illinois	Jr	12	612	672	112	872	2268	189.00
Jay Bailey, Austin Peay	Sr	12	1687	85	0	381	2153	179.42
Ari Confesor, Holy Cross	Jr	12	113	721	322	841	1997	166.42
Fred Amey, Cal St–Sacramento	So	11	31	989	278	514	1812	164.73

DIVISION II

SCORING

	CLASS	GP	TD	XP	FG	PTS	PTS/GAME
David Kircus, Grand Valley St	Sr	14	35	1	0	212	15.14
Ian Smart, C.W. Post	Sr	12	30	0	0	180	15.00
Ben Nelson, St. Cloud St	Sr	11	23	0	0	138	12.55
Kegan Coleman, Central Missouri St	So	12	24	0	0	144	12.00
DaMarcus Blount, N Alabama	Fr	11	20	0	0	120	10.91

FIELD GOALS

	CLASS	GP	FGA	FG	PCT	FG/GAME
Henrik Juul-Nielsen, Nebraska-Kearney	Sr	11	24	20	83.3	1.82
Andrew Keippela, Western Oregon	So	9	23	14	60.9	1.56
J.W. Boren, Tarleton St	Sr	11	25	17	68.0	1.55
Austin Wellock, Ashland	Fr	11	19	15	78.9	1.36
Keith Witt, S Dakota St	Fr	10	25	13	52.0	1.30

DIVISION II (CONT.)

TOTAL OFFENSE

	CLASS	GP	YDS	YDS/GAME
Andrew Webb, Fort Lewis	Jr	11	4245	385.91
Dusty Burk, Truman	Sr	11	3441	312.82
Josh Chapman, MO Southern St	Sr	11	3408	309.82
Zak Hill, Central Washington	Jr	9	2692	299.11
Brett Gilliland, W Alabama	Jr	11	3213	292.10

RUSHING

	CLASS	GP	CAR	YDS	TD	YDS/GAME
Ian Smart, C.W. Post	Sr	12	287	2023	30	168.63
LeVar Ammons, Quincy	So	10	249	1650	13	165.00
Darrin Davis, Southern Conn St	Sr	11	327	1620	15	147.33
Mike Miller, Nebraska-Kearney	So	11	333	1600	13	145.50
Robert Campbell, Findlay	Jr	11	341	1575	16	143.20

PASSING EFFICIENCY

	CLASS	GP	ATT	COMP	PCT COMP	YDS	TD	INT	RATING PTS
Curt Anes, Grand Valley St	Sr	14	414	278	67.2	3692	47	6	176.6
Brian Eyerman, Indiana (PA)	Sr	12	290	173	59.7	2724	36	7	174.7
Ricky Fritz, Minnesota-Duluth	Sr	12	287	160	55.8	2760	34	13	166.6
Ryan Flanigan, UC–Davis	Jr	12	253	166	65.6	2397	20	10	163.4
Zak Hill, Central Washington	Jr	9	308	209	67.9	2694	22	7	160.4

Note: Minimum 15 attempts per game.

RECEPTIONS PER GAME

	CLASS	GP	NO.	YDS	TD	REC/G
Andrew Blakley, Truman	Sr	11	96	965	6	8.70
Gerald Gales, W Alabama	Jr	11	96	994	4	8.70
Chris Brewer, Fort Lewis	So	11	85	1274	18	7.70
Marc Green, SW Baptist	Jr	11	85	1014	4	7.70
Jamal Allen, Fort Lewis	Sr	11	80	939	5	7.30

RECEIVING YARDS PER GAME

	CLASS	GP	NO.	YDS	TD	YDS/G
Chris Brewer, Fort Lewis	So	11	85	1274	18	115.8
Nikolas Lewis, Southern Arkansas	So	11	65	1239	14	112.6
Nate Washington, Tiffin	So	10	53	1120	11	112.0
Ryshaun Ward, Concord	Sr	11	67	1214	11	110.4
Kyle Henderson, W Alabama	Sr	11	58	1190	14	108.2

INTERCEPTIONS

	CLASS	GP	NO.	YDS	INT/GAME
Nicholas Murray, Johnson Smith	Jr	10	10	97	1.0
Rico Cody, Fort Valley St	Sr	11	10	73	0.9
Jon Arnold, California (PA)	Jr	11	9	48	0.8
Ryan Bowers, Presbyterian	Sr	11	9	43	0.8
Jamel Jackson, Catawba	Jr	9	7	130	0.8

PUNTING

	CLASS	NO.	AVG
Michael Koenen, Western Wash	So	43	44.4
Sean McNicholas, Edinboro	Sr	58	44.2
Eric Roth, Washburn	Sr	53	42.5
Jeff Williams, Adams St	Fr	65	42.3
Daniel de la Corte, Fort Lewis	So	53	41.8
Ryan Wettstein, Northern Michigan	Jr	60	41.8

Note: Minimum 3.6 per game.

DIVISION III

SCORING

	CLASS	GP	TD	XP	FG	PTS	PTS/GAME
Dan Pugh, Mount Union	Sr	14	41	2	0	250	17.86
David Russell, Linfield	Sr	11	30	0	0	180	16.36
Fredrick Jackson, Coe	Sr	12	29	0	0	174	14.50
Greg Wood, Worcester St.	Jr	11	26	1	0	158	14.36
Ryan Soule, Hartwick	Sr	10	22	0	0	132	13.20

FIELD GOALS

	CLASS	GP	FGA	FG	PCT	FG/GAME
Ben Lambert, Washington (MO)	So	10	21	15	71.4	1.50
Alex Espinoza, California Luteran	Jr	9	19	13	68.4	1 44
Christopher Reed, Muhlenberg	Sr	12	21	16	76.2	1.33
Pat Dunne, Lake Forest	Sr	11	22	14	63.6	1.27

Three tied with 1.20

TOTAL OFFENSE

	CLASS	GP	YDS	YDS/GAME
Adam King, Howard Payne	So	10	3613	361.3
Tom Stetzer, WI-Platteville	Jr	9	3136	348.4
Eli Grant, Case Reserve	Jr	10	3192	319.2
Dan Cole, RPI	Jr	10	3173	317.3
Roy Hampton, Trinity (TX)	Sr	14	4418	315.6

RUSHING

	CLASS	GP	CAR	YDS	TD	YDS/GAME
Aaron Stepka, Colby	So	8	293	1370	11	171.3
David McNeal, Merchant Marine	Jr	11	338	1860	17	169.1
Randal Baker, Carthage	Sr	10	286	1680	16	168.0
Dan Pugh, Mount Union	Sr	14	384	2300	35	164.3
Luke Hagel, Ripon	Sr	10	265	1616	19	161.6

PASSING EFFICIENCY

	CLASS	GP	ATT	COMP	PCT COMP	YDS	TD	INT	RATING PTS
Roy Hampton, Trinity (TX)	Sr	14	397	260	65.5	4095	43	6	184.9
Rob Adamson, Mount Union	Sr	11	231	139	60.2	2424	30	9	183.4
Eli Grant, Case Reserve	Jr	10	345	220	63.8	3265	33	7	170.8
Matt Trickey, Ripon	So	10	217	126	58.1	2228	23	13	167.3
Mike Donnenwerth, Simpson	Jr	10	258	158	61.2	2318	22	5	161.0

Note: Minimum 15 attempts per game.

RECEPTIONS PER GAME

	CLASS	GP	NO.	YDS	TD	REC/GAME
Luis Uresti, Sul Ross St	Sr	9	87	1082	4	9.7
Conrad Singh, Hampden-Sydney	Jr	10	86	831	5	8.6
Blake Elliott, St. John's (MN)	Jr	14	120	1484	22	8.6
Jim Raptis, Chicago	Jr	9	77	983	4	8.6
Dwayne Tawney, Whitworth	Jr	10	83	1226	8	8.3
Mark Boehms, Alma	Sr	11	91	1116	11	8.3

RECEIVING YARDS PER GAME

	CLASS	GP	NO.	YDS	TD	YDS/GAME
Ryan Soule, Hartwick	Sr	10	76	1550	20	155.0
Lewis Howes, Principia	So	9	71	1218	10	135.3
Matt Kent, WI-Platteville	Jr	9	65	1139	13	126.6
Dwayne Tawney, Whitworth	Jr	10	83	1226	8	122.6
Nick Bublavi, Catholic	So	10	62	1206	14	120.6

2002 NCAA INDIVIDUAL LEADERS (CONT.)

DIVISION III (CONT.)

INTERCEPTIONS

	CLASS	GP	NO.	YDS	INT/G
Jeff Thomas, Redlands	Sr	10	13	127	1.3
James Patrick, Stillman	Jr	10	11	146	1.1
David Simpson, Alma	Sr	11	12	134	1.1
Kyle Hausler, Capital	Fr	10	10	158	1.0
Five tied with 0.9					

PUNTING

	CLASS	NO.	AVG
Scott Verhalen, E Texas Baptist	Jr	39	43.3
Cory Ohnesorge, Occidental	Fr	39	42.2
Sean Lipscomb, Redlands	Sr	45	41.7
Dusty Lehr, Juniata	Sr	48	40.0
Philip Stuebs, Martin Luther	Jr	34	39.9

Note: Minimum 3.6 per game.

2002 NCAA DIVISION I-A TEAM LEADERS

OFFENSE

SCORING

	GP	PTS	AVG
Boise St	13	593	45.62
Kansas St	13	582	44.77
Bowling Green	12	490	40.83
Miami (FL)	13	527	40.54
Oklahoma	14	541	38.64
Texas Tech	14	537	38.36
Iowa	13	484	37.23
Hawaii	14	502	35.86
Southern California	13	465	35.77
California	12	427	35.58

RUSHING

	GP	CAR	YDS	AVG	TD	YDS/GAME
Air Force	13	786	4001	5.1	41	307.8
W Virginia	13	714	3687	5.2	39	283.6
Navy	12	652	3249	5.0	34	270.8
Nebraska	14	724	3762	5.2	29	268.7
Kansas St	13	655	3433	5.2	53	264.1
Rice	11	606	2725	4.5	24	247.7
Wake Forest	13	718	3135	4.4	33	241.2
Ohio	12	649	2878	4.4	30	239.8
Colorado	14	652	3259	5.0	28	232.8
Penn St	13	526	2972	5.7	36	228.62

TOTAL OFFENSE

	GP	PLAYS	YDS	AVG	TD*	YDS/GAME
Boise St	13	950	6519	6.86	79	501.46
Hawaii	14	1039	6939	6.68	66	495.64
Marshall	13	991	6439	6.50	59	495.31
Texas Tech	14	1155	6835	5.92	71	488.21
Toledo	14	1033	6611	6.40	66	472.21
Miami (FL)	13	887	6056	6.83	70	465.85
Purdue	13	1034	5879	5.69	51	452.23
Southern California	13	1009	5840	5.79	60	449.23
Bowling Green	12	898	5387	6.00	65	448.92
Illinois	12	915	5356	5.85	43	446.33

*Defensive and special teams TDs not included.

PASSING

	GP	ATT	COMP	YDS	PCT COMP	YDS/ATT	TD	INT	YDS/GAME
Texas Tech	14	770	515	5444	66.88	7.07	50	15	388.9
Hawaii	14	731	407	5406	55.68	7.40	35	26	386.1
Marshall	13	575	383	4804	66.61	8.35	35	15	369.5
Washington	13	621	372	4501	59.90	7.25	28	14	346.2
San Diego St	13	584	352	4302	60.27	7.37	24	10	330.9
Central Florida	12	442	270	3837	61.09	8.68	31	17	319.8
Utah St	11	487	258	3388	52.98	6.96	21	16	308.0
Southern California	13	494	313	3988	63.36	8.07	33	10	306.8
Arizona St	14	558	306	4254	54.84	7.62	31	16	303.9
Louisiana Tech	12	527	305	3633	57.87	6.89	19	19	302.8

SINGLE-GAME HIGHS

Points Scored: 77—Kentucky, Sept 7 (vs Texas–El Paso).
Net Rushing Yards: 536—W Virginia, Sept 28 (vs E Carolina).
Passing Yards: 559—Arizona St, Oct 19 (vs Oregon).
Rushing and Passing Yards: 733—Marshall, Oct 12 (vs Buffalo).
Fewest Rushing and Passing Yards Allowed: 60—Oklahoma, Oct 19 (vs Iowa St).

2002 NCAA DIVISION I-A TEAM LEADERS

DEFENSE

SCORING

	GP	PTS	AVG
Kansas St	13	154	11.8
Ohio St	14	183	13.1
N Texas	13	192	14.8
Georgia	14	212	15.1
Alabama	13	200	15.4
Oklahoma	14	216	15.4
Maryland	14	228	16.3
Texas	13	212	16.3
Notre Dame	13	217	16.7
N Carolina St	14	238	17.0

TOTAL DEFENSE

	GP	PLAYS	YDS	AVG	YDS/GAME
Texas Christian	12	799	2882	3.61	240.25
Kansas St	13	864	3237	3.75	249.00
Alabama	13	764	3345	4.38	257.31
Troy St	12	784	3322	4.24	276.83
Tennessee	13	840	3703	4.41	284.85
Southern Cal	13	842	3704	4.40	284.92
Miami (FL)	13	935	3705	3.96	285.00
Louisiana St	13	825	3728	4.52	286.77
N Texas	13	870	3778	4.34	290.62
Oklahoma	14	928	4104	4.42	293.14

RUSHING

	GP	CAR	YDS	AVG	TD	YDS/GAME
Texas Christian	12	393	778	1.98	9	64.8
Kansas St	13	446	904	2.03	7	69.5
Ohio St	14	418	1088	2.60	5	77.7
Alabama	13	390	1042	2.67	10	80.2
Iowa	13	416	1065	2.56	17	81.9
Southern Cal	13	388	1081	2.79	9	83.2
S Florida	11	420	959	2.28	8	87.2
Washington St	13	453	1134	2.50	11	87.2
Oregon St	13	479	1225	2.56	13	94.2
Notre Dame	13	439	1238	2.82	11	95.2

TURNOVER MARGIN

	GP	TURNOVERS GAINED			TURNOVERS LOST			MARGIN/GAME
		FUM	INT	TOTAL	FUM	INT	TOTAL	
S Florida	11	14	22	36	10	5	15	1.91
Tulane	13	21	22	43	11	10	21	1.69
California	12	21	15	36	8	10	18	1.50
W Virginia	13	15	19	34	6	9	15	1.46
Southern Cal	13	19	17	36	8	10	18	1.38
Wake Forest	13	21	13	34	10	6	16	1.38
Oklahoma	14	12	24	36	6	11	17	1.36
Texas	13	13	22	35	6	12	18	1.31
Wisconsin	14	13	22	35	9	8	17	1.29
Texas Christian	12	20	22	42	14	13	27	1.25

PASSING EFFICIENCY DEFENSE

	GP	ATT	COMP	YDS	PCT COMP	YDS/ATT	TD	PCT TD	INT	PCT INT	RATING PTS
Miami (FL)	13	353	163	1556	46.18	4.41	8	2.27	12	3.40	83.91
Texas Christian	12	406	158	2105	38.92	5.18	16	3.94	22	5.42	84.62
Kansas State	13	418	191	2333	45.69	5.58	11	2.63	20	4.78	91.70
Southern Mississippi	13	379	177	2195	46.70	5.79	6	1.58	16	4.22	92.13
Louisiana State	13	361	163	1985	45.15	5.50	13	3.60	17	4.71	93.85
Oregon St	13	456	222	2591	48.68	5.68	10	2.19	20	4.39	94.89
Texas	13	400	192	2147	48.00	5.37	17	4.25	22	5.50	96.11
Marshall	13	366	175	2099	47.81	5.73	10	2.73	15	4.10	96.79
Oklahoma	14	432	206	2594	47.69	6.00	13	3.01	24	5.56	96.96
Notre Dame	13	452	223	2662	49.34	5.89	12	2.65	21	4.65	98.24

NATIONAL CHAMPIONS

YEAR	CHAMPION	RECORD	BOWL GAME	HEAD COACH
1883..	Yale	8-0-0	No bowl	Ray Tompkins (Captain)
1884..	Yale	9-0-0	No bowl	Eugene L. Richards (Captain)
1885..	Princeton	9-0-0	No bowl	Charles DeCamp (Captain)
1886..	Yale	9-0-1	No bowl	Robert N. Corwin (Captain)
1887..	Yale	9-0-0	No bowl	Harry W. Beecher (Captain)
1888..	Yale	13-0-0	No bowl	Walter Camp
1889..	Princeton	10-0-0	No bowl	Edgar Poe (Captain)
1890..	Harvard	11-0-0	No bowl	George A. Stewart/George C. Adams
1891..	Yale	13-0-0	No bowl	Walter Camp
1892..	Yale	13-0-0	No bowl	Walter Camp
1893..	Princeton	11-0-0	No bowl	Tom Trenchard (Captain)
1894..	Yale	16-0-0	No bowl	William C. Rhodes
1895..	Pennsylvania	14-0-0	No bowl	George Woodruff
1896..	Princeton	10-0-1	No bowl	Garrett Cochran
1897..	Pennsylvania	15-0-0	No bowl	George Woodruff
1898..	Harvard	11-0-0	No bowl	W. Cameron Forbes
1899..	Harvard	10-0-1	No bowl	Benjamin H. Dibblee
1900..	Yale	12-0-0	No bowl	Malcolm McBride
1901..	Michigan	11-0-0	Won Rose	Fielding Yost
1902..	Michigan	11-0-0	No bowl	Fielding Yost
1903..	Princeton	11-0-0	No bowl	Art Hillebrand
1904..	Pennsylvania	12-0-0	No bowl	Carl Williams
1905..	Chicago	11-0-0	No bowl	Amos Alonzo Stagg
1906..	Princeton	9-0-1	No bowl	Bill Roper
1907..	Yale	9-0-1	No bowl	Bill Knox
1908..	Pennsylvania	11-0-1	No bowl	Sol Metzger
1909..	Yale	10-0-0	No bowl	Howard Jones
1910..	Harvard	8-0-1	No bowl	Percy Houghton
1911..	Princeton	8-0-2	No bowl	Bill Roper
1912..	Harvard	9-0-0	No bowl	Percy Houghton
1913..	Harvard	9-0-0	No bowl	Percy Houghton
1914..	Army	9-0-0	No bowl	Charley Daly
1915..	Cornell	9-0-0	No bowl	Al Sharpe
1916..	Pittsburgh	8-0-0	No bowl	Pop Warner
1917..	Georgia Tech	9-0-0	No bowl	John Heisman
1918..	Pittsburgh	4-1-0	No bowl	Pop Warner
1919..	Harvard	9-0-1	Won Rose	Bob Fisher
1920..	California	9-0-0	Won Rose	Andy Smith
1921..	Cornell	8-0-0	No bowl	Gil Dobie
1922..	Cornell	8-0-0	No bowl	Gil Dobie
1923..	Illinois	8-0-0	No bowl	Bob Zuppke
1924..	Notre Dame	10-0-0	Won Rose	Knute Rockne
1925..	Alabama (H)	10-0-0	Won Rose	Wallace Wade
	Dartmouth (D)	8-0-0	No bowl	Jesse Hawley
1926..	Alabama (H)	9-0-1	Tied Rose	Wallace Wade
	Stanford (D)(H)	10-0-1	Tied Rose	Pop Warner
1927..	Illinois	7-0-1	No bowl	Bob Zuppke
1928..	Georgia Tech (H)	10-0-0	Won Rose	Bill Alexander
	Southern Cal (D)	9-0-1	No bowl	Howard Jones
1929..	Notre Dame	9-0-0	No bowl	Knute Rockne
1930..	Notre Dame	10-0-0	No bowl	Knute Rockne
1931..	Southern Cal	10-1-0	Won Rose	Howard Jones
1932..	Southern Cal (H)	10-0-0	Won Rose	Howard Jones
	Michigan (D)	8-0-0	No bowl	Harry Kipke
1933..	Michigan	7-0-1	No bowl	Harry Kipke
1934..	Minnesota	8-0-0	No bowl	Bernie Bierman
1935..	Minnesota (H)	8-0-0	No bowl	Bernie Bierman
	Southern Methodist (D)	12-1-0	Lost Rose	Matty Bell
1936..	Minnesota	7-1-0	No bowl	Bernie Bierman

NATIONAL CHAMPIONS (CONT.)

YEAR	CHAMPION	RECORD	BOWL GAME	HEAD COACH
1937	Pittsburgh	9-0-1	No bowl	Jock Sutherland
1938	Texas Christian (AP)	11-0-0	Won Sugar	Dutch Meyer
	Notre Dame (D)	8-1-0	No bowl	Elmer Layden
1939	Southern Cal (D)	8-0-2	Won Rose	Howard Jones
	Texas A&M (AP)	11-0-0	Won Sugar	Homer Norton
1940	Minnesota	8-0-0	No bowl	Bernie Bierman
1941	Minnesota	8-0-0	No bowl	Bernie Bierman
1942	Ohio St	9-1-0	No bowl	Paul Brown1943
	Notre Dame	9-1-0	No bowl	Frank Leahy
1943	Notre Dame	9-1-0	No bowl	Frank Leahy
1944	Army	9-0-0	No bowl	Red Blaik
1945	Army	9-0-0	No bowl	Red Blaik
1946	Notre Dame	8-0-1	No bowl	Frank Leahy
1947	Notre Dame	9-0-0	No bowl	Frank Leahy
	Michigan*	10-0-0	Won Rose	Fritz Crisler
1948	Michigan	9-0-0	No bowl	Bennie Oosterbaan
1949	Notre Dame	10-0-0	No bowl	Frank Leahy
1950	Oklahoma	10-1-0	Lost Sugar	Bud Wilkinson
1951	Tennessee	10-1-0	Lost Sugar	Bob Neyland
1952	Michigan St	9-0-0	No bowl	Biggie Munn
1953	Maryland	10-1-0	Lost Orange	Jim Tatum
1954	Ohio St	10-0-0	Won Rose	Woody Hayes
	UCLA (UPI)	9-0-0	No bowl	Red Sanders
1955	Oklahoma	11-0-0	Won Orange	Bud Wilkinson
1956	Oklahoma	10-0-0	No bowl	Bud Wilkinson
1957	Auburn	10-0-0	No bowl	Shug Jordan
	Ohio St (UPI)	9-1-0	Won Rose	Woody Hayes
1958	Louisiana St	11-0-0	Won Sugar	Paul Dietzel
1959	Syracuse	11-0-0	Won Cotton	Ben Schwartzwalder
1960	Minnesota	8-2-0	Lost Rose	Murray Warmath
1961	Alabama	11-0-0	Won Sugar	Bear Bryant
1962	Southern Cal	11-0-0	Won Rose	John McKay
1963	Texas	11-0-0	Won Cotton	Darrell Royal
1964	Alabama	10-1-0	Lost Orange	Bear Bryant
1965	Alabama	9-1-1	Won Orange	Bear Bryant
	Michigan St (UPI)	10-1-0	Lost Rose	Duffy Daugherty
1966	Notre Dame	9-0-1	No bowl	Ara Parseghian
1967	Southern Cal	10-1-0	Won Rose	John McKay
1968	Ohio St	10-0-0	Won Rose	Woody Hayes
1969	Texas	11-0-0	Won Cotton	Darrell Royal
1970	Nebraska	11-0-1	Won Orange	Bob Devaney
	Texas (UPI)	10-1-0	Lost Cotton	Darrell Royal
1971	Nebraska	13-0-0	Won Orange	Bob Devaney
1972	Southern Cal	12-0-0	Won Rose	John McKay
1973	Notre Dame	11-0-0	Won Sugar	Ara Parseghian
	Alabama (UPI)	11-1-0	Lost Sugar	Bear Bryant
1974	Oklahoma	11-0-0	No bowl	Barry Switzer
	Southern Cal (UPI)	10-1-1	Won Rose	John McKay
1975	Oklahoma	11-1-0	Won Orange	Barry Switzer
1976	Pittsburgh	12-0-0	Won Sugar	Johnny Majors
1977	Notre Dame	11-1-0	Won Cotton	Dan Devine
1978	Alabama	11-1-0	Won Sugar	Bear Bryant
	Southern Cal (UPI)	12-1-0	Won Rose	John Robinson
1979	Alabama	12-0-0	Won Sugar	Bear Bryant
1980	Georgia	12-0-0	Won Sugar	Vince Dooley
1981	Clemson	12-0-0	Won Orange	Danny Ford
1982	Penn St	11-1-0	Won Sugar	Joe Paterno
1983	Miami (FL)	11-1-0	Won Orange	Howard Schnellenberger
1984	Brigham Young	13-0-0	Won Holiday	LaVell Edwards
1985	Oklahoma	11-1-0	Won Orange	Barry Switzer
1986	Penn St	12-0-0	Won Fiesta	Joe Paterno
1987	Miami (FL)	12-0-0	Won Orange	Jimmy Johnson
1988	Notre Dame	12-0-0	Won Fiesta	Lou Holtz

NATIONAL CHAMPIONS (CONT.)

YEAR	CHAMPION	RECORD	BOWL GAME	HEAD COACH
1989	Miami (FL)	11-1-0	Won Sugar	Dennis Erickson
1990	Colorado	11-1-1	Won Orange	Bill McCartney
	Georgia Tech (UPI)	11-0-1	Won Citrus	Bobby Ross
1991	Miami (FL)	12-0-0	Won Orange	Dennis Erickson
	Washington (CNN)	12-0-0	Won Rose	Don James
1992	Alabama	13-0-0	Won Sugar	Gene Stallings
1993	Florida St	12-1-0	Won Orange	Bobby Bowden
1994	Nebraska	13-0-0	Won Orange	Tom Osborne
1995	Nebraska	12-0-0	Won Fiesta	Tom Osborne
†1996	Florida	12–1	Won Sugar	Steve Spurrier
1997	Michigan	12–0	Won Rose	Lloyd Carr
	Nebraska (ESPN)	13–0	Won Orange	Tom Osborne
1998	Tennessee	13–0	Won Fiesta	Phillip Fulmer
1999	Florida St	12–0	Won Sugar	Bobby Bowden
2000	Oklahoma	13–0	Won Orange	Bob Stoops
2001	Miami (FL)	12–0	Won Rose	Larry Coker
2002	Ohio St	14–0	Won Fiesta	Jim Tressel

*The AP, which had voted Notre Dame No. 1, took a second vote, giving the national title to Michigan after its 49–0 win over Southern Cal in the Rose Bowl.   Note: Selectors: Helms Athletic Foundation (H) 1883–1935, The Dickinson System (D) 1924–40, The Associated Press (AP) 1936–present, United Press International (UPI) 1958–90, USA Today/CNN (CNN) 1991–96, and USA Today/ESPN (ESPN) 1997–present. †In 1996 the NCAA introduced overtime to break ties.

RESULTS OF MAJOR BOWL GAMES

ROSE BOWL

1-1-02 ......Michigan 49, Stanford 0
1-1-16 ......Washington St 14, Brown 0
1-1-17 ......Oregon 14, Pennsylvania 0
1-1-18 ......Mare Island 19, Camp Lewis 7
1-1-19 ......Great Lakes 17, Mare Island 0
1-1-20 ......Harvard 7, Oregon 6
1-1-21 ......California 28, Ohio St 0
1-2-22 ......Washington & Jefferson 0, California 0
1-1-23 ......Southern Cal 14, Penn St 3
1-1-24 ......Navy 14, Washington 14
1-1-25 ......Notre Dame 27, Stanford 10
1-1-26 ......Alabama 20, Washington 19
1-1-27 ......Alabama 7, Stanford 7
1-2-28 ......Stanford 7, Pittsburgh 6
1-1-29 ......Georgia Tech 8, California 7
1-1-30 ......Southern Cal 47, Pittsburgh 14
1-1-31 ......Alabama 24, Washington St 0
1-1-32 ......Southern Cal 21, Tulane 12
1-2-33 ......Southern Cal 35, Pittsburgh 0
1-1-34 ......Columbia 7, Stanford 0
1-1-35 ......Alabama 29, Stanford 13
1-1-36 ......Stanford 7, Southern Methodist 0
1-1-37 ......Pittsburgh 21, Washington 0
1-1-38 ......California 13, Alabama 0
1-2-39 ......Southern Cal 7, Duke 3
1-1-40 ......Southern Cal 14, Tennessee 0
1-1-41 ......Stanford 21, Nebraska 13
1-1-42 ......Oregon St 20, Duke 16

1-1-43 ......Georgia 9, UCLA 0
1-1-44 ......Southern Cal 29, Washington 0
1-1-45 ......Southern Cal 25, Tennessee 0
1-1-46 ......Alabama 34, Southern Cal 14
1-1-47 ......Illinois 45, UCLA 14
1-1-48 ......Michigan 49, Southern Cal 0
1-1-49 ......Northwestern 20, California 14
1-2-50 ......Ohio St 17, California 14
1-1-51 ......Michigan 14, California 6
1-1-52 ......Illinois 40, Stanford 7
1-1-53 ......Southern Cal 7, Wisconsin 0
1-1-54 ......Michigan St 28, UCLA 20
1-1-55 ......Ohio St 20, Southern Cal 7
1-2-56 ......Michigan St 17, UCLA 14
1-1-57 ......Iowa 35, Oregon St 19
1-1-58 ......Ohio St 10, Oregon 7
1-1-59 ......Iowa 38, California 12
1-1-60 ......Washington 44, Wisconsin 8
1-2-61 ......Washington 17, Minnesota 7
1-1-62 ......Minnesota 21, UCLA 3
1-1-63 ......Southern Cal 42, Wisconsin 37
1-1-64 ......Illinois 17, Washington 7
1-1-65 ......Michigan 34, Oregon St 7
1-1-66 ......UCLA 14, Michigan St 12
1-2-67 ......Purdue 14, Southern Cal 13
1-1-68 ......Southern Cal 14, Indiana 3
1-1-69 ......Ohio St 27, Southern Cal 16
1-1-70 ......Southern Cal 10, Michigan 3

Note: The Fiesta, Orange, Rose and Sugar Bowls constitute the Bowl Alliance, formed in 1995. The Alliance holds eight berths: one each for the champions of the ACC, Big 10, Big 12, Big East, Pac 10, and SEC, and two at-large, reserved for any Division I-A team with at least nine wins and ranked in the top 12 of the BCS rankings. Of the eight teams, the two highest-ranked go to the Fiesta Bowl in 2003, and the Sugar Bowl in 2004. Once these four BCS matches have been set conferences may place the remaining qualified teams in the other bowls. Teams that have won at least six games against Division I-A teams qualify.

Get Your
Game On

By Hank Hersch

I T IS A REVERED VILLAGE not found on any map, a sought-after spot with no amenities, a weather-whipped place that represents all that is good and insane about college sports. From January until the end of March, hundreds of students at Duke forsake the comforts of their dorms and apartments for a tent city named after the Blue Devils' vaunted basketball coach. Huddled in sleeping bags and living off pizza and beer, struggling to keep their GPA's from plummeting in lockstep with the Durham, N.C., temperatures, the good citizens of Krzyzewskiville stake their places outside Cameron Indoor Stadium for the rights to roughly 1,200 undergrad tickets set aside for prime games. Student line monitors

Duke hoop fans came to praise Shane Battier as his number was retired in 2001, but they usually try to bury opposing players under a blizzard of derisive signs.

Blue Fan Group: The craziest of the Cameron Crazies stopped at nothing to support Blue Devil hoopsters like Dahntay Jones (right, with ball).

patrol the tentropolis, outfitted with cell phones, bullhorns and official windbreakers. Dwellers are allowed to leave without forfeiting their positions, to attend a class or a sporting event, for occasional half-hour "grace periods," or when the thermometer drops significantly below freezing.

To those fervent hundreds, their hardships are no worse than what Charlie endured to enter the chocolate factory, and the wonders that await them inside the arena are as great: Instead of orange-skinned Oompa Loompas, there are blue-painted undergrads; instead of wild Willie Wonka, there's the Crazy Towel Guy, a retired executive whose whipping towel stirs the fans into a frenzy. While most big-time hoops programs have in recent years built larger facilities to keep pace with the demand for

seats, Duke has resisted that trend. Opened in 1940, Cameron holds only 9,314, a capacity half that of many rival schools. The pulse of that crowd is set by the erstwhile Krzyzewskivilleans, who, snuggled into nine rows of bleachers, dedicate themselves to passionately cheering on their powerhouse team—and making the opposition's life unbearable.

Over the years the Cameron Crazies have exhibited a flair for topicality (chanting at North Carolina guard Steve Hale, who had recently recovered from a punctured lung, "In Hale! . . . Ex Hale!"), taunts (wearing a skullcap depicting a fuel gauge with the arrow on empty to deride bald Maryland coach Lefty Driesell) and tastelessness (tossing condoms and women's underwear at Maryland forward Herman Veal, who had been accused of—but never charged with—sexual misconduct). Perhaps most important, the Crazies' dedication has become a self-perpetuating attraction at

Reenacting an age-old, if occasionally hazardous, tradition, Ohio State fans tore down the goalposts following their victory over archrival Michigan in November 2002.

Duke, one that enticed hotly recruited guard J.J. Redick to commit to Mike Krzyzewski's Blue Devils as a high school junior. "Once I saw all that intensity," he said, "I knew I wanted to be a part of it."

True, the heady and intoxicating brew concocted inside Cameron is unique, but the Dookies haven't patented the ingredients that make U.S. college sports so special: passion and tradition, rivalry and loyalty. The words posted at Virginia's Aquatic & Fitness Center—GIVE ABOUT 2 HOURS EVERYDAY TO EXERCISE, FOR HEALTH MUST NOT BE SACRI-

FICED TO LEARNING—were written centuries ago by university founder Thomas Jefferson, and while they remain a dictum to heed, students these days are likely to set aside additional time to watching others exercise and finding clever ways to exhort them. When the opposing lineup is introduced at Kansas basketball games, for instance, fans at the Allen Field House express their disinterest by holding newspapers in front of their faces. When the Jayhawks' starters are announced, they tear those papers into shreds and use them as confetti.

FIGHT SONGS HAVE BEEN A part of college sports since their inception, and much like other traditions, they range in character from venerable to rowdy to oddly compelling. In the first category are the rallying cries of such schools as Michigan ("Hail to the victors"),

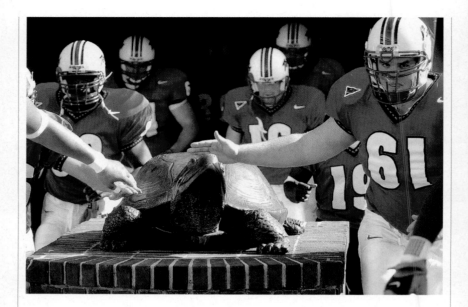

Wisconsin ("On Wisconsin! Plunge right through that line!"; official song rights, incidentally, owned by Michael Jackson) and Notre Dame ("Cheer Cheer for old Notre Dame/ Wake up the echoes cheering her name.") In the second category you'll

Maryland football players touch a bronze terrapin for good luck; fans of Kansas hoops players like Keith Langford (right) rank with the most passionate, and inventive, in the nation.

find Georgia Tech's song, which seems to have been written at the local pub: "I'm a ramblin' wreck from Georgia Tech . . . Like all good fellows, I drink my whiskey clear." And spearheading the third category is the Kansas fight song, which begins softly and builds, like a Gregorian chant: "Rock chalk, Jayhawk, KU." The Rock Chalk chant was adopted in 1866; Teddy Roosevelt called it the finest college cheer he had ever heard.

TAKE A CURSORY LOOK at almost any college football program and you'll find an unusual ritual. For good luck, players at Maryland rub the nose of one of the bronze terrapin statues on campus; at Louisiana Tech, they rub a bronze bulldog; at Clemson, they rub a large rock. Since 1915, freshmen at Georgia Tech have received beanies on which to write the Yellow Jackets' football scores over the next four years. Pieces of turf—some of it artificial—lie at Florida State's sod ceme-

tery, interred mementos of upsets and bowl victories. Before each Texas A&M home game the Aggies hold midnight yell practice at Kyle Field. Toward the end of practice, the stadium lights are turned off, which is a cue to kiss your date. "If you know the engi-

Minnesota players like Terry Jackson (above, left) battle annually for a bronze hog and a brown jug, not to be confused with the Old Oaken Bucket (opposite), for which Purdue defeated Indiana in 2002.

neer," says sports information director Alan Cannon, "you can slip him a few extra bucks to keep the lights off a few extra moments."

GAME DAYS ARE RESERVED for even more spine-tingling stuff. For more than a half-century as many as 25,000 supporters have gathered on 10 acres of oak-shaded lawn known as the Grove when Ole Miss kicks off in Oxford. Many revelers dress formally, picnic with silver candelabras and return after the game to revel until midnight—even though they've arrived as early as 4 a.m. Celebrations at Wisconsin begin at the more civil hour of nine, when an antique fire engine called the Bucky Wagon winds through campus, roaring and honking.

Hundreds of Tennessee fans arrive at Neyland Stadium by boat, decked

out in orange and white, and dock along the banks of the Tennessee River at the Volunteer Landing for one of the nation's most raucous pregame bashes. Before taking the field at Nebraska, the players walk backward through a long tunnel, eyeing plaques and images of past Cornhuskers stars on the walls. Their walk is shown on a big screen at Memorial Stadium; when the team emerges, the stands erupt.

AT STAKE IN MANY CASES are whimsical trophies with intriguing origins. Take Floyd of Rosedale, a 21-by-15-inch bronze sculpture of a hog. In 1935, Iowa's football program was returning from a suspension for using a slush fund; the Hawkeyes had accused neighboring Minnesota of dirty play the previous year. To promote sportsmanship, the two states' governors wagered a prize swine on the outcome of their next game, which the Golden Gophers won 18–6. The pig was rescued from Rosedale Farms near Fort Dodge, Iowa, and presented to the winning governor, Floyd Olson. Thereafter, a replica of the inaugural hog would change hands.

Other such coveted artifacts include the Little Brown Jug (for which Michigan and Minnesota have vied since 1903), the Old Oaken Bucket (on which wins by Indiana and Purdue are symbolized by I and P chain links attached to the bucket's handle) and the Bronze Boot (over which Colorado State and Wyoming annually battle). In 1960 Stephen F. Austin of Texas and Northwestern State of Louisiana agreed that whichever team lost the next matchup would fell a tree near the school and send the trunk to the winning school, which would carve it into a statue. Northwestern State prevailed, received a 2,000-pound black gum log and created 7'6", 320-pound Chief Caddo, named for a Native American whose tribe settled the areas where both schools are located.

Before Tennessee's 48–0 win over Ken-

Their cuddly appearances aside, mascots such as Navy's Billy the goat, Iowa's Herky the hawk (below), and Texas Tech's Raider Red (right) are not afraid to mix it up if they have to.

tucky in 1993, Vols defensive tackle Paul Yatkowski was asked who on his team is in charge of the prize at stake in their rivalry, the Beer Barrel Trophy. "I don't know," he said. "If it's full, probably me."

Mascots have been around since Yale bought the bulldog Handsome Dan from a New Haven blacksmith for five dollars in 1889—or 798 dog years ago. That pooch led the Elis to 125 victories in 131 football games and inspired Cole Porter, class of 1913, to write the song "Bulldog." Ralphie, the buffalo at Colorado; Mike, the tiger at LSU; Bevo, the steer at Texas; and Billy, the goat at Navy, have all become talismans for their storied schools, succeeded by animals inheriting their stature and name, with roman numerals attached. Handsome Dan XV is now ensconced at Yale, but his status as top dog has been surpassed. Georgia's bulldog,

UGA, gained more cachet than any other campus canine in 1982, when he accompanied Herschel Walker to the Heisman Trophy banquet in Manhattan. For that occasion UGA forsook his usual red letter sweater for a white collar and black bowtie.

The rising prominence of college sports has not only increased the profile of mascots but, if Hollywood's taste is any indication, bands (*Drumline*) and cheerleaders (*Bring It On*; though the cheerleaders in that one were high-schoolers) as well. For decades there have been few gigs as prestigious—and none more prestigious among sousaphone players—than being chosen to high-step solo at Ohio Stadium and dot the I in the marching band's signature formation, "Script Ohio." Wisconsin, Michigan and Notre Dame, to name just a few, perform fight songs that have reduced grown men to tears. Florida A&M's Marching 100 (which actually numbers more than 300) may be the most famous college band in the land, though its supremacy is constantly challenged by other traditionally black colleges. The competition is fierce: At halftime of a 1998 game, the band members at Southern, feeling that their exit march had been blocked, and their counterparts at Prairie View A&M, feeling that their formation had been sabotaged, engaged in an all-out brawl that lasted 20 minutes and destroyed three sousaphones.

Nor is cheerleading now for the weak of heart. More than 200 colleges and junior colleges offer full and partial rewards for cheerleaders, whose elaborate and acrobatic maneuvers often require them to drill longer and harder than the varsity teams they support. Kentucky, a seven-time national basketball champ, awards full in-state tuition scholarships, with grueling tryouts that attract flocks of girls. As Wildcats adviser T. Lynn Williamson puts it, "We're trying to be an inspiration to our basketball team."

This is part of what makes college sports so constantly refreshing, and there's always the other extreme, which does its part, too. The requirements for joining the cheerleading crew at all-male Division III St. John's of Collegeville, Minn., aren't nearly as stringent as Kentucky's (though in both cases participants are expected to don women's clothing.) Duties as a Rat Pack member include doing goofy dances and throwing sausages into the stands to rally the crowd for the Johnnies. The students at UC Davis show their support for the Aggies with even more sophisticated devotion, chanting: "Bossy Cow Cow [pause], Honey BeeBee [pause], Oleo Margarine, Oleo Butterine, Alfalfa [long pause], *hay!*"

Huh? The intent of the cheer, said one Davis student, "is to confuse the opposition and their cheering section. It works remarkably well." Why didn't the Cameron Crazies think of that?

Borrowing a page from Kansas's book, Maryland hoop fans check the papers during player introductions for the opposing team.

BILL VAUGHAN/ICON SMI

RESULTS OF MAJOR BOWL GAMES (CONT.)

ROSE BOWL (CONT.)

1-1-71 ......Stanford 27, Ohio St 17
1-1-72 ......Stanford 13, Michigan 12
1-1-73 ......Southern Cal 42, Ohio St 17
1-1-74 ......Ohio St 42, Southern Cal 21
1-1-75 ......Southern Cal 18, Ohio St 17
1-1-76 ......UCLA 23, Ohio St 10
1-1-77 ......Southern Cal 14, Michigan 6
1-2-78 ......Washington 27, Michigan 20
1-1-79 ......Southern Cal 17, Michigan 10
1-1-80 ......Southern Cal 17, Ohio St 16
1-1-81 ......Michigan 23, Washington 6
1-1-82 ......Washington 28, Iowa 0
1-1-83 ......UCLA 24, Michigan 14
1-2-84 ......UCLA 45, Illinois 9
1-1-85 ......Southern Cal 20, Ohio St 17
1-1-86 ......UCLA 45, Iowa 28
1-1-87 ......Arizona St 22, Michigan 15
1-1-88 ......Michigan St 20, Southern Cal 17
1-2-89 ......Michigan 22, Southern Cal 14
1-1-90 ......Southern Cal 17, Michigan 10
1-1-91 ......Washington 46, Iowa 34
1-1-92 ......Washington 34, Michigan 14
1-1-93 ......Michigan 38, Washington 31
1-1-94 ......Wisconsin 21, UCLA 16
1-2-95 ......Penn St 38, Oregon 20
1-1-96 ......Southern Cal 41, Northwestern 32
1-1-97 ......Ohio St 20, Arizona St 17
1-1-98 ......Michigan 21, Washington St 16
1-1-99 ......Wisconsin 38, UCLA 31
1-1-00 ......Wisconsin 17, Stanford 9
1-1-01 ......Washington 34, Purdue 24
1-3-02 ......Miami 37, Nebraska 14
1-1-03 ......Oklahoma 34, Washington St 14

City: Pasadena. Stadium: Rose Bowl, capacity 96,576.
Playing Sites: Tournament Park (1902, 1916–22), Rose Bowl (1923–41, since 1943), Duke Stadium, Durham, NC (1942).

ORANGE BOWL

1-1-35 ....Bucknell 26, Miami (FL) 0
1-1-36 ....Catholic 20, Mississippi 19
1-1-37 ....Duquesne 13, Mississippi St 12
1-1-38 ....Auburn 6, Michigan St 0
1-2-39 ....Tennessee 17, Oklahoma 0
1-1-40 ....Georgia Tech 21, Missouri 7
1-1-41 ....Mississippi St 14, Georgetown 7
1-1-42 ....Georgia 40, Texas Christian 26
1-1-43 ....Alabama 37, Boston College 21
1-1-44 ....Louisiana St 19, Texas A&M 14
1-1-45 ....Tulsa 26, Georgia Tech 12
1-1-46 ....Miami (FL) 13, Holy Cross 6
1-1-47 ....Rice 8, Tennessee 0
1-1-48 ....Georgia Tech 20, Kansas 14
1-1-49 ....Texas 41, Georgia 28
1-2-50 ....Santa Clara 21, Kentucky 13
1-1-51 ....Clemson 15, Miami (FL) 14
1-1-52 ....Georgia Tech 17, Baylor 14
1-1-53 ....Alabama 61, Syracuse 6
1-1-54 ....Oklahoma 7, Maryland 0
1-1-55 ....Duke 34, Nebraska 7
1-2-56 ....Oklahoma 20, Maryland 6
1-1-57 ....Colorado 27, Clemson 21

ORANGE BOWL (CONT.)

1-1-58 ....Oklahoma 48, Duke 21
1-1-59 ....Oklahoma 21, Syracuse 6
1-1-60 ....Georgia 14, Missouri 0
1-2-61 ....Missouri 21, Navy 14
1-1-62 ....Louisiana St 25, Colorado 7
1-1-63 ....Alabama 17, Oklahoma 0
1-1-64 ....Nebraska 13, Auburn 7
1-1-65 ....Texas 21, Alabama 17
1-1-66 ....Alabama 39, Nebraska 28
1-2-67 ....Florida 27, Georgia Tech 12
1-1-68 ....Oklahoma 26, Tennessee 24
1-1-69 ....Penn St 15, Kansas 14
1-1-70 ....Penn St 10, Missouri 3
1-1-71 ....Nebraska 17, Louisiana St 12
1-1-72 ....Nebraska 38, Alabama 6
1-1-73 ....Nebraska 40, Notre Dame 6
1-1-74 ....Penn St 16, Louisiana St 9
1-1-75 ....Notre Dame 13, Alabama 11
1-1-76 ....Oklahoma 14, Michigan 6
1-1-77 ....Ohio St 27, Colorado 10
1-2-78 ....Arkansas 31, Oklahoma 6
1-1-79 ....Oklahoma 31, Nebraska 24
1-1-80 ....Oklahoma 24, Florida St 7
1-1-81 ....Oklahoma 18, Florida St 17
1-1-82 ....Clemson 22, Nebraska 15
1-1-83 ....Nebraska 21, Louisiana St 20
1-2-84 ....Miami (FL) 31, Nebraska 30
1-1-85 ....Washington 28, Oklahoma 17
1-1-86 ....Oklahoma 25, Penn St 10
1-1-87 ....Oklahoma 42, Arkansas 8
1-1-88 ....Miami (FL) 20, Oklahoma 14
1-2-89 ....Miami (FL) 23, Nebraska 3
1-1-90 ....Notre Dame 21, Colorado 6
1-1-91 ....Colorado 10, Notre Dame 9
1-1-92 ....Miami (FL) 22, Nebraska 0
1-1-93 ....Florida St 27, Nebraska 14
1-1-94 ....Florida St 18, Nebraska 16
1-1-95 ....Nebraska 24, Miami (FL) 17
1-1-96 ....Florida St 31, Notre Dame 26
12-31-96 ....Nebraska 41, Virginia Tech 21
1-2-98 ....Nebraska 42, Tennessee 17
1-2-99 ....Florida 31, Syracuse 10
1-1-00 ....Michigan 35, Alabama 34 (ot)
1-3-01 ....Oklahoma 13, Florida St 2
1-2-02 ....Florida 56, Maryland 23
1-2-03 ....Southern Cal 38, Iowa 17

City: Miami. Stadium: Pro Player Stadium, capacity 75,192. Playing Sites: Orange Bowl (1935–96), Pro Player Stadium (since 1996).

SUGAR BOWL

1-1-35 ....Tulane 20, Temple 14
1-1-36 ....Texas Christian 3, Louisiana St 2
1-1-37 ....Santa Clara 21, Louisiana St 14
1-1-38 ....Santa Clara 6, Louisiana St 0
1-2-39 ....Texas Christian 15, Carnegie Tech 7
1-1-40 ....Texas A&M 14, Tulane 13
1-1-41 ....Boston Col 19, Tennessee 13
1-1-42 ....Fordham 2, Missouri 0
1-1-43 ....Tennessee 14, Tulsa 7
1-1-44 ....Georgia Tech 20, Tulsa 18
1-1-45 ....Duke 29, Alabama 26

RESULTS OF MAJOR BOWL GAMES (CONT.)

SUGAR BOWL (CONT.)

1-1-46 ....Oklahoma St 33, St. Mary's (CA) 13
1-1-47 ....Georgia 20, N Carolina 10
1-1-48 ....Texas 27, Alabama 7
1-1-49 ....Oklahoma 14, N Carolina 6
1-2-50 ....Oklahoma 35, Louisiana St 0
1-1-51 ....Kentucky 13, Oklahoma 7
1-1-52 ....Maryland 28, Tennessee 13
1-1-53 ....Georgia Tech 24, Mississippi 7
1-1-54 ....Georgia Tech 42, W Virginia 19
1-1-55 ....Navy 21, Mississippi 0
1-2-56 ....Georgia Tech 7, Pittsburgh 0
1-1-57 ....Baylor 13, Tennessee 7
1-1-58 ....Mississippi 39, Texas 7
1-1-59 ....Louisiana St 7, Clemson 0
1-1-60 ....Mississippi 21, Louisiana St 0
1-2-61 ....Mississippi 14, Rice 6
1-1-62 ....Alabama 10, Arkansas 3
1-1-63 ....Mississippi 17, Arkansas 13
1-1-64 ....Alabama 12, Mississippi 7
1-1-65 ....Louisiana St 13, Syracuse 10
1-1-66 ....Missouri 20, Florida 18
1-2-67 ....Alabama 34, Nebraska 7
1-1-68 ....Louisiana St 20, Wyoming 13
1-1-69 ....Arkansas 16, Georgia 2
1-1-70 ....Mississippi 27, Arkansas 22
1-1-71 ....Tennessee 34, Air Force 13
1-1-72 ....Oklahoma 40, Auburn 22
12-31-72 ....Oklahoma 14, Penn St 0
12-31-73 ....Notre Dame 24, Alabama 23
12-31-74 ....Nebraska 13, Florida 10
12-31-75 ....Alabama 13, Penn St 6
1-1-77 ....Pittsburgh 27, Georgia 3
1-2-78 ....Alabama 35, Ohio St 6
1-1-79 ....Alabama 14, Penn St 7
1-1-80 ....Alabama 24, Arkansas 9
1-1-81 ....Georgia 17, Notre Dame 10
1-1-82 ....Pittsburgh 24, Georgia 20
1-1-83 ....Penn St 27, Georgia 23
1-2-84 ....Auburn 9, Michigan 7
1-1-85 ....Nebraska 28, Louisiana St 10
1-1-86 ....Tennessee 35, Miami (FL) 7
1-1-87 ....Nebraska 30, Louisiana St 15
1-1-88 ....Syracuse 16, Auburn 16
1-2-89 ....Florida St 13, Auburn 7
1-1-90 ....Miami (FL) 33, Alabama 25
1-1-91 ....Tennessee 23, Virginia 22
1-1-92 ....Notre Dame 39, Florida 28
1-1-93 ....Alabama 34, Miami (FL) 13
1-1-94 ....Florida 41, West Virginia 7
1-2-95 ....Florida St 23, Florida 17
12-31-95 ....Virginia Tech 28, Texas 10
1-2-97 ....Florida 52, Florida St 20
1-1-98 ....Florida St 31, Ohio St 14
1-1-99 ....Ohio St 24, Texas A&M 14
1-4-00 ....Florida St 46, Virginia Tech 29
1-2-01 ....Miami (FL) 37, Florida 20
1-1-02 ....Louisiana St 47, Illinois 34
1-1-03 ....Georgia 26, Florida St 13

City: New Orleans. Stadium: Louisiana Superdome, capacity 76,791.

Playing Sites: Tulane Stadium (1935–74), Louisiana Superdome (since 1975).

COTTON BOWL

1-1-37 ....Texas Christian 16, Marquette 6
1-1-38 ....Rice 28, Colorado 14
1-2-39 ....St. Mary's (CA) 20, Texas Tech 13
1-1-40 ....Clemson 6, Boston Col 3
1-1-41 ....Texas A&M 13, Fordham 12
1-1-42 ....Alabama 29, Texas A&M 21
1-1-43 ....Texas 14, Georgia Tech 7
1-1-44 ....Texas 7, Randolph Field 7
1-1-45 ....Oklahoma St 34, Texas Christian 0
1-1-46 ....Texas 40, Missouri 27
1-1-47 ....Arkansas 0, Louisiana St 0
1-1-48 ....Southern Methodist 13, Penn St 13
1-1-49 ....Southern Methodist 21, Oregon 13
1-2-50 ....Rice 27, N Carolina 13
1-1-51 ....Tennessee 20, Texas 14
1-1-52 ....Kentucky 20, Texas Christian 7
1-1-53 ....Texas 16, Tennessee 0
1-1-54 ....Rice 28, Alabama 6
1-1-55 ....Georgia Tech 14, Arkansas 6
1-2-56 ....Mississippi 14, Texas Christian 13
1-1-57 ....Texas Christian 28, Syracuse 27
1-1-58 ....Navy 20, Rice 7
1-1-59 ....Texas Christian 0, Air Force 0
1-1-60 ....Syracuse 23, Texas 14
1-2-61 ....Duke 7, Arkansas 6
1-1-62 ....Texas 12, Mississippi 7
1-1-63 ....Louisiana St 13, Texas 0
1-1-64 ....Texas 28, Navy 6
1-1-65 ....Arkansas 10, Nebraska 7
1-1-66 ....Louisiana St 14, Arkansas 7
12-31-66 ....Georgia 24, Southern Methodist 9
1-1-68 ....Texas A&M 20, Alabama 16
1-1-69 ....Texas 36, Tennessee 13
1-1-70 ....Texas 21, Notre Dame 17
1-1-71 ....Notre Dame 24, Texas 11
1-1-72 ....Penn St 30, Texas 6
1-1-73 ....Texas 17, Alabama 13
1-1-74 ....Nebraska 19, Texas 3
1-1-75 ....Penn St 41, Baylor 20
1-1-76 ....Arkansas 31, Georgia 10
1-1-77 ....Houston 30, Maryland 21
1-2-78 ....Notre Dame 38, Texas 10
1-1-79 ....Notre Dame 35, Houston 34
1-1-80 ....Houston 17, Nebraska 14
1-1-81 ....Alabama 30, Baylor 2
1-1-82 ....Texas 14, Alabama 12
1-1-83 ....SMU 7, Pittsburgh 3
1-2-84 ....Georgia 10, Texas 9
1-1-85 ....Boston Col 45, Houston 28
1-1-86 ....Texas A&M 36, Auburn 16
1-1-87 ....Ohio St 28, Texas A&M 12
1-1-88 ....Texas A&M 35, Notre Dame 10
1-2-89 ....UCLA 17, Arkansas 3
1-1-90 ....Tennessee 31, Arkansas 27
1-1-91 ....Miami (FL) 46, Texas 3
1-1-92 ....Florida St 10, Texas A&M 2
1-1-93 ....Notre Dame 28, Texas A&M 3
1-1-94 ....Notre Dame 24, Texas A&M 21
1-2-95 ....Southern Cal 55, Texas Tech 14
1-1-96 ....Colorado 38, Oregon 6
1-1-97 ....Brigham Young 19, Kansas St 15
1-1-98 ....UCLA 29, Texas A&M 23

COTTON BOWL (CONT.)

1-1-99 ....Texas 38, Mississippi St 11
1-1-00 ....Arkansas 27, Texas 6
1-1-01 ....Kansas St 35, Tennessee 21
1-1-02 ....Oklahoma 10, Arkansas 3
1-1-03 ....Texas 35, Louisiana St 20
City: Dallas. Stadium: Cotton Bowl, capacity 68,252.

SUN BOWL

1-1-36 ....Hardin-Simmons 14, New Mexico St 14
1-1-37 ....Hardin-Simmons 34, UTEP 6
1-1-38 ....W Virginia 7, Texas Tech 6
1-2-39 ....Utah 26, New Mexico 0
1-1-40 ....Catholic 0, Arizona St 0
1-1-41 ....Case Reserve 26, Arizona St 13
1-1-42 ....Tulsa 6, Texas Tech 0
1-1-43 ....2nd Air Force 13, Hardin-Simmons 7
1-1-44 ....Southwestern (TX) 7, New Mexico 0
1-1-45 ....Southwestern (TX) 35, New Mexico 0
1-1-46 ....New Mexico 34, Denver 24
1-1-47 ....Cincinnati 18, Virginia Tech 6
1-1-48 ....Miami (OH) 13, Texas Tech 12
1-1-49 ....W Virginia 21, UTEP 12
1-2-50 ....UTEP 33, Georgetown 20
1-1-51 ....W Texas St 14, Cincinnati 13
1-1-52 ....Texas Tech 25, Pacific 14
1-1-53 ....Pacific 26, Southern Miss 7
1-1-54 ....UTEP 37, Southern Miss 14
1-1-55 ....UTEP 47, Florida St 20
1-2-56 ....Wyoming 21, Texas Tech 14
1-1-57 ....George Washington 13, UTEP 0
1-1-58 ....Louisville 34, Drake 20
12-31-58 ...Wyoming 14, Hardin-Simmons 6
12-31-59 ...New Mexico St 28, N Texas 8
12-31-60 ...New Mexico St 20, Utah St 13
12-30-61 ...Villanova 17, Wichita St 9
12-31-62 ...W Texas St 15, Ohio 14
12-31-63 ...Oregon 21, Southern Methodist 14
12-26-64 ...Georgia 7, Texas Tech 0
12-31-65 ...UTEP 13, Texas Christian 12
12-24-66 ...Wyoming 28, Florida St 20
12-30-67 ...UTEP 14, Mississippi 7
12-28-68 ...Auburn 34, Arizona 10
12-20-69 ...Nebraska 45, Georgia 6
12-19-70 ...Georgia Tech 17, Texas Tech 9
12-18-71 ...Louisiana St 33, Iowa St 15
12-30-72 ...N Carolina 32, Texas Tech 28
12-29-73 ...Missouri 34, Auburn 17
12-28-74 ...Mississippi St 26, N Carolina 24
12-26-75 ...Pittsburgh 33, Kansas 19
1-2-77 ....Texas A&M 37, Florida 14
12-31-77 ...Stanford 24, Louisiana St 14
12-23-78 ...Texas 42, Maryland 0
12-22-79 ...Washington 14, Texas 7
12-27-80 ...Nebraska 31, Mississippi St 17
12-26-81 ...Oklahoma 40, Houston 14
12-25-82 ...N Carolina 26, Texas 10
12-24-83 ...Alabama 28, Southern Methodist 7
12-22-84 ...Maryland 28, Tennessee 27
12-28-85 ...Georgia 13, Arizona 13
12-25-86 ...Alabama 28, Washington 6

SUN BOWL (CONT.)

12-25-87 ...Oklahoma St 35, W Virginia 33
12-24-88 ...Alabama 29, Army 28
12-30-89 ...Pittsburgh 31, Texas A&M 28
12-31-90 ...Michigan St 17, Southern Cal 16
12-31-91 ...UCLA 6, Illinois 3
12-31-92 ...Baylor 20, Arizona 15
12-24-93 ...Oklahoma 41, Texas Tech 10
12-30-94 ...Texas 35, N Carolina 31
12-29-95 ...Iowa 38, Washington 18
12-31-96 ...Stanford 38, Michigan St 0
12-31-97 ...Arizona St 17, Iowa 7
12-31-98 ...Texas Christian 28, Southern Cal 19
12-31-99 ...Oregon 24, Minnesota 20
12-29-00 ...Wisconsin 21, UCLA 20
12-31-01 ...Washington St 33, Purdue 27
12-31-02 ...Purdue 34, Washington 24
City: El Paso. Stadium: Sun Bowl, capacity 51,270.
Name Changes: Sun Bowl (1936–86; 94–), John Hancock Sun Bowl (1987–88), John Hancock Bowl (1989–93).
Playing Sites: Kidd Field (1936–62), Sun Bowl (since 1963).

GATOR BOWL

1-1-46 ....Wake Forest 26, S Carolina 14
1-1-47 ....Oklahoma 34, N Carolina St 13
1-1-48 ....Maryland 20, Georgia 20
1-1-49 ....Clemson 24, Missouri 23
1-2-50 ....Maryland 20, Missouri 7
1-1-51 ....Wyoming 20, Washington & Lee 7
1-1-52 ....Miami (FL) 14, Clemson 0
1-1-53 ....Florida 14, Tulsa 13
1-1-54 ....Texas Tech 35, Auburn 13
12-31-54 ....Auburn 33, Baylor 13
12-31-55 ....Vanderbilt 25, Auburn 13
12-29-56 ....Georgia Tech 21, Pittsburgh 14
12-28-57 ....Tennessee 3, Texas A&M 0
12-27-58 ....Mississippi 7, Florida 3
1-2-60 ....Arkansas 14, Georgia Tech 7
12-31-60 ....Florida 13, Baylor 12
12-30-61 ....Penn St 30, Georgia Tech 15
12-29-62 ....Florida 17, Penn St 7
12-28-63 ....N Carolina 35, Air Force 0
1-2-65 ....Florida St 36, Oklahoma 19
12-31-65 ....Georgia Tech 31, Texas Tech 21
12-31-66 ....Tennessee 18, Syracuse 12
12-30-67 ....Penn St 17, Florida St 17
12-28-68 ....Missouri 35, Alabama 10
12-27-69 ....Florida 14, Tennessee 13
1-2-71 ....Auburn 35, Mississippi 28
12-31-71 ....Georgia 7, N Carolina 3
12-30-72 ....Auburn 24, Colorado 3
12-29-73 ....Texas Tech 28, Tennessee 19
12-30-74 ....Auburn 27, Texas 3
12-29-75 ....Maryland 13, Florida 0
12-27-76 ....Notre Dame 20, Penn St 9
12-30-77 ....Pittsburgh 34, Clemson 3
12-29-78 ....Clemson 17, Ohio St 15
12-28-79 ....N Carolina 17, Michigan 15
12-29-80 ....Pittsburgh 37, S Carolina 9
12-28-81 ....N Carolina 31, Arkansas 27

RESULTS OF MAJOR BOWL GAMES (CONT.)

GATOR BOWL (CONT.)

12-30-82 ....Florida St 31, W Virginia 12
12-30-83 ....Florida 14, Iowa 6
12-28-84 ....Oklahoma St 21, S Carolina 14
12-30-85 ....Florida St 34, Oklahoma St 23
12-27-86 ....Clemson 27, Stanford 21
12-31-87 ....Louisiana St 30, S Carolina 13
1-1-89 ....Georgia 34, Michigan St 27
12-30-89 ....Clemson 27, W Virginia 7
1-1-91 ....Michigan 35, Mississippi 3
12-29-91 ....Oklahoma 48, Virginia 14
12-31-92 ....Florida 27, N Carolina St 10
12-31-93 ....Alabama 24, North Carolina 10
12-30-94 ....Tennessee 45, Virginia Tech 23
1-1-96 ....Syracuse 41, Clemson 0
1-1-97 ....N Carolina 20, W Virginia 13
1-1-98 ....N Carolina 42, Viginia Tech 13
1-1-99 ....Georgia Tech 35, Notre Dame 28
1-1-00 ....Miami 27, Georgia Tech 13
1-1-01 ....Virginia Tech 41, Clemson 20
1-1-02 ....Florida St 30, Virginia Tech 17
1-1-03 ....N Carolina St 28, Notre Dame 6

City: Jacksonville, FL. Stadium: Alltel Stadium, capacity 76,976.

FLORIDA CITRUS BOWL

1-1-47 . . . . Catawba 31, Maryville (TN) 6
1-1-48 . . . . Catawba 7, Marshall 0
1-1-49 . . . . Murray St 21, Sul Ross St 21
1-2-50 . . . . St. Vincent 7, Emory & Henry 6
1-1-51 . . . . Morris Harvey 35, Emory & Henry 14
1-1-52 . . . . Stetson 35, Arkansas St 20
1-1-53 . . . . E Texas St 33, Tennessee Tech 0
1-1-54 . . . . E Texas St 7, Arkansas St 7
1-1-55 . . . . NE-Omaha 7, Eastern Kentucky 6
1-2-56 . . . . Juniata 6, Missouri Valley 6
1-1-57 . . . . W Texas St 20, Southern Miss 13
1-1-58 . . . . E Texas St 10, Southern Miss 9
12-27-58 . . E Texas St 26, Missouri Valley 7
1-1-60 . . . . Middle Tenn St 21, Presbyterian 12
12-30-60 . . Citadel 27, Tennessee Tech 0
12-29-61 . . Lamar 21, Middle Tennessee St 14
12-22-62 . . Houston 49, Miami (OH) 21
12-28-63 . . Western Kentucky 27, Coast Guard 0
12-12-64 . . E Carolina 14, Massachusetts 13
12-11-65 . . E Carolina 31, Maine 0
12-10-66 . . Morgan St 14, W Chester 6
12-16-67 . . TN-Martin 25, W Chester 8
12-27-68 . . Richmond 49, Ohio 42
12-26-69 . . Toledo 56, Davidson 33
12-28-70 . . Toledo 40, William & Mary 12
12-28-71 . . Toledo 28, Richmond 3
12-29-72 . . Tampa 21, Kent St 18
12-22-73 . . Miami (OH) 16, Florida 7
12-21-74 . . Miami (OH) 21, Georgia 10
12-20-75 . . Miami (OH) 20, S Carolina 7
12-18-76 . . Oklahoma St 49, Brigham Young 21
12-23-77 . . Florida St 40, Texas Tech 17
12-23-78 . . N Carolina St 30, Pittsburgh 17
12-22-79 . . Louisiana St 34, Wake Forest 10
12-20-80 . . Florida 35, Maryland 20
12-19-81 . . Missouri 19, Southern Miss 17

FLORIDA CITRUS BOWL (CONT.)

12-18-82 ....Auburn 33, Boston Col 26
12-17-83 ....Tennessee 30, Maryland 23
12-22-84 ....Georgia 17, Florida St 17
12-28-85 ....Ohio St 10, Brigham Young 7
1-1-87 ....Auburn 16, Southern Cal 7
1-1-88 ....Clemson 35, Penn St 10
1-2-89 ....Clemson 13, Oklahoma 6
1-1-90 ....Illinois 31, Virginia 21
1-1-91 ....Georgia Tech 45, Nebraska 21
1-1-92 ....California 37, Clemson 13
1-1-93 ....Georgia 21, Ohio State 14
1-1-94 ....Penn State 31, Tennessee 13
1-2-95 ....Alabama 24, Ohio St 17
1-1-96 ....Tennessee 20, Ohio St 14
1-1-97 ....Tennessee 48, Northwestern 28
1-1-98 ....Florida 21, Penn St 6
1-1-99 ....Michigan 45, Arkansas 31
1-1-00 ....Michigan St 37, Florida 34
1-1-01 ....Michigan 31, Auburn 28
1-1-02 ....Tennessee 45, Michigan 17
1-1-03 ....Auburn 13, Penn St 9

City: Orlando, FL. Stadium: Florida Citrus Bowl, capacity 70,000.

Name Change: Tangerine Bowl (1947–82).

Playing Sites: Tangerine Bowl (1947–72, 1974–82); Florida Field, Gainesville (1973); Orlando Stadium/Florida Citrus Bowl-Orlando (since 1983).

LIBERTY BOWL

12-19-59 ....Penn St 7, Alabama 0
12-17-60 ....Penn St 41, Oregon 12
12-16-61 ....Syracuse 15, Miami (FL) 14
12-15-62 ....Oregon St 6, Villanova 0
12-21-63 ....Mississippi St 16, N Carolina St 12
12-19-64 ....Utah 32, W Virginia 6
12-18-65 ....Mississippi 13, Auburn 7
12-10-66 ....Miami (FL) 14, Virginia Tech 7
12-16-67 ....N Carolina St 14, Georgia 7
12-14-68 ....Mississippi 34, Virginia Tech 17
12-13-69 ....Colorado 47, Alabama 33
12-12-70 ....Tulane 17, Colorado 3
12-20-71 ....Tennessee 14, Arkansas 13
12-18-72 ....Georgia Tech 31, Iowa St 30
12-17-73 ....N Carolina St 31, Kansas 18
12-16-74 ....Tennessee 7, Maryland 3
12-22-75 ....Southern Cal 20, Texas A&M 0
12-20-76 ....Alabama 36, UCLA 6
12-19-77 ....Nebraska 21, N Carolina 17
12-23-78 ....Missouri 20, Louisiana St 15
12-22-79 ....Penn St 9, Tulane 6
12-27-80 ....Purdue 28, Missouri 25
12-30-81 ....Ohio St 31, Navy 28
12-29-82 ....Alabama 21, Illinois 15
12-29-83 ....Notre Dame 19, Boston Col 18
12-27-84 ....Auburn 21, Arkansas 15
12-27-85 ....Baylor 21, Louisiana St 7
12-29-86 ....Tennessee 21, Minnesota 14
12-29-87 ....Georgia 20, Arkansas 17
12-28-88 ....Indiana 34, S Carolina 10

LIBERTY BOWL (CONT.)

12-28-89 ....Mississippi 42, Air Force 29
12-27-90 ....Air Force 23, Ohio St 11
12-29-91 ....Air Force 38, Mississippi St 15
12-31-92 ....Mississippi 13, Air Force 0
12-28-93 ....Louisville 18, Michigan St 7
12-31-94 ....Illinois 30, E Carolina 0
12-30-95 ....East Carolina 19, Stanford 13
12-27-96 ....Syracuse 30, Houston 17
12-31-97 ....Southern Miss 41, Pittsburgh 7
12-31-98 ....Tulane 41, Brigham Young 27
12-31-99 ....Southern Miss 23, Colorado St 17
12-29-01 ....Colorado St 22, Louisville 17
12-31-01 ....Louisville 28, Brigham Young 10
12-31-02 ....Texas Christian 17, Colorado St 3

City: Memphis (since 1965). Stadium: Liberty Bowl Memorial Stadium, capacity 62,921.

Playing Sites: Philadelphia (Municipal Stadium, 1959–63), Atlantic City (Convention Center, 1964).

BLUEBONNET BOWL

12-19-59 ....Clemson 23, Texas Christian 7
12-17-60 ....Texas 3, Alabama 3
12-16-61 ....Kansas 33, Rice 7
12-22-62 ....Missouri 14, Georgia Tech 10
12-21-63 ....Baylor 14, LSU 7
12-19-64 ....Tulsa 14, Mississippi 7
12-18-65 ....Tennessee 27, Tulsa 6
12-17-66 ....Texas 19, Mississippi 0
12-23-67 ....Colorado 31, Miami (FL) 21
12-31-68 ....Southern Methodist 28, Oklahoma 27
12-31-69 ....Houston 36, Auburn 7
12-31-70 ....Alabama 24, Oklahoma 24
12-31-71 ....Colorado 29, Houston 17
12-30-72 ....Tennessee 24, Louisiana St 17
12-29-73 ....Houston 47, Tulane 7
12-23-74 ....N Carolina St 31, Houston 31
12-27-75 ....Texas 38, Colorado 21
12-31-76 ....Nebraska 27, Texas Tech 24
12-31-77 ....Southern Cal 47, Texas A&M 28
12-31-78 ....Stanford 25, Georgia 22
12-31-79 ....Purdue 27, Tennessee 22
12-31-80 ....N Carolina 16, Texas 7
12-31-81 ....Michigan 33, UCLA 14
12-31-82 ....Arkansas 28, Florida 24
12-31-83 ....Oklahoma St 24, Baylor 14
12-31-84 ....W Virginia 31, Texas Christian 14
12-31-85 ....Air Force 24, Texas 16
12-31-86 ....Baylor 21, Colorado 9
12-31-87 ....Texas 32, Pittsburgh 27

City: Houston. Playing sites: Rice Stadium (1959–67; 1985–86), Astrodome (1968–84, 1987).

Name change: Astro-Bluebonnet Bowl (1968–76). Bowl was discontinued after 1987.

PEACH BOWL

12-30-68 ....Louisiana St 31, Florida St 27
12-30-69 ....W Virginia 14, S Carolina 3
12-30-70 ....Arizona St 48, N Carolina 26
12-30-71 ....Mississippi 41, Georgia Tech 18
12-29-72 ....N Carolina St 49, W Virginia 13
12-28-73 ....Georgia 17, Maryland 16

PEACH BOWL (CONT.)

12-28-74 ....Vanderbilt 6, Texas Tech 6
12-31-75 ....W Virginia 13, N Carolina St 10
12-31-76 ....Kentucky 21, N Carolina 0
12-31-77 ....N Carolina St 24, Iowa St 14
12-25-78 ....Purdue 41, Georgia Tech 21
12-31-79 ....Baylor 24, Clemson 18
1-2-81 ....Miami (FL) 20, Virginia Tech 10
12-31-81 ....W Virginia 26, Florida 6
12-31-82 ....Iowa 28, Tennessee 22
12-30-83 ....Florida St 28, N Carolina 3
12-31-84 ....Virginia 27, Purdue 24
12-31-85 ....Army 31, Illinois 29
12-31-86 ....Virginia Tech 25, N Carolina St 24
1-2-88 ....Tennessee 27, Indiana 22
12-31-88 ....N Carolina St 28, Iowa 23
12-30-89 ....Syracuse 19, Georgia 18
12-29-90 ....Auburn 27, Indiana 23
1-1-92 ....E Carolina 37, N Carolina St 34
1-2-93 ....N Carolina 21, Mississippi St 17
12-31-93 ....Clemson 14, Kentucky 13
1-1-95 ....N Carolina St 28, Mississippi St 24
12-30-95 ....Virginia 34, Georgia 27
12-28-96 ....Louisiana St 10, Clemson 7
1-2-98 ....Auburn 21, Clemson 17
12-31-98 ....Georgia 35, Virginia 33
12-30-99 ....Mississippi St 17, Clemson 7
12-29-00 ....Louisiana St 28, Georgia Tech 14
12-31-01 ....N Carolina 16, Auburn 10
12-31-02 ....Maryland 30, Tennessee 3

City: Atlanta. Stadium: Georgia Dome, capacity 71,500.

Playing Sites: Grant Field (1968–70), Atlanta–Fulton County Stadium (1971–92), Georgia Dome (since 1993).

FIESTA BOWL

12-27-71 ....Arizona St 45, Florida St 38
12-23-72 ....Arizona St 49, Missouri 35
12-21-73 ....Arizona St 28, Pittsburgh 7
12-28-74 ....Oklahoma St 16, Brigham Young 6
12-26-75 ....Arizona St 17, Nebraska 14
12-25-76 ....Oklahoma 41, Wyoming 7
12-25-77 ....Penn St 42, Arizona St 30
12-25-78 ....Arkansas 10, UCLA 10
12-25-79 ....Pittsburgh 16, Arizona 10
12-26-80 ....Penn St 31, Ohio St 19
1-1-82 ....Penn St 26, Southern Cal 10
1-1-83 ....Arizona St 32, Oklahoma 21
1-2-84 ....Ohio St 28, Pittsburgh 23
1-1-85 ....UCLA 39, Miami (FL) 37
1-1-86 ....Michigan 27, Nebraska 23
1-2-87 ....Penn St 14, Miami (FL) 10
1-1-88 ....Florida St 31, Nebraska 28
1-2-89 ....Notre Dame 34, W Virginia 21
1-1-90 ....Florida St 41, Nebraska 17
1-1-91 ....Louisville 34, Alabama 7
1-1-92 ....Penn St 42, Tennessee 17
1-1-93 ....Syracuse 26, Colorado 22
1-1-94 ....Arizona 29, Miami (FL) 0
1-2-95 ....Colorado 41, Notre Dame 24
1-2-96 ....Nebraska 62, Florida 24
1-1-97 ....Penn St 38, Texas 15
12-31-97 ....Kansas St 35, Syracuse 18

RESULTS OF MAJOR BOWL GAMES (CONT.)

FIESTA BOWL (CONT.)

1-4-99 ....Tennessee 23, Florida St 16
1-2-00 ....Nebraska 31, Tennessee 21
1-1-01 ....Oregon St 41, Notre Dame 9
1-1-02 ....Oregon 38, Colorado 16
1-3-03 ....Ohio St 31, Miami (FL) 24 [2OT]

City: Tempe, AZ. Stadium: Sun Devil Stadium, capacity 73,471.

INDEPENDENCE BOWL

12-13-76 ....McNeese St 20, Tulsa 16
12-17-77 ....Louisiana Tech 24, Louisville 14
12-16-78 ....E Carolina 35, Louisiana Tech 13
12-15-79 ....Syracuse 31, McNeese St 7
12-13-80 ....Southern Miss 16, McNeese St 14
12-12-81 ....Texas A&M 33, Oklahoma St 16
12-11-82 ....Wisconsin 14, Kansas St 3
12-10-83 ....Air Force 9, Mississippi 3
12-15-84 ....Air Force 23, Virginia Tech 7
12-21-85 ....Minnesota 20, Clemson 13
12-20-86 ....Mississippi 20, Texas Tech 17
12-19-87 ....Washington 24, Tulane 12
12-23-88 ....Southern Miss 38, UTEP 18
12-16-89 ....Oregon 27, Tulsa 24
12-15-90 ....Louisiana Tech 34, Maryland 34
12-29-91 ....Georgia 24, Arkansas 15
12-31-92 ....Wake Forest 39, Oregon 35
12-31-93 ....Virginia Tech 45, Indiana 20
12-28-94 ....Virginia 20, Texas Christian 10
12-29-95 ....Louisiana St 45, Michigan St 26
12-31-96 ....Auburn 32, Army 29
12-28-97 ....Louisiana St 27, Notre Dame 9
12-31-98 ....Mississippi 35, Texas Tech 18
12-31-99 ....Mississippi 27, Oklahoma 25
12-31-00 ....Mississippi St 43, Texas A&M 41
12-27-01 ....Alabama 14, Iowa St 13
12-27-02 ....Mississippi 27, Nebraska 23

City: Shreveport, LA. Stadium: Independence Stadium, capacity 50,459.

ALL-AMERICAN BOWL

12-22-77 ....Maryland 17, Minnesota 7
12-20-78 ....Texas A&M 28, Iowa St 12
12-29-79 ....Missouri 24, S Carolina 14
12-27-80 ....Arkansas 34, Tulane 15
12-31-81 ....Mississippi St 10, Kansas 0
12-31-82 ....Air Force 36, Vanderbilt 28
12-22-83 ....W Virginia 20, Kentucky 16
12-29-84 ....Kentucky 20, Wisconsin 19
12-31-85 ....Georgia Tech 17, Michigan St 14
12-31-86 ....Florida St 27, Indiana 13
12-22-87 ....Virginia 22, Brigham Young 16
12-29-88 ....Florida 14, Illinois 10
12-28-89 ....Texas Tech 49, Duke 21
12-28-90 ....N Carolina St 31, Southern Miss. 27

City: Birmingham, AL. Stadium: Legion Field.

Name Change: Hall of Fame Classic (1977–84). Bowl was discontinued after 1990.

HOLIDAY BOWL

12-22-78 ....Navy 23, Brigham Young 16
12-21-79 ....Indiana 38, Brigham Young 37
12-19-80 ....Brigham Young 46, SMU45
12-18-81 ....Brigham Young 38, Washington St 36
12-17-82 ....Ohio St 47, Brigham Young 17
12-23-83 ....Brigham Young 21, Missouri 17
12-21-84 ....Brigham Young 24, Michigan 17
12-22-85 ....Arkansas 18, Arizona St 17
12-30-86 ....Iowa 39, San Diego St 38
12-30-87 ....Iowa 20, Wyoming 19
12-30-88 ....Oklahoma St 62, Wyoming 14
12-29-89 ....Penn St 50, Brigham Young 39
12-29-90 ....Texas A&M 65, Brigham Young 14
12-30-91 ....Iowa 13, Brigham Young 13
12-30-92 ....Hawaii 27, Illinois 17
12-30-93 ....Ohio St 28, Brigham Young 21
12-30-94 ....Michigan 24, Colorado St 14
12-29-95 ....Kansas St 54, Colorado St 21
12-30-96 ....Colorado 33, Washington 21
12-29-97 ....Colorado St 35, Missouri 24
12-30-98 ....Arizona 23, Nebraska 20
12-29-99 ....Kansas St 24, Washington 20
12-29-00 ....Oregon 35, Texas 30
12-28-01 ....Texas 47, Washington 43
12-27-02 ....Kansas St 34, Arizona St 27

City: San Diego. Stadium: Qualcomm Stadium, capacity 70,000.

LAS VEGAS BOWL

12-19-81 ...Toledo 27, San Jose St 25
12-18-82 ...Fresno St 29, Bowling Green 28
12-17-83 ...Northern Illinois 20, Cal St–Fullerton 13
12-15-84 ...UNLV 30, Toledo 13*
12-14-85 ...Fresno St 51, Bowling Green 7
12-13-86 ...San Jose St 37, Miami (OH) 7
12-12-87 ...Eastern Michigan 30, San Jose St 27
12-10-88 ...Fresno St 35, Western Michigan 30
12-9-89 .....Fresno St 27, Ball St 6
12-8-90 .....San Jose St 48, Central Michigan 24
12-14-91 ...Bowling Green 28, Fresno St 21
12-18-92 ...Bowling Green 35, Nevada 34
12-17-93 ...Utah St 42, Ball St 33
12-15-94 ...UNLV 52, Central Michigan 24
12-14-95 ...Toledo 40, Nevada 37
12-19-96 ...Nevada 18, Ball St 15
12-19-97 ...Oregon 41, Air Force 13
12-19-98 ...N Carolina 20, San Diego St 13
12-18-99 ...Utah 17, Fresno St 16
12-21-00 ...UNLV 31, Arkansas 14
12-25-01 ...Utah 10, Southern Cal 6
12-25-02 ...UCLA 27, New Mexico 13

* Toledo won later by forfeit.

City: Las Vegas (since 1992). Stadium: Sam Boyd Silver Bowl Stadium, capacity 40,000.

Name change: California Bowl (1981–91).

Playing sites: Fresno, CA (Bulldog Stadium, 1981–91), Las Vegas.

RESULTS OF MAJOR BOWL GAMES (CONT.)

ALOHA BOWL

12-25-82 ..Washington 21, Maryland 20
12-26-83 ..Penn St 13, Washington 10
12-29-84 ..Southern Methodist 27, Notre Dame 20
12-28-85 ..Alabama 24, Southern Cal 3
12-27-86 ..Arizona 30, N Carolina 21
12-25-87 ..UCLA 20, Florida 16
12-25-88 ..Washington St 24, Houston 22
12-25-89 ..Michigan St 33, Hawaii 13
12-25-90 ..Syracuse 28, Arizona 0
12-25-91 ..Georgia Tech 18, Stanford 17
12-25-92 ..Kansas 23, Brigham Young 20
12-25-93 ..Colorado 41, Fresno St 30
12-25-94 ..Boston College 12, Kansas St 7
12-25-95 ..Kansas 51, UCLA 30
12-25-96 ..Navy 42, California 38
12-25-97 ..Washington 51, Michigan St 23
12-25-98 ..Colorado 51, Oregon 43
12-25-99 ..Wake Forest 23, Arizona St 3
12-25-00 ..Boston College 31, Arizona St 17

City: Honolulu. Stadium: Aloha Stadium. Bowl was discontinued after 2000.

FREEDOM BOWL

12-16-84 ....Iowa 55, Texas 17
12-30-85 ....Washington 20, Colorado 17
12-30-86 ....UCLA 31, Brigham Young 10
12-30-87 ....Arizona St 33, Air Force 28
12-29-88 ....Brigham Young 20, Colorado 17
12-30-89 ....Washington 34, Florida 7
12-29-90 ....Colorado St 32, Oregon 31
12-30-91 ....Tulsa 28, San Diego St 17
12-29-92 ....Fresno St 24, Southern Cal 7
12-30-93 ....Southern Cal 28, Utah 21
12-29-94 ....Utah 16, Arizona 13

City: Anaheim. Stadium: Anaheim Stadium. Bowl was discontinued after 1994.

OUTBACK BOWL

12-23-86 ....Boston College 27, Georgia 24
1-2-88 ....Michigan 28, Alabama 24
1-2-89 ....Syracuse 23, Louisiana St 10
1-1-90 ....Auburn 31, Ohio St 14
1-1-91 ....Clemson 30, Illinois 0
1-1-92 ....Syracuse 24, Ohio St 17
1-1-93 ....Tennessee 38, Boston College 23
1-1-94 ....Michigan 42, N Carolina St 7
1-2-95 ....Wisconsin 34, Duke 20
1-1-96 ....Penn St 43, Auburn 14
1-1-97 ....Alabama 17, Michigan 14
1-1-98 ....Georgia 33, Wisconsin 6
1-1-99 ....Penn St 26, Kentucky 14
1-1-00 ....Georgia 28, Purdue 25
1-1-01 ....S Carolina 24, Ohio St 7
1-1-02 ....S Carolina 31, Ohio St 28
1-1-03 ....Michigan 38, Florida 30

City: Tampa. Stadium: Raymond James Stadium, capacity 75,000. Name change: Hall of Fame Bowl (1986–95).

INSIGHT.COM BOWL

12-31-89 ....Arizona 17, N Carolina St 10
12-31-90 ....California 17, Wyoming 15
12-31-91 ....Indiana 24, Baylor 0
12-29-92 ....Washington St 31, Utah 28
12-29-93 ....Kansas St 52, Wyoming 17
12-29-94 ....Brigham Young 31, Oklahoma 6
12-27-95 ....Texas Tech 55, Air Force 41
12-27-96 ....Wisconsin 38, Utah 10
12-27-97 ....Arizona 20, New Mexico 14
12-26-98 ....Missouri 34, West Virginia 31
12-31-99 ....Colorado 62, Boston College 28
12-28-00 ....Iowa St 37, Pittsburgh 29
12-29-01 ....Syracuse 26, Kansas St 3
12-26-02 ....Pittsburgh 38, Oregon St 13

City: Tucson. Stadium: Arizona Stadium, capacity 55,883. Name change: Copper Bowl 1989–97.

TANGERINE BOWL

12-28-90 ....Florida St 24, Penn St 17
12-28-91 ....Alabama 30, Colorado 25
1-1-93 ....Stanford 24, Penn St 3
1-1-94 ....Boston College 31, Virginia 13
1-2-95 ....S Carolina 24, W Virginia 21
12-30-95 ....N Carolina 20, Arkansas 10
12-27-96 ....Miami (FL) 31, Virginia 21
12-29-97 ....Georgia Tech 35, W Virginia 30
12-29-98 ....Miami (FL) 46, N Carolina St 23
12-30-99 ....Illinois 62, Virginia 21
12-28-00 ....N Carolina St 38, Minnesota 30
12-20-01 ....Pittsburgh 34, N Carolina St 19
12-23-02 ....Texas Tech 55, Clemson 15

City: Miami. Stadium: Pro Player Stadium, capacity 75,192. Name change: Blockbuster Bowl (1990–93), Carquest Bowl (1994–97), Micron PC Bowl (1998–00).

ALAMO BOWL

12-31-93 ....California 37, Iowa 3
12-31-94 ....Washington St 10, Baylor 3
12-28-95 ....Texas A&M 22, Michigan 20
12-29-96 ....Iowa 27, Texas Tech 0
12-30-97 ....Purdue 33, Oklahoma St 20
12-29-98 ....Purdue 37, Kansas St 34
12-28-99 ....Penn St 24, Texas A&M 0
12-30-00 ....Nebraska 66, Northwestern 17
12-29-01 ....Iowa 16, Texas Tech 13
12-28-02 ....Wisconsin 31, Colorado 28 (OT)

City: San Antonio, TX. Stadium: Alamodome, capacity 67,000.

ANNUAL ASSOCIATED PRESS TOP 20

1936

		RECORD	COACH
1.	Minnesota	7-1-0	Bernie Bierman
2.	Louisiana St	9-0-1	Bernie Moore
3.	Pittsburgh	7-1-1	Jack Sutherland
4.	Alabama	8-0-1	Frank Thomas
5.	Washington	7-1-1	Jimmy Phelan
6.	Santa Clara	7-1-0	Buck Shaw
7.	Northwestern	7-1-0	Pappy Waldorf
8.	Notre Dame	6-2-1	Elmer Layden
9.	Nebraska	7-2-0	Dana X. Bible
10.	Pennsylvania	7-1-0	Harvey Harman
11.	Duke	9-1-0	Wallace Wade
12.	Yale	7-1-0	Ducky Pond
13.	Dartmouth	7-1-1	Red Blaik
14.	Duquesne	7-2-0	John Smith
15.	Fordham	5-1-2	Jim Crowley
16.	Texas Christian	8-2-2	Dutch Meyer
17.	Tennessee	6-2-2	Bob Neyland
18.	Arkansas	7-3-0	Fred Thomsen
19.	Navy	6-3-0	Tom Hamilton
20.	Marquette	7-1-0	Frank Murray

1937

		RECORD	COACH
1.	Pittsburgh	9-0-1	Jack Sutherland
2.	California	9-0-1	Stub Allison
3.	Fordham	7-0-1	Jim Crowley
4.	Alabama	9-0-0	Frank Thomas
5.	Minnesota	6-2-0	Bernie Bierman
6.	Villanova	8-0-1	Clipper Smith
7.	Dartmouth	7-0-2	Red Blaik
8.	Louisiana St	9-1-0	Bernie Moore
9.	Notre Dame	6-2-1	Elmer Layden
	Santa Clara	8-0-0	Buck Shaw
11.	Nebraska	6-1-2	Biff Jones
12.	Yale	6-1-1	Ducky Pond
13.	Ohio St	6-2-0	Francis Schmidt
14.	Holy Cross	8-0-2	Eddie Anderson
	Arkansas	6-2-2	Fred Thomsen
16.	Texas Christian	4-2-2	Dutch Meyer
17.	Colorado	8-0-0	Bunnie Oakes
18.	Rice	5-3-2	Jimmy Kitts
19.	N Carolina	7-1-1	Ray Wolf
20.	Duke	7-2-1	Wallace Wade

1938

		RECORD	COACH
1.	Texas Christian	10-0-0	Dutch Meyer
2.	Tennessee	10-0-0	Bob Neyland
3.	Duke	9-0-0	Wallace Wade
4.	Oklahoma	10-0-0	Tom Stidham
5.	#Notre Dame	8-1-0	Elmer Layden
6.	Carnegie Tech	7-1-0	Bill Kern
7.	Southern Cal	8-2-0	Howard Jones
8.	Pittsburgh	8-2-0	Jack Sutherland
9.	Holy Cross	8-1-0	Eddie Anderson
10.	Minnesota	6-2-0	Bernie Bierman
11.	Texas Tech	10-0-0	Pete Cawthon
12.	Cornell	5-1-1	Carl Snavely
13.	Alabama	7-1-1	Frank Thomas
14.	California	10-1-0	Stub Allison

1938 (CONT.)

		RECORD	COACH
15.	Fordham	6-1-2	Jim Crowley
16.	Michigan	6-1-1	Fritz Crisler
17.	Northwestern	4-2-2	Pappy Waldorf
18.	Villanova	8-0-1	Clipper Smith
19.	Tulane	7-2-1	Red Dawson
20.	Dartmouth	7-2-0	Red Blaik

#Selected No. 1 by the Dickinson System.

1939

		RECORD	COACH
1.	Texas A&M	10-0-0	Homer Norton
2.	Tennessee	10-0-0	Bob Neyland
3.	#Southern Cal	7-0-2	Howard Jones
4.	Cornell	8-0-0	Carl Snavely
5.	Tulane	8-0-1	Red Dawson
6.	Missouri	8-1-0	Don Faurot
7.	UCLA	6-0-4	Babe Horrell
8.	Duke	8-1-0	Wallace Wade
9.	Iowa	6-1-1	Eddie Anderson
10.	Duquesne	8-0-1	Buff Donelli
11.	Boston College	9-1-0	Frank Leahy
12.	Clemson	8-1-0	Jess Neely
13.	Notre Dame	7-2-0	Elmer Layden
14.	Santa Clara	5-1-3	Buck Shaw
15.	Ohio St	6-2-0	Francis Schmidt
16.	Georgia Tech	7-2-0	Bill Alexander
17.	Fordham	6-2-0	Jim Crowley
18.	Nebraska	7-1-1	Biff Jones
19.	Oklahoma	6-2-1	Tom Stidham
20.	Michigan	6-2-0	Fritz Crisler

#Selected No. 1 by the Dickinson System.

1940

		RECORD	COACH
1.	Minnesota	8-0-0	Bernie Bierman
2.	Stanford	9-0-0	C. Shaughnessy
3.	Michigan	7-1-0	Fritz Crisler
4.	Tennessee	10-0-0	Bob Neyland
5.	Boston College	10-0-0	Frank Leahy
6.	Texas A&M	8-1-0	Homer Norton
7.	Nebraska	8-1-0	Biff Jones
8.	Northwestern	6-2-0	Pappy Waldorf
9.	Mississippi St	9-0-1	Allyn McKeen
10.	Washington	7-2-0	Jimmy Phelan
11.	Santa Clara	6-1-1	Buck Shaw
12.	Fordham	7-1-0	Jim Crowley
13.	Georgetown	8-1-0	Jack Hagerty
14.	Pennsylvania	6-1-1	George Munger
15.	Cornell	6-2-0	Carl Snavely
16.	SMU	8-1-1	Matty Bell
17.	Hard.-Simmons	9-0-0	Abe Woodson
18.	Duke	7-2-0	Wallace Wade
19.	Lafayette	9-0-0	Hooks Mylin
20.	—		

Only 19 teams selected.

1941

		RECORD	COACH
1.	Minnesota	8-0-0	Bernie Bierman
2.	Duke	9-0-0	Wallace Wade
3.	Notre Dame	8-0-1	Frank Leahy
4.	Texas	8-1-1	Dana X. Bible
5.	Michigan	6-1-1	Fritz Crisler
6.	Fordham	7-1-0	Jim Crowley
7.	Missouri	8-1-0	Don Faurot
8.	Duquesne	8-0-0	Buff Donelli
9.	Texas A&M	9-1-0	Homer Norton
10.	Navy	7-1-1	Swede Larson
11.	Northwestern	5-3-0	Pappy Waldorf
12.	Oregon St	7-2-0	Lon Stiner
13.	Ohio St	6-1-1	Paul Brown
14.	Georgia	8-1-1	Wally Butts
15.	Pennsylvania	7-1-1	George Munger
16.	Mississippi St	8-1-1	Allyn McKeen
17.	Mississippi	6-2-1	Harry Mehre
18.	Tennessee	8-2-0	John Barnhill
19.	Washington St	6-4-0	Babe Hollingbery
20.	Alabama	8-2-0	Frank Thomas

1942

		RECORD	COACH
1.	Ohio St	9-1-0	Paul Brown
2.	Georgia	10-1-0	Wally Butts
3.	Wisconsin	8-1-1	H. Stuhldreher
4.	Tulsa	10-0-0	Henry Frnka
5.	Georgia Tech	9-1-0	Bill Alexander
6.	Notre Dame	7-2-2	Frank Leahy
7.	Tennessee	8-1-1	John Barnhill
8.	Boston College	8-1-0	Denny Myers
9.	Michigan	7-3-0	Fritz Crisler
10.	Alabama	7-3-0	Frank Thomas
11.	Texas	8-2-0	Dana X. Bible
12.	Stanford	6-4-0	Marchie Schwartz
13.	UCLA	7-3-0	Babe Horrell
14.	William & Mary	9-1-1	Carl Voyles
15.	Santa Clara	7-2-0	Buck Shaw
16.	Auburn	6-4-1	Jack Meagher
17.	Washington St	6-2-2	Babe Hollingbery
18.	Mississippi St	8-2-0	Allyn McKeen
19.	Minnesota	5-4-0	George Hauser
	Holy Cross	5-4-1	Ank Scanlon
	Penn St	6-1-1	Bob Higgins

1943

		RECORD	COACH
1.	Notre Dame	9-1-0	Frank Leahy
2.	Iowa Pre-Flight	9-1-0	Don Faurot
3.	Michigan	8-1-0	Fritz Crisler
4.	Navy	8-1-0	Billick Whelchel
5.	Purdue	9-0-0	Elmer Burnham
6.	Great Lakes	10-2-0	Tony Hinkle
7.	Duke	8-1-0	Eddie Cameron
8.	Del Monte P-F	7-1-0	Bill Kern
9.	Northwestern	6-2-0	Pappy Waldorf
10.	March Field	9-1-0	Paul Schissler

1943 (CONT.)

		RECORD	COACH
11.	Army	7-2-1	Red Blaik
12.	Washington	4-0-0	Ralph Welch
13.	Georgia Tech	7-3-0	Bill Alexander
14.	Texas	7-1-0	Dana X. Bible
15.	Tulsa	6-0-1	Henry Frnka
16.	Dartmouth	6-1-0	Earl Brown
17.	Bainbridge NTS	7-0-0	Joe Maniaci
18.	Colorado College	7-0-0	Hal White
19.	Pacific	7-2-0	Amos A. Stagg
20.	Pennsylvania	6-2-1	George Munger

1944

		RECORD	COACH
1.	Army	9-0-0	Red Blaik
2.	Ohio St	9-0-0	Carroll Widdoes
3.	Randolph Field	11-0-0	Frank Tritico
4.	Navy	6-3-0	Oscar Hagberg
5.	Bainbridge NTS	9-0-0	Joe Maniaci
6.	Iowa Pre-Flight	10-1-0	Jack Meagher
7.	Southern Cal	7-0-2	Jeff Cravath
8.	Michigan	8-2-0	Fritz Crisler
9.	Notre Dame	8-2-0	Ed McKeever
10.	March Field	7-1-2	Paul Schissler
11.	Duke	5-4-0	Eddie Cameron
12.	Tennessee	8-0-1	John Barnhill
13.	Georgia Tech	8-2-0	Bill Alexander
	Norman P-F	6-0-0	John Gregg
15.	Illinois	5-4-1	Ray Eliot
16.	El Toro Marines	8-1-0	Dick Hanley
17.	Great Lakes	9-2-1	Paul Brown
18.	Fort Pierce	9-0-0	Hamp Pool
19.	St. Mary's P-F	4-4-0	Jules Sikes
20.	2nd Air Force	7-2-1	Bill Reese

1945

		RECORD	COACH
1.	Army	9-0-0	Red Blaik
2.	Alabama	9-0-0	Frank Thomas
3.	Navy	7-1-1	Oscar Hagberg
4.	Indiana	9-0-1	Bo McMillan
5.	Oklahoma A&M	8-0-0	Jim Lookabaugh
6.	Michigan	7-3-0	Fritz Crisler
7.	St. Mary's (CA)	7-1-0	Jimmy Phelan
8.	Pennsylvania	6-2-0	George Munger
9.	Notre Dame	7-2-1	Hugh Devore
10.	Texas	9-1-0	Dana X. Bible
11.	Southern Cal	7-3-0	Jeff Cravath
12.	Ohio St	7-2-0	Carroll Widdoes
13.	Duke	6-2-0	Eddie Cameron
14.	Tennessee	8-1-0	John Barnhill
15.	Louisiana St	7-2-0	Bernie Moore
16.	Holy Cross	8-1-0	John DeGrosa
17.	Tulsa	8-2-0	Henry Frnka
18.	Georgia	8-2-0	Wally Butts
19.	Wake Forest	4-3-1	Peahead Walker
20.	Columbia	8-1-0	Lou Little

Note: Except where indicated with an asterisk, the polls from 1936 through 1964 were taken before the bowl games and those from 1965 through the present were taken after the bowl games.

1946

		RECORD	COACH
1.	Notre Dame	8-0-1	Frank Leahy
2.	Army	9-0-1	Red Blaik
3.	Georgia	10-0-0	Wally Butts
4.	UCLA	10-0-0	B. LaBrucherie
5.	Illinois	7-2-0	Ray Eliot
6.	Michigan	6-2-1	Fritz Crisler
7.	Tennessee	9-1-0	Bob Neyland
8.	Louisiana St	9-1-0	Bernie Moore
9.	N Carolina	8-1-1	Carl Snavely
10.	Rice	8-2-0	Jess Neely
11.	Georgia Tech	8-2-0	Bobby Dodd
12.	Yale	7-1-1	Howard Odell
13.	Pennsylvania	6-2-0	George Munger
14.	Oklahoma	7-3-0	Jim Tatum
15.	Texas	8-2-0	Dana X. Bible
16.	Arkansas	6-3-1	John Barnhill
17.	Tulsa	9-1-0	J.O. Brothers
18.	N Carolina St	8-2-0	Beattie Feathers
19.	Delaware	9-0-0	Bill Murray
20.	Indiana	6-3-0	Bo McMillan

1947

		RECORD	COACH
1.	Notre Dame	9-0-0	Frank Leahy
2.	#Michigan	9-0-0	Fritz Crisler
3.	SMU	9-0-1	Matty Bell
4.	Penn St	9-0-0	Bob Higgins
5.	Texas	9-1-0	Blair Cherry
6.	Alabama	8-2-0	Red Drew
7.	Pennsylvania	7-0-1	George Munger
8.	Southern Cal	7-1-1	Jeff Cravath
9.	N Carolina	8-2-0	Carl Snavely
10.	Georgia Tech	9-1-0	Bobby Dodd
11.	Army	5-2-2	Red Blaik
12.	Kansas	8-0-2	George Sauer
13.	Mississippi	8-2-0	Johnny Vaught
14.	William & Mary	9-1-0	Rube McCray
15.	California	9-1-0	Pappy Waldorf
16.	Oklahoma	7-2-1	Bud Wilkinson
17.	N Carolina St	5-3-1	Beattie Feathers
18.	Rice	6-3-1	Jess Neely
19.	Duke	4-3-2	Wallace Wade
20.	Columbia	7-2-0	Lou Little

#The AP, which had voted Notre Dame No. 1 before the bowl games, took a second vote, giving the title to Michigan after its 49–0 win over Southern Cal in the Rose Bowl.

1948

		RECORD	COACH
1.	Michigan	9-0-0	Bennie Oosterbaan
2.	Notre Dame	9-0-1	Frank Leahy
3.	N Carolina	9-0-1	Carl Snavely
4.	California	10-0-0	Pappy Waldorf
5.	Oklahoma	9-1-0	Bud Wilkinson
6.	Army	8-0-1	Red Blaik
7.	Northwestern	7-2-0	Bob Voigts
8.	Georgia	9-1-0	Wally Butts
9.	Oregon	9-1-0	Jim Aiken

1948 (CONT.)

		RECORD	COACH
10.	SMU	8-1-1	Matty Bell
11.	Clemson	10-0-0	Frank Howard
12.	Vanderbilt	8-2-1	Red Sanders
13.	Tulane	9-1-0	Henry Frnka
14.	Michigan St	6-2-2	Biggie Munn
15.	Mississippi	8-1-0	Johnny Vaught
16.	Minnesota	7-2-0	Bernie Bierman
17.	William & Mary	6-2-2	Rube McCray
18.	Penn St	7-1-1	Bob Higgins
19.	Cornell	8-1-0	Lefty James
20.	Wake Forest	6-3-0	Peahead Walker

1949

		RECORD	COACH
1.	Notre Dame	10-0-0	Frank Leahy
2.	Oklahoma	10-0-0	Bud Wilkinson
3.	California	10-0-0	Pappy Waldorf
4.	Army	9-0-0	Red Blaik
5.	Rice	9-1-0	Jess Neely
6.	Ohio St	6-1-2	Wes Fesler
7.	Michigan	6-2-1	Bennie Oosterbaan
8.	Minnesota	7-2-0	Bernie Bierman
9.	Louisiana St	8-2-0	Gaynell Tinsley
10.	Pacific	11-0-0	Larry Siemering
11.	Kentucky	9-2-0	Bear Bryant
12.	Cornell	8-1-0	Lefty James
13.	Villanova	8-1-0	Jim Leonard
14.	Maryland	8-1-0	Jim Tatum
15.	Santa Clara	7-2-1	Len Casanova
16.	N Carolina	7-3-0	Carl Snavely
17.	Tennessee	7-2-1	Bob Neyland
18.	Princeton	6-3-0	Charlie Caldwell
19.	Michigan St	6-3-0	Biggie Munn
20.	Missouri	7-3-0	Don Faurot
	Baylor	8-2-0	Bob Woodruff

1950

		RECORD	COACH
1.	Oklahoma	10-0-0	Bud Wilkinson
2.	Army	8-1-0	Red Blaik
3.	Texas	9-1-0	Blair Cherry
4.	Tennessee	10-1-0	Bob Neyland
5.	California	9-0-1	Pappy Waldorf
6.	Princeton	9-0-0	Charlie Caldwell
7.	Kentucky	10-1-0	Bear Bryant
8.	Michigan St	8-1-0	Biggie Munn
9.	Michigan	5-3-1	Bennie Oosterbaan
10.	Clemson	8-0-1	Frank Howard
11.	Washington	8-2-0	Howard Odell
12.	Wyoming	9-0-0	Bowden Wyatt
13.	Illinois	7-2-0	Ray Eliot
14.	Ohio St	6-3-0	Wes Fesler
15.	Miami (FL)	9-0-1	Andy Gustafson
16.	Alabama	9-2-0	Red Drew
17.	Nebraska	6-2-1	Bill Glassford
18.	Washington & Lee	8-2-0	George Barclay
19.	Tulsa	9-1-1	J.O. Brothers
20.	Tulane	6-2-1	Henry Frnka

ANNUAL ASSOCIATED PRESS TOP 20 (CONT.)

1951

		RECORD	COACH
1.	Tennessee	10-0-0	Bob Neyland
2.	Michigan St	9-0-0	Biggie Munn
3.	Maryland	9-0-0	Jim Tatum
4.	Illinois	8-0-1	Ray Eliot
5.	Georgia Tech	10-0-0	Bobby Dodd
6.	Princeton	9-0-0	Charlie Caldwell
7.	Stanford	9-1-0	Chuck Taylor
8.	Wisconsin	7-1-1	Ivy Williamson
9.	Baylor	8-1-1	George Sauer
10.	Oklahoma	8-2-0	Bud Wilkinson
11.	Texas Christian	6-4-0	Dutch Meyer
12.	California	8-2-0	Pappy Waldorf
13.	Virginia	8-1-0	Art Guepe
14.	San Francisco	9-0-0	Joe Kuharich
15.	Kentucky	7-4-0	Bear Bryant
16.	Boston University	6-4-0	Buff Donelli
17.	UCLA	5-3-1	Red Sanders
18.	Washington St	7-3-0	Forest Evashevski
19.	Holy Cross	8-2-0	Eddie Anderson
20.	Clemson	7-2-0	Frank Howard

1952

		RECORD	COACH
1.	Michigan St	9-0-0	Biggie Munn
2.	Georgia Tech	11-0-0	Bobby Dodd
3.	Notre Dame	7-2-1	Frank Leahy
4.	Oklahoma	8-1-1	Bud Wilkinson
5.	Southern Cal	9-1-0	Jess Hill
6.	UCLA	8-1-0	Red Sanders
7.	Mississippi	8-0-2	Johnny Vaught
8.	Tennessee	8-1-1	Bob Neyland
9.	Alabama	9-2-0	Red Drew
10.	Texas	8-2-0	Ed Price
11.	Wisconsin	6-2-1	Ivy Williamson
12.	Tulsa	8-1-1	J.O. Brothers
13.	Maryland	7-2-0	Jim Tatum
14.	Syracuse	7-2-0	Ben Schwartzwalder
15.	Florida	7-3-0	Bob Woodruff
16.	Duke	8-2-0	Bill Murray
17.	Ohio St	6-3-0	Woody Hayes
18.	Purdue	4-3-2	Stu Holcomb
19.	Princeton	8-1-0	Charlie Caldwell
20.	Kentucky	5-4-2	Bear Bryant

1953

		RECORD	COACH
1.	Maryland	10-0-0	Jim Tatum
2.	Notre Dame	9-0-1	Frank Leahy
3.	Michigan St	8-1-0	Biggie Munn
4.	Oklahoma	8-1-1	Bud Wilkinson
5.	UCLA	8-1-0	Red Sanders
6.	Rice	8-2-0	Jess Neely
7.	Illinois	7-1-1	Ray Eliot
8.	Georgia Tech	8-2-1	Bobby Dodd
9.	Iowa	5-3-1	Forest Evashevski
10.	W Virginia	8-1-0	Art Lewis
11.	Texas	7-3-0	Ed Price
12.	Texas Tech	10-1-0	DeWitt Weaver
13.	Alabama	6-2-3	Red Drew
14.	Army	7-1-1	Red Blaik

1953 (CONT.)

		RECORD	COACH
15.	Wisconsin	6-2-1	Ivy Williamson
16.	Kentucky	7-2-1	Bear Bryant
17.	Auburn	7-2-1	Shug Jordan
18.	Duke	7-2-1	Bill Murray
19.	Stanford	6-3-1	Chuck Taylor
20.	Michigan	6-3-0	Bennie Oosterbaan

1954

		RECORD	COACH
1.	Ohio St	9-0-0	Woody Hayes
2.	#UCLA	9-0-0	Red Sanders
3.	Oklahoma	10-0-0	Bud Wilkinson
4.	Notre Dame	9-1-0	Terry Brennan
5.	Navy	7-2-0	Eddie Erdelatz
6.	Mississippi	9-1-0	Johnny Vaught
7.	Army	7-2-0	Red Blaik
8.	Maryland	7-2-1	Jim Tatum
9.	Wisconsin	7-2-0	Ivy Williamson
10.	Arkansas	8-2-0	Bowden Wyatt
11.	Miami (FL)	8-1-0	Andy Gustafson
12.	W Virginia	8-1-0	Art Lewis
13.	Auburn	7-3-0	Shug Jordan
14.	Duke	7-2-1	Bill Murray
15.	Michigan	6-3-0	Bennie Oosterbaan
16.	Virginia Tech	8-0-1	Frank Moseley
17.	Southern Cal	8-3-0	Jess Hill
18.	Baylor	7-3-0	George Sauer
19.	Rice	7-3-0	Jess Neely
20.	Penn St	7-2-0	Rip Engle

#Selected No. 1 by UP.

1955

		RECORD	COACH
1.	Oklahoma	10-0-0	Bud Wilkinson
2.	Michigan St	8-1-0	Duffy Daugherty
3.	Maryland	10-0-0	Jim Tatum
4.	UCLA	9-1-0	Red Sanders
5.	Ohio St	7-2-0	Woody Hayes
6.	Texas Christian	9-1-0	Abe Martin
7.	Georgia Tech	8-1-1	Bobby Dodd
8.	Auburn	8-1-1	Shug Jordan
9.	Notre Dame	8-2-0	Terry Brennan
10.	Mississippi	9-1-0	Johnny Vaught
11.	Pittsburgh	7-3-0	John Michelosen
12.	Michigan	7-2-0	Bennie Oosterbaan
13.	Southern Cal	6-4-0	Jess Hill
14.	Miami (FL)	6-3-0	Andy Gustafson
15.	Miami (OH)	9-0-0	Ara Parseghian
16.	Stanford	6-3-1	Chuck Taylor
17.	Texas A&M	7-2-1	Bear Bryant
18.	Navy	6-2-1	Eddie Erdelatz
19.	W Virginia	8-2-0	Art Lewis
20.	Army	6-3-0	Red Blaik

Note: Except where indicated with an asterisk, the polls from 1936 through 1964 were taken before the bowl games and those from 1965 through the present were taken after the bowl games.

1956

		RECORD	COACH
1.	Oklahoma	10-0-0	Bud Wilkinson
2.	Tennessee	10-0-0	Bowden Wyatt
3.	Iowa	8-1-0	Forest Evashevski
4.	Georgia Tech.	9-1-0	Bobby Dodd
5.	Texas A&M	9-0-1	Bear Bryant
6.	Miami (FL)	8-1-1	Andy Gustafson
7.	Michigan	7-2-0	Bennie Oosterbaan
8.	Syracuse	7-1-0	Ben Schwartzwalder
9.	Michigan St	7-2-0	Duffy Daugherty
10.	Oregon St	7-2-1	Tommy Prothro
11.	Baylor	8-2-0	Sam Boyd
12.	Minnesota	6-1-2	Murray Warmath
13.	Pittsburgh	7-2-1	John Michelosen
14.	Texas Christian	7-3-0	Abe Martin
15.	Ohio St	6-3-0	Woody Hayes
16.	Navy	6-1-2	Eddie Erdelatz
17.	George Wash	7-1-1	Gene Sherman
18.	Southern Cal	8-2-0	Jess Hill
19.	Clemson	7-1-2	Frank Howard
20.	Colorado	7-2-1	Dallas Ward
	Penn St	6-2-1	Rip Engle

1957

		RECORD	COACH
1.	Auburn	10-0-0	Shug Jordan
2.	#Ohio St	8-1-0	Woody Hayes
3.	Michigan St	8-1-0	Duffy Daugherty
4.	Oklahoma	9-1-0	Bud Wilkinson
5.	Navy	8-1-1	Eddie Erdelatz
6.	Iowa	7-1-1	Forest Evashevski
7.	Mississippi	8-1-1	Johnny Vaught
8.	Rice	7-3-0	Jess Neely
9.	Texas A&M	8-2-0	Bear Bryant
10.	Notre Dame	7-3-0	Terry Brennan
11.	Texas	6-3-1	Darrell Royal
12.	Arizona St	10-0-0	Dan Devine
13.	Tennessee	7-3-0	Bowden Wyatt
14.	Mississippi St	6-2-1	Wade Walker
15.	N Carolina St	7-1-2	Earle Edwards
16.	Duke	6-2-2	Bill Murray
17.	Florida	6-2-1	Bob Woodruff
18.	Army	7-2-0	Red Blaik
19.	Wisconsin	6-3-0	Milt Brunt
20.	VMI	9-0-1	John McKenna

#Selected No. 1 by UP.

1958

		RECORD	COACH
1.	Louisiana St	10-0-0	Paul Dietzel
2.	Iowa	7-1-1	Forest Evashevski
3.	Army	8-0-1	Red Blaik
4.	Auburn	9-0-1	Shug Jordan
5.	Oklahoma	9-1-0	Bud Wilkinson
6.	Air Force	9-0-1	Ben Martin
7.	Wisconsin	7-1-1	Milt Bruhn
8.	Ohio St	6-1-2	Woody Hayes
9.	Syracuse	8-1-0	Ben Schwartzwalder
10.	Texas Christian	8-2-0	Abe Martin

1958 (CONT.)

		RECORD	COACH
11.	Mississippi	8-2-0	Johnny Vaught
12.	Clemson	8-2-0	Frank Howard
13.	Purdue	6-1-2	Jack Mollenkopf
14.	Florida	6-3-1	Bob Woodruff
15.	S Carolina	7-3-0	Warren Giese
16.	California	7-3-0	Pete Elliott
17.	Notre Dame	6-4-0	Terry Brennan
18.	SMU	6-4-0	Bill Meek
19.	Oklahoma St	7-3-0	Cliff Speegle
20.	Rutgers	8-1-0	John Stiegman

1959

		RECORD	COACH
1.	Syracuse	10-0-0	Ben Schwartzwalder
2.	Mississippi	9-1-0	Johnny Vaught
3.	Louisiana St	9-1-0	Paul Dietzel
4.	Texas	9-1-0	Darrell Royal
5.	Georgia	9-1-0	Wally Butts
6.	Wisconsin	7-2-0	Milt Bruhn
7.	Texas Christian	8-2-0	Abe Martin
8.	Washington	9-1-0	Jim Owens
9.	Arkansas	8-2-0	Frank Broyles
10.	Alabama	7-1-2	Bear Bryant
11.	Clemson	8-2-0	Frank Howard
12.	Penn St	8-2-0	Rip Engle
13.	Illinois	5-3-1	Ray Eliot
14.	Southern Cal	8-2-0	Don Clark
15.	Oklahoma	7-3-0	Bud Wilkinson
16.	Wyoming	9-1-0	Bob Devaney
17.	Notre Dame	5-5-0	Joe Kuharich
18.	Missouri	6-4-0	Dan Devine
19.	Florida	5-4-1	Bob Woodruff
20.	Pittsburgh	6-4-0	John Michelosen

1960

		RECORD	COACH
1.	Minnesota	8-1-0	Murray Warmath
2.	Mississippi	9-0-1	Johnny Vaught
3.	Iowa	8-1-0	Forest Evashevski
4.	Navy	9-1-0	Wayne Hardin
5.	Missouri	9-1-0	Dan Devine
6.	Washington	9-1-0	Jim Owens
7.	Arkansas	8-2-0	Frank Broyles
8.	Ohio St	7-2-0	Woody Hayes
9.	Alabama	8-1-1	Bear Bryant
10.	Duke	7-3-0	Bill Murray
11.	Kansas	7-2-1	Jack Mitchell
12.	Baylor	8-2-0	John Bridgers
13.	Auburn	8-2-0	Shug Jordan
14.	Yale	9-0-0	Jordan Oliver
15.	Michigan St	6-2-1	Duffy Daugherty
16.	Penn St	6-3-0	Rip Engle
17.	New Mexico St.	10-0-0	Warren Woodson
18.	Florida	8-2-0	Ray Graves
19.	Syracuse	7-2-0	Ben Schwartzwalder
	Purdue	4-4-1	Jack Mollenkopf

ANNUAL ASSOCIATED PRESS TOP 20 (CONT.)

1961

		RECORD	COACH
1.	Alabama	10-0-0	Bear Bryant
2.	Ohio St	8-0-1	Woody Hayes
3.	Texas	9-1-0	Darrell Royal
4.	Louisiana St	9-1-0	Paul Dietzel
5.	Mississippi	9-1-0	Johnny Vaught
6.	Minnesota	7-2-0	Murray Warmath
7.	Colorado	9-1-0	Sonny Grandelius
8.	Michigan St	7-2-0	Duffy Daugherty
9.	Arkansas	8-2-0	Frank Broyles
10.	Utah St	9-0-1	John Ralston
11.	Missouri	7-2-1	Dan Devine
12.	Purdue	6-3-0	Jack Mollenkopf
13.	Georgia Tech	7-3-0	Bobby Dodd
14.	Syracuse	7-3-0	Ben Schwartzwalder
15.	Rutgers	9-0-0	John Bateman
16.	UCLA	7-3-0	Bill Barnes
	Rice	7-3-0	Jess Neely
	Penn St	7-3-0	Rip Engle
	Arizona	8-1-1	Jim LaRue
20.	Duke	7-3-0	Bill Murray

1962

		RECORD	COACH
1.	Southern Cal	10-0-0	John McKay
2.	Wisconsin	8-1-0	Milt Bruhn
3.	Mississippi	9-0-0	Johnny Vaught
4.	Texas	9-0-1	Darrell Royal
5.	Alabama	9-1-0	Bear Bryant
6.	Arkansas	9-1-0	Frank Broyles
7.	Louisiana St	8-1-1	Charlie McClendon
8.	Oklahoma	8-2-0	Bud Wilkinson
9.	Penn St	9-1-0	Rip Engle
10.	Minnesota	6-2-1	Murray Warmath
11–20: UPI			
11.	Georgia Tech	7-2-1	Bobby Dodd
12.	Missouri	7-1-2	Dan Devine
13.	Ohio St	6-3-0	Woody Hayes
14.	Duke	8-2-0	Bill Murray
	Washington	7-1-2	Jim Owens
16.	Northwestern	7-2-0	Ara Parseghian
	Oregon St	8-2-0	Tommy Prothro
18.	Arizona St	7-2-1	Frank Kush
	Miami (FL)	7-3-0	Andy Gustafson
	Illinois	2-7-0	Pete Elliott

1963

		RECORD	COACH
1.	Texas	10-0-0	Darrell Royal
2.	Navy	9-1-0	Wayne Hardin
3.	Illinois	7-1-1	Pete Elliott
4.	Pittsburgh	9-1-0	John Michelosen
5.	Auburn	9-1-0	Shug Jordan
6.	Nebraska	9-1-0	Bob Devaney
7.	Mississippi	7-0-2	Johnny Vaught
8.	Alabama	8-2-0	Bear Bryant
9.	Oklahoma	8-2-0	Bud Wilkinson
10.	Michigan St	6-2-1	Duffy Daugherty
11–20: UPI			
11.	Mississippi St	6-2-2	Paul Davis

1963 (CONT.)

		RECORD	COACH
12.	Syracuse	8-2-0	Ben Schwartzwalder
13.	Arizona St	8-1-0	Frank Kush
14.	Memphis St	9-0-1	Billy J. Murphy
15.	Washington	6-4-0	Jim Owens
16.	Penn St	7-3-0	Rip Engle
	Southern Cal	7-3-0	John McKay
	Missouri	7-3-0	Dan Devine
19.	N Carolina	8-2-0	Jim Hickey
20.	Baylor	7-3-0	John Bridgers

1964

		RECORD	COACH
1.	Alabama	10-0-0	Bear Bryant
2.	Arkansas	10-0-0	Frank Broyles
3.	Notre Dame	9-1-0	Ara Parseghian
4.	Michigan	8-1-0	Bump Elliott
5.	Texas	9-1-0	Darrell Royal
6.	Nebraska	9-1-0	Bob Devaney
7.	Louisiana St	7-2-1	Charlie McClendon
8.	Oregon St	8-2-0	Tommy Prothro
9.	Ohio St	7-2-0	Woody Hayes
10.	Southern Cal	7-3-0	John McKay
11–20: UPI			
11.	Florida St	8-1-1	Bill Peterson
12.	Syracuse	7-3-0	Ben Schwartzwalder
13.	Princeton	9-0-0	Dick Colman
14.	Penn St	6-4-0	Rip Engle
	Utah	8-2-0	Ray Nagel
16.	Illinois	6-3-0	Pete Elliott
	New Mexico	9-2-0	Bill Weeks
18.	Tulsa	8-2-0	Glenn Dobbs
19.	Missouri	6-3-1	Dan Devine
20.	Mississippi	5-4-1	Johnny Vaught
	Michigan St	4-5-1	Duffy Daugherty

1965

		RECORD	COACH
1.	Alabama	9-1-1	Bear Bryant
2.	#Michigan St	10-1-0	Duffy Daugherty
3.	Arkansas	10-1-0	Frank Broyles
4.	UCLA	8-2-1	Tommy Prothro
5.	Nebraska	10-1-0	Bob Devaney
6.	Missouri	8-2-1	Dan Devine
7.	Tennessee	8-1-2	Doug Dickey
8.	Louisiana St	8-3-0	Charlie McClendon
9.	Notre Dame	7-2-1	Ara Parseghian
10.	Southern Cal	7-2-1	John McKay
11–20: UPI			
11.	Texas Tech	8-2-0	J.T. King
12.	Ohio St	7-2-0	Woody Hayes
13.	Florida	7-3-0	Ray Graves
14.	Purdue	7-2-1	Jack Mollenkopf
15.	Georgia	6-4-0	Vince Dooley
16.	Tulsa	8-2-0	Glenn Dobbs
17.	Mississippi	6-4-0	Johnny Vaught

1965 (CONT.)

		RECORD	COACH
18.	Kentucky	6-4-0	Charlie Bradshaw
19	Syracuse	7-3-0	Ben Schwartzwalder
20.	Colorado	6-2-2	Eddie Crowder

#Selected No. 1 by UPI.

1966*

		RECORD	COACH
1.	Notre Dame	9-0-1	Ara Parseghian
2.	Michigan St	9-0-1	Duffy Daugherty
3.	Alabama	10-0-0	Bear Bryant
4.	Georgia	9-1-0	Vince Dooley
5.	UCLA	9-1-0	Tommy Prothro
6.	Nebraska	9-1-0	Bob Devaney
7.	Purdue	8-2-0	Jack Mollenkopf
8.	Georgia Tech	9-1-0	Bobby Dodd
9.	Miami (FL)	7-2-1	Charlie Tate
10.	SMU	8-2-0	Hayden Fry

11–20: UPI

		RECORD	COACH
11.	Florida	8-2-0	Ray Graves
12.	Mississippi	8-2-0	Johnny Vaught
13.	Arkansas	8-2-0	Frank Broyles
14.	Tennessee	7-3-0	Doug Dickey
15.	Wyoming	9-1-0	Lloyd Eaton
16.	Syracuse	8-2-0	Ben Schwartzwalder
17.	Houston	8-2-0	Bill Yeoman
18.	Southern Cal	7-3-0	John McKay
19.	Oregon St	7-3-0	Dee Andros
20.	Virginia Tech	8-1-1	Jerry Claiborne

1967*

		RECORD	COACH
1.	Southern Cal	9-1-0	John McKay
2.	Tennessee	9-1-0	Doug Dickey
3.	Oklahoma	9-1-0	Chuck Fairbanks
4.	Indiana	9-1-0	John Pont
5.	Notre Dame	8-2-0	Ara Parseghian
6.	Wyoming	10-0-0	Lloyd Eaton
7.	Oregon St	7-2-1	Dee Andros
8.	Alabama	8-1-1	Bear Bryant
9.	Purdue	8-2-0	Jack Mollenkopf
10.	Penn St	8-2-0	Joe Paterno

11–20: UPI†

		RECORD	COACH
11.	UCLA	7-2-1	Tommy Prothro
12.	Syracuse	8-2-0	Ben Schwartzwalder
13.	Colorado	8-2-0	Eddie Crowder
14.	Minnesota	8-2-0	Murray Warmath
15.	Florida St	7-2-1	Bill Peterson
16.	Miami (FL)	7-3-0	Charlie Tate
17.	N Carolina St	8-2-0	Earle Edwards
18.	Georgia	7-3-0	Vince Dooley
19.	Houston	9-2-0	Bill Yeoman
20.	Arizona St	8-2-0	Frank Kush

†UPI ranked Penn St 11th and did not rank Alabama, which was on probation.

Note: Except where indicated with an asterisk, the polls from 1936 through 1964 were taken before the bowl games and those from 1965 through the present were taken after the bowl games.

1968

		RECORD	COACH
1.	Ohio St	10-0-0	Woody Hayes
2.	Penn St	11-0-0	Joe Paterno
3.	Texas	9-1-1	Darrell Royal
4.	Southern Cal	9-1-1	John McKay
5.	Notre Dame	7-2-1	Ara Parseghian
6.	Arkansas	10-1-0	Frank Broyles
7.	Kansas	9-2-0	Pepper Rodgers
8.	Georgia	8-1-2	Vince Dooley
9.	Missouri	8-3-0	Dan Devine
10.	Purdue	8-2-0	Jack Mollenkopf
11.	Oklahoma	7-4-0	Chuck Fairbanks
12.	Michigan	8-2-0	Bump Elliott
13.	Tennessee	8-2-1	Doug Dickey
14.	SMU	8-3-0	Hayden Fry
15.	Oregon St	7-3-0	Dee Andros
16.	Auburn	7-4-0	Shug Jordan
17.	Alabama	8-3-0	Bear Bryant
18.	Houston	6-2-2	Bill Yeoman
19.	Louisiana St	8-3-0	Charlie McClendon
20.	Ohio	10-1-0	Bill Hess

1969

		RECORD	COACH
1.	Texas	11-0-0	Darrell Royal
2.	Penn St	11-0-0	Joe Paterno
3.	Southern Cal	10-0-1	John McKay
4.	Ohio St	8-1-0	Woody Hayes
5.	Notre Dame	8-2-1	Ara Parseghian
6.	Missouri	9-2-0	Dan Devine
7.	Arkansas	9-2-0	Frank Broyles
8.	Mississippi	8-3-0	Johnny Vaught
9.	Michigan	8-3-0	Bo Schembechler
10.	Louisiana St	9-1-0	Charlie McClendon
11.	Nebraska	9-2-0	Bob Devaney
12.	Houston	9-2-0	Bill Yeoman
13.	UCLA	8-1-1	Tommy Prothro
14.	Florida	9-1-1	Ray Graves
15.	Tennessee	9-2-0	Doug Dickey
16.	Colorado	8-3-0	Eddie Crowder
17.	W Virginia	10-0-1	Jim Carlen
18.	Purdue	8-2-0	Jack Mollenkopf
19.	Stanford	7-2-1	John Ralston
20.	Auburn	8-3-0	Shug Jordan

1970

		RECORD	COACH
1.	Nebraska	11-0-1	Bob Devaney
2.	Notre Dame	10-1-0	Ara Parseghian
3.	#Texas	10-1-0	Darrell Royal
4.	Tennessee	11-0-1	Bill Battle
5.	Ohio St	9-1-0	Woody Hayes
6.	Arizona St	11-0-0	Frank Kush
7.	Louisiana St	9-3-0	Charlie McClendon
8.	Stanford	9-3-0	John Ralston
9.	Michigan	9-1-0	Bo Schembechler
10.	Auburn	9-2-0	Shug Jordan
11.	Arkansas	9-2-0	Frank Broyles
12.	Toledo	12-0-0	Frank Lauterbur

ANNUAL ASSOCIATED PRESS TOP 20 (CONT.)

1970 (CONT.)

		RECORD	COACH
13.	Georgia Tech	9-3-0	Bud Carson
14.	Dartmouth	9-0-0	Bob Blackman
15.	Southern Cal	6-4-1	John McKay
16.	Air Force	9-3-0	Ben Martin
17.	Tulane	8-4-0	Jim Pittman
18.	Penn St	7-3-0	Joe Paterno
19.	Houston	8-3-0	Bill Yeoman
20.	Oklahoma	7-4-1	Chuck Fairbanks
	Mississippi	7-4-0	Johnny Vaught

#Selected No. 1 by UPI.

1971

		RECORD	COACH
1.	Nebraska	13-0-0	Bob Devaney
2.	Oklahoma	11-1-0	Chuck Fairbanks
3.	Colorado	10-2-0	Eddie Crowder
4.	Alabama	11-1-0	Bear Bryant
5.	Penn St	11-1-0	Joe Paterno
6.	Michigan	11-1-0	Bo Schembechler
7.	Georgia	11-1-0	Vince Dooley
8.	Arizona St	11-1-0	Frank Kush
9.	Tennessee	10-2-0	Bill Battle
10.	Stanford	9-3-0	John Ralston
11.	Louisiana St	9-3-0	Charlie McClendon
12.	Auburn	9-2-0	Shug Jordan
13.	Notre Dame	8-2-0	Ara Parseghian
14.	Toledo	12-0-0	John Murphy
15.	Mississippi	10-2-0	Billy Kinard
16.	Arkansas	8-3-1	Frank Broyles
17.	Houston	9-3-0	Bill Yeoman
18.	Texas	8-3-0	Darrell Royal
19.	Washington	8-3-0	Jim Owens
20.	Southern Cal	6-4-1	John McKay

1972

		RECORD	COACH
1.	Southern Cal	12-0-0	John McKay
2.	Oklahoma	11-1-0	Chuck Fairbanks
3.	Texas	10-1-0	Darrell Royal
4.	Nebraska	9-2-1	Bob Devaney
5.	Auburn	10-1-0	Shug Jordan
6.	Michigan	10-1-0	Bo Schembechler
7.	Alabama	10-2-0	Bear Bryant
8.	Tennessee	10-2-0	Bill Battle
9.	Ohio St	9-2-0	Woody Hayes
10.	Penn St	10-2-0	Joe Paterno
11.	Louisiana St	9-2-1	Charlie McClendon
12.	N Carolina	11-1-0	Bill Dooley
13.	Arizona St	10-2-0	Frank Kush
14.	Notre Dame	8-3-0	Ara Parseghian
15.	UCLA	8-3-0	Pepper Rodgers
16.	Colorado	8-4-0	Eddie Crowder
17.	N Carolina St	8-3-1	Lou Holtz
18.	Louisville	9-1-0	Lee Corso
19.	Washington St	7-4-0	Jim Sweeney
20.	Georgia Tech	7-4-1	Bill Fulcher

1973

		RECORD	COACH
1.	Notre Dame	11-0-0	Ara Parseghian
2.	Ohio St	10-0-1	Woody Hayes
3.	Oklahoma	10-0-1	Barry Switzer
4.	#Alabama	11-1-0	Bear Bryant
5.	Penn St	12-0-0	Joe Paterno
6.	Michigan	10-0-1	Bo Schembechler
7.	Nebraska	9-2-1	Tom Osborne
8.	Southern Cal	9-2-1	John McKay
9.	Arizona St	11-1-0	Frank Kush
	Houston	11-1-0	Bill Yeoman
11.	Texas Tech	11-1-0	Jim Carlen
12.	UCLA	9-2-0	Pepper Rodgers
13.	Louisiana St	9-3-0	Charlie McClendon
14.	Texas	8-3-0	Darrell Royal
15.	Miami (OH)	11-0-0	Bill Mallory
16.	N Carolina St	9-3-0	Lou Holtz
17.	Missouri	8-4-0	Al Onofrio
18.	Kansas	7-4-1	Don Fambrough
19.	Tennessee	8-4-0	Bill Battle
20.	Maryland	8-4-0	Jerry Claiborne
	Tulane	9-3-0	Bennie Ellender

#Selected No. 1 by UPI.

1974

		RECORD	COACH
1.	Oklahoma	11-0-0	Barry Switzer
2.	#Southern Cal	10-1-1	John McKay
3.	Michigan	10-1-0	Bo Schembechler
4.	Ohio St	10-2-0	Woody Hayes
5.	Alabama	11-1-0	Bear Bryant
6.	Notre Dame	10-2-0	Ara Parseghian
7.	Penn St	10-2-0	Joe Paterno
8.	Auburn	10-2-0	Shug Jordan
9.	Nebraska	9-3-0	Tom Osborne
10.	Miami (OH)	10-0-1	Dick Crum
11.	N Carolina St	9-2-1	Lou Holtz
12.	Michigan St	7-3-1	Denny Stolz
13.	Maryland	8-4-0	Jerry Claiborne
14.	Baylor	8-4-0	Grant Teaff
15.	Florida	8-4-0	Doug Dickey
16.	Texas A&M	8-3-0	Emory Ballard
17.	Mississippi St	9-3-0	Bob Tyler
	Texas	8-4-0	Darrell Royal
19.	Houston	8-3-1	Bill Yeoman
20.	Tennessee	7-3-2	Bill Battle

#Selected No. 1 by UPI.

1975

		RECORD	COACH
1.	Oklahoma	11-1-0	Barry Switzer
2.	Arizona St	12-0-0	Frank Kush
3.	Alabama	11-1-0	Bear Bryant
4.	Ohio St	11-1-0	Woody Hayes
5.	UCLA	9-2-1	Dick Vermeil
6.	Texas	10-2-0	Darrell Royal
7.	Arkansas	10-2-0	Frank Broyles
8.	Michigan	8-2-2	Bo Schembechler
9.	Nebraska	10-2-0	Tom Osborne
10.	Penn St	9-3-0	Joe Paterno

1975 (CONT.)

		RECORD	COACH
11.	Texas A&M	10-2-0	Emory Bellard
12.	Miami (OH)	11-1-0	Dick Crum
13.	Maryland	9-2-1	Jerry Claiborne
14.	California	8-3-0	Mike White
15.	Pittsburgh	8-4-0	Johnny Majors
16.	Colorado	9-3-0	Bill Mallory
17.	Southern Cal	8-4-0	John McKay
18.	Arizona	9-2-0	Jim Young
19.	Georgia	9-3-0	Vince Dooley
20.	W Virginia	9-3-0	Bobby Bowden

1976

		RECORD	COACH
1.	Pittsburgh	12-0-0	Johnny Majors
2.	Southern Cal	11-1-0	John Robinson
3.	Michigan	10-2-0	Bo Schembechler
4.	Houston	10-2-0	Bill Yeoman
5.	Oklahoma	9-2-1	Barry Switzer
6.	Ohio St	9-2-1	Woody Hayes
7.	Texas A&M	10-2-0	Emory Bellard
8.	Maryland	11-1-0	Jerry Claiborne
9.	Nebraska	9-3-1	Tom Osborne
10.	Georgia	10-2-0	Vince Dooley
11.	Alabama	9-3-0	Bear Bryant
12.	Notre Dame	9-3-0	Dan Devine
13.	Texas Tech	10-2-0	Steve Sloan
14.	Oklahoma St	9-3-0	Jim Stanley
15.	UCLA	9-2-1	Terry Donahue
16.	Colorado	8-4-0	Bill Mallory
17.	Rutgers	11-0-0	Frank Burns
18.	Kentucky	9-3-0	Fran Curci
19.	Iowa St	8-3-0	Earle Bruce
20.	Mississippi St	9-2-0	Bob Tyler

1977

		RECORD	COACH
1.	Notre Dame	11-1-0	Dan Devine
2.	Alabama	11-1-0	Bear Bryant
3.	Arkansas	11-1-0	Lou Holtz
4.	Texas	11-1-0	Fred Akers
5.	Penn St	11-1-0	Joe Paterno
6.	Kentucky	10-1-0	Fran Curci
7.	Oklahoma	10-2-0	Barry Switzer
8.	Pittsburgh	9-2-1	Jackie Sherrill
9.	Michigan	10-2-0	Bo Schembechler
10.	Washington	10-2-0	Don James
11.	Ohio St	9-3-0	Woody Hayes
12.	Nebraska	9-3-0	Tom Osborne
13.	Southern Cal	8-4-0	John Robinson
14.	Florida St	10-2-0	Bobby Bowden
15.	Stanford	9-3-0	Bill Walsh
16.	San Diego St	10-1-0	Claude Gilbert
17.	N Carolina	8-3-1	Bill Dooley
18.	Arizona St	9-3-0	Frank Kush
19.	Clemson	8-3-1	Charley Pell
20.	Brigham Young	9-2-0	LaVell Edwards

1978

		RECORD	COACH
1.	Alabama	11-1-0	Bear Bryant
2.	#Southern Cal	12-1-0	John Robinson
3.	Oklahoma	11-1-0	Barry Switzer
4.	Penn St	11-1-0	Joe Paterno
5.	Michigan	10-2-0	Bo Schembechler
6.	Clemson	11-1-0	Charley Pell
7.	Notre Dame	9-3-0	Dan Devine
8.	Nebraska	9-3-0	Tom Osborne
9.	Texas	9-3-0	Fred Akers
10.	Houston	9-3-0	Bill Yeoman
11.	Arkansas	9-2-1	Lou Holtz
12.	Michigan St	8-3-0	Darryl Rogers
13.	Purdue	9-2-1	Jim Young
14.	UCLA	8-3-1	Terry Donahue
15.	Missouri	8-4-0	Warren Powers
16.	Georgia	9-2-1	Vince Dooley
17.	Stanford	8-4-0	Bill Walsh
18.	N Carolina St	9-3-0	Bo Rein
19.	Texas A&M	8-4-0	Emory Bellard (4–2) Tom Wilson (4–2)
20.	Maryland	9-3-0	Jerry Claiborne

#Selected No. 1 by UPI.

1979

		RECORD	COACH
1.	Alabama	12-0-0	Bear Bryant
2.	Southern Cal	11-0-1	John Robinson
3.	Oklahoma	11-1-0	Barry Switzer
4.	Ohio St	11-1-0	Earle Bruce
5.	Houston	11-1-0	Bill Yeoman
6.	Florida St	11-1-0	Bobby Bowden
7.	Pittsburgh	11-1-0	Jackie Sherrill
8.	Arkansas	10-2-0	Lou Holtz
9.	Nebraska	10-2-0	Tom Osborne
10.	Purdue	10-2-0	Jim Young
11.	Washington	10-1-0	Don James
12.	Texas	9-3-0	Fred Akers
13.	Brigham Young	11-1-0	LaVell Edwards
14.	Baylor	8-4-0	Grant Teaff
15.	N Carolina	8-3-1	Dick Crum
16.	Auburn	8-3-0	Doug Barfield
17.	Temple	10-2-0	Wayne Hardin
18.	Michigan	8-4-0	Bo Schembechler
19.	Indiana	8-4-0	Lee Corso
20.	Penn St	8-4-0	Joe Paterno

1980

		RECORD	COACH
1.	Georgia	12-0-0	Vince Dooley
2.	Pittsburgh	11-1-0	Jackie Sherrill
3.	Oklahoma	10-2-0	Barry Switzer
4.	Michigan	10-2-0	Bo Schembechler
5.	Florida St	10-2-0	Bobby Bowden
6.	Alabama	10-2-0	Bear Bryant
7.	Nebraska	10-2-0	Tom Osborne
8.	Penn St	10-2-0	Joe Paterno
9.	Notre Dame	9-2-1	Dan Devine
10.	N Carolina	11-1-0	Dick Crum
11.	Southern Cal	8-2-1	John Robinson

1980 (CONT.)

		RECORD	COACH
12.	Brigham Young	12-1-0	LaVell Edwards
13.	UCLA	9-2-0	Terry Donahue
14.	Baylor	10-2-0	Grant Teaff
15.	Ohio St	9-3-0	Earle Bruce
16.	Washington	9-3-0	Don James
17.	Purdue	9-3-0	Jim Young
18.	Miami (FL)	9-3-0	H. Schnellenberger
19.	Mississippi St	9-3-0	Emory Bellard
20.	SMU	8-4-0	Ron Meyer

1981

		RECORD	COACH
1.	Clemson	12-0-0	Danny Ford
2.	Texas	10-1-1	Fred Akers
3.	Penn St	10-2-0	Joe Paterno
4.	Pittsburgh	11-1-0	Jackie Sherrill
5.	SMU	10-1-0	Ron Meyer
6.	Georgia	10-2-0	Vince Dooley
7.	Alabama	9-2-1	Bear Bryant
8.	Miami (FL)	9-2-0	H. Schnellenberger
9.	N Carolina	10-2-0	Dick Crum
10.	Washington	10-2-0	Don James
11.	Nebraska	9-3-0	Tom Osborne
12.	Michigan	9-3-0	Bo Schembechler
13.	Brigham Young	11-2-0	LaVell Edwards
14.	Southern Cal	9-3-0	John Robinson
15.	Ohio St	9-3-0	Earle Bruce
16.	Arizona St	9-2-0	Darryl Rogers
17.	W Virginia	9-3-0	Don Nehlen
18.	Iowa	8-4-0	Hayden Fry
19.	Missouri	8-4-0	Warren Powers
20.	Oklahoma	7-4-1	Barry Switzer

1982

		RECORD	COACH
1.	Penn St	11-1-0	Joe Paterno
2.	SMU	11-0-1	Bobby Collins
3.	Nebraska	12-1-0	Tom Osborne
4.	Georgia	11-1-0	Vince Dooley
5.	UCLA	10-1-1	Terry Donahue
6.	Arizona St	10-2-0	Darryl Rogers
7.	Washington	10-2-0	Don James
8.	Clemson	9-1-1	Danny Ford
9.	Arkansas	9-2-1	Lou Holtz
10.	Pittsburgh	9-3-0	Foge Fazio
11.	Louisiana St	8-3-1	Jerry Stovall
12.	Ohio St	9-3-0	Earle Bruce
13.	Florida St	9-3-0	Bobby Bowden
14.	Auburn	9-3-0	Pat Dye
15.	Southern Cal	8-3-0	John Robinson
16.	Oklahoma	8-4-0	Barry Switzer
17.	Texas	9-3-0	Fred Akers
18.	N Carolina	8-4-0	Dick Crum
19.	W Virginia	9-3-0	Don Nehlen
20.	Maryland	8-4-0	Bobby Ross

1983

		RECORD	COACH
1.	Miami (FL)	11-1-0	H. Schnellenberger
2.	Nebraska	12-1-0	Tom Osborne
3.	Auburn	11-1-0	Pat Dye
4.	Georgia	10-1-1	Vince Dooley
5.	Texas	11-1-0	Fred Akers
6.	Florida	9-2-1	Charlie Pell
7.	Brigham Young	11-1-0	LaVell Edwards
8.	Michigan	9-3-0	Bo Schembechler
9.	Ohio St	9-3-0	Earle Bruce
10.	Illinois	10-2-0	Mike White
11.	Clemson	9-1-1	Danny Ford
12.	SMU	10-2-0	Bobby Collins
13.	Air Force	10-2-0	Ken Hatfield
14.	Iowa	9-3-0	Hayden Fry
15.	Alabama	8-4-0	Ray Perkins
16.	W Virginia	9-3-0	Don Nehlen
17.	UCLA	7-4-1	Terry Donahue
18.	Pittsburgh	8-3-1	Foge Fazio
19.	Boston College	9-3-0	Jack Bicknell
20.	E Carolina	8-3-0	Ed Emory

1984

		RECORD	COACH
1.	Brigham Young	13-0-0	LaVell Edwards
2.	Washington	11-1-0	Don James
3.	Florida	9-1-1	Chas Pell (0-1-1) Galen Hall (9-0)
4.	Nebraska	10-2-0	Tom Osborne
5.	Boston College	10-2-0	Jack Bicknell
6.	Oklahoma	9-2-1	Barry Switzer
7.	Oklahoma St	10-2-0	Pat Jones
8.	SMU	10-2-0	Bobby Collins
9.	UCLA	9-3-0	Terry Donahue
10.	Southern Cal	10-3-0	Ted Tollner
11.	S Carolina	10-2-0	Joe Morrison
12.	Maryland	9-3-0	Bobby Ross
13.	Ohio St	9-3-0	Earle Bruce
14.	Auburn	9-4-0	Pat Dye
15.	Louisiana St	8-3-1	Bill Arnsparger
16.	Iowa	8-4-1	Hayden Fry
17.	Florida St	7-3-2	Bobby Bowden
18.	Miami (FL)	8-5-0	Jimmy Johnson
19.	Kentucky	9-3-0	Jerry Claiborne
20.	Virginia	8-2-2	George Welsh

1985

		RECORD	COACH
1.	Oklahoma	11-1-0	Barry Switzer
2.	Michigan	10-1-1	Bo Schembechler
3.	Penn St	11-1-0	Joe Paterno
4.	Tennessee	9-1-2	Johnny Majors
5.	Florida	9-1-1	Galen Hall
6.	Texas A&M	10-2-0	Jackie Sherrill
7.	UCLA	9-2-1	Terry Donahue
8.	Air Force	12-1-0	Fisher DeBerry
9.	Miami (FL)	10-2-0	Jimmy Johnson
10.	Iowa	10-2-0	Hayden Fry
11.	Nebraska	9-3-0	Tom Osborne
12.	Arkansas	10-2-0	Ken Hatfield
13.	Alabama	9-2-1	Ray Perkins
14.	Ohio St	9-3-0	Earle Bruce

ANNUAL ASSOCIATED PRESS TOP 20 (CONT.)

1985 (CONT.)

		RECORD	COACH
15.	Florida St	9-3-0	Bobby Bowden
16.	Brigham Young	11-3-0	LaVell Edwards
17.	Baylor	9-3-0	Grant Teaff
18.	Maryland	9-3-0	Bobby Ross
19.	Georgia Tech	9-2-1	Bill Curry
20.	Louisiana St	9-2-1	Bill Arnsparger

1986

		RECORD	COACH
1.	Penn St	12-0-0	Joe Paterno
2.	Miami (FL)	11-1-0	Jimmy Johnson
3.	Oklahoma	11-1-0	Barry Switzer
4.	Arizona St	10-1-1	John Cooper
5.	Nebraska	10-2-0	Tom Osborne
6.	Auburn	10-2-0	Pat Dye
7.	Ohio St	10-3-0	Earle Bruce
8.	Michigan	11-2-0	Bo Schembechler
9.	Alabama	10-3-0	Ray Perkins
10.	Louisiana St	9-3-0	Bill Arnsparger
11.	Arizona	9-3-0	Larry Smith
12.	Baylor	9-3-0	Grant Teaff
13.	Texas A&M	9-3-0	Jackie Sherrill
14.	UCLA	8-3-1	Terry Donahue
15.	Arkansas	9-3-0	Ken Hatfield
16.	Iowa	9-3-0	Hayden Fry
17.	Clemson	8-2-2	Danny Ford
18.	Washington	8-3-1	Don James
19.	Boston College	9-3-0	Jack Bicknell
20.	Virginia Tech	9-2-1	Bill Dooley

1987

		RECORD	COACH
1.	Miami (FL)	12-0-0	Jimmy Johnson
2.	Florida St	11-1-0	Bobby Bowden
3.	Oklahoma	11-1-0	Barry Switzer
4.	Syracuse	11-0-1	Dick MacPherson
5.	Louisiana St	10-1-1	Mike Archer
6.	Nebraska	10-2-0	Tom Osborne

1987 (CONT.)

		RECORD	COACH
7.	Auburn	9-1-2	Pat Dye
8.	Michigan St	9-2-1	George Perles
9.	UCLA	10-2-0	Terry Donahue
10.	Texas A&M	10-2-0	Jackie Sherrill
11.	Oklahoma St	10-2-0	Pat Jones
12.	Clemson	10-2-0	Danny Ford
13.	Georgia	9-3-0	Vince Dooley
14.	Tennessee	10-2-1	Johnny Majors
15.	S Carolina	8-4-0	Joe Morrison
16.	Iowa	10-3-0	Hayden Fry
17.	Notre Dame	8-4-0	Lou Holtz
18.	Southern Cal	8-4-0	Larry Smith
19.	Michigan	8-4-0	Bo Schembechler
20.	Arizona St	7-4-1	John Cooper

1988

		RECORD	COACH
1.	Notre Dame	12-0-0	Lou Holtz
2.	Miami (FL)	11-1-0	Jimmy Johnson
3.	Florida St	11-1-0	Bobby Bowden
4.	Michigan	9-2-1	Bo Schembechler
5.	W Virginia	11-1-0	Don Nehlen
6.	UCLA	10-2-0	Terry Donahue
7.	Southern Cal	10-2-0	Larry Smith
8.	Auburn	10-2-0	Pat Dye
9.	Clemson	10-2-0	Danny Ford
10.	Nebraska	11-2-0	Tom Osborne
11.	Oklahoma St	10-2-0	Pat Jones
12.	Arkansas	10-2-0	Ken Hatfield
13.	Syracuse	10-2-0	Dick MacPherson
14.	Oklahoma	9-3-0	Barry Switzer
15.	Georgia	9-3-0	Vince Dooley
16.	Washington St	9-3-0	Dennis Erickson
17.	Alabama	9-3-0	Bill Curry
18.	Houston	9-3-0	Jack Pardee
19.	Louisiana St	8-4-0	Mike Archer
20.	Indiana	8-3-1	Bill Mallory

ANNUAL ASSOCIATED PRESS TOP 25

†1989

		RECORD	COACH
1.	Miami (FL)	11-1-0	Dennis Erickson
2.	Notre Dame	12-1-0	Lou Holtz
3.	Florida St	10-2-0	Bobby Bowden
4.	Colorado	11-1-0	Bill McCartney
5.	Tennessee	11-1-0	Johnny Majors
6.	Auburn	10-2-0	Pat Dye
7.	Michigan	10-2-0	Bo Schembechler
8.	Southern Cal	9-2-1	Larry Smith
9.	Alabama	10-2-0	Bill Curry
10.	Illinois	10-2-0	John Mackovic
11.	Nebraska	10-2-0	Tom Osborne
12.	Clemson	10-2-0	Danny Ford
13.	Arkansas	10-2-0	Ken Hatfield
14.	Houston	9-2-0	Jack Pardee

†1989 (CONT.)

		RECORD	COACH
15.	Penn St	8-3-1	Joe Paterno
16.	Michigan St	8-4-0	George Perles
17.	Pittsburgh	8-3-1	Mike Gottfried
18.	Virginia	10-3-0	George Welsh
19.	Texas Tech	9-3-0	Spike Dykes
20.	Texas A&M	8-4-0	R.C. Slocum
21.	W Virginia	8-3-1	Don Nehlen
22.	Brigham Young	10-3-0	LaVell Edwards
23.	Washington	8-4-0	Don James
24.	Ohio St	8-4-0	John Cooper
25.	Arizona	8-4-0	Dick Tomey

1990

		RECORD	COACH
1.	Colorado	11-1-1	Bill McCartney
2.	#Georgia Tech	11-0-1	Bobby Ross

†In 1989 the AP expanded its final poll to 25 teams.

ANNUAL ASSOCIATED PRESS TOP 25 (CONT.)

1990 (CONT.)

		RECORD	COACH
3.	Miami (FL)	10-2-0	Dennis Erickson
4.	Florida St	10-2-0	Bobby Bowden
5.	Washington	10-2-0	Don James
6.	Notre Dame	9-3-0	Lou Holtz
7.	Michigan	9-3-0	Gary Moeller
8.	Tennessee	9-2-2	Johnny Majors
9.	Clemson	10-2-0	Ken Hatfield
10.	Houston	10-1-0	John Jenkins
11.	Penn St	9-3-0	Joe Paterno
12.	Texas	10-2-0	David McWilliams
13.	Florida	9-2-0	Steve Spurrier
14.	Louisville	10-1-1	H. Schnellenberger
15.	Texas A&M	9-3-1	R.C. Slocum
16.	Michigan St	8-3-1	George Perles
17.	Oklahoma	8-3-0	Gary Gibbs
18.	Iowa	8-4-0	Hayden Fry
19.	Auburn	8-3-1	Pat Dye
20.	Southern Cal	8-4-1	Larry Smith
21.	Mississippi	9-3-0	Billy Brewer
22.	Brigham Young	10-3-0	LaVell Edwards
23.	Virginia	8-4-0	George Wells
24.	Nebraska	9-3-0	Tom Osborne
25.	Illinois	8-4-0	John Mackovic

#Selected No. 1 by UPI.

1991

		RECORD	COACH
1.	Miami (FL)	12-0-0	Dennis Erickson
2.	#Washington	12-0-0	Don James
3.	Penn St	11-2-0	Joe Paterno
4.	Florida St	11-2-0	Bobby Bowden
5.	Alabama	11-1-0	Gene Stallings
6.	Michigan	10-2-0	Gary Moeller
7.	Florida	10-2-0	Steve Spurrier
8.	California	10-2-0	Bruce Snyder
9.	E Carolina	11-1-0	Bill Lewis
10.	Iowa	10-1-1	Hayden Fry
11.	Syracuse	10-2-0	Paul Pasqualoni
12.	Texas A&M	10-2-0	R.C. Slocum
13.	Notre Dame	10-3-0	Lou Holtz
14.	Tennessee	9-3-0	Johnny Majors
15.	Nebraska	9-2-1	Tom Osborne
16.	Oklahoma	9-3-0	Gary Gibbs
17.	Georgia	9-3-0	Ray Goff
18.	Clemson	9-2-1	Ken Hatfield
19.	UCLA	9-3-0	Terry Donahue
20.	Colorado	8-3-1	Bill McCartney
21.	Tulsa	10-2-0	David Rader
22.	Stanford	8-4-0	Dennis Green
23.	Brigham Young	8-3-2	LaVell Edwards
24.	N Carolina St	9-3-0	Dick Sheridan
25.	Air Force	10-3-0	Fisher DeBerry

#Selected No. 1 by USA Today/ CNN.

1992

		RECORD	COACH
1.	Alabama	13-0-0	Gene Stallings
2.	Florida St	11-1-0	Bobby Bowden
3.	Miami	11-1-0	Dennis Erickson
4.	Notre Dame	10-1-1	Lou Holtz
5.	Michigan	9-0-3	Gary Moeller

1992 (CONT.)

		RECORD	COACH
6.	Syracuse	10-2-0	Paul Pasqualoni
7.	Texas A&M	12-1-0	R.C. Slocum
8.	Georgia	10-2-0	Ray Goff
9.	Stanford	10-3-0	Bill Walsh
10.	Florida	9-4-0	Steve Spurrier
11.	Washington	9-3-0	Don James
12.	Tennessee	9-3-0	Johnny Majors
13.	Colorado	9-2-1	Bill McCartney
14.	Nebraska	9-3-0	Tom Osborne
15.	Washington St	9-3-0	Mike Price
16.	Mississippi	9-3-0	Billy Brewer
17.	N Carolina St	9-3-1	Dick Sheridan
18.	Ohio St	8-3-1	John Cooper
19.	N Carolina	9-3-0	Mack Brown
20.	Hawaii	11-2-0	Bob Wagner
21.	Boston College	8-3-1	Tom Coughlin
22.	Kansas	8-4-0	Glen Mason
23.	Mississippi St	7-5-0	Jackie Sherrill
24.	Fresno St	9-4-0	Jim Sweeney
25.	Wake Forest	8-4-0	Bill Dooley

1993

		RECORD	COACH
1.	Florida St	12-1-0	Bobby Bowden
2.	Notre Dame	11-1-0	Lou Holtz
3.	Nebraska	11-1-0	Tom Osborne
4.	Auburn	11-0-0	Terry Bowden
5.	Florida	11-2-0	Steve Spurrier
6.	Wisconsin	10-1-1	Barry Alvarez
7.	W Virginia	11-1-0	Don Nehlen
8.	Penn St	10-2-0	Joe Paterno
9.	Texas A&M	10-2-0	R.C. Slocum
10.	Arizona	10-2-0	Dick Tomey
11.	Ohio St	10-1-1	John Cooper
12.	Tennessee	9-2-1	Phil Fulmer
13.	Boston College	9-3-0	Tom Coughlin
14.	Alabama	9-3-1	Gene Stallings
15.	Miami	9-3-0	Dennis Erickson
16.	Colorado	8-3-1	Bill McCartney
17.	Oklahoma	9-3-0	Gary Gibbs
18.	UCLA	8-4-0	Terry Donahue
19.	N Carolina	10-3-0	Mack Brown
20.	Kansas St	9-2-1	Bill Snyder
21.	Michigan	8-4-0	Gary Moeller
22.	Virginia Tech	9-3-0	Frank Beamer
23.	Clemson	9-3-0	Ken Hatfield
24.	Louisville	9-3-0	H. Schnellenberger
25.	California	9-4-0	Keith Gilbertson

1994

		RECORD	COACH
1.	Nebraska	13-0-0	Tom Osborne
2.	Penn St	12-0-0	Joe Paterno
3.	Colorado	11-1-0	Bill McCartney
4.	Florida St	10-1-1	Bobby Bowden
5.	Alabama	12-1-0	Gene Stallings
6.	Miami (FL)	10-2-0	Dennis Erickson
7.	Florida	10-2-1	Steve Spurrier
8.	Texas A&M	10-0-1	R.C. Slocum
9.	Auburn	9-1-1	Terry Bowden
10.	Utah	10-2-0	Ron McBride

1994 (CONT.)

		RECORD	COACH
11.	Oregon	9-4-0	Rich Brooks
12.	Michigan	8-4-0	Gary Moeller
13.	Southern Cal	8-3-1	John Robinson
14.	Ohio St	9-4-0	John Cooper
15.	Virginia	9-3-0	George Welsh
16.	Colorado St	10-2-0	Sonny Lubick
17.	N Carolina St	9-3-0	Mike O'Cain
18.	Brigham Young	10-3-0	LaVell Edwards
19.	Kansas St	9-3-0	Bill Snyder
20.	Arizona	8-4-0	Dick Tomey
21.	Washington St	8-4-0	Mike Price
22.	Tennessee	8-4-0	Phillip Fulmer
23.	Boston College	7-4-1	Dan Henning
24.	Mississippi St	8-4-0	Jackie Sherrill
25.	Texas	8-4-0	John Mackovic

1995

		RECORD	COACH
1.	Nebraska	12-0-0	Tom Osborne
2.	Florida	12-1-0	Steve Spurrier
3.	Tennessee	11-1-0	Phillip Fulmer
4.	Florida St	10-2-0	Bobby Bowden
5.	Colorado	10-2-0	Rick Neuheisel
6.	Ohio St	11-2-0	John Cooper
7.	Kansas St	10-2-0	Bill Snyder
8.	Northwestern	10-2-0	Gary Barnett
9.	Kansas	10-2-0	Glen Mason
10.	Virginia Tech	10-2-0	Frank Beamer
11.	Notre Dame	9-3-0	Lou Holtz
12.	Southern Cal	9-2-1	John Robinson
13.	Penn St	9-3-0	Joe Paterno
14.	Texas	10-2-1	John Mackovic
15.	Texas A&M	9-3-0	S.C. Slocum
16.	Virginia	9-4-0	George Welsh
17.	Michigan	9-4-0	Lloyd Carr
18.	Oregon	9-3-0	Mike Bellotti
19.	Syracuse	9-3-0	Paul Pasqualoni
20.	Miami (FL)	8-3-0	Butch Davis
21.	Alabama	8-3-0	Gene Stallings
22.	Auburn	8-4-0	Terry Bowden
23.	Texas Tech	9-3-0	Spike Dykes
24.	Toledo	11-0-1	Gary Pinkel
25.	Iowa	8-4-0	Hayden Fry

1996

		RECORD	COACH
1.	Florida	12-1	Steve Spurrier
2.	Ohio St	11-1	John Cooper
3.	Florida St	11-1	Bobby Bowden
4.	Arizona St	11-1	Bruce Snyder
5.	Brigham Young	14-1	LaVell Edwards
6.	Nebraska	11-2	Tom Osborne
7.	Penn St	11-2	Joe Paterno
8.	Colorado	10-2	Rick Neuheisel
9.	Tennessee	10-2	Phillip Fulmer
10.	N Carolina	10-2	Mack Brown
11.	Alabama	10-3	Gene Stallings
12.	Louisiana St	10-2	Gerry DiNardo

*In 1996 the NCAA introduced overtime to break ties.

1996 (CONT.)

		RECORD	COACH
13.	Virginia Tech	10-2	Frank Beamer
14.	Miami (FL)	9-3	Butch Davis
15.	Northwestern	9-3	Gary Barnett
16.	Washington	9-3	Jim Lambright
17.	Kansas St	9-3	Bill Snyder
18.	Iowa	9-3	Hayden Fry
19.	Notre Dame	8-3	Lou Holtz
20.	Michigan	8-4	Lloyd Carr
21.	Syracuse	9-3	Paul Pasqualoni
22.	Wyoming	10-2	Joe Tiller
23.	Texas	8-5	John Mackovic
24.	Auburn	8-4	Terry Bowden
25.	Army	10-2	Bob Sutton

1997

		RECORD	COACH
1.	Michigan	12-0	Lloyd Carr
2.	Nebraska	13-0	Tom Osborne
3.	Florida St	11-1	Bobby Bowden
4.	Florida	10-2	Steve Spurrier
5.	UCLA	10-2	Bob Toledo
6.	N Carolina	11-1	Mack Brown
7.	Tennessee	11-2	Phillip Fulmer
8.	Kansas St	11-1	Bill Snyder
9.	Washington St	10-2	Mike Price
10.	Georgia	10-2	Jim Donnan
11.	Auburn	10-3	Terry Bowden
12.	Ohio St	10-3	John Cooper
13.	Louisiana St	9-3	Gerry DiNardo
14.	Arizona St	8-3	Bruce Snyder
15.	Purdue	9-3	Joe Tiller
16.	Penn St	9-3	Joe Paterno
17.	Colorado St	11-2	Sonny Lubick
18.	Washington	8-4	Jim Lambright
19.	Southern Miss	9-3	Jeff Bower
20.	Texas A&M	9-4	R. C. Slocum
21.	Syracuse	9-4	Paul Pasqualoni
22.	Mississippi	8-4	Tommy Tuberville
23.	Missouri	7-5	Larry Smith
24.	Oklahoma St	8-4	Bob Simmons
25.	Georgia Tech	7-5	George O'Leary

1998

		RECORD	COACH
1.	Tennessee	13-0	Phillip Fulmer
2.	Ohio St	11-1	John Cooper
3.	Florida St	11-2	Bobby Bowden
4.	Arizona	12-1	Dick Tomey
5.	Florida	10-2	Steve Spurrier
6.	Wisconsin	11-1	Barry Alvarez
7.	Tulane	12-0	Tommy Bowden
8.	UCLA	10-2	Bob Toledo
9.	Georgia Tech	10-2	George O'Leary
10.	Kansas St	11-2	Bill Snyder
11.	Texas A&M	11-3	R.C. Slocum
12.	Michigan	10-3	Lloyd Carr
13.	Air Force	12-1	Fisher DeBerry
14.	Georgia	9-3	Jim Donnan
15.	Texas	9-3	Mack Brown
16.	Arkansas	9-3	Houston Nutt
17.	Penn St	9-3	Joe Paterno

ANNUAL ASSOCIATED PRESS TOP 25 (CONT.)

1998 (CONT.)

		RECORD	COACH
18.	Virginia	9–3	George Welsh
19.	Nebraska	9–4	Frank Solich
20.	Miami (FL)	9–3	Butch Davis
21.	Missouri	8–4	Larry Smith
22.	Notre Dame	9–3	Bob Davie
23.	Virginia Tech	9–3	Frank Beamer
24.	Purdue	9–4	Joe Tiller
25.	Syracuse	8–4	Paul Pasqualoni

1999

		RECORD	COACH
1.	Florida St	12–0	Bobby Bowden
2.	Virginia Tech	11–1	Frank Beamer
3.	Nebraska	12–1	Frank Solich
4.	Wisconsin	10–2	Barry Alvarez
5.	Michigan	10–2	Lloyd Carr
6.	Kansas St	11–1	Bill Snyder
7.	Michigan St	10–2	Nick Saban
8.	Alabama	10–3	Mike DuBose
9.	Tennessee	9–3	Phillip Fulmer
10.	Marshall	13–0	Bob Pruett
11.	Penn St	10–3	Joe Paterno
12.	Florida	9–4	Steve Spurrier
13.	Mississippi St	10–2	Jackie Sherrill
14.	Southern Miss	9–3	Jeff Bower
15.	Miami (FL)	9–4	Butch Davis
16.	Georgia	8–4	Jim Donnan
17.	Arkansas	8–4	Houston Nutt
18.	Minnesota	8–4	Glen Mason
19.	Oregon	9–3	Mike Bellotti
20.	Georgia Tech	8–4	Goerge O'Leary
21.	Texas	9–5	Mack Brown
22.	Mississippi	8–4	David Cutcliffe
23.	Texas A&M	8–4	R.C. Slocum
24.	Illinois	8–4	Ron Turner
25.	Purdue	7–5	Joe Tiller

2000

		RECORD	COACH
1.	Oklahoma	13–0	Bob Stoops
2.	Miami (FL)	11–1	Butch Davis
3.	Washington	11–1	Rick Neuheisel
4.	Oregon St	11–1	Dennis Erickson
5.	Florida St	11–2	Bobby Bowden
6.	Virginia Tech	11–1	Frank Beamer
7.	Oregon	10–2	Mike Belotti
8.	Nebraska	10–2	Frank Solich
9.	Kansas St	11–3	Bill Snyder
10.	Florida	10–3	Steve Spurrier
11.	Michigan	9–3	Lloyd Carr
12.	Texas	9–3	Mack Brown
13.	Purdue	8–4	Joe Tiller
14.	Colorado St	10–2	Sonny Lubeck
15.	Notre Dame	9–3	Bob Davie
16.	Clemson	9–3	Tommy Bowden
17.	Georgia Tech	9–3	George O'Leary
18.	Auburn	9–4	Tommy Tuberville
19.	S Carolina	8–4	Lou Holtz
20.	Georgia	8–4	Jim Donnan
21.	Texas Christian	10–2	Dennis Franchione
22.	Louisiana State	8–4	Nick Saban

2000 (CONT.)

		RECORD	COACH
23.	Wisconsin	9–4	Barry Alvarez
24.	Mississippi St	8–4	Jackie Sherrill
25.	Iowa St	9–3	Dan McCarney

2001

		RECORD	COACH
1.	Miami (FL)	12–0	Larry Coker
2.	Oregon	11–1	Mike Belotti
3.	Florida	10–2	Steve Spurrier
4.	Tennessee	11–2	Phillip Fulmer
5.	Texas	11–2	Mack Brown
6.	Oklahoma	11–2	Bob Stoops
7.	Louisiana St	10–3	Nick Saban
8.	Nebraska	11–2	Frank Solich
9.	Colorado	10–3	Gary Barnett
10.	Washington St	10–2	Mike Price
11.	Maryland	10–2	Ralph Friedgen
12.	Illinois	10–2	Ron Turner
13.	S Carolina	9–3	Lou Holtz
14.	Syracuse	10–3	Paul Pasqualoni
15.	Florida St	8–4	Bobby Bowden
16.	Stanford	9–3	Tyrone Willingham
17.	Louisville	11–2	John Smith
18.	Virginia Tech	8–4	Frank Beamer
19.	Washington	8–4	Rick Neuheisel
20.	Michigan	8–4	Lloyd Carr
21.	Boston College	8–4	Tom O'Brien
22.	Georgia	8–4	Mark Richt
23.	Toledo	10–2	Tom Amstutz
24.	Georgia Tech	8–5	George O'Leary
25.	Brigham Young	12–2	Gary Crowton

2002

		RECORD	COACH
1.	Ohio St	14–0	Jim Tressel
2.	Miami (FL)	12–1	Larry Coker
3.	Georgia	13–1	Mark Richt
4.	Southern Cal	11–2	Pete Carroll
5.	Oklahoma	12–2	Bob Stoops
6.	Texas	11–2	Mack Brown
7.	Kansas St	11–2	Bill Snyder
8.	Iowa	11–2	Kirk Ferentz
9.	Michigan	10–3	Lloyd Carr
10.	Washington St	10–3	Mike Price
11.	Alabama	10–3	Dennis Franchione
12.	N Carolina St	11–3	Chuck Amato
13.	Maryland	11–3	Ralph Friedgen
14.	Auburn	9–4	Tommy Tuberville
15.	Boise St	12–1	Dan Hawkins
16.	Penn St	9–4	Joe Paterno
17.	Notre Dame	10–3	Tyrone Willingham
18.	Virginia Tech	10–4	Frank Beamer
19.	Pittsburgh	9–4	Walt Harris
20.	Colorado	9–5	Gary Barnett
21.	Florida St	9–5	Bobby Bowden
22.	Viriginia	9–5	Al Groh
23.	Texas Christian	10–2	Gary Patterson
24.	Marshall	11–2	Bob Pruett
25.	W Virginia	9–4	Rich Rodriguez

NCAA DIVISIONAL CHAMPIONSHIPS

DIVISION I-AA

YEAR	WINNER	RUNNER-UP	SCORE
1978	Florida A&M	Massachusetts	35–28
1979	Eastern Kentucky	Lehigh	30–7
1980	Boise St	Eastern Kentucky	31–29
1981	Idaho St	Eastern Kentucky	34–23
1982	Eastern Kentucky	Delaware	17–14
1983	Southern Illinois	Western Carolina	43–7
1984	Montana St	Louisiana Tech	19–6
1985	Georgia Southern	Furman	44–42
1986	Georgia Southern	Arkansas St	48–21
1987	NE Louisiana	Marshall	43–42
1988	Furman	Georgia Southern	17–12
1989	Georgia Southern	Stephen F. Austin St	37–34
1990	Georgia Southern	NV-Reno	36–13
1991	Youngstown St	Marshall	25–17
1992	Marshall	Youngstown St	31–28
1993	Youngstown St	Marshall	17–5
1994	Youngstown St	Boise St	28–14
1995	Montana	Marshall	22–20
1996	Marshall	Montana	49–29
1997	Youngstown St	McNesse St	10–9
1998	Massachusetts	Georgia Southern	55–43
1999	Georgia Southern	Youngstown St	59–24
2000	Georgia Southern	Montana	27–25
2001	Montana	Furman	13–6
2002	Western Kentucky	McNeese St	34–14

DIVISION II

YEAR	WINNER	RUNNER-UP	SCORE
1973	Louisiana Tech	Western Kentucky	34–0
1974	Central Michigan	Delaware	54–14
1975	Northern Michigan	Western Kentucky	16–14
1976	Montana St	Akron	24–13
1977	Lehigh	Jacksonville St	33–0
1978	Eastern Illinois	Delaware	10–9
1979	Delaware	Youngstown St	38–21
1980	Cal Poly SLO	Eastern Illinois	21–13
1981	SW Texas St	N Dakota St	42–13
1982	SW Texas St	UC–Davis	34–9
1983	N Dakota St	Central St (OH)	41–21
1984	Troy St	N Dakota St	18–17
1985	N Dakota St	N Alabama	35–7
1986	N Dakota St	S Dakota	27–7
1987	Troy St	Portland St	31–17
1988	N Dakota St	Portland St	35–21
1989	Mississippi College	Jacksonville St	3–0
1990	N Dakota St	Indiana (PA)	51–11
1991	Pittsburg St	Jacksonville St	23–6
1992	Jacksonville St	Pittsburg St	17–13
1993	N Alabama	Indiana (PA)	41–34
1994	N Alabama	Texas A&M–Kingsville	16–10
1995	N Alabama	Pittsburg St	27–7
1996	Northern Colorado	Carson-Newman	23–14
1997	Northern Colorado	New Haven	51–0
1998	NW Missouri St	Carson-Newman	24–6
1999	NW Missouri St	Carson-Newman	58–52 (OT)
2000	Delta St	Bloomsburg	63–34
2001	Grand Valley St	N Dakota	17–14
2002	Grand Valley St	Valdosta St	31–24

NCAA DIVISIONAL CHAMPIONSHIPS (CONT.)

DIVISION III

YEAR	WINNER	RUNNER-UP	SCORE
1973	Wittenberg	Juniata	41–0
1974	Central (IA)	Ithaca	10–8
1975	Wittenberg	Ithaca	28–0
1976	St. John's (MN)	Towson St	31–28
1977	Widener	Wabash	39–36
1978	Baldwin-Wallace	Wittenberg	24–10
1979	Ithaca	Wittenberg	14–10
1980	Dayton	Ithaca	63–0
1981	Widener	Dayton	17–10
1982	W Georgia	Augustana (IL)	14–0
1983	Augustana (IL)	Union (NY)	21–17
1984	Augustana (IL)	Central (IA)	21–12
1985	Augustana (IL)	Ithaca	20–7
1986	Augustana (IL)	Salisbury St	31–3
1987	Wagner	Dayton	19–3
1988	Ithaca	Central (IA)	39–24
1989	Dayton	Union (NY)	17–7
1990	Allegheny	Lycoming	21–14 (OT)
1991	Ithaca	Dayton	34–20
1992	WI-LaCrosse	Washington & Jefferson	16–12
1993	Mount Union	Rowan	34–24
1994	Albion	Washington & Jefferson	38–15
1995	WI-LaCrosse	Rowan	36–7
1996	Mount Union	Rowan	56–24
1997	Mount Union	Lycoming	61–12
1998	Mount Union	Rowan	44–24
1999	Pacific Lutheran	Rowan	42–13
2000	Mount Union	St. John's	10–7
2001	Mount Union	Bridgewater	30–27
2002	Mount Union	Trinity (TX)	48–7

NAIA DIVISIONAL CHAMPIONSHIPS

DIVISION I

YEAR	WINNER	RUNNER-UP	SCORE
1956	St. Joseph's (IN)/ Montana St		0–0
1957	Pittsburg St (KS)	Hillsdale (MI)	27–26
1958	NE Oklahoma	Northern Arizona	19–13
1959	Texas A&I	Lenoir-Rhyne (NC)	20–7
1960	Lenoir-Rhyne (NC)	Humboldt St (CA)	15–14
1961	Pittsburg St (KS)	Linfield (OR)	12–7
1962	Central St (OK)	Lenoir-Rhyne (NC)	28–13
1963	St. John's (MN)	Prairie View (TX)	33–27
1964	Concordia-Moorhead/ Sam Houston		7–7
1965	St. John's (MN)	Linfield (OR)	33–0
1966	Waynesburg (PA)	WI-Whitewater	42–21
1967	Fairmont St (WV)	Eastern Washington	28–21
1968	Troy St (MI)	Texas A&I	43–35
1969	Texas A&I	Concordia-Moorhead (MN)	32–7
1970	Texas A&I	Wofford (SC)	48–7
1971	Livingston (AL)	Arkansas Tech	14–12
1972	E Texas St	Carson-Newman (TN)	21–18
1973	Abilene Christian	Elon (NC)	42–14
1974	Texas A&I	Henderson St (AR)	34–23
1975	Texas A&I	Salem (WV)	37–0
1976	Texas A&I	Central Arkansas	26–0
1977	Abilene Christian	SW Oklahoma	24–7
1978	Angelo St (TX)	Elon (NC)	34–14

NAIA DIVISIONAL CHAMPIONSHIPS (CONT.)

DIVISION I (CONT.)

YEAR	WINNER	RUNNER-UP	SCORE
1979	Texas A&I	Central St (OK)	20–14
1980	Elon (NC)	NE Oklahoma	17–10
1981	Elon (NC)	Pittsburg St	3–0
1982	Central St (OK)	Mesa (CO)	14–11
1983	Carson-Newman (TN)	Mesa (CO)	36–28
1984	Carson-Newman (TN)/Central Arkansas		19–19
1985	Central Arkansas/ Hillsdale (MI)		10–10
1986	Carson-Newman (TN)	Cameron (OK)	17–0
1987	Cameron (OK)	Carson-Newman (TN)	30–2
1988	Carson-Newman (TN)	Adams St (CO)	56–21
1989	Carson-Newman (TN)	Emporia St (KS)	34–20
1990	Central St (OH)	Mesa St (CO)	38–16
1991	Central Arkansas	Central St (OH)	19–16
1992	Central St (OH)	Gardner-Webb (NC)	19–16
1993	E Central (OK)	Glenville St (WV)	49–35
1994	Northeastern St (OK)	Arkansas–Pine Bluff	13–12
1995	Central St (OH)	Northeastern St (OK)	37–7
1996	SW Oklahoma St	Montana Tech	33–31
1997	Findlay (OH)	Willamette (OR)	14–7
1998	Azusa Pacific	Olivet Nazarene	17–14
1999	Northwestern Oklahoma St	Georgetown (KY)	34–26
2000	Georgetown (KY)	Northwestern Oklahoma St	20–0
2001	Georgetown (KY)	Sioux Falls	49–27
2002	Carroll (MN)	Georgetown (KY)	28–7

DIVISION II

YEAR	WINNER	RUNNER-UP	SCORE
1970	Westminster (PA)	Anderson (IN)	21–16
1971	California Lutheran	Westminster (PA)	30–14
1972	Missouri Southern	Northwestern (IA)	21–14
1973	Northwestern (IA)	Glenville St (WV)	10–3
1974	Texas Lutheran	Missouri Valley	42–0
1975	Texas Lutheran	California Lutheran	34–8
1976	Westminster (PA)	Redlands (CA)	20–13
1977	Westminster (PA)	California Lutheran	17–9
1978	Concordia-Moorhead (MN)	Findlay (OH)	7–0
1979	Findlay (OH)	Northwestern (IA)	51–6
1980	Pacific Lutheran	Wilmington (OH)	38–10
1981	Austin Coll./ Concordia-Moorhead (MN)		24–24
1982	Linfield (OR)	William Jewell (MO)	33–15
1983	Northwestern (IA)	Pacific Lutheran	25–21
1984	Linfield (OR)	Northwestern (IA)	33–22
1985	WI-La Crosse	Pacific Lutheran	24–7
1986	Linfield (OR)	Baker (KS)	17–0
1987	Pacific Lutheran	WI-Stevens Point*	16–16
1988	Westminster (PA)	WI-La Crosse	21–14
1989	Westminster (PA)	WI-La Crosse	51–30
1990	Peru St (NE)	Westminster (PA)	17–7
1991	Georgetown (KY)	Pacific Lutheran	28–20
1992	Findlay (OH)	Linfield (OR)	26–13
1993	Pacific Lutheran (WA)	Westminster (PA)	50–20
1994	Westminster (PA)	Pacific Lutheran	27–7
1995	Findlay (OH)/ Central Washington		21–21
1996	Sioux Falls (SD)	Western Washington	47–25

*Forfeited 1987 season due to use of an ineligible player.   †In 1997 the NAIA consolidated its two divisions into one.

AWARDS

HEISMAN MEMORIAL TROPHY

Awarded to the best college player by the Downtown Athletic Club of New York City. The trophy is named after John W. Heisman, who coached Georgia Tech to the national championship in 1917 and later served as DAC athletic director.

YEAR WINNER, COLLEGE, POSITION	WINNER'S SEASON STATISTICS	RUNNER-UP, COLLEGE
1935..Jay Berwanger, Chicago, HB	Rush: 119 Yds: 577 TD: 6	Monk Meyer, Army
1936..Larry Kelley, Yale, E	Rec: 17 Yds: 372 TD: 6	Sam Francis, Nebraska
1937..Clint Frank, Yale, HB	Rush: 157 Yds: 667 TD: 11	Byron White, Colorado
1938..†Davey O'Brien,	Att/Comp: 194/110 Yds: 1733	Marshall Goldberg, Pittsburgh
Texas Christian, QB	TD: 19	
1939..Nile Kinnick, Iowa, HB	Rush: 106 Yds: 374 TD: 5	Tom Harmon, Michigan
1940..Tom Harmon, Michigan, HB	Rush: 191 Yds: 852 TD: 16	John Kimbrough, Texas A&M
1941..†Bruce Smith, Minnesota, HB	Rush: 98 Yds: 480 TD: 6	Angelo Bertelli, Notre Dame
1942..Frank Sinkwich, Georgia, HB	Att/Comp: 166/84 Yds: 1392	Paul Governali, Columbia
	TD: 10	
1943..Angelo Bertelli, Notre Dame, QB	Att/Comp: 36/25 Yds: 511 TD: 10	Bob Odell, Pennsylvania
1944..Les Horvath, Ohio State, QB	Rush: 163 Yds: 924 TD: 12	Glenn Davis, Army
1945..*†Doc Blanchard, Army, FB	Rush: 101 Yds: 718 TD: 13	Glenn Davis, Army
1946..Glenn Davis, Army, HB	Rush: 123 Yds: 712 TD: 7	Charley Trippi, Georgia
1947..†John Lujack, Notre Dame, QB	Att/Comp: 109/61 Yds: 777 TD: 9	Bob Chappius, Michigan
1948..*Doak Walker,	Rush: 108 Yds: 532 TD: 8	Charlie Justice, N Carolina
Southern Methodist, HB		
1949..†Leon Hart, Notre Dame, E	Rec: 19 Yds: 257 TD: 5	Charlie Justice, N Carolina
1950..*Vic Janowicz, Ohio St, HB	Att/Comp: 77/32 Yds: 561 TD: 12	Kyle Rote, Southern Methodist
1951..Dick Kazmaier, Princeton, HB	Rush: 149 Yds: 861 TD: 9	Hank Lauricella, Tennessee
1952..Billy Vessels, Oklahoma, HB	Rush: 167 Yds: 1072 TD: 17	Jack Scarbath, Maryland
1953..John Lattner, Notre Dame, HB	Rush: 134 Yds: 651 TD: 6	Paul Giel, Minnesota
1954..Alan Ameche, Wisconsin, FB	Rush: 146 Yds: 641 TD: 9	Kurt Burris, Oklahoma
1955..Howard Cassady, Ohio St, HB	Rush: 161 Yds: 958 TD: 15	Jim Swink, Texas Christian
1956..Paul Hornung, Notre Dame, QB	Att/Comp: 111/59 Yds: 917 TD: 3	Johnny Majors, Tennessee
1957..John David Crow, Texas A&M, HB	Rush: 129 Yds: 562 TD: 10	Alex Karras, Iowa
1958..Pete Dawkins, Army, HB	Rush: 78 Yds: 428 TD: 6	Randy Duncan, Iowa
Year...Winner, College, Position	Winner's Season Statistics	Runner-Up, College
1959..Billy Cannon, Louisiana St, HB	Rush: 139 Yds: 598 TD: 6	Rich Lucas, Penn St
1960..Joe Bellino, Navy, HB	Rush: 168 Yds: 834 TD: 18	Tom Brown, Minnesota
1961..Ernie Davis, Syracuse, HB	Rush: 150 Yds: 823 TD: 15	Bob Ferguson, Ohio St
1962..Terry Baker, Oregon St, QB	Att/Comp: 203/112 Yds: 1738	Jerry Stovall, Louisiana St
	TD: 15	
1963..*Roger Staubach, Navy, QB	Att/Comp: 161/107 Yds: 1474	Billy Lothridge, Georgia Tech
	TD: 7	
1964..John Huarte, Notre Dame, QB	Att/Comp: 205/114 Yds: 2062	Jerry Rhome, Tulsa
	TD: 16	
1965..Mike Garrett, Southern Cal, HB	Rush: 267 Yds: 1440 TD: 16	Howard Twilley, Tulsa
1966..Steve Spurrier, Florida, QB	Att/Comp: 291/179 Yds: 2012	Bob Griese, Purdue
	TD: 16	
1967..Gary Beban, UCLA, QB	Att/Comp: 156/87 Yds: 1359	O.J. Simpson, Southern Cal
	TD: 8	
1968..O.J. Simpson, Southern Cal, HB	Rush: 383 Yds: 1880 TD: 23	Leroy Keyes, Purdue
1969..Steve Owens, Oklahoma, FB	Rush: 358 Yds: 1523 TD: 23	Mike Phipps, Purdue
1970..Jim Plunkett, Stanford, QB	Att/Comp: 358/191 Yds: 2715	Joe Theismann, Notre Dame
	TD: 18	
1971..Pat Sullivan, Auburn, QB	Att/Comp: 281/162 Yds: 2012	Ed Marinaro, Cornell
	TD: 20	
1972..Johnny Rodgers, Nebraska, FL	Rec: 55 Yds: 942 TD: 17	Greg Pruitt, Oklahoma
1973..John Cappelletti, Penn St, HB	Rush: 286 Yds: 1522 TD: 17	John Hicks, Ohio St
1974..*Archie Griffin, Ohio St, HB	Rush: 256 Yds: 1695 TD: 12	Anthony Davis, Southern Cal
1975..Archie Griffin, Ohio St, HB	Rush: 262 Yds: 1450 TD: 4	Chuck Muncie, California
1976..†Tony Dorsett, Pittsburgh, HB	Rush: 370 Yds: 2150 TD: 23	Ricky Bell, Southern Cal
1977..Earl Campbell, Texas, FB	Rush: 267 Yds: 1744 TD: 19	Terry Miller, Oklahoma St
1978..*Billy Sims, Oklahoma, HB	Rush: 231 Yds: 1762 TD: 20	Chuck Fusina, Penn St
1979..Charles White, Southern Cal, HB	Rush: 332 Yds: 1803 TD: 19	Billy Sims, Oklahoma
1980..George Rogers, S Carolina, HB	Rush: 324 Yds: 1894 TD: 14	Hugh Green, Pittsburgh
1981..Marcus Allen, Southern Cal, HB	Rush: 433 Yds: 2427 TD: 23	Herschel Walker, Georgia

AWARDS (CONT.)

HEISMAN MEMORIAL TROPHY (CONT.)

YEAR WINNER, COLLEGE, POSITION	WINNER'S SEASON STATISTICS	RUNNER-UP, COLLEGE
1982..*Herschel Walker, Georgia, HB	Rush: 335 Yds: 1752 TD: 17	John Elway, Stanford
1983..Mike Rozier, Nebraska, HB	Rush: 275 Yds: 2148 TD: 29	Steve Young, Brigham Young
1984..Doug Flutie, Boston College, QB	Att/Comp: 396/233 Yds: 3454 TD: 27	Keith Byars, Ohio St
1985..Bo Jackson, Auburn, HB	Rush: 278 Yds: 1786 TD: 17	Chuck Long, Iowa
1986..Vinny Testaverde, Miami (FL), QB	Att/Comp: 276/175 Yds: 2557 TD: 26	Paul Palmer, Temple
1987..Tim Brown, Notre Dame, WR	Rec: 39 Yds: 846 TD: 7	Don McPherson, Syracuse
1988..*Barry Sanders, Oklahoma St, RB	Rush: 344 Yds: 2628 TD: 39	Rodney Peete, Southern Cal
1989..*Andre Ware, Houston, QB	Att/Comp: 578/365 Yds: 4699 TD: 46	Anthony Thompson, Indiana
1990..*Ty Detmer, Brigham Young, QB	Att/Comp: 562/361 Yds: 5188 TD: 41	Raghib Ismail, Notre Dame
1991..*Desmond Howard, Michigan, WR	Rec: 61 Yds: 950 TD: 23	Casey Weldon, Florida St
1992..Gino Torretta, Miami (FL), QB	Att/Comp: 402/228 Yds: 3060 TD: 19	Marshall Faulk, San Diego St
1993..†Charlie Ward, Florida St, QB	Att/Comp: 380/264 Yds: 3032 TD: 27	Heath Shuler, Tennessee
1994..Rashaan Salaam, Colorado, RB	Rush: 298 Yds: 2055 TD: 24	Ki-Jana Carter, Penn St
1995..Eddie George, Ohio State, RB	Rush: 303 Yds: 1826 TD: 23	Tommie Frazier, Nebraska
1996..†Danny Wuerffel, Florida, QB	Att/Comp: 360/207 Yds: 3625 TD: 39	Troy Davis, Iowa St
1997..†Charles Woodson, Michigan, CB/ WR	7 interceptions; Rec: 11 Yds: 231 TD: 4	Peyton Manning, Tennessee
1998..Ricky Williams, Texas, RB	Rush: 361 Yds: 2124 TD: 28	Michael Bishop, Kansas St
1999..Ron Dayne, Wisconsin, RB	Rush: 303 Yds: 1834 TD: 19	Joe Hamilton, Georgia Tech
2000..Chris Weinke, Florida St, QB	Att/Comp: 431/266 Yds: 4167 TD: 33	Josh Heupel, Oklahoma
2001..Eric Crouch, Nebraska, QB	Att/Comp: 189/105 Yds: 1510 TD: 7; Rush: 1115 Yds, 18 TD	Rex Grossman, Florida
2002..Carson Palmer, Southern Cal, QB	Att/Comp: 458/288 Yds: 3639 TD: 32	Brad Banks, Iowa

*Juniors (all others seniors).   †Winners who played for national championship teams the same year.

Note: Former Heisman winners and national media cast votes, with ballots allowing for three names (3 points for first, 2 for second and 1 for third).

MAXWELL AWARD

Given to the nation's outstanding college football player by the Maxwell Football Club of Philadelphia.

YEAR	PLAYER, COLLEGE, POSITION	YEAR	PLAYER, COLLEGE, POSITION
1937	Clint Frank, Yale, HB	1958	Pete Dawkins, Army, HB
1938	Davey O'Brien, Texas Christian, QB	1959	Rich Lucas, Penn St, QB
1939	Nile Kinnick, Iowa, HB	1960	Joe Bellino, Navy, HB
1940	Tom Harmon, Michigan, HB	1961	Bob Ferguson, Ohio St, FB
1941	Bill Dudley, Virginia, HB	1962	Terry Baker, Oregon St, QB
1942	Paul Governali, Columbia, QB	1963	Roger Staubach, Navy, QB
1943	Bob Odell, Pennsylvania, HB	1964	Glenn Ressler, Penn St, C
1944	Glenn Davis, Army, HB	1965	Tommy Nobis, Texas, LB
1945	Doc Blanchard, Army, FB	1966	Jim Lynch, Notre Dame, LB
1946	Charley Trippi, Georgia, HB	1967	Gary Beban, UCLA, QB
1947	Doak Walker, Southern Meth, HB	1968	O.J. Simpson, Southern Cal, RB
1948	Chuck Bednarik, Pennsylvania, C	1969	Mike Reid, Penn St, DT
1949	Leon Hart, Notre Dame, E	1970	Jim Plunkett, Stanford, QB
1950	Reds Bagnell, Pennsylvania, HB	1971	Ed Marinaro, Cornell, RB
1951	Dick Kazmaier, Princeton, HB	1972	Brad Van Pelt, Michigan St, DB
1952	John Lattner, Notre Dame, HB	1973	John Cappelletti, Penn St, RB
1953	John Lattner, Notre Dame, HB	1974	Steve Joachim, Temple, QB
1954	Ron Beagle, Navy, E	1975	Archie Griffin, Ohio St, RB
1955	Howard Cassady, Ohio St, HB	1976	Tony Dorsett, Pittsburgh, RB
1956	Tommy McDonald, Oklahoma, HB	1977	Ross Browner, Notre Dame, DE
1957	Bob Reifsnyder, Navy, T		

AWARDS (CONT.)

MAXWELL AWARD (CONT.)

YEAR	PLAYER, COLLEGE, POSITION
1978	Chuck Fusina, Penn St, QB
1979	Charles White, Southern Cal, RB
1980	Hugh Green, Pittsburgh, DE
1981	Marcus Allen, Southern Cal, RB
1982	Herschel Walker, Georgia, RB
1983	Mike Rozier, Nebraska, RB
1984	Doug Flutie, Boston College, QB
1985	Chuck Long, Iowa, QB
1986	Vinny Testaverde, Miami (FL), QB
1987	Don McPherson, Syracuse, QB
1988	Barry Sanders, Oklahoma St, RB
1989	Anthony Thompson, Indiana, RB
1990	Ty Detmer, Brigham Young, QB
1991	Desmond Howard, Michigan, WR
1992	Gino Torretta, Miami (FL), QB
1993	Charlie Ward, Florida St, QB
1994	Kerry Collins, Penn St, QB
1995	Eddie George, Ohio St, RB
1996	Danny Wuerffel, Florida, QB
1997	Peyton Manning, Tennessee, QB
1998	Ricky Williams, Texas, RB
1999	Ron Dayne, Wisconsin, RB
2000	Drew Brees, Purdue, QB
2001	Ken Dorsey, Miami (FL), QB
2002	Larry Johnson, Penn St, RB

DAVEY O'BRIEN NATIONAL QUARTERBACK AWARD

Given to the top quarterback in the nation by the Davey O'Brien Educational and Charitable Trust of Fort Worth. Named for Texas Christian Hall of Fame quarterback Davey O'Brien (1936–38).

YEAR	PLAYER, COLLEGE
1981	Jim McMahon, Brigham Young
1982	Todd Blackledge, Penn St
1983	Steve Young, Brigham Young
1984	Doug Flutie, Boston College
1985	Chuck Long, Iowa
1986	Vinny Testaverde, Miami (FL)
1987	Don McPherson, Syracuse
1988	Troy Aikman, UCLA
1989	Andre Ware, Houston
1990	Ty Detmer, Brigham Young
1991	Ty Detmer, Brigham Young
1992	Gino Torretta, Miami (FL)
1993	Charlie Ward, Florida St
1994	Kerry Collins, Penn St
1995	Danny Wuerffel, Florida
1996	Danny Wuerffel, Florida
1997	Peyton Manning, Tennessee
1998	Michael Bishop, Kansas St
1999	Joe Hamilton, Georgia Tech
2000	Chris Weinke, Florida St
2001	Eric Crouch, Nebraska
2002	Brad Banks, Iowa

Note: Originally honored the outstanding football player in the Southwest as follows: 1977—Earl Campbell, Texas, RB; 1978—Billy Sims, Oklahoma, RB; 1979—Mike Singletary, Baylor, LB; 1980—Mike Singletary, Baylor, LB.

VINCE LOMBARDI/ROTARY AWARD

Given to the outstanding college lineman of the year, the award is sponsored by the Rotary Club of Houston.

YEAR	PLAYER, COLLEGE, POSITION
1970	Jim Stillwagon, Ohio St, MG
1971	Walt Patulski, Notre Dame, DE
1972	Rich Glover, Nebraska, MG
1973	John Hicks, Ohio St, OT
1974	Randy White, Maryland, DT
1975	Lee Roy Selmon, Oklahoma, DT
1976	Wilson Whitley, Houston, DT
1977	Ross Browner, Notre Dame, DE
1978	Bruce Clark, Penn St, DT
1979	Brad Budde, Southern Cal, G
1980	Hugh Green, Pittsburgh, DE
1981	Kenneth Sims, Texas, DT
1982	Dave Rimington, Nebraska, C
1983	Dean Steinkuhler, Nebraska, G
1984	Tony Degrate, Texas, DT
1985	Tony Casillas, Oklahoma, NG
1986	Cornelius Bennett, Alabama, LB
1987	Chris Spielman, Ohio St, LB
1988	Tracy Rocker, Auburn, DT
1989	Percy Snow, Michigan St, LB
1990	Chris Zorich, Notre Dame, NG
1991	Steve Emtman, Washington, DT
1992	Marvin Jones, Florida St, LB
1993	Aaron Taylor, Notre Dame, OT
1994	Warren Sapp, Miami (FL), DT
1995	Orlando Pace, Ohio St, OT
1996	Orlando Pace, Ohio St, OT
1997	Grant Wistrom, Nebraska, DE
1998	Dat Nguyen, Texas A&M, LB
1999	Corey Moore, Virginia Tech, DE
2000	Jamal Reynolds, Florida St, DE
2001	Julius Peppers, N Carolina, DE
2002	Terrell Suggs, Arizona St, DL

AWARDS (CONT.)

OUTLAND TROPHY

Given to the outstanding interior lineman, selected by the Football Writers Association of America.

YEAR	PLAYER, COLLEGE, POSITION
1946	George Connor, Notre Dame, T
1947	Joe Steffy, Army, G
1948	Bill Fischer, Notre Dame, G
1949	Ed Bagdon, Michigan St, G
1950	Bob Gain, Kentucky, T
1951	Jim Weatherall, Oklahoma, T
1952	Dick Modzelewski, Maryland, T
1953	J.D. Roberts, Oklahoma, G
1954	Bill Brooks, Arkansas, G
1955	Calvin Jones, Iowa, G
1956	Jim Parker, Ohio St, G
1957	Alex Karras, Iowa, T
1958	Zeke Smith, Auburn, G
1959	Mike McGee, Duke, T
1960	Tom Brown, Minnesota, G
1961	Merlin Olsen, Utah St, T
1962	Bobby Bell, Minnesota, T
1963	Scott Appleton, Texas, T
1964	Steve DeLong, Tennessee, T
1965	Tommy Nobis, Texas, G
1966	Loyd Phillips, Arkansas, T
1967	Ron Yary, Southern Cal, T
1968	Bill Stanfill, Georgia, T
1969	Mike Reid, Penn St, DT
1970	Jim Stillwagon, Ohio St, MG
1971	Larry Jacobson, Nebraska, DT
1972	Rich Glover, Nebraska, MG
1973	John Hicks, Ohio St, OT
1974	Randy White, Maryland, DE
1975	Lee Roy Selmon, Oklahoma, DT
1976	Ross Browner, Notre Dame, DE
1977	Brad Shearer, Texas, DT
1978	Greg Roberts, Oklahoma, G
1979	Jim Ritcher, N Carolina St, C
1980	Mark May, Pittsburgh, OT
1981	Dave Rimington, Nebraska, C
1982	Dave Rimington, Nebraska, C
1983	Dean Steinkuhler, Nebraska, G
1984	Bruce Smith, Virginia Tech, DT
1985	Mike Ruth, Boston College, NG
1986	Jason Buck, Brigham Young, DT
1987	Chad Hennings, Air Force, DT
1988	Tracy Rocker, Auburn, DT
1989	Mohammed Elewonibi, Brigham Young, G
1990	Russell Maryland, Miami (FL), DT
1991	Steve Emtman, Washington, DT
1992	Will Shields, Nebraska, G
1993	Rob Waldrop, Arizona, NG
1994	Zach Wiegert, Nebraska, G
1995	Jonathan Ogden, UCLA, OT
1996	Orlando Pace, Ohio St, OT
1997	Aaron Taylor, Nebraska, G
1998	Kris Farris, UCLA, OL
1999	Chris Samuels, Alabama, OL
2000	John Henderson, Tennessee, DT
2001	Bryant McKinnie, Miami (FL), OT
2002	Rien Long, Washington St, DL

BUTKUS AWARD

Given to the top collegiate linebacker, the award was established by the Downtown Athletic Club of Orlando and named for college Hall of Famer Dick Butkus of Illinois.

YEAR	PLAYER, COLLEGE
1985	Brian Bosworth, Oklahoma
1986	Brian Bosworth, Oklahoma
1987	Paul McGowan, Florida St
1988	Derrick Thomas, Alabama
1989	Percy Snow, Michigan St
1990	Alfred Williams, Colorado
1991	Erick Anderson, Michigan
1992	Marvin Jones, Florida St
1993	Trev Alberts, Nebraska
1994	Dana Howard, Illinois
1995	Kevin Hardy, Illinois
1996	Matt Russell, Colorado
1997	Andy Katzenmoyer, Ohio St
1998	Chris Claiborne, Southern Cal
1999	LaVar Arrington, Penn St
2000	Dan Morgan, Miami (FL)
2001	Rocky Calmus, Oklahoma
2002	E.J. Henderson, Maryland

JIM THORPE AWARD

Given to the best defensive back of the year, the award is presented by the Jim Thorpe Athletic Club of Oklahoma City.

YEAR	PLAYER, COLLEGE
1986	Thomas Everett, Baylor
1987	Bennie Blades, Miami (FL)
	Rickey Dixon, Oklahoma
1988	Deion Sanders, Florida St
1989	Mark Carrier, Southern Cal
1990	Darryl Lewis, Arizona
1991	Terrell Buckley, Florida St
1992	Deon Figures, Colorado
1993	Antonio Langham, Alabama
1994	Chris Hudson, Colorado
1995	Greg Myers, Colorado St
1996	Lawrence Wright, Florida
1997	Charles Woodson, Michigan
1998	Antoine Winfield, Ohio St
1999	Tyrone Carter, Minnesota
2000	Jamar Fletcher, Wisconsin
2001	Roy Williams, Oklahoma
2002	Terence Newman, Kansas St

AWARDS (CONT.)

WALTER PAYTON PLAYER OF THE YEAR AWARD

Given to the top Division I-AA player as voted by Division I-AA sports information directors. Sponsored by Sports Network.

YEAR	PLAYER, COLLEGE, POSITION	YEAR	PLAYER, COLLEGE, POSITION
1987	Kenny Gamble, Colgate, RB	1995	Dave Dickenson, Montana, QB
1988	Dave Meggett, Towson St, RB	1996	Archie Amerson, Northern Arizona, RB
1989	John Friesz, Idaho, QB	1997	Brian Finneran, Villanova, WR
1990	Walter Dean, Grambling, RB	1998	Jerry Azumah, New Hampshire, RB
1991	Jamie Martin, Weber St, QB	1999	Adrian Peterson, Georgia Southern, RB
1992	Michael Payton, Marshall, QB	2000	Louis Ivory, Furman, RB
1993	Doug Nussmeier, Idaho, QB	2001	Brian Westbrook, Villanova, RB
1994	Steve McNair, Alcorn St, QB	2002	Tony Romo, Eastern Illinois, QB

NCAA DIVISION I-A INDIVIDUAL RECORDS

CAREER

SCORING

Most Points Scored: 468—Travis Prentice, Miami (OH), 1996–99
Most Points Scored per Game: 12.1—Marshall Faulk, San Diego St, 1991–93
Most Touchdowns Scored: 78—Travis Prentice, Miami (OH), 1996–99
Most Touchdowns Scored per Game: 2.0—Marshall Faulk, San Diego St, 1991–93
Most Touchdowns Scored, Rushing: 73—Travis Prentice, Miami (OH), 1996–99
Most Touchdowns Scored, Passing: 121—Ty Detmer, Brigham Young, 1988–91
Most Touchdowns Scored, Receiving: 50— Troy Edwards, Louisiana Tech, 1996–98
Most Touchdowns Scored, Interception Returns: 5—Ken Thomas, San Jose St, 1979–82; Jackie Walker, Tennessee, 1969–71; Deltha O'Neal, California, 1996–99
Most Touchdowns Scored, Punt Returns: 7—Johnny Rodgers, Nebraska, 1970–72; Jack Mitchell, Oklahoma, 1946–48; David Allen, Kansas St, 1997–99
Most Touchdowns Scored, Kickoff Returns: 6—Anthony Davis, Southern Cal, 1972–74

TOTAL OFFENSE

Most Plays: 1,917—Antwaan Randle El, Indiana, 1998–01
Most Plays per Game: 48.5—Doug Gaynor, Long Beach St, 1984–85
Most Yards Gained: 14,665—Ty Detmer, Brigham Young, 1988–91 (15,031 passing, -366 rushing)
Most Yards Gained per Game: 382.4—Tim Rattay, Louisiana Tech, 1997–99
Most 300+ Yard Games: 33 —Ty Detmer, Brigham Young, 1988–91

Note: All career records entering 2002 season.

RUSHING

Most Rushes: 1,215—Steve Bartalo, Colorado St, 1983–86 (4813 yds)
Most Rushes per Game: 34.0—Ed Marinaro, Cornell, 1969–71
Most Yards Gained: 6,397—Ron Dayne, Wisconsin, 1996–99
Most Yards Gained per Game: 174.6—Ed Marinaro, Cornell, 1969–71
Most 100+ Yard Games: 33—Tony Dorsett, Pittsburgh, 1973–76; Archie Griffin, Ohio St, 1972–75
Most 200+ Yard Games: 11—Marcus Allen, Southern Cal, 1978–81; Ricky Williams, Texas, 1995–98; Ron Dayne, Wisconsin, 1996–99

PASSING

Highest Passing Efficiency Rating: 163.6—Danny Wuerffel, Florida, 1993–96 (1,170 attempts, 708 completions, 42 interceptions, 10,875 yards, 114 touchdown passes)
Most Passes Attempted: 1,679—Chris Redman, Louisville, 1996–99
Most Passes Attempted per Game: 47.0—Tim Rattay, Louisiana Tech, 1997–99
Most Passes Completed: 1,031—Chris Redman, Louisville, 1996–99
Most Passes Completed per Game: 30.8—Tim Rattay, Louisiana Tech, 1997–99
*Highest Completion Percentage: 67.1—Tim Couch, Kentucky, 1996–98
Most Yards Gained: 15,031—Ty Detmer, Brigham Young, 1988–91
Most Yards Gained per Game: 386.2—Tim Rattay, Louisiana Tech, 1997–99

*Minimum 1,000 attempts.

CAREER (CONT.)

RECEIVING

Most Passes Caught: 300—Arnold Jackson, Louisville, 1997–00
Most Passes Caught per Game: 10.5—Emmanuel Hazard, Houston, 1989–90
Most Yards Gained: 5,005—Trevor Insley, Nevada, 1996–99
Most Yards Gained per Game: 140.9—Alex Van Dyke, Nevada, 1994–95
Highest Average Gain per Reception: 25.7—Wesley Walker, California, 1973–75

ALL-PURPOSE RUNNING

Most Plays: 1,347—Steve Bartalo, Colorado St, 1983-86 (1,215 rushes, 132 receptions)
Most Yards Gained: 7,206—Ricky Williams, Texas, 1995–98 (6,279 rushing, 927 receiving)
Most Yards Gained per Game: 237.8—Ryan Benjamin, Pacific, 1990–92
Highest Average Gain per Play: 17.4—Anthony Carter, Michigan, 1979–82

INTERCEPTIONS

Most Passes Intercepted: 29—Al Brosky, Illinois, 1950–52
Most Passes Intercepted per Game: 1.1—Al Brosky, Illinois, 1950–52
Most Yards on Interception Returns: 501—Terrell Buckley, Florida St, 1989–91
Highest Average Gain per Interception: 26.5—Tom Pridemore, W Virginia, 1975–77

SPECIAL TEAMS

Highest Punt Return Average: 23.6—Jack Mitchell, Oklahoma, 1946–48
Highest Kickoff Return Average: 36.2—Forrest Hall, San Francisco, 1946–47
Highest Average Yards per Punt: 46.3—Todd Sauerbrun, W Virginia, 1991–94

SINGLE SEASON

SCORING

Most Points Scored: 234—Barry Sanders, Oklahoma St, 1988
Most Points Scored per Game: 21.3—Barry Sanders, Oklahoma St, 1988
Most Touchdowns Scored: 39—Barry Sanders, Oklahoma St, 1988
Most Touchdowns Scored, Rushing: 37—Barry Sanders, Oklahoma St, 1988
Most Touchdowns Scored, Passing: 54—David Klingler, Houston, 1990
Most Touchdowns Scored, Receiving: 27—Troy Edwards, Louisiana Tech, 1998
Most Touchdowns Scored, Interception Returns: 4—Deltha O'Neal, California, 1999
Most Touchdowns Scored, Punt Returns: 4—Santana Moss, Miami (FL), 2000; David Allen, Kansas St, 1998; Quinton Spotwood, Syracuse, 1997; Tinker Keck, Cincinnati, 1997; James Henry, Southern Miss, 1987; Golden Richards, Brigham Young, 1971; Cliff Branch, Colorado, 1971
Most Touchdowns Scored, Kickoff Returns: 3—Leland McElroy, Texas A&M, 1993; Terance Mathis, New Mexico, 1989; Willie Gault, Tennessee, 1980; Anthony Davis, Southern Cal, 1974; Stan Brown, Purdue, 1970; Forrest Hall, San Francisco, 1946

TOTAL OFFENSE

Most Plays: 704—David Klingler, Houston, 1990
Most Yards Gained: 5,221—David Klingler, Houston, 1990
Most Yards Gained per Game: 474.6—David Klingler, Houston, 1990
Most 300+ Yard Games: 12—Ty Detmer, Brigham Young, 1990

RUSHING

Most Rushes: 403—Marcus Allen, Southern Cal, 1981
Most Rushes per Game: 39.6—Ed Marinaro, Cornell, 1971
Most Yards Gained: 2,628—Barry Sanders, Oklahoma St, 1988
Most Yards Gained per Game: 238.9—Barry Sanders, Oklahoma St, 1988
Most 100+ Yard Games: 11—By 14 players, most recently Ahman Green, Nebraska, 1997

PASSING

Highest Passing Efficiency Rating: 183.3—Shaun King, Tulane, 1998 (328 attempts, 223 completions, 6 interceptions, 3,232 yards, 36 TD passes)
Most Passes Attempted: 643—David Klingler, Houston, 1990
Most Passes Attempted per Game: 58.5—David Klingler, Houston, 1990
Most Passes Completed: 400—Tim Couch, Kentucky, 1998
Most Passes Completed per Game: 36.4—Tim Couch, Kentucky, 1998
Highest Completion Percentage: 73.6—Daunte Culpepper, Central Florida, 1998
Most Yards Gained: (12 games) 5,188—Ty Detmer, Brigham Young, 1990; (11 games) 5,140—David Klingler, Houston, 1990
Most Yards Gained per Game: 467.3—David Klingler, Houston, 1990

NCAA DIVISION I-A INDIVIDUAL RECORDS (CONT.)

SINGLE SEASON (CONT.)

RECEIVING

Most Passes Caught: 142—Emmanuel Hazard, Houston, 1989
Most Passes Caught per Game: 13.4—Howard Twilley, Tulsa, 1965
Most Yards Gained: 2,060—Trevor Insley, Nevada, 1999
Most Yards Gained per Game: 187.3—Trevor Insley, Nevada, 1999
Highest Average Gain per Reception: 27.9—Elmo Wright, Houston, 1968 (min. 30 receptions)

ALL-PURPOSE RUNNING

Most Plays: 432—Marcus Allen, Southern Cal, 1981
Most Yards Gained: 3,250—Barry Sanders, Oklahoma St, 1988
Most Yards Gained per Game: 295.5—Barry Sanders, Oklahoma St, 1988
Highest Average Gain per Play: 18.5—Henry Bailey, UNLV, 1992

INTERCEPTIONS

Most Passes Intercepted: 14 — Al Worley, Washington, 1968
Most Yards on Interception Returns: 302 — Charles Phillips, Southern Cal, 1974
Highest Average Gain per Interception: 50.6 — Norm Thompson, Utah, 1969

SPECIAL TEAMS

Highest Punt Return Average: 25.9 — Bill Blackstock, Tennessee, 1951
Highest Kickoff Return Average: 40.1 — Paul Allen, Brigham Young, 1961
Highest Average Yards per Punt: 50.3 — Chad Kessler, Louisiana St, 1997

SINGLE GAME

SCORING

Most Points Scored: 48—Howard Griffith, Illinois, 1990 (vs Southern Illinois)
Most Field Goals: 7—Dale Klein, Nebraska, 1985 (vs Missouri); Mike Prindle, Western Michigan, 1934 (vs Marshall)
Most Extra Points (Kick): 13—Derek Mahoney, Fresno St, 1991 (vs New Mexico); Terry Leiweke, Houston, 1968 (vs Tulsa)
Most Extra Points (2-Pts): 6—Jim Pilot, New Mexico St, 1961 (vs Hardin-Simmons)

TOTAL OFFENSE

Most Yards Gained: 732—David Klingler, Houston, 1990 (vs Arizona St)

RUSHING

Most Yards Gained: 406—LaDainian Tomlinson, Texas Christian, 1999 (vs UTEP)
Most Touchdowns Rushed: 8—Howard Griffith, Illinois, 1990 (vs Southern Illinois)

PASSING

Most Passes Completed: 55—Rusty LaRue, Wake Forest, 1995 (vs Duke); Drew Brees, Purdue, 1998 (vs Wisconsin)
Most Yards Gained: 716—David Klingler, Houston, 1990 (vs Arizona St)
Most Touchdown Passes: 11—David Klingler, Houston, 1990 [vs Eastern Washington (I-AA)]

RECEIVING

Most Passes Caught: 23—Randy Gatewood, UNLV, 1994 (vs Idaho)
Most Yards Gained: 405—Troy Edwards, Louisiana Tech, 1998 (vs Nebraska)
Most Touchdown Catches: 6—Tim Delaney, San Diego St, 1969 (vs New Mexico St)

NCAA DIVISION I-AA INDIVIDUAL RECORDS

CAREER

SCORING

Most Points Scored: 544—Brian Westbrook, Villanova, 1998-2001
Most Touchdowns Scored: 89—Brian Westbrook, Villanova, 1998-2001
Most Touchdowns Scored, Rushing: 84—Adrian Peterson, Georgia Southern, 1998–2001
Most Touchdowns Scored, Passing: 139—Willie Totten, Mississippi Valley, 1982–85
Most Touchdowns Scored, Receiving: 50—Jerry Rice, Mississippi Valley, 1981–84

RUSHING

Most Rushes: 1,124—Charles Roberts, Cal St–Sacramento, 1997–2000
Most Rushes per Game: 38.2—Arnold Mickens, Butler, 1994–95
Most Yards Gained: 6,559—Adrian Peterson, Georgia Southern, 1998–2001
Most Yards Gained per Game: 190.7—Arnold Mickens, Butler, 1994–95

Note: Career records entering 2002 season.

PASSING

Highest Passing Efficiency Rating: 170.8—Shawn Knight, William & Mary, 1991–94
Most Passes Attempted: 1,680—Marcus Brady, Cal St–Northridge, 1998-2001; Steve McNair, Alcorn St, 1991–94
Most Passes Completed: 1,039—Marcus Brady, Cal St–Northridge, 1998-2001
Most Passes Completed per Game: 26.5—Chris Sanders, Chattanooga, 1999–2000
Highest Completion Percentage: 67.3—Dave Dickenson, Montana, 1992–95
Most Yards Gained: 14,496—Steve McNair, Alcorn St, 1991–94
Most Yards Gained per Game: 350.0—Neil Lomax, Portland St, 1978–80

RECEIVING

Most Passes Caught: 317—Jacquay Nunnally, Florida A&M, 1997–2000
Most Yards Gained: 4,693—Jerry Rice, Mississippi Valley, 1981–84
Most Yards Gained per Game: 116.9—Derrick Ingram, Alabama–Birmingham, 1993–94
Highest Average Gain per Reception: 24.3—John Taylor, Delaware St, 1982–85

SINGLE SEASON

SCORING

Most Points Scored: 176—Brian Westbrook, Villanova, 2001
Most Touchdowns Scored: 29—Adrian Peterson, Georgia Southern, 1999; Brian Westbrook, Villanova, 2001
Most Touchdowns Scored, Rushing: 28—Adrian Peterson, Georgia Southern, 1999
Most Touchdowns Scored, Passing: 56—Willie Totten, Mississippi Valley, 1984
Most Touchdowns Scored, Receiving: 27—Jerry Rice, Mississippi Valley, 1984

RUSHING

Most Rushes: 409—Arnold Mickens, Butler, 1994
Most Rushes per Game: 40.9—Arnold Mickens, Butler, 1994
Most Yards Gained: 2,260—Charles Roberts, Cal St–Sacramento, 1998
Most Yards Gained per Game: 225.5—Arnold Mickens, Butler, 1994

PASSING

Highest Passing Efficiency Rating: 204.6—Shawn Knight, William & Mary, 1993
Most Passes Attempted: 577—Joe Lee, Towson, 1999
Most Passes Completed: 324—Willie Totten, Mississippi Valley, 1984
Most Passes Completed per Game: 32.4—Willie Totten, Mississippi Valley, 1984
Highest Completion Percentage: 70.6—Giovanni Carmazzi, Hofstra, 1997
Most Yards Gained: 4,863—Steve McNair, Alcorn St, 1994
Most Yards Gained per Game: 455.7—Willie Totten, Mississippi Valley, 1984

RECEIVING

Most Passes Caught: 120—Stephen Campbell, Brown, 2000
Most Yards Gained: 1,712—Eddie Conti, Delaware, 1998
Most Yards Gained per Game: 168.2—Jerry Rice, Mississippi Valley, 1984
Highest Average Gain per Reception: 28.9—Mikhael Ricks, Stephen F. Austin, 1997; (min. 35 receptions)

NCAA DIVISION I-AA INDIVIDUAL RECORDS (CONT.)

SINGLE GAME

SCORING

Most Points Scored: 42—Jesse Burton, McNeese St, 1998 (vs Southern Utah); Archie Amerson, Northern Arizona, 1996 (vs Weber St)
Most Field Goals: 8—Goran Lingmerth, Northern Arizona, 1986 (vs Idaho)

RUSHING

Most Yards Gained: 437—Maurice Hicks, N Carolina A&T, 2001 (vs Morgan St)
Most Touchdowns Rushed: 7—Archie Amerson, Northern Arizona, 1996 (vs Weber St)

PASSING

Most Passes Completed: 48—Clayton Millis, Cal St–Northridge, 1995 (vs St. Mary's [CA])
Most Yards Gained: 624—Jamie Martin, Weber St, 1991 (vs Idaho St)
Most Touchdown Passes: 9—Willie Totten, Mississippi Valley, 1984 (vs Kentucky St)

RECEIVING

Most Passes Caught: 24—Chas Gessner, Brown, 2002 (vs Rhode Island); Jerry Rice, Mississippi Valley, 1983 (vs Southern–BR)
Most Yards Gained: 376—Kassim Osgood, Cal Poly, 2000 (vs Northern Iowa)
Most Touchdown Catches: 6—Cos DeMatteo, Chattanooga, 2000 (vs Mississippi Valley)

NCAA DIVISION II INDIVIDUAL RECORDS

CAREER

SCORING

Most Points Scored: 544—Brian Shay, Emporia St, 1995–98
Most Touchdowns Scored: 88—Brian Shay, Emporia St, 1995–98
Most Touchdowns Scored, Rushing: 81—Brian Shay, Emporia St, 1995–98
Most Touchdowns Scored, Passing: 116—Chris Hatcher, Valdosta St, 1991–94
Most Touchdowns Scored, Receiving: 49—Bruce Cerone, Yankton/Emporia St, 1965–69

RUSHING

Most Rushes: 1,131—Josh Ranek, S Dakota St, 1997–01
Most Rushes per Game: 29.8—Bernie Peeters, Luther, 1968–71
Most Yards Gained: 6,958—Brian Shay, Emporia St, 1995–98
Most Yards Gained per Game: 183.4—Anthony Gray, Western NM, 1997–98

PASSING

Highest Passing Efficiency Rating: 190.8—Dusty Bonner, Valdosta St, 2000–01
Most Passes Attempted: 1,719—Bob McLaughlin, Lock Haven, 1992–95
Most Passes Completed: 1,001—Chris Hatcher, Valdosta St, 1991–94
Most Passes Completed per Game: 25.7—Chris Hatcher, Valdosta St, 1991–94
Highest Completion Percentage: 72.7—Dusty Bonner, Valdosta St, 2000–01
Most Yards Gained: 11,213—Justin Coleman, Nebraska–Kearney, 1997–00
Most Yards Gained per Game: 323.7—Dusty Bonner, Valdosta St, 2000–01

Note: Career records entering 2002 season.

RECEIVING

Most Passes Caught: 323—Clarence Coleman, Ferris St, 1998–01
Most Yards Gained: 4,983—Clarence Coleman, Ferris St, 1998–01
Most Yards Gained per Game: 160.8—Chris George, Glenville St, 1993–94
Highest Average Gain per Reception: 22.8—Tyrone Johnson, Western St (CO), 1990–93

SINGLE SEASON

SCORING

Most Points Scored: 212—David Kircus, Grand Valley St, 2002
Most Touchdowns Scored: 35—David Kircus, Grand Valley St, 2002
Most Touchdowns Scored, Rushing: 33—Ian Smart, C.W. Post, 2001
Most Touchdowns Scored, Passing: 54—Dusty Bonner, Valdosta St, 2000
Most Touchdowns Scored, Receiving: 35—David Kircus, Grand Valley St, 2002

RUSHING

Most Rushes: 385—Joe Gough, Wayne St (MI), 1994
Most Rushes per Game: 38.6—Mark Perkins, Hobart, 1968
Most Yards Gained: 2,653—Kavin Gailliard, American International, 1999
Most Yards Gained per Game: 222.0—Anthony Gray, Western New Mexico, 1997

SINGLE SEASON (CONT.)

PASSING

Highest Passing Efficiency Rating: 221.63—Curt Anes, Grand Valley St, 2001
Most Passes Attempted: 544— Lance Funderburk, Valdosta St, 1995
Most Passes Completed: 356— Lance Funderburk, Valdosta St, 1995
Most Passes Completed per Game: 32.4—Lance Funderburk, Valdosta St, 1995
Highest Completion Percentage: 74.7— Chris Hatcher, Valdosta St, 1994
Most Yards Gained: 4,189—Wilkie Perez, Glenville St, 1997
Most Yards Gained per Game: 393.4— Grady Benton, W Texas A&M, 1994

RECEIVING

Most Passes Caught: 119—Brad Bailey, W Texas A&M, 1994
Most Yards Gained: 1,876—Chris George, Glenville St, 1993
Most Yards Gained per Game: 187.6— Chris George, Glenville St, 1993
Highest Average Gain per Reception: 32.5— Tyrone Johnson, Western St, 1991 (min. 30 receptions)

SINGLE GAME

SCORING

Most Points Scored: 48—Paul Zaeske, N Park, 1968 (vs N Central); Junior Wolf, Panhandle St, 1958 (vs St. Mary [KS])
Most Field Goals: 6—Steve Huff, Central Missouri St, 1985 (vs SE Missouri St)

SCORING

Most Yards Gained: 405—Alvon Brown, Kentucky St, 2000 (vs Kentucky Wesleyan)
Most Touchdowns Rushed: 8—Junior Wolf, Panhandle St, 1958 (vs St. Mary [KS])

PASSING

Most Passes Completed: 56—Jarrod DeGeorgia, Wayne St (NE),1996 (vs Drake)
Most Yards Gained: 642—Wilkie Perez, Glenville St, 1997, (vs Concord)
Most Touchdowns Passed: 10—Bruce Swanson, N Park, 1968 (vs N Central)

RECEIVING

Most Passes Caught: 23—Chris George, Glenville St, 1994 (vs WV Wesleyan); Barry Wagner, Alabama A&M, 1989 (vs Clark Atlanta)
Most Yards Gained: 401—Kevin Ingram, W Chester, 1998 (vs Clarion)
Most Touchdown Catches: 8—Paul Zaeske, N Park, 1968 (vs N Central)

ZANIEST CHEERLEADERS

VINCENT MUZIK

[ST JOHN'S (Minn.)]

They do wacky tumbling stunts and goofy dances, throw sausages into the stands and sometimes don women's clothing. The handful of students known as the Rat Pack lead the cheers at their all-male, sports-mad Division III school in the pine woods of central Minnesota. The appreciative home crowds often include scores of Benedictine monks from a monastery on campus. The Rat Pack, which began in the 1950s and got its name by pestering opponents, is looking forward to having a national football audience this fall. That's when Johnnies football coach John Gagliardi is expected to break Eddie Robinson's record for most college victories (408).

NCAA DIVISION III INDIVIDUAL RECORDS

CAREER

SCORING

Most Points Scored: 562—R.J. Bowers, Grove City, 1997–00
Most Touchdowns Scored: 92—R.J. Bowers, Grove City, 1997–00
Most Touchdowns Scored, Rushing: 91—R.J. Bowers, Grove City, 1997–00
Most Touchdowns Scored, Passing: 148—Justin Peery, Westminster (MO), 1996–99
Most Touchdowns Scored, Receiving: 75—Scott Pingel, Westminster (MO), 1996–99

RUSHING

Most Rushes: 1,190—Steve Tardif, Maine Maritime, 1996–99
Most Rushes per Game: 32.7—Chris Sizemore, Bridgewater (VA), 1972–74
Most Yards Gained: 7,353—R.J. Bowers, Grove City, 1997–00
Most Yards Gained per Game: 183.8—R.J. Bowers, Grove City, 1997–00

PASSING

Highest Passing Efficiency Rating: 194.2—Bill Borchert, Mount Union, 1994–97
Most Passes Attempted: 1,696—Kirk Baumgartner, WI–Stevens Point, 1986–89
Most Passes Completed: 1,012—Justin Peery, Westminster (MO), 1996–99
Most Passes Completed per Game: 25.9—Justin Peery, Westminster (MO), 1996–99
Highest Completion Percentage: 67.0—Gary Smeck, Mount Union, 1997–00
Most Yards Gained: 13,262—Justin Peery, Westminster (MO), 1996–99
Most Yards Gained per Game: 340.1—Justin Peery, Westminster (MO), 1996–99

RECEIVING

Most Passes Caught: 436—Scott Pingel, Westminster (MO), 1996–99
Most Yards Gained: 6,108—Scott Pingel, Westminster (MO), 1996–99
Most Yards Gained per Game: 156.6—Scott Pingel, Westminster (MO), 1996–99
Highest Average Gain per Reception: 22.9—Kirk Aikens, Hartwick, 1995–98

Note: Career leaders entering 2002 season.

SINGLE SEASON

SCORING

Most Points Scored: 250—Dan Pugh, Mt. Union, 2002
Most Points Scored per Game: 20.8—James Regan, Pomona-Pitzer, 1997
Most Touchdowns Scored: 41—Dan Pugh, Mt. Union, 2002
Most Touchdowns Scored, Rushing: 34—Dan Pugh, Mt. Union, 2002
Most Touchdowns Scored, Passing: 54—Justin Peery, Westminster (MO), 1999
Most Touchdowns Scored, Receiving: 26—Scott Pingel, Westminster (MO), 1998

RUSHING

Most Rushes: 384—Dan Pugh, Mt. Union, 2002
Most Rushes per Game: 38.0—Mike Birosak, Dickinson, 1989
Most Yards Gained: 2,385—Dante Brown, Marietta, 1996

PASSING

Highest Passing Efficiency Rating: 225.0—Mike Simpson, Eureka, 1994
Most Passes Attempted: 527—Kirk Baumgartner, WI–Stevens Point, 1988
Most Passes Completed: 329—Justin Peery, Westminster (MO), 1999
Most Passes Completed per Game: 32.9—Justin Peery, Westminster (MO), 1999
Highest Completion Percentage: 72.9—Jim Ballard, Mount Union, 1993
Most Yards Gained: 4,501—Justin Peery, Westminster (MO), 1998
Most Yards Gained per Game: 450.1—Justin Peery, Westminster (MO), 1998

RECEIVING

Most Passes Caught: 136—Scott Pingel, Westminster (MO), 1999
Most Yards Gained: 2,157—Scott Pingel, Westminster, (MO), 1998
Most Yards Gained per Game: 215.7—Scott Pingel, Westminster, (MO), 1998
Highest Average Gain per Reception: 26.9—Marty Redlawsk, Concordia (IL), 1985

NCAA DIVISION III INDIVIDUAL RECORDS (CONT.)

SINGLE GAME

SCORING
Most Field Goals: 6—Jim Hever, Rhodes, 1984 (vs Millsaps)

PASSING
Most Passes Completed: 51—Scott Kello, Sul Ross St, 2002 (vs Howard Payne)
Most Yards Gained: 731—Zamir Amin, Menlo, 2000 (vs California Lutheran)
Most Touchdown Passes: 9—Joe Zarlinga, Ohio Northern, 1998 (vs Capital)

RUSHING
Most Yards Gained: 441—Dante Brown, Marietta, 1996 (vs Baldwin-Wallace)
Most Touchdowns Rushed: 8—Carey Bender, Coe, 1994 (vs Beloit)

RECEIVING
Most Passes Caught: 23—Sean Munroe, Mass-Boston, 1992 (vs Mass-Maritime)
Most Yards Gained: 418—Lewis Howes, Principia, 2002 (vs Martin Luther)
Most Touchdown Catches: 7—Matt Perceval, Wesleyan (CT), 1998 (vs Middlebury)

NCAA DIVISION I-A ALLTIME INDIVIDUAL LEADERS

CAREER (ENTERING 2002 SEASON)

SCORING

POINTS (KICKERS)	YEARS	PTS
Roman Anderson, Houston	1988–91	423
Carlos Huerta, Miami (FL)	1988–91	397
Jason Elam, Hawaii	1988–92	395
Derek Schmidt, Florida St	1984–87	393
Kris Brown, Nebraska	1995–98	388

POINTS (NON-KICKERS)	YEARS	PTS
Miami (OH)	1996–99	468
Ricky Williams, Texas	1995–98	452
Anthony Thompson, Indiana	1986–89	394
Ron Dayne, Wisconsin	1996–99	378
Marshall Faulk, San Diego St	1991–93	376

POINTS PER GAME (NON-KICKERS)	YEARS	PTS/GAME
Marshall Faulk, San Diego St	1991–93	12.1
Ed Marinaro, Cornell	1969–71	11.8
Bill Burnett, Arkansas	1968–70	11.3
Steve Owens, Oklahoma	1967–69	11.2
Eddie Talboom, Wyoming	1948–50	10.8

TOTAL OFFENSE

YARDS GAINED	YEARS	YDS
Ty Detmer, Brigham Young	1988–91	14,665
Tim Rattay, Louisiana Tech	1997–99	12,618
Chris Redman, Louisville	1996–99	12,129
Drew Brees, Purdue	1997–00	11,815
David Neill, Nevada	1998–01	11,664

YARDS PER GAME	YEARS	YDS/GME
Tim Rattay, Louisiana Tech	1997–99	382.4
Chris Vargas, Nevada	1992–93	320.9
Ty Detmer, Brigham Young	1988–91	318.8
Daunte Culpepper, Central Florida	1996–98	313.5
Mike Perez, San Jose St	1986–87	309.1

RUSHING

YARDS GAINED	YEARS	YDS
Ron Dayne, Wisconsin	1996–99	6,397
Ricky Williams, Texas	1995–98	6,279
Tony Dorsett, Pittsburgh	1973–76	6,082
Charles White, Southern Cal	1976–79	5,598
Travis Prentice, Miami (OH)	1996–99	5,596

RUSHING (CONT.)

YARDS PER GAME	YEARS	YDS/GAME
Ed Marinaro, Cornell	1969–71	174.6
O.J. Simpson, Southern Cal	1967–68	164.4
Herschel Walker, Georgia	1980–82	159.4
LeShon Johnson, Northern Illinois	1992–93	150.6
Ron Dayne, Wisconsin	1996–99	148.8

TOUCHDOWNS RUSHING	YEARS	TD
Travis Prentice, Miami (OH)	1996–99	73
Ricky Williams, Texas	1995–98	72
Anthony Thompson, Indiana	1986–89	64
Ron Dayne, Wisconsin	1996–99	63
Eric Crouch, Nebraska	1998–2001	59

PASSING

PASSING EFFICIENCY	YEARS	RATING
Danny Wuerffel, Florida	1993–96	163.6
Ty Detmer, Brigham Young	1988–91	162.7
Steve Sarkisian, Brigham Young	1995–96	162.0
Billy Blanton, San Diego St	1993–96	157.1
Jim McMahon, Brigham Young	1977–78, 80–81	156.9

Note: Minimum 500 completions.

YARDS GAINED	YEARS	YDS
Ty Detmer, Brigham Young	1988–91	15,031
Tim Rattay, Louisiana Tech	1997–99	12,746
Chris Redman, Louisville	1996–99	12,541
Todd Santos, San Diego St	1984–87	11,425
Tim Lester, Western Michigan	1997–99	11,299

COMPLETIONS	YEARS	COMP
Chris Redman, Louisville	1996–99	1,031
Tim Rattay, Louisiana Tech	1997–99	1,015
Ty Detmer, Brigham Young	1988–91	958
Drew Brees, Purdue	1997–2000	942
Todd Santos, San Diego St	1984–87	910

TOUCHDOWNS PASSING	YEARS	TD
Ty Detmer, Brigham Young	1988–91	121
Tim Rattay, Louisiana Tech	1997–99	115
Danny Wuerffel, Florida	1993–96	114
Chad Pennington, Marshall	1997–99	100
David Klingler, Houston	1988–91	91

CAREER (CONT.)

RECEIVING

CATCHES	YEARS	NO.
Arnold Jackson, Louisville	1997–2000	300
Trevor Insley, Nevada	1996–99	298
Geoff Noisy, Nevada	1995–98	295
Troy Edwards, Louisiana Tech	1996–98	280
Aaron Turner, Pacific	1989–92	266

CATCHES PER GAME	YEARS	AVG
Emmanuel Hazard, Houston	1989–90	10.5
Alex Van Dyke, Nevada	1994–95	10.3
Howard Twilley, Tulsa	1963–65	10.0
Jason Phillips, Houston	1987–88	9.4
Troy Edwards, Louisiana Tech	1996–98	8.2

YARDS GAINED	YEARS	YDS
Trevor Insley, Nevada	1996–99	5,005
Marcus Harris, Wyoming	1993–96	4,518
Ryan Yarborough, Wyoming	1990–93	4,357
Troy Edwards, Louisiana Tech	1996–98	4,352
Aaron Turner, Pacific	1989–92	4,345

TOUCHDOWN CATCHES	YEARS	TD
Troy Edwards, Louisiana Tech	1996–98	50
Aaron Turner, Pacific	1989–92	43
Ryan Yarborough, Wyoming	1990–93	42
Marcus Harris, Wyoming	1993–96	38
Clarkston Hines, Duke	1986–89	38

ALL-PURPOSE RUNNING

YARDS GAINED	YEARS	YDS
Ricky Williams, Texas	1996–98	7,206
Napoleon McCallum, Navy	1981–85	7,172
Darrin Nelson, Stanford	1977–78, 80–81	6,885
Kevin Faulk, Louisiana St.	1995–98	6,833
Ron Dayne, Wisconsin	1996–99	6,701

YARDS PER GAME	YEARS	AVG
Ryan Benjamin, Pacific	1990–92	237.8
Sheldon Canley, San Jose St	1988–90	205.8
Howard Stevens, Louisville	1971–72	193.7
O.J. Simpson, Southern Cal	1967–68	192.9
Alex Van Dyke, Nevada	1994–95	188.5

INTERCEPTIONS

PLAYER/SCHOOL	YEARS	INT
Al Brosky, Illinois	1950–52	29
John Provost, Holy Cross	1972–74	27
Martin Bayless, Bowling Green	1980–83	27
Tom Curtis, Michigan	1967–69	25
Tony Thurman, Boston Col.	1981–84	25
Tracy Saul, Texas Tech	1989–92	25

PUNTING AVERAGE

PLAYER/SCHOOL	YEARS	AVG
Todd Sauerbrun, W Virginia	1991–94	46.3
Reggie Roby, Iowa	1979–82	45.6
Greg Montgomery, Michigan St	1985–87	45.4
Tom Tupa, Ohio St	1984–87	45.2
Barry Helton, Colorado	1984–87	44.9

Note: At least 150 punts.

PUNT RETURN AVERAGE

PLAYER/SCHOOL	YEARS	AVG
Jack Mitchell, Oklahoma	1946–48	23.6
Gene Gibson, Cincinnati	1949–50	20.5
Eddie Macon, Pacific	1949–51	18.9
Jackie Robinson, UCLA	1939–40	18.8
Bobby Dillon, Texas	1949–51	17.7

Note: At least 30 returns.

KICKOFF RETURN AVERAGE

PLAYER/SCHOOL	YEARS	AVG
Anthony Davis, Southern Cal	1972–74	35.1
Eric Booth, Southern Miss	1994–97	32.4
Overton Curtis, Utah St	1957–58	31.0
Fred Montgomery, New Mexico St	1991–92	30.5
Altie Taylor, Utah St	1966–68	29.3

Note: At least 30 returns.

SINGLE SEASON

SCORING

POINTS	YEAR	PTS
Barry Sanders, Oklahoma St	1988	234
Troy Edwards, Louisiana Tech	1998	188
Mike Rozier, Nebraska	1983	174
Lydell Mitchell, Penn St	1971	174
Brock Forsey, Boise St	2002	174

FIELD GOALS	YEAR	FG
John Lee, UCLA	1984	29
Paul Woodside, W Virginia	1982	28
Luis Zendejas, Arizona St	1983	28
Fuad Reveiz, Tennessee	1982	27
Sebastian Janikowski, Florida St	1998	27

Four tied with 25.

ALL-PURPOSE RUNNING

YARDS GAINED	YEAR	YDS
Barry Sanders, Oklahoma St	1988	3,250
Troy Edwards, Louisiana Tech	1998	2,794
Ryan Benjamin, Pacific	1991	2,995
Mike Pringle, Fullerton St	1989	2,690
Paul Palmer, Temple	1986	2,633

YARDS PER GAME	YEAR	AVG
Barry Sanders, Oklahoma St	1988	295.5
Ryan Benjamin, Pacific	1991	249.6
Byron (Whizzer) White, Colorado	1937	246.3
Mike Pringle, Fullerton St	1989	244.6
Paul Palmer, Temple	1986	239.4

NCAA DIVISION I-A ALLTIME INDIVIDUAL LEADERS (CONT.)

SINGLE SEASON

TOTAL OFFENSE

YARDS GAINED	YEAR	YDS
David Klingler, Houston	1990	5,221
Ty Detmer, Brigham Young	1990	5,022
Tim Rattay, Louisiana Tech	1998	4,840
Andre Ware, Houston	1989	4,661
Jim McMahon, Brigham Young	1980	4,627

YARDS PER GAME	YEAR	AVG
David Klingler, Houston	1990	474.6
Andre Ware, Houston	1989	423.7
Ty Detmer, Brigham Young	1990	418.5
Tim Rattay, Louisiana Tech	1998	403.3
Mike Maxwell, Nevada	1995	402.6

RUSHING

YARDS GAINED	YEAR	YDS
Barry Sanders, Oklahoma St	1988	2,628
Marcus Allen, Southern Cal	1981	2,342
Troy Davis, Iowa St	1996	2,185
LaDainian Tomlinson, TCU	2000	2,158
Mike Rozier, Nebraska	1983	2,148

YARDS PER GAME	YEAR	AVG
Barry Sanders, Oklahoma St	1988	238.9
Marcus Allen, Southern Cal	1981	212.9
Ed Marinaro, Cornell	1971	209.0
Troy Davis, Iowa St	1996	198.6
LaDainian Tomlinson, TCU	2000	196.2

TOUCHDOWNS RUSHING	YEAR	TD
Barry Sanders, Oklahoma St	1988	37
Mike Rozier, Nebraska	1983	29
Ricky Williams, Texas	1998	27
Lee Suggs, Virginia Tech	2000	27
Willis McGahee, Miami	2002	27

PASSING

PASSING EFFICIENCY	YEAR	RATING
Shaun King, Tulane	1998	183.3
Michael Vick, Virginia Tech	1999	180.4
Danny Wuerffel, Florida	1995	178.4
Jim McMahon, Brigham Young	1980	176.9
Ty Detmer, Brigham Young	1989	175.6

YARDS GAINED	YEAR	YDS
Ty Detmer, Brigham Young	1990	5,188
David Klingler, Houston	1990	5,140
Tim Rattay, Louisiana Tech	1998	4,943
Andre Ware, Houston	1989	4,699
Jim McMahon, Brigham Young	1980	4,571

COMPLETIONS	YEAR	ATT	COMP
Tim Couch, Kentucky	1998	553	400
Tim Rattay, Louisiana Tech	1998	559	380
David Klingler, Houston	1990	643	374
Andre Ware, Houston	1989	578	365
Tim Couch, Kentucky	1997	547	363

PASSING (CONT.)

TOUCHDOWNS PASSING	YEAR	TD
David Klingler, Houston	1990	54
Jim McMahon, Brigham Young	1980	47
Andre Ware, Houston	1989	46
Tim Rattay, Louisiana Tech	1998	46
David Carr, Fresno St	2001	42

RECEIVING

CATCHES	YEAR	GP	NO.
Emmanuel Hazard, Houston	1989	11	142
Troy Edwards, Louisiana Tech	1998	12	140
Nate Burleson, Nevada	2002	12	138
Howard Twilley, Tulsa	1965	10	134
Trevor Insley, Nevada	1999	11	134

CATCHES PER GAME	YEAR	NO.	NO./ GAME
Howard Twilley, Tulsa	1965	134	13.4
Emmanuel Hazard, Houston	1989	142	12.9
Trevor Insley, Nevada	1999	134	12.2
Troy Edwards, Louisiana Tech	1998	140	11.7
Alex Van Dyke, Nevada	1995	129	11.7

YARDS GAINED	YEAR	YDS
Trevor Insley, Nevada	1999	2,060
Troy Edwards, Louisiana Tech	1998	1,996
Alex Van Dyke, Nevada	1995	1,854
J.R. Tolver, San Diego St	2002	1,785
Howard Twilley, Tulsa	1965	1,779

TOUCHDOWN CATCHES	YEAR	TD
Troy Edwards, Louisiana Tech	1998	27
Randy Moss, Marshall	1997	25
Emmanuel Hazard, Houston	1989	22
Desmond Howard, Michigan	1991	19
Ashley Lelie, Hawaii	2001	19

NCAA DIVISION I-A ALLTIME INDIVIDUAL LEADERS (CONT.)

SINGLE GAME

SCORING

POINTS	OPPONENT	YEAR	PTS
Howard Griffith, Illinois	Southern Illinois	1990	48
Marshall Faulk, San Diego St	Pacific	1991	44
Jim Brown, Syracuse	Colgate	1956	43
Showboat Boykin, Mississippi	Mississippi St	1951	42
Fred Wendt, UTEP*	New Mexico St	1948	42

*UTEP was Texas Mines in 1948.

FIELD GOALS	OPPONENT	YEAR	FG
Dale Klein, Nebraska	Missouri	1985	7
Mike Prindle, Western Michigan	Marshall	1984	7

Note: 13 tied with 6.
Klein's distances were 32-22-43-44-29-43-43. Prindle's distances were 32-44-42-23-48-41-27.

TOTAL OFFENSE

YARDS GAINED	OPPONENT	YEAR	YDS
David Klingler, Houston	Arizona St	1990	732
Matt Vogler, TCU	Houston	1990	696
Brian Lindgren, Idaho	Middle Tenn St	2001	657
David Klingler, Houston	Texas Christian	1990	625
Scott Mitchell, Utah	Air Force	1988	625

PASSING

YARDS GAINED	OPPONENT	YEAR	YDS
David Klingler, Houston	Arizona St	1990	716
Matt Vogler, TCU	Houston	1990	690
Brian Lindgren, Idaho	Middle Tenn St	2001	637
Scott Mitchell, Utah	Air Force	1988	631
Jeremy Leach, New Mexico	Utah	1989	622

COMPLETIONS	OPPONENT	YEAR	COMP
Drew Brees, Purdue	Wisconsin	1998	55
Rusty LaRue, Wake Forest	Duke	1995	55
Rusty LaRue, Wake Forest	NC St	1995	50
Brian Lindgren, Idaho	Middle Tenn St	2001	49
Kliff Kingsbury, Texas Tech	Missouri/Texas A&M	2002	49

TOUCHDOWNS PASSING	OPPONENT	YEAR	TD
David Klingler, Houston	E Wash	1990	11

Note: Klingler's TD passes were 5-48-29-7-3-7-40-10-7-8-51.

RUSHING

YARDS GAINED	OPPONENT	YEAR	YDS
LaDainian Tomlinson, Texas Christian	UTEP	1999	406
Tony Sands, Kansas	Missouri	1991	396
Marshall Faulk, San Diego St	Pacific	1991	386
Robbie Mixon, Central Michigan	Eastern Michigan	2002	382
Troy Davis, Iowa St	Missouri	1996	378

TOUCHDOWNS RUSHING	OPPONENT	YEAR	TD
Howard Griffith, Illinois	Southern Illinois	1990	8

Note: Griffith's TD runs were 5-51-7-41-5-18-5-3.

SINGLE GAME (CONT.)

RECEIVING

CATCHES	OPPONENT	YEAR	NO.
Randy Gatewood, UNLV	Idaho	1994	23
Jay Miller, Brigham Young	New Mexico	1973	22
Troy Edwards, La. Tech	Nebraska	1998	21
Chris Daniels, Purdue	Michigan St	1999	21
Rick Eber, Tulsa	Idaho St	1967	20
Kenny Christian, Eastern Michigan	Temple	2000	20

YARDS GAINED	OPPONENT	YEAR	YDS
Troy Edwards, Louisiana Tech	Nebraska	1998	405
Randy Gatewood, UNLV	Idaho	1994	363
Chuck Hughes, UTEP*	N Texas St	1965	349
Nate Burleson, Nevada	San Jose St	2001	326
Rick Eber, Tulsa	Idaho St	1967	322

*UTEP was Texas Western in 1965.

TOUCHDOWN CATCHES	OPPONENT	YEAR	TD
Tim Delaney, San Diego St	New Mex. St	1969	6

Note: Delaney's TD catches were 2-22-34-31-30-9.

LONGEST PLAYS (SINCE 1941)

PASSING	OPPONENT	YEAR	YDS
Fred Owens to Jack Ford, Portland	St. Mary's (CA)	1947	99
Bo Burris to Warren McVea, Houston	Washington St	1966	99
Colin Clapton to Eddie Jenkins, Holy Cross	Boston U	1970	99
Terry Peel to Robert Ford,| Houston	Syracuse	1970	99
Terry Peel to Robert Ford, Houston	San Diego St	1972	99
Cris Collinsworth to Derrick Gaffney, Florida	Rice	1977	99
Scott Ankrom to James Maness, Texas Christian	Rice	1984	99
Gino Toretta to Horace Copeland, Miami (FL)	Arkansas	1991	99
John Paci to Thomas Lewis, Indiana	Penn St	1993	99
Troy DeGar to Wes Caswell, Tulsa	Oklahoma	1996	99
Drew Brees to Vinny Sutherland, Purdue	Northwestern	1999	99
Dan Urban to Justin McCariens, Northern Illinois	Ball St	2000	99
Jason Johnson to Brandon Marshall, Arizona	Idaho	2001	99

RUSHING	OPPONENT	YEAR	YDS
Gale Sayers, Kansas	Nebraska	1963	99
Max Anderson, Arizona St	Wyoming	1967	99
Ralph Thompson, W Texas St	Wichita St	1970	99
Kelsey Finch, Tennessee	Florida	1977	99
Eric Vann, Kansas	Oklahoma	1997	99

FIELD GOALS	OPPONENT	YEAR	YDS
Steve Little, Arkansas	Texas	1977	67
Russell Erxleben, Texas	Rice	1977	67
Joe Williams, Wichita St	Southern IL	1978	67
Martin Gramatica, Kansas St	Northern IL	1998	65
Tony Franklin, Texas A&M	Baylor	1976	65

PUNTS	OPPONENT	YEAR	YDS
Pat Brady, Nevada*	Loyola (CA)	1950	99
George O'Brien, Wisconsin	Iowa	1952	96
John Hadl, Kansas	Oklahoma	1959	94
Carl Knox, Texas Christian	Oklahoma St	1947	94
Preston Johnson, SMU	Pittsburgh	1940	94

*Nevada was Nevada-Reno in 1950.

NOTABLE ACHIEVEMENTS

DIVISION I-A WINNINGEST TEAMS

ALLTIME WINNING PERCENTAGE

	YRS	W	L	T	PCT	GP	BOWL RECORD
Notre Dame	113	781	247	42	.750	1,070	13-11-0
Michigan	123	813	266	36	.745	1,115	16-16-0
Alabama	107	744	281	43	.717	1,068	29-19-3
Nebraska	112	764	301	40	.710	1,105	20-20-0
Oklahoma	107	713	280	53	.707	1,046	21-12-1
Texas	109	755	304	33	.707	1,092	19-20-2
Ohio St	112	731	292	53	.704	1,076	14-19-0
Tennessee	105	718	294	52	.699	1,064	23-19-0
Penn St	115	744	318	41	.693	1,103	23-11-2
Southern Cal	109	684	294	54	.689	1,032	25-15-0
Florida St	55	400	189	17	.674	606	18-10-2
Boise St	34	259	133	2	.660	394	2-0-0
Washington	112	625	341	50	.640	1,016	14-13-1
Miami (OH)	113	604	337	44	.636	985	5-2-0
Georgia	108	649	366	54	.632	1,069	19-15-3
Miami (FL)	75	484	282	19	.629	785	15-11-0
Louisiana St	108	628	363	47	.628	1,038	16-16-1
Arizona St	89	494	297	24	.621	815	10-7-1
Central Michigan	101	515	309	36	.620	860	0-2-0
Auburn	109	617	370	47	.619	1,034	14-12-2
Army	112	621	382	51	.613	1,054	2-2-0
Florida	95	574	349	40	.617	963	13-15-0
Colorado	112	621	379	36	.617	1,036	11-13-0
Texas A&M	107	617	390	48	.608	1,055	13-14-0
Syracuse	112	648	414	49	.605	1,111	12-8-1

Note: Includes bowl games.

ALLTIME VICTORIES

Michigan	813	Georgia	649	N Carolina	608
Notre Dame	781	Syracuse	648	Miami (OH)	604
Nebraska	764	Louisiana St	628	Pittsburgh	603
Texas	755	Washington	625	Arkansas	601
Penn St	744	Army	621	Minnesota	591
Alabama	744	Colorado	621	Virginia Tech	587
Ohio St	731	Auburn	617	Navy	579
Tennessee	718	Texas A&M	617	Clemson	578
Oklahoma	713	Georgia Tech	609	Florida	574
Southern Cal	684	W Virginia	606	Michigan St	568

NUMBER ONE VS NUMBER TWO

The No. 1 and No. 2 teams, according to the Associated Press Poll, have met 33 times, including 13 bowl games, since the poll's inception in 1936. The No. 1 teams have a 20-11-2 record in these matchups. Notre Dame (4-3-2) has played in nine of the games.

DATE	RESULTS	STADIUM
10-9-43	No. 1 Notre Dame 35, No. 2 Michigan 12	Michigan (Ann Arbor)
11-20-43	No. 1 Notre Dame 14, No. 2 Iowa Pre-Flight 13	Notre Dame (South Bend)
12-2-44	No. 1 Army 23, No. 2 Navy 7	Municipal (Baltimore)
11-10-45	No. 1 Army 48, No. 2 Notre Dame 0	Yankee (New York)
12-1-45	No. 1 Army 32, No. 2 Navy 13	Municipal (Philadelphia)
11-9-46	No. 1 Army 0, No. 2 Notre Dame 0	Yankee (New York)
1-1-63	No. 1 Southern Cal 42, No. 2 Wisconsin 37 (Rose Bowl)	Rose Bowl (Pasadena)
10-12-63	No. 2 Texas 28, No. 1 Oklahoma 7	Cotton Bowl (Dallas)
1-1-64	No. 1 Texas 28, No. 2 Navy 6 (Cotton Bowl)	Cotton Bowl (Dallas)
11-19-66	No. 1 Notre Dame 10, No. 2 Michigan St 10	Spartan (E Lansing)
9-28-68	No. 1 Purdue 37, No. 2 Notre Dame 22	Notre Dame (South Bend)
1-1-69	No. 1 Ohio St 27, No. 2 Southern Cal 16 (Rose Bowl)	Rose Bowl (Pasadena)
12-6-69	No. 1 Texas 15, No. 2 Arkansas 14	Razorback (Fayetteville)

NOTABLE ACHIEVEMENTS (CONT.)

NUMBER ONE VS NUMBER TWO (CONT.)

DATE	RESULTS	STADIUM
11-25-71	No. 1 Nebraska 35, No. 2 Oklahoma 31	Owen Field (Norman)
1-1-72	No. 1 Nebraska 38, No. 2 Alabama 6 (Orange Bowl)	Orange Bowl (Miami)
1-1-79	No. 2 Alabama 14, No. 1 Penn St 7 (Sugar Bowl)	Sugar Bowl (New Orleans)
9-26-81	No. 1 Southern Cal 28, No. 2 Oklahoma 24	Coliseum (Los Angeles)
1-1-83	No. 2 Penn St 27, No. 1 Georgia 23 (Sugar Bowl)	Sugar Bowl (New Orleans)
10-19-85	No. 1 Iowa 12, No. 2 Michigan 10	Kinnick (Iowa City)
9-27-86	No. 2 Miami (FL) 28, No. 1 Oklahoma 16	Orange Bowl (Miami)
1-2-87	No. 2 Penn St 14, No. 1 Miami (FL) 10 (Fiesta Bowl)	Sun Devil (Tempe)
11-21-87	No. 2 Oklahoma 17, No. 1 Nebraska 7	Memorial (Lincoln)
1-1-88	No. 2 Miami (FL) 20, No. 1 Oklahoma 14 (Orange Bowl)	Orange Bowl (Miami)
11-26-88	No. 1 Notre Dame 27, No. 2 Southern Cal 10	Coliseum (Los Angeles)
9-16-89	No. 1 Notre Dame 24, No. 2 Michigan 19	Michigan (Ann Arbor)
11-16-91	No. 2 Miami (FL) 17, No. 1 Florida St 16	Campbell (Tallahassee)
1-1-93	No. 2 Alabama 34, No. 1 Miami (FL) 13 (Sugar Bowl)	Superdome (New Orleans)
11-13-93	No. 2 Notre Dame 31, No. 1 Florida St 24	Notre Dame (South Bend)
1-1-94	No. 1 Florida St 18, No. 2 Nebraska 16 (Orange Bowl)	Orange Bowl (Miami)
1-2-96	No. 1 Nebraska 62, No. 2 Florida 24 (Fiesta Bowl)	Sun Devil (Tempe)
11-30-96	No. 2 Florida St 24, No. 1 Florida 21	Campbell (Tallahassee)
1-4-99	No. 1 Tennessee 23, No. 2 Florida St 16 (Fiesta Bowl)	Sun Devil (Tempe)
1-4-00	No. 1 Florida St 46, No. 2 Virginia Tech 29 (Sugar Bowl)	Superdome (New Orleans)

LONGEST DIVISION I-A WINNING STREAKS

WINS	TEAM	YRS	ENDED BY	SCORE
47	Oklahoma	1953–57	Notre Dame	7–0
39	Washington	1908–14	Oregon St	0–0
37	Yale	1890–93	Princeton	6–0
37	Yale	1887–89	Princeton	10–0
35	Toledo	1969–71	Tampa	21–0
34	Pennsylvania	1894–96	Lafayette	6–4
31	Oklahoma	1948–50	Kentucky	13–7
31	Pittsburgh	1914–18	Cleveland Naval Reserve	10–9
31	Pennsylvania	1896–98	Harvard	10–0
30	Texas	1968–70	Notre Dame	24–11

LONGEST DIVISION I-A UNBEATEN STREAKS

NO.	W	T	TEAM	YRS	ENDED BY	SCORE
63	59	4	Washington	1907–17	California	27–0
56	55	1	Michigan	1901–05	Chicago	2–0
50	46	4	California	1920–25	Olympic Club	15–0
48	47	1	Oklahoma	1953–57	Notre Dame	7–0
48	47	1	Yale	1885–89	Princeton	10–0
47	42	5	Yale	1879–85	Princeton	6–5
44	42	2	Yale	1894–96	Princeton	24–6
42	39	3	Yale	1904–08	Harvard	4–0
39	37	2	Notre Dame	1946–50	Purdue	28–14
37	36	1	Oklahoma	1972–75	Kansas	23–3
37	37	0	Yale	1890–93	Princeton	6–0
35	35	0	Toledo	1969–71	Tampa	21–0
35	34	1	Minnesota	1903–05	Wisconsin	16–12
34	33	1	Nebraska	1912–16	Kansas	7–3
34	34	0	Pennsylvania	1894–96	Lafayette	6–4
34	32	2	Princeton	1884–87	Harvard	12–0
34	29	5	Princeton	1877–82	Harvard	1–0
33	30	3	Tennessee	1926–30	Alabama	18–6
33	31	2	Georgia Tech	1914–18	Pittsburgh	32–0
33	30	3	Harvard	1911–15	Cornell	10–0
32	31	1	Nebraska	1969–71	UCLA	20–17
32	30	2	Army	1944–47	Columbia	21–20
32	31	1	Harvard	1898–1900	Yale	28–0
31	30	1	Penn St	1967–70	Colorado	41–13

NOTABLE ACHIEVEMENTS (CONT.)

LONGEST DIVISION I-A UNBEATEN STREAKS (CONT.)

NO.	W	T	TEAM	YRS	ENDED BY	SCORE
31	30	1	San Diego St	1967–70	Long Beach St	27–11
31	29	2	Georgia Tech	1950–53	Notre Dame	27–14
31	31	0	Oklahoma	1948–50	Kentucky	13–7
31	31	0	Pittsburgh	1914–18	Cleveland Naval	10–9
31	31	0	Pennsylvania	1896–98	Harvard	10–0

Note: Includes bowl games.

LONGEST DIVISION I-A LOSING STREAKS

LOSSES		SEASONS	ENDED AGAINST	SCORE
34	Northwestern	1979–82	Northern Illinois	31–6
28	Virginia	1958–61	William & Mary	21–6
28	Kansas St	1945–48	Arkansas St	37–6
27	New Mexico St	1988–90	Cal St–Fullerton	43–9
27	Eastern Michigan	1980–82	Kent St	9–7

MOST-PLAYED DIVISION I-A RIVALRIES

GP	OPPONENTS (SERIES LEADER LISTED FIRST)	RECORD	FIRST GAME
111	Minnesota-Wisconsin	58-45-8	1890
110	Missouri-Kansas	51-50-9	1891
108	Nebraska-Kansas	84-21-3	1892
108	Texas–Texas A&M	69-34-5	1894
106	Miami (OH)–Cincinnati	56-43-7	1888
106	N Carolina–Virginia	56-46-4	1892
105	Auburn-Georgia	51-46-8	1892
105	Oregon–Oregon St	53-42-10	1894
104	Purdue-Indiana	63-35-6	1891
104	Stanford-California	54-39-11	1892
103	Baylor–Texas Christian*	49-47-7	1899
102	Army-Navy	49-46-7	1890
101	Utah–Utah St	69-28-4	1892
99	Clemson–S Carolina	59-36-4	1896
99	Kansas–Kansas St	61-33-5	1902
98	N Carolina–Wake Forest	65-31-2	1888
98	Michigan–Ohio St	56-36-6	1897
98	Mississippi–Miss St	55-37-6	1901
97	Oklahoma-Kansas	64-27-6	1903
97	Tennessee-Kentucky	65-23-9	1893
96	Penn St–Pittsburgh	50-42-4	1893
96	Georgia–Georgia Tech	53-38-5	1893

*Have not met since 1996.

Note: Notable Achievements entering 2002 season.

NCAA COACHES' RECORDS (ENTERING 2002 SEASON)

ALLTIME WINNINGEST DIVISION I-A COACHES

COACH (ALMA MATER)	COLLEGES COACHED	YRS	W	L	T	PCT
Knute Rockne (Notre Dame '14)†	Notre Dame 1918–30	13	105	12	5	.881
Frank W. Leahy (Notre Dame '31)†	Boston Col 1939–40; Notre Dame 1941–43, 1946–53	13	107	13	9	.864
George W. Woodruff (Yale 1889)†	Pennsylvania 1892–01; Illinois 1903; Carlisle 1905	12	142	25	2	.846
Barry Switzer (Arkansas '60)	Oklahoma 1973–88	16	157	29	4	.837
Tom Osborne (Hastings '59)†	Nebraska 1973–98	25	255	49	3	.836
Percy D. Haughton (Harvard 1899)†	Cornell 1899–1900; Harvard 1908–16; Columbia 1923–24	13	96	17	6	.832

NCAA COACHES' RECORDS (CONT.)

ALLTIME WINNINGEST DIVISION I-A COACHES (CONT.)

COACH (ALMA MATER)	COLLEGES COACHED	YRS	W	L	T	PCT
Bob Neyland (Army '16)†	Tennessee 1926–34, 1936–40, 1946–52	21	173	31	12	.829
Fielding Yost (W Virginia 1895)†	Ohio Wesleyan 1897; Nebraska 1898; Kansas 1899; Stanford 1900; Michigan 1901–23, 1925–26	29	196	36	12	.828
*Phillip Fulmer (Tennessee '71)	Tennessee 1992–	10	95	20	0	.826
Bud Wilkinson (Minnesota '37)†	Oklahoma 1947–63	17	145	29	4	.826
Jock Sutherland (Pittsburgh '18)†	Lafayette 1919–23; Pittsburgh 1924–38	20	144	28	14	.812
Bob Devaney (Alma, MI '39)†	Wyoming 1957–61; Nebraska 1962–72	16	136	30	7	.806
Frank W. Thomas (Notre Dame '23)†	Tenn.-Chattanooga 1925–28; Alabama 1931–42, 1944–46	19	141	33	9	.795
Henry L. Williams (Yale 1891)†	Army 1891; Minnesota 1900–21	23	141	34	12	.786
Gil Dobie (Minnesota '02)†	N Dakota St 1906–07; Washington 1908-16; Navy 1917–19; Cornell 1920–35; Boston College 1936–38	33	180	45	15	.781
Bear Bryant (Alabama '36)†	Maryland 1945, Kentucky 1946–53, Texas A&M 1954–57, Alabama 1958–82	38	323	85	17	.780

*Active. †Hall of Fame member.
Note: Minimum 10 years as head coach at Division I institutions; record at four-year colleges only; bowl games included; ties computed as half won, half lost.

BY VICTORIES

	YRS	W	L	T	PCT		YRS	W	L	T	PCT
*Joe Paterno	36	327	96	3	.771	Bo Schembechler	27	234	65	8	.775
Paul (Bear) Bryant	38	323	85	17	.780	*Lou Holtz	30	233	113	7	.670
*Bobby Bowden	36	323	91	4	.778	Hayden Fry	37	232	178	10	.564
Glenn (Pop) Warner	44	319	106	32	.733	Jess Neely	40	207	176	19	.539
Amos Alonzo Stagg	57	314	199	35	.605	Warren Woodson	31	203	95	14	.673
LaVell Edwards	29	257	100	3	.718	Don Nehlen	30	202	128	8	.609
Tom Osborne	25	255	49	3	.836	Vince Dooley	25	201	77	10	.715
Woody Hayes	33	238	72	10	.759	Eddie Anderson	39	201	128	15	.606

*Active.

MOST BOWL VICTORIES

	W	L	T		W	L	T
*Joe Paterno	20	9	1	Barry Switzer	8	5	0
*Bobby Bowden	18	6	1	*Jackie Sherrill	8	6	0
Paul (Bear) Bryant	15	12	2	Darrell Royal	8	7	1
Jim Wacker	13	2	0	Vince Dooley	8	10	2
*Lou Holtz	12	8	2	Pat Dye	7	2	1
Tom Osborne	12	13	0	Bob Devaney	7	3	0
Don James	10	5	0	Dan Devine	7	3	0
John Vaught	10	8	0	Earle Bruce	7	5	0
Bobby Dodd	9	4	0	Charlie McClendon	7	6	0
Johnny Majors	9	7	0	Hayden Fry	7	9	1
*John Robinson	8	1	0	LaVell Edwards	7	14	1
Terry Donahue	8	4	1	*Active.			

NCAA COACHES' RECORDS (CONT.)

WINNINGEST ACTIVE DIVISION I-A COACHES
BY PERCENTAGE

COACH, COLLEGE	YRS	W	L	T	PCT#	BOWLS		
						W	L	T
Bob Pruett, Marshall	6	69	11	0	.863	4	1	0
Phillip Fulmer, Tennessee	10	95	20	0	.826	6	4	0
Bobby Bowden, Florida St	36	323	91	4	.778	18	6	1
Joe Paterno, Penn St	36	327	96	3	.771	20	9	1
Lloyd Carr, Michigan	7	66	20	0	.767	4	3	0
R. C. Slocum, Texas A&M	13	117	41	2	.738	3	8	0
Dennis Erickson, Oregon St	16	136	51	1	.722	5	4	0
Rick Neuheisel, Washington	7	59	24	0	.711	4	2	0
Tommy Bowden, Clemson	5	40	18	0	.690	1	2	0
Paul Pasqualoni, Syracuse	16	125	56	1	.690	6	2	0

#Bowl games included in overall record. Ties computed as half win, half loss..
Note: Minimum five years as Division I-A head coach; record at four-year colleges only.

BY VICTORIES

Joe Paterno, Penn St	327	Frank Beamer, Virginia Tech	149
Bobby Bowden, Florida St	323	Dennis Franchione, Alabama	145
Lou Holtz, S Carolina	233	Fisher DeBerry, Air Force	141
Jackie Sherrill, Mississippi St	175	Dennis Erickson, Oregon St	136
Ken Hatfield, Rice	155	Paul Pasqualoni, Syracuse	125

WINNINGEST ACTIVE DIVISION I-AA COACHES
BY PERCENTAGE

COACH, COLLEGE	YRS	W	L	T	PCT*
Mike Kelly, Dayton	21	195	40	1	.828
Al Bagnoli, Pennsylvania	20	154	50	0	.755
Greg Gattuso, Duquesne	9	71	24	0	.747
Pete Richardson, Southern	14	120	41	1	.744
Joe Walton, Robert Morris	8	58	21	1	.731
Joe Gardi, Hofstra	12	99	36	2	.730
Roy Kidd, Eastern Kentucky	38	307	119	8	.717
Billy Joe, Florida A&M	28	221	89	4	.710
Joe Taylor, Hampton	19	146	59	4	.708
Walt Hameline, Wagner	21	150	67	2	.690

*Playoff games included.
Note: Minimum five years as a Division I-A and/or Division I-AA head coach; record at four-year colleges only.

BY VICTORIES

Roy Kidd, Eastern Kentucky	307	Al Bagnoli, Pennsylvania	154
Billy Joe, Florida A&M	221	Walt Hameline, Wagner	150
Ron Randleman, Sam Houston St	201	Jimmye Laycock, William & Mary	148
Mike Kelly, Dayton	195	Joe Taylor, Hampton	146
Bill Hayes, N Carolina A&T	191	Bob Ricca, St. John's (NY)	146

NCAA COACHES' RECORDS (CONT.)

WINNINGEST ACTIVE DIVISION II COACHES
BY PERCENTAGE

COACH, COLLEGE	YRS	W	L	T	PCT*
Chuck Broyles, Pittsburg St (KS)	12	123	23	2	.838
Ken Sparks, Carson-Newman	22	211	51	2	.803
John Luckhardt, California (PA)	17	137	37	2	.784
Bob Babich, N Dakota St	5	44	14	0	.759
Bob Biggs, UC–Davis	9	81	27	1	.748
Dale Lennon, N Dakota	5	43	15	0	.741
Danny Hale, Bloomsburg	14	113	42	1	.728
Brian Kelly, Grand Valley St	11	90	34	2	.722
Peter Yetten, Bentley	14	98	39	1	.714
Frank Cignetti, Indiana (PA)	20	165	67	1	.710

*Ties computed as half win, half loss. Playoff games included.
Note: Minimum five years as a college head coach; record at four-year colleges only.

BY VICTORIES

Ken Sparks, Carson-Newman	211
Willard Bailey, Virginia Union	199
Bud Elliott, Eastern New Mexico	185
Frank Cignetti, Indiana (PA)	165
Dennis Douds, E Stroudsburg	162
Gary Howard, Central Oklahoma	155
John Luckhardt, California (PA)	137
Jerry Vandergriff, Angelo St	136
Mel Tjeerdsma, NW Missouri St	135
Monte Cater, Shepherd	130

WINNINGEST ACTIVE DIVISION III
BY PERCENTAGE

COACH, COLLEGE	YRS	W	L	T	PCT*
Larry Kehres, Mount Union	16	178	17	3	.907
Joe Fincham, Wittenberg	6	63	7	0	.900
Rich Kacmarynski, Central (IA)	5	49	8	0	.860
Dick Farley, Williams	15	101	16	3	.854
Rick Willis, Wartburg	5	43	8	0	.843
Chris Creighton, Wabash	5	40	9	0	.816
Bill Zwaan, Widener	5	45	13	0	.776
E. J. Mills, Amherst	5	31	9	0	.775
John Gagliardi, St. John's (MN)	53	388	112	11	.770
Frosty Westering, Pacific Lutheran	37	294	89	7	.763

*Ties computed as half won, half lost. Playoff games included.
Note: Minimum five years as a college head coach; record at four-year colleges only.

BY VICTORIES

John Gagliardi, St John's (MN)	388
Frosty Westering, Pacific Lutheran	294
Frank Girardi, Lycoming	226
Peter Mazzaferro, Bridgewater (MA)	193
Larry Kehres, Mount Union	178
Tom Gilburg, Franklin & Marshall	156
Eric Hamilton, College of New Jersey	153
Lou Wacker, Emory & Henry	151
Wayne Perry, Hanover	140
Rick Giancola, Montclair St	134

NAIA COACHES' RECORDS (ENTERING 2002 SEASON)

WINNINGEST ACTIVE NAIA COACHES

BY PERCENTAGE

COACH, COLLEGE	YRS	W	L	T	PCT*
Ted Kessinger, Bethany (KS)	26	208	50	1	.805
Hank Biesiot, Dickinson St (ND)	27	182	66	1	.733
Carl Poelker, McKendree (IL)	20	129	58	1	.689
Bob Young, Sioux Falls (SD)	20	137	66	3	.672
Geno DeMarco, Geneva (PA)	6	41	21	0	.661
Larry Wilcox, Benedictine (KS)	23	159	82	0	.660
Orv Otten, Northwestern (IA)	7	48	26	0	.649
Vic Wallace, Lambuth (TN)	20	139	75	4	.647
Todd Sturdy, St. Ambrose (IA)	7	44	26	0	.629
John Frangoulis, Baker (KS)	6	38	25	0	.603

*Playoff games included.
Note: Minimum five years as a collegiate head coach and includes record against four-year institutions only.

BY VICTORIES

Ted Kessinger, Bethany (KS)	208	Bob Young, Sioux Falls (SD)	137
Hank Biesiot, Dickinson St (ND)	182	Carl Poelker, McKendree (IL)	129
Larry Wilcox, Benedictine (KS)	159	Jim Dennison, Walsh (OH)	127
Kevin Donley, St. Francis (IN)	144	Fran Schwenk, Doane (NE)	103
Vic Wallace, Lambuth (TN)	139	Bob Green, Montana Tech	91

☆ LARGEST FOOTBALL TROPHY ☆

[CHIEF CADDO]

DARREN CARROLL

In 1960, interstate rivals Stephen F. Austin of Texas and Northwestern State of Louisiana agreed that whichever school lost the next year's football matchup would fell a tree near its campus and send the trunk to the winning school, where a statue would be carved. Northwestern State won and created 7' 6", 320-pound Chief Caddo (named for a Caddo Indian whose tribe settled the areas where both schools are located) from a 2,000-pound black gum log. The Chief, held by the winner of the annual game, is on display in the field house at Northwestern State, awaiting this year's Nov. 22 showdown.

Midfielder Adolfo Gregorio returns to the defending champion Bruins, who landed the nation's top recruiting class.

The Rich
GET RICHER

College Cup 2003 should have plenty of familiar faces as most of the nation's top teams enjoyed stellar recruiting years

IKE NCAA basketball, men's college soccer is being reshaped at the dawn of the 21st century. The most talented players in the sport are jumping to the professional ranks at earlier and earlier ages, and the exodus is having a significant impact on the game. Indeed, the very best youth soccer players in the U.S. are bypassing college altogether these days, the better to keep pace with their counterparts around the world, who typically enter a professional environment in their early teens.

And as in basketball, the drain off its top has made the college soccer talent pool shallower, increased parity in the game, and given handicappers nightmares. That said, there are still some clear cut favorites in the field, as well as some players with professional careers in their futures.

On the women's side, the days of the regular season constituting little more than a prelude to the coronation of North Carolina appear to be over. The 16-time champion Tar Heels, who won nine national titles in a row from 1986 to '94, have not won the women's championship in two years. The balance of power may not have shifted, exactly—UNC still made it to the final four in 2002—but the women's game has become more than a one-horse race in recent years.

FAVORITES

Last year's men's semifinalists, UCLA, Stanford, Maryland and Creighton, all appear poised to make another run at the College Cup, which will be held in December 2003 at the Home Depot Center in Carson, Calif., the sparkling new headquarters of the U.S. national team.

According to *Soccer America*, **UCLA**, which won the 2002 title with a 1–0 victory over Pac-10 rival Stanford, landed the best recruiting class in the nation, reeling in four members of the U.S. under-18 national team and two from the U.S. under-17s. The Bruins lost five seniors from last year's team, including All-America forward Tim Pierce (12 goals, 7 assists in 2002), but this

year's recruiting class should, as coach Tom Fitzgerald says, "allow us to again challenge for the NCAA title."

Leading the way are forward Chad Barrett, who had 32 goals and 21 assists during his senior year at Southridge High School in Beavertown, Ore., speedy defender Brandon Owen, currently in residence with U-17 team in Bradenton, Fla., and midfielder Jose Gomez, whom Fitzgerald calls "one of the best midfield passers

Marshall (14) scored the double-overtime winner that sent the Cardinal into last year's College Cup final.

of anyone wh has ever come through the under-17 program." After five and a half years as head coach of Major League Soccer's Columbus Crew, Fitzgerald came to Westwood in 2002 and won a national title in his first season on the job. This year, it appears the rich get richer.

Stanford coach Bret Simon calls his 2003 recruiting class "talented and deep . . . one of the best in the country." He may need all of that talent and depth to replace the four players he lost to the MLS draft after the 2002 season, in which the Cardinal went 18-5-2 and reached the College Cup final. Simon's prize recruits include midfielder Marcus Ryan and goalkeeper Andrew Kartunen. Ryan, who ranks 10th on *Soccer America*'s list of the nation's Top 25 recruits, is a member of the Region IV Olympic Development team. A mainstay of U.S. youth teams since the under-14 level, Kartunen will line up behind the Cardinal's rock-solid central defender, Chad Marshall. As a freshman last season, Marshall scored the winner in double overtime against Creighton to give the Cardinal a 2–1 victory in the national semifinals and a berth in the championship game.

That defeat was especially tough for **Creighton**, since the Blue Jays were facing their former coach in the Cardinal's Simon. They hope to make amends in 2003. Returning seven starters from last year's team, which went 18-4-2, Creighton has a good chance to do just that. They lost senior Mike Tranchilla (15 goals 7 assists in '02) to graduation but will still have a potent attack, spearheaded by Julian Nash (8 g, 8 a) and Damian Westfield (8 g, 4 a), and their midfield, anchored by David Wagenfuhr (5 g, 4 a) and Mehdi Ballouchy (5 g, 4 a), should be one of the best in the nation.

The Blue Jays will be tested in late August, when Butler, Furman and last year's other national semifinalists, **Maryland**, come to town for an early-season tournament. Maryland, which lost 1–0 to UCLA in the 2002 semis, may be the most dangerous of the pre-season favorites. If it can survive its brutal schedule, that is. The Terps will face 14 teams that qualified for the 2002 NCAAs, including—in their opener, no less—the defending champion Bruins. But with first team All-America midfielder Sumed Ibrahim, a healthy Domenic Mediate, and produc-

tive striker Abe Thompson returning to the fold, coach Sasho Cirovski is confident the Terps will be equal to the daunting task. "It's an incredible schedule and I can't wait to get started," he said. At the end of it, following games against 2002 NCAA quarterfinalists Connecticut and Penn State, and its usual slate of foes from the ACC, the nation's toughest conference (it put six teams in the NCAA tournament last year), Maryland could well be raising a trophy at the Home Depot Center.

But as we've said, college soccer is even more wide open than NCAA hoops, so there are several other teams that qualify as favorites. Maryland's ACC rivals Wake Forest were the No. 1 seed in last year's tournament and only lost three players to graduation. **Clemson**, a perennial power which went 14-5-3 in 2002 and lost to Stanford in the NCAA quarterfinals, has reloaded with a stellar recruiting class, including goalkeeper Phillip Marfuggi and attacking midfielder Olatomiwa Ogunsola, both with the U.S. under-17 team in Bradenton. **St. John's** will be battle-tested by their Big East schedule (the conference placed the Red Storm, Connecticut and Boston College among the top eight seeds in last year's NCAAs) come tournament time, with All-America senior midfielder Chris Wingert leading the way. Wingert, a candidate for the 2004 Olympic team, would like nothing more than to close his college career with an NCAA title.

The 2002 women's championship was noteworthy as the first time since 1995 that Anson Dorrance's **North**

Carolina Tar Heels did not reach the title game. Falling 2–1 to Santa Clara in the semis, the Tar Heels saw their string of championships stopped at two. But fear not for Dorrance and the Chapel Hill faithful: They landed the top recruit in the country in East Brunswick, N.J.'s Heather O'Reilly, who has already played for the U.S. women's national team. The Tar Heels could well begin another run of titles in 2003.

After edging UNC last season, **Santa Clara** went on to lose the national final 2–1 in double overtime to Portland, but will welcome the best crop of freshman in the nation in the fall of 2003. Chief among the Broncos recruits is goalkeeper Julie Ryder, a "difference maker," according to coach Jerry Smith, who should step right into the starting job. **Portland** will challenge for the College Cup again, with the likes of forward Angie Woznuk and defender Stephanie Lopez, two players with world-class potential, joining the team. A No. 1 seed in last year's tournament, **Stanford** returns seven starters from a team that went 21–2. The Cardinal's Pac-10 rival **UCLA** loses just one player to graduation and has added five recruits with U.S. youth national team experience. The Bruins should improve upon their 2002 performance, which saw them finish 18–4 after a defeat on penalty kicks to Texas A&M in the third round of the NCAAs.

DARKHORSES

No one will take them lightly, since they won the men's national championship in 2001, but the **North Carolina** Tar Heels would probably call 2003 a rebuilding year. And how coach Elmar Bolowich has rebuilt: He will welcome a class of 13 players, several of whom should compete for playing time right away. In attacking midfielder Corey Ashe, Bolowich may have the best recruit in the country. After being baptized by the ACC fires, the Tar Heels could be ready to pull some postseason surprises.

Vying with Ashe for the title of top recruit is **Southern Methodist** signee Ramon Nunez, a midfielder from Dallas. Nunez joins a Mustangs team that went 16-3-3 last season and is eager to improve upon its third-round showing at the NCAAs. **Furman** lost All-America midfielder Ricardo Clark to MLS's MetroStars but returns eight starters from last year's 19-3-1 team.

Connecticut and **Boston College** could join St. John's in competing at the national level, though BC lost its alltime leading scorer, Casey Schmidt (now with Colorado of MLS), and UConn lost Damani Ralph (now with Chicago). Still, the cupboard is by no means bare at either school. The same can be said for **Indiana** (see SIDELINES) and **Virginia**. The Cavaliers had another fine recruiting year, but lost one of the best players in school history, Alecko Eskandarian, who departed early for MLS along with midfielder Jacob LeBlanc.

In the women's game, **Nebraska**, which landed top recruit Brittany Timko, a starter on the Canadian national team, is a program showing steady improvement. **Notre Dame** hopes to rebound from its injury-riddled 13–8 campaign in 2002, and **Penn State**, which made a surprising run to

CHRIS HOWELL/ICON SMI

College soccer will say goodbye to a legend in Yeagley, who founded Indiana's program and led it to five NCAA titles.

the final four of the NCAAs last season, will have to adjust to life without superstar Christie Welsh. But with four seniors starting in 2003, the Nittany Lions will take their chances.

SIDELINES

After 30 years and 527 victories, the most among active coaches, Indiana men's coach Jerry Yeagley has announced that he will retire following the 2003 season, his 31st. Yeagley's teams have won five national titles and set a record by reaching the semifinals of the NCAA tournament for five consecutive seasons, from 1997 to 2001, winning the championship in 1998 and '99.

Yeagley stands 17 wins shy of the NCAA record for coaching victories, held by San Francisco's Steve Negoesco (544 wins in 39 seasons). That's a margin that would be difficult for any team to close in one season., much less a team that lost seven players to graduation last year, including Big Ten Player of the Year Pat Noonan, now with New England of MLS. To be sure, the Hoosiers will field a talented crop of players in 2003, with eight quality recruits added to the mix, and the pursuit of the record, however distant it may be, will surely add motivation to Yeagley's charges. But the coach, who founded IU's soccer program, maintains that the record did not figure prominently in his decision. "There are things I want to do with my wife Marilyn and my family," he said. "I know I will miss it. But I'll be close by."

NCAA MEN'S DIVISION I CHAMPIONSHIP GAME

UCLA   0   1—1
Stanford   0   0—0

Goal: Aaron Lopez, 89.

UCLA: Zach Wells, Tim Pierce, Aaron Lopez, Cliff McKinley, Chadd Davis, Jimmy Frazelle, Adolfo Gregorio, Leonard Griffin, Mike Enfield, Scot Thompson, Tony Lawson.

Stanford: Robby Fulton, James Twellman, Roger Levesque, Todd Dunivant, Taylor Graham, Chad Marshall, Abe Geiger, Mike Wilson, Johanes Maliza, Darren Fernandez, Aaron Maines.

NCAA MEN'S DIVISION I INDIVIDUAL LEADERS

GOALS

PLAYER AND TEAM	CLASS	GP	G	AVG
Alecko Eskandarian, Virginia	Jr	20	25	1.25
Antou Jallow, WI-Milwaukee	So	20	24	1.20
Joseph Ngwenya, Coastal Carolina	Jr	24	27	1.13
Jeff Deren, Massachusetts	Sr	20	22	1.10
Dimelon Westfield, Clemson	Sr	20	20	1.00
T.J. Rolfing, Radford	Sr	20	19	0.95
Arnar Johannsson, George Washington	Jr	19	18	0.95
Francis Wakhisi, Winthrop	Sr	23	21	0.91
Rob Friend, UC–Santa Barbara	Sr	22	20	0.91
Chris Goos, UNC-Greensboro	Sr	22	20	0.91

ASSISTS

PLAYER AND TEAM	CLASS	GP	A	AVG
Chris Goos, UNC-Greensboro	Sr	22	20	0.91
Memo Arzate, UC-Santa Barbara	Jr	21	18	0.86
Garret Pickard, Centenary (LA)	Jr	19	16	0.84
Matt Crawford, N Carolina	Sr	21	16	0.76
Adam Bruh, Michigan	Fr	18	13	0.72
David McGill, UC-Santa Barbara	Jr	21	15	0.71
Rhian Dodds, Robert Morris	Sr	17	11	0.65
Roger Levesque, Stanford	Sr	21	13	0.62
Kevin Wickart, St. Louis	Jr	20	12	0.60
Andrew Dorman, Boston U	Jr	17	10	0.59
Jonathan Hemmert, Bucknell	So	17	10	0.59

POINTS

PLAYER AND TEAM	CLASS	GP	G	A	PTS	PTS/G
Chris Goos, UNC-Greensboro	Sr	22	20	20	60	2.73
Alecko Eskandarian, Virginia	Jr	20	25	4	54	2.70
Antou Jallow, WI-Milwaukee	So	20	24	5	53	2.65
Joseph Ngwenya, Coastal Carolina	Jr	24	27	9	63	2.63
Jeff Deren, Massachusetts	Sr	20	22	7	51	2.55
Dimelon Westfield, Clemson	Sr	20	20	5	45	2.25
Matthew Osborne, George Wash	Sr	22	19	11	49	2.23
Arnar Johannsson, George Wash	Jr	19	18	6	42	2.21
T.J. Rolfing, Radford	Sr	20	19	5	43	2.15
Ryan Kneipper, N Carolina	Sr	21	18	9	45	2.14

NCAA MEN'S DIVISION I INDIVIDUAL LEADERS (CONT.)

GOALS AGAINST AVERAGE

PLAYER AND TEAM	CLASS	GP	MIN	G	GAA
Robby Fulton, Stanford	So	18	1681	8	0.43
Bill Gaudette, St. John's (NY)	Jr	21	1985	10	0.45
Chris Dadaian, WI-Milwaukee	Sr	17	1491	9	0.54
John Moschella, St. Peter's	Fr	14	967	6	0.56
Kevin Baker, Holy Cross	Jr	19	1792	12	0.60
Adam Edwards, Bucknell	Fr	19	1747	12	0.62
Matthew Haefner, Pennsylvania	Jr	17	1598	11	0.62
Alex Maslow, Furman	So	15	1281	9	0.63
William Hesmer, Wake Forest	Jr	19	1794	13	0.65
Steven Burns, Fairfield	Fr	11	900	7	0.70

NCAA WOMEN'S DIVISION I CHAMPIONSHIP GAME

Portland	0	1	0	1—2
Santa Clara	0	1	0	0—1

Goals: Santa Clara: Devvyn Hawkins, 53; Portland: Christine Sinclair, 61, 104.

Portland: Lauren Arase, Betsy Barr, Imani Dorsey, Kristen Moore, Erin Misaki, Kristen Rogers, Wanda Rozwadowska, Emily Patterson, Christine Sinclair, Lauren Orlandos, Lindsey Huie, Rebekah Patrick.

Santa Clara: Alyssa Sobolik, Megan Kakadelas, Veronica Zepeda, Micaela Esquivel, Aly Wagner, Lana Bowen, Jessica Ballweg, Devvyn Hawkins, Bree Horvath, Chardonnay Poole, Kristi Candau.

NCAA WOMEN'S DIVISION I INDIVIDUAL LEADERS

GOALS

PLAYER AND TEAM	CLASS	GP	G	AVG
Rosie Luzak, Niagara	Jr	18	25	1.39
Marilyn Marin, N Texas	Jr	19	26	1.37
Ranieka Bean, Howard	So	16	21	1.31
Krystal Sandza, UC–Santa Barbara	So	20	25	1.25
Christine Sinclair, Portland	So	21	26	1.24

ASSISTS

PLAYER AND TEAM	CLASS	GP	A	AVG
Kelly Parker, Texas–El Paso	Sr	19	19	1.00
Robyn Vince, Tennessee Tech	So	18	17	0.94
Melissa Bennett, Washington	Jr	20	18	0.90
Marilyn Marin, N Texas	Jr	19	15	0.79
Julie Ferguson, Florida Atlantic	Fr	17	13	0.76

POINTS

PLAYER AND TEAM	CLASS	GP	G	A	PTS	PTS/G
Marilyn Marin, N Texas	Jr	19	26	15	67	3.53
Rosie Luzak, Niagara	Jr	18	25	7	57	3.17
Krystal Sandza, UC–Santa Barbara	So	20	25	8	58	2.90
Holly Cohen, Texas–El Paso	Sr	18	22	7	51	2.83
Ranieka Bean, Howard	So	16	21	2	44	2.75

GOALS AGAINST AVERAGE

PLAYER AND TEAM	CLASS	GP	MIN	G	GAA
Nicole Barnhart, Stanford	So	23	2047	4	0.18
Kim Bonafede, Navy	So	21	1756	7	0.36
Lauren Arase, Portland	Sr	21	1929	8	0.37
Laura Finley, W Virginia	Jr	14	1202	6	0.45
Morgan Bennett, Army	Fr	15	1285	7	0.49

NCAA MEN'S DIVISION II CHAMPIONSHIP GAME

Sonoma St	1	3	—4
Southern New Hampshire	2	1	—3

Goals:

Sonoma State: Brian Coyne, 35; Brandon Boone, 49; Michael Nathan, 74; Tony Bussard, 77.

Southern New Hampshire: Anthony Augustine, 15; Mounir Tajiou, 36; Romelle Burgess, 90.

NCAA MEN'S DIVISION II INDIVIDUAL LEADERS

GOALS

PLAYER AND TEAM	CLASS	GP	G	AVG
Paul Hopkins, Tusculum	So	21	28	1.33
Ricky Charles, SC-Spartanburg	Jr	22	25	1.14
Juan Trujillo, Limestone	Fr	18	20	1.11
Kyle Clancy, Dominican (NY)	Fr	20	22	1.10
Lance Snodgrass, Regis (CO)	Jr	16	17	1.06

ASSISTS

PLAYER AND TEAM	CLASS	GP	A	AVG
Jose Palladino, Clayton St	Sr	18	17	0.94
David Ormesher, Tusculum	Sr	21	19	0.90
Oliver Carias, Queens (NC)	So	20	18	0.90
Avi Scabini, Barry	Jr	18	14	0.78
Derek Thomas, Limestone	Sr	19	14	0.74

POINTS

PLAYER AND TEAM	CLASS	GP	G	A	PTS	PTS/G
Paul Hopkins, Tusculum	So	21	28	13	69	3.29
Ricky Charles, SC-Spartanburg	Jr	22	25	13	63	2.86
Derek Thomas, Limestone	Sr	19	19	14	52	2.74
David Ormesher, Tusculum	Sr	21	18	19	55	2.62
Lance Snodgrass, Regis (CO)	Jr	16	17	7	41	2.56
Juan Trujillo, Limsetone	Fr	18	20	6	46	2.56

GOALS AGAINST AVERAGE

PLAYER AND TEAM	CLASS	GP	MIN	G	GAA
Kevin Street, Lynn	Fr	12	855	5	0.53
Tony Swaminathan, Tusculum	Sr	20	1767	12	0.61
Jorge Geddes, W Virginia Wesleyan	Sr	22	2009	14	0.63
Andrew Shaffer, West Chester	So	19	1283	9	0.63
Brian Flebbe, Queens (NC)	Sr	20	1761	13	0.66

CHEERS

"Differential Y, differential X, to hell with differentials, we want sex!"

—Georgia Tech

NCAA MEN'S DIVISION III CHAMPIONSHIP GAME

Otterbein	0	0	—0
Messiah	1	0	—1

Goal: Troy Sauer, 18.

Otterbein: Jeffrey Rust, Jason Manly, Brett Neiderman, Kyle Daniel, Drew Cheesman, Angelo Manzo, Dennis Duryea, Jesse Rose, Mark Welp, Auston Bland, Mike Lochner, Jason Shelton, Eli Wynkoop, Adam Rothermel.

Messiah: Dave Casper, Haden Woodworth, Aaron Casper, Kevin Schneider, Troy Sauer, Matt Bills, Aaron Faro, Andy Rosamilia, Sam Casey, Brown Vincent, Matt Snavely, Seth Lehman, Bill Crompton, Hylton Kipe, Brandon Fisher, Bryan Mohney, Chris Claasen.

NCAA MEN'S DIVISION III INDIVIDUAL LEADERS

GOALS

PLAYER AND TEAM	CLASS	GP	G	AVG
Jason Ross, Augustana (IL)	Jr	20	30	1.50
Tim Trava, St. Joseph's (LI)	Jr	22	32	1.45
Rudy Lormil, Kean	Sr	20	25	1.25
Adam Ivankovic, Cal St–Hayward	Sr	13	16	1.23
Alex Blake, Williams	Sr	20	24	1.20

ASSISTS

PLAYER AND TEAM	CLASS	GP	A	AVG
Brandon Migitsch, Pitt-Greensburg	Sr	20	19	0.95
Mike Egan, Gordon	Sr	18	15	0.83
Justin Cryder, Blackburn	Jr	17	13	0.76
Alex Blake, Williams	Sr	20	15	0.75
Dan Antoniuk, Wheaton (MA)	Sr	15	11	0.73

POINTS

PLAYER AND TEAM	CLASS	GP	G	A	PTS	PTS/G
Tim Trava, St. Joseph's (LI)	Jr	22	32	10	74	3.36
Alex Blake, Williams	Sr	20	24	15	63	3.15
Jason Ross, Augustana (IL)	Jr	20	30	3	63	3.15
Rudy Lormil, Kean	Sr	20	25	6	56	2.80
Kyle Marvin, Fredonia St	Sr	16	17	8	42	2.63

GOALS AGAINST AVERAGE

PLAYER AND TEAM	CLASS	GP	MIN	G	GAA
Josh Rosenblum, Trinity (TX)	Jr	20	1209	5	0.37
Dave Casper, Messiah	So	26	2036	9	0.40
Michael Madigan, Macalester	Sr	21	1549	8	0.46
David Treleven, Wooster	Fr	14	1330	7	0.47
Tom Paparounis, Salisbury	Sr	12	939	5	0.48
Jason Thurman, NE-Wesleyan	Sr	21	1679	9	0.48

MEN'S DIVISION I

YEAR	CHAMPION	COACH	SCORE	RUNNER-UP
1959	St. Louis	Bob Guelker	5–2	Bridgeport
1960	St. Louis	Bob Guelker	3–2	Maryland
1961	West Chester	Mel Lorback	2–0	St. Louis
1962	St. Louis	Bob Guelker	4–3	Maryland
1963	St. Louis	Bob Guelker	3–0	Navy
1964	Navy	F.H. Warner	1–0	Michigan St
1965	St. Louis	Bob Guelker	1–0	Michigan St
1966	San Francisco	Steve Negoesco	5–2	LIU–Brooklyn
1967	Michigan St	Gene Kenney	0–0	Game called due to
	St. Louis	Harry Keough		inclement weather
1968	Maryland	Doyle Royal	2–2 (2 OT)	
	Michigan St	Gene Kenney		
1969	St. Louis	Harry Keough	4–0	San Francisco
1970	St. Louis	Harry Keough	1–0	UCLA
1971	Vacated		3–2	St. Louis
1972	St. Louis	Harry Keough	4–2	UCLA
1973	St. Louis	Harry Keough	2–1 (OT)	UCLA
1974	Howard	Lincoln Phillips	2–1 (4 OT)	St. Louis
1975	San Francisco	Steve Negoesco	4–0	SIU–Edwardsville
1976	San Francisco	Steve Negoesco	1–0	Indiana
1977	Hartwick	Jim Lennox	2–1	San Francisco
1978	Vacated		2–0	Indiana
1979	SIU–Edwardsville	Bob Guelker	3–2	Clemson
1980	San Francisco	Steve Negoesco	4–3 (OT)	Indiana
1981	Connecticut	Joe Morrone	2–1 (OT)	Alabama A&M
1982	Indiana	Jerry Yeagley	2–1 (8 OT)	Duke
1983	Indiana	Jerry Yeagley	1–0 (2 OT)	Columbia
1984	Clemson	I.M. Ibrahim	2–1	Indiana
1985	UCLA	Sigi Schmid	1–0 (8 OT)	American
1986	Duke	John Rennie	1–0	Akron
1987	Clemson	I.M. Ibrahim	2–0	San Diego St
1988	Indiana	Jerry Yeagley	1–0	Howard
1989	Santa Clara	Steve Sampson	1–1 (2 OT)	
	Virginia	Bruce Arena		
1990	UCLA	Sigi Schmid	1–0 (OT)	Rutgers
1991	Virginia	Bruce Arena	0–0*	Santa Clara
1992	Virginia	Bruce Arena	2–0	San Diego
1993	Virginia	Bruce Arena	2–0	S Carolina
1994	Virginia	Bruce Arena	1–0	Indiana
1995	Wisconsin	Jim Launder	2–0	Duke
1996	St. John's (NY)	Dave Masur	4–1	Florida International
1997	UCLA	Sigi Schmid	2–1	Virginia
1998	Indiana	Jerry Yeagley	3–1	Stanford
1999	Indiana	Jerry Yeagley	1–0	Santa Clara
2000	Connecticut	Ray Reid	2–0	Creighton
2001	N Carolina	Elmar Bolowich	2–0	Indiana
2002	UCLA	Tom Fitzgerald	1–0	Stanford

*Under a rule passed in 1991, the NCAA determined that when a score is tied after regulation and overtime, and the championship is determined by penalty kicks, the official score will be 0–0.

MEN'S DIVISION II

YEAR	CHAMPION	YEAR	CHAMPION
1972	SIU–Edwardsville	1988	Florida Tech
1973	MO–St. Louis	1989	New Hampshire College
1974	Adelphi	1990	Southern Connecticut St
1975	Baltimore	1991	Florida Tech
1976	Loyola (MD)	1992	Southern Connecticut St
1977	Alabama A&M	1993	Seattle Pacific
1978	Seattle Pacific	1994	Tampa
1979	Alabama A&M	1995	Southern Connecticut St
1980	Lock Haven	1996	Grand Canyon
1981	Tampa	1997	Cal St-Bakersfield
1982	Florida International	1998	Southern Connecticut St
1983	Seattle Pacific	1999	Southern Connecticut St
1984	Florida International	2000	Cal St–Dominguez Hills
1985	Seattle Pacific	2001	Tampa
1986	Seattle Pacific	2002	Sonoma St
1987	Southern Connecticut St		

MEN'S DIVISION III

YEAR	CHAMPION	YEAR	CHAMPION
1974	Brockport St	1989	Elizabethtown
1975	Babson	1990	Glassboro St
1976	Brandeis	1991	UC–San Diego
1977	Lock Haven	1992	Kean
1978	Lock Haven	1993	UC–San Diego
1979	Babson	1994	Bethany (WV)
1980	Babson	1995	Williams
1981	Glassboro St	1996	College of New Jersey
1982	NC–Greensboro	1997	Wheaton (IL)
1983	NC–Greensboro	1998	Ohio Wesleyan
1984	Wheaton (IL)	1999	St. Lawrence
1985	NC–Greensboro	2000	Messiah
1986	NC–Greensboro	2001	Richard Stockton
1987	NC–Greensboro	2002	Messiah
1988	UC–San Diego		

WOMEN'S DIVISION I

YEAR	CHAMPION	COACH	SCORE	RUNNER-UP
1982 ....N Carolina		Anson Dorrance	2–0	Central Florida
1983 ....N Carolina		Anson Dorrance	4–0	George Mason
1984 ....N Carolina		Anson Dorrance	2–0	Connecticut
1985 ....George Mason		Hank Leung	2–0	N Carolina
1986 ....N Carolina		Anson Dorrance	2–0	Colorado College
1987 ....N Carolina		Anson Dorrance	1–0	Massachusetts
1988 ....N Carolina		Anson Dorrance	4–1	N Carolina St
1989 ....N Carolina		Anson Dorrance	2–0	Colorado College
1990 ....N Carolina		Anson Dorrance	6–0	Connecticut
1991 ....N Carolina		Anson Dorrance	3–1	Wisconsin
1992 ....N Carolina		Anson Dorrance	9–1	Duke
1993 ....N Carolina		Anson Dorrance	6–0	George Mason
1994 ....N Carolina		Anson Dorrance	5–0	Notre Dame
1995 ....Notre Dame		Chris Petrucelli	1–0	Portland
1996 ....N Carolina		Anson Dorrance	1–0	Notre Dame
1997 ....N Carolina		Anson Dorrance	2–0	Connecticut
1998 ....Florida		Becky Burleigh	1–0	N Carolina
1999 ....N Carolina		Anson Dorrance	2–0	Notre Dame
2000 ....N Carolina		Anson Dorrance	2–1	UCLA
2001 ....Santa Clara		Jerry Smith	1–0	N Carolina
2002 ....Portland		Clive Charles	2–1	Santa Clara

GO FIGURE

33 Goals scored by the Nebraska Wesleyan women's team against Dana in a 1996 match, the most goals ever scored in a single intercollegiate contest, either male or female.

12 Number of Division I soccer programs eliminated in the last 10 years. In the past year two schools, Charleston Southern, and TCU shut down their men's teams. Fresno State shut down its program in April 2003, but reversed the decision and reinstated it in May.

2.71 Goals scored per game during the 1980 season by Appalachian State's Thompson Usiyan, the most prolific scorer in Division I history. Usiyan hit net 46 times in 17 games. He holds the career record with 109 goals in 49 career matches.

1.25 Goals scored per game by Virginia junior Alecko Eskandarian, the nation's goal scoring leader in 2002, who has since departed for D.C. United of MLS.

204 Number of games, out of 205, in which the University of North Carolina women's team went unbeaten from Sept. 30, 1986, to Oct. 16, 1994. The only blemish between unbeaten streaks of 103 and 101 games during that span was a 3–2 loss at the University of Connecticut. During its history the Tar Heels' women's program has also had unbeaten streaks of 70, 56 and 35 games.

WOMEN'S DIVISION II

YEAR	CHAMPION	YEAR	CHAMPION
1988	Cal St–Hayward	1996	Franklin Pierce
1989	Barry	1997	Franklin Pierce
1990	Sonoma St	1998	Lynn
1991	Cal St–Dominguez Hills	1999	Franklin Pierce
1992	Barry	2000	UC–San Diego
1993	Barry	2001	UC–San Diego
1994	Franklin Pierce	2002	Christian Brothers
1995	Franklin Pierce		

WOMEN'S DIVISION III

YEAR	CHAMPION	YEAR	CHAMPION
1986	Rochester	1995	UC–San Diego
1987	Rochester	1996	UC–San Diego
1988	William Smith	1997	UC–San Diego
1989	UC–San Diego	1998	Macalester
1990	Ithaca	1999	UC–San Diego
1991	Ithaca	2000	College of New Jersey*
1992	Cortland St	2001	Ohio Wesleyan
1993	Trenton St	2002	Ohio Wesleyan
1994	Trenton St		

*Formerly Trenton St.

 # CREATIVE THINKING

Frustrated by its inability to attain varsity status, the BYU men's soccer team purchased a franchise for $40,000 in the Premier Development League, a Third Division U.S. pro circuit. In spring 2003 the Cougars became the first college team in any sport to play in a league with pro squads. After winning seven club championships in 10 years, BYU coach Chris Watkins said he wanted tougher competition, but because of Title IX restrictions the school wouldn't add a men's varsity sport. Joining the Premier League also allows players to travel internationally without being subject to NCAA restrictions, which would have made it difficult for student athletes to follow the Mormon precepts about preaching the faith. "I'm not sure about other teams, but it fits BYU," Watkins told SI.

After scoring 33 points in the final against Texas to lead Syracuse to its first national championship, Anthony, a freshman, declared himself eligible for the NBA draft.

Marching On

The NBA may be draining college basketball's top talent, but that hasn't made March any less mad

IKE A FLOWERING bush whose top branches are greened regularly, the talent in NCAA basketball has grown outward instead of upward in recent years. The gardener in this case is the National Basketball Association, which trims the upper reaches of the college basketball plant every June, claiming stars such as Carmelo Anthony of 2002–03 national champion Syracuse and leaving the NCAA game with plenty of good players, but fewer and fewer great ones.

The 2003 offseason saw the trend continue as Anthony, Texas guard T.J. Ford, and Marquette junior Dwayne Wade all made themselves eligible for the NBA draft. Indeed, every one of the 15 AP All-Americas from 2002–03 have departed the college ranks, and the top

young player in the country, LeBron James, is going straight from St. Vincent–St. Mary high school in Akron, Ohio, to the NBA's Cleveland Cavaliers.

The result of this youth exodus is that the NCAA title race is excitingly wide open, and handicapping it—several months ahead of time, no less—is a losing proposition. But we'll take a crack at it anyway. As for the NCAA women, they have no such problem of stars leaving early for the WNBA—at least not yet—so their fortunes should be a little easier to predict.

FAVORITES

With big man Emeka Okafor and guard Ben Gordon returning to a team that finished 23–10 and made it to the Sweet 16 of the NCAAs in 2002–03, **Connecticut** is the consensus preseason

The nation's leader in blocks last season, with 4.7 per game, Connecticut junior Okafor is also a first-rate rebounder and scorer.

No. 1 among college hoops wags. Okafor may be the country's premier rebounder and shot blocker, having averaged 11.2 boards a game last year, and 4.7 blocks, and he can also score (15.9 ppg). Gordon is a silky scorer also blessed with explosiveness, intelligence and strength. He grabbed 4.7 rebounds a game last season to go with his 4.7 assists and 19.5 points per game.

If the Huskies add star recruit Charlie Villanueva next season, well, in the words of Villanueva himself, "It's over." The 6'10" Villanueva, from Blair Academy in New Jersey, is one of the nation's top prospects, but he made himself eligible for the NBA draft, stating that if he can get a team to guarantee that it will draft him in the first round, he will skip college altogether. If not, he'll make UConn that much stronger. As we went to press, fans in Storrs, Conn., and the rest of the Big East's cities, were still holding their breath over the matter.

Villanueva may be confident of Connecticut's dominance should he join the team, but there will be other schools with something to say about it next winter. Chief among them could be **Kentucky**, which will lose Marquis Estill (11.6 points and 5.9 rebounds a game in 2002–03) to the NBA draft, but welcomes back Erik Daniels (9.7 ppg 5.0 rpg) and Chuck Hayes (8.5 ppg, 6.7 rpg) to suit up alongside talented players such as Cliff Hawkins, Antwain Barbour and Kelenna Azubuike. The Wildcats may lack size in 2003–04, but they will make up for it with a balanced, speedy attack.

Texas lost national player of the year Ford to the professional ranks, but still has enough talent—in Brandon Mouton, Brian Boddicker, Royal Ivey and Brad Buckman—to make a return trip to the Final Four. The Longhorn hoopsters, fresh from their appearance in the 2003 national semis (a 95–84 loss to Syracuse) are winning daily converts in football-mad Texas. **Duke**, which hasn't missed the NCAA tournament since 1995, will look to Chris Duhon, one of the top guards in the country, Shavlik Randolph, a 6'10" sophomore who can shoot and handle the ball, and guard J.J. Redick, who averaged 14.5 points a game as a freshman in 2002–03, to improve upon last season's "off" year, when the Blue Devils finished 26–7. Duke also landed top recruit Luol Deng, a versatile talent who played with Villanueva at Blair Academy.

Another team to keep an eye on is **Michigan State**, which will dress two dangerous big men, Paul Davis and Erazem Lorbek, who are only sophomores. A very young team in 2002–03, the Spartans lost to Texas in the Elite Eight of the NCAAs. Guards Chris Hill (13.7 ppg in 2002–03) and Alan Anderson should be even better as juniors, and the Spartans added coveted prospect Shannon Brown to join them in the backcourt.

If the Conecticut men with Villanueva in their ranks are a good bet to dominate the men's game in 2003–04, the UConn women, who started two freshmen and no seniors in 2002–03—and went 37–1 and won their third national title in four years—are practically a sure thing. They lose no one from their entire roster, and guard Diana Taurasi, the 2003 Final Four's most outstanding player and the consensus player of the year, will be a savvy senior looking to win her third title in four years at **Connecticut**. If she does, Taurasi will have to merit consideration as one the best women's college players of all time. Joining the UConn women in the ranks of favorites are its archrival **Tennessee**, which lost to the Huskies 71–68 in the 2003 national title game; **Duke**, which went 28–1 in 2002–03 and reached the Final Four; and **Texas**, which narrowly lost to Connecticut in the semis. The Longhorns will lose two seniors, but they went 8–3 against Top 25 teams in 2002–03, including a victory over Tennessee. They will look to build on that success in 2003–04.

DARKHORSES

Remember the **North Carolina** men's fast start in 2002–03? They didn't remember it very long in Chapel Hill, either, as

Daniels leads a solid corps of returnees to Kentucky, which finished 32-4 last year, reaching the Elite Eight of the NCAAs.

Williams led Kansas to the national final, then took the job at North Carolina, where he had apprenticed to Dean Smith.

third-year coach Matt Doherty stepped down after the team finished 19–16 following a 5–0 opening salvo last fall. That start included victories over Kansas and Stanford en route to the preseason NIT title. The Tar Heels cooled off after that as their youth and inexperience—they featured three freshman—caught up with them. Now those three freshmen, Rashad McCants, Raymond Felton and Sean May, are sophomores; and the Tar Heels have a new coach, Roy Williams—fresh from leading Kansas to last year's final—and the rest of the ACC is wary.

Arizona lost Jason Gardner, Luke Walton and Rick Anderson to graduation, but still has the improving, 6' 10" junior Channing Frye in the frontcourt, and plenty of talent to complement him. The Wildcats also welcome point guard Mustafa Shakur, a highly touted recruit, and may line up Ndudi Ebi, one of the top prospects in the U.S.,

alongside Frye. Ebi declared for the draft but, like Villanueva, still holds college out as an option.

On the heels of reaching the national championship game, **Kansas** lost its coach, Williams, who departed for Chapel Hill, and its senior leaders, Kirk Hinrich and Nick Collison, but don't count them out: They still have Keith Langford (15.9 ppg last season) and Wayne Simien (14.8 ppg, 8.2 rpg), and will add center David Padgett, one of the top prospects in the nation.

Competition in the women's game is much more top heavy than in the men's; the favorites tend to look down on the rest of the nation's teams from a fair height. The Elite Eight of the 2003 women's tournament, for example, was populated entirely by No. 1 and No. 2 seeds. But the gap is narrowing, as evidenced by the presence of seven teams seeded fifth or lower in the Sweet 16—a first. There are several teams capable of springing some surprises. **Georgia** was a fifth seed in the 2003 tournament but reached the Sweet 16, where it was edged by Duke 66–63. The Lady Bulldogs had just one senior on their roster last season and hope to go farther in 2004. **Minnesota** returns second-team AP All-America guard Lindsay Whelan, and looks to improve upon its best season in the NCAA era, when it knocked off Stanford to reach the Sweet 16. **Louisiana State**, **Purdue** and **Texas Tech**, all top seeds in the 2003 tournament, should make some noise again in 2003–04, and **Louisiana Tech**, a powerhouse during the 1980s, made a strong

Roy Williams leaving Kansas for North Carolina, where he was a longtime assistant for Dean Smith, and where he recruited outgoing Tar Heels coach Matt Doherty.

There were still others that we heard more about than we probably wanted to, such as coach Larry Eustachy, whose drunken misadventures led to his departure from Iowa State. He was replaced by his former assistant Wayne Morgan. Also in this category were the perplexing goings-on at Georgia, where coach Jim Harrick left yet another program after allegations of NCAA violations, including academic fraud. Harrick, who had departed UCLA and Rhode Island under similar circumstances, was replaced by Dennis Felton.

Harrick's successor at UCLA, Steve Lavin, left that fabled program after a 10–19 season and was succeeded by Ben Howland, fresh from leading Pittsburgh to the Sweet 16 of the 2003 NCAA tournament. Former Illinois coach Bill Self made a similar move, departing the competitive Illini program to succeed Roy Williams at Kansas.

run in the 2003 NCAAs, losing to in-state rival LSU in the Sweet 16. The Lady Techsters lost just one player to graduation in '03.

SIDELINES

From Alcorn State to Wright State, the college basketball coaching carousel spun especially quickly this offseason, as a whopping 43 Division I schools made coaching changes. Some flew under the average fan's radar, like Billy Lee being replaced by Robbie Laing at Campbell, while others constituted landmark moments in the game, like

NCAA CHAMPIONSHIP GAME BOX SCORE

SYRACUSE 81

SYRACUSE	MIN	FG M–A	FT M–A	Reb O–T	A	PF	TP
Warrick	31	2–4	2–4	0–2	1	3	6
Anthony	37	7–16	3–4	4–10	7	2	20
Forth	24	3–4	0–1	1–3	0	5	6
McNamara	34	6–13	0–0	0–0	1	2	18
Duany	13	4–6	1–2	3–4	0	3	11
Pace	21	4–9	0–0	1–8	2	2	8
Edelin	27	4–10	4–6	0–2	2	1	12
McNeil	13	0–1	0–0	2–5	0	4	0
Totals	200	30–63	10–17	11–34	13	22	81

Percentages: FG—.476, FT—.588. 3-pt goals: 11–18, .611 (Anthony 3–5, McNamara 6–10, Duany 2–3). Team rebounds: 2. Blocked shots: 7 (Warrick 2, Forth 3, McNeil 2). Turnovers: 17 (Warrick 3, Anthony 3, McNamara 3, Duany 2, Pace 2, Edelin 2, McNeil 2). Steals: 10 (Edelin 3, Pace 3, Anthony, Forth, McNamara, Duany).

Halftime: Syracuse 53, Kansas 42.   A: 54,524.

KANSAS 78

KANSAS	MIN	FG M–A	FT M–A	Reb O–T	A	PF	TP
Collison	40	8–14	3–10	8–21	3	5	19
Langford	23	7–9	5–10	2–2	0	5	19
Graves	37	7–13	2–7	11–16	3	2	16
Hinrich	38	6–20	1–1	1–2	4	1	16
Miles	34	1–5	0–0	1–6	7	1	2
Lee	23	2–8	0–0	1–1	1	1	5
Nash	5	0–2	1–2	0–1	0	1	1
Totals	200	31–71	12–30	24–49	18	16	78

Percentages: FG—.437, FT—.400. 3-pt goals: 4–20, .200 (Langford 0–1, Hinrich 3–12, Miles 0–2, Lee 1–5). Team rebounds: 3. Blocked shots: 4 (Collison 3, Hinrich). Turnovers: 18 (Collison 5, Miles 4, Langford 3, Hinrich 3, Graves 2, Lee). Steals: 9 (Collison 3, Lee 2, Langford, Graves, Hinrich, Miles).

Officials: Dick Cartmell, Gerald Boudreaux, Reggie Cofer.

FINAL AP TOP 25

1. Kentucky (70)	29–3	14. Louisville	24–6
2. Arizona (1)	25–3	15. Creighton	29–4
3. Oklahoma	24–6	16. Dayton	25–5
4. Pittsburgh	26–4	17. Maryland	19–9
5. Texas	22–6	18. Stanford	23–8
6. Kansas	25–7	19. Memphis	23–6
7. Duke	24–6	20. Mississippi St	21–9
8. Wake Forest	24–5	21. Wisconsin	22–7
9. Marquette	23–5	22. Notre Dame	22–9
10. Florida	24–7	23. Connecticut	21–9
11. Illinois	24–6	24. Missouri	21–10
12. Xavier	25–5	25. Georgia	19–8
13. Syracuse	24–5		

Poll taken before NCAA Tournament.

NATIONAL INVITATION TOURNAMENT SCORES

Opening round: College of Charleston 71, Kent St 66; Providence 67, Richmond 49; Temple 98, Drexel 59; Boston College 90, Fairfield 78; Siena 74, Villanova 59; Western Michigan 63, IL-Chicago 62; Iowa St 76, Wichita St 65; Iowa 62, Valparaiso 60.
First round: Wyoming 78, Eastern Washington 71; N Carolina 83, DePaul 72; Georgetown 70, Tennessee 60; Providence 68, College of Charleston 64; Temple 75, Boston College 62; Rhode Island 61, Seton Hall 60; Minnesota 62, St. Louis 52; Hawaii 85, UNLV 68; St. John's 62, Boston University 57; Virginia 89, Brown 73; Alabama-Birmingham 82, Louisiana-Lafayette 80; Siena 68, Western Michigan 62; Iowa 54, Iowa St 53; Georgia Tech 72, Ohio St 58; San Diego St 67, UCSB 62; Texas Tech 66, Nevada 54.
Second round: N Carolina 90, Wyoming 74; Georgetown 67, Providence 58; Temple 61; Rhode Island 53; Minnesota 84, Hawaii 70; St. John's 73, Virginia 63; Alabama-Birmingham 80, Siena 71; Georgia Tech 79, Iowa 78; Texas Tech 57, San Diego St 48.
Third round: Georgetown 79, N Carolina 74; Minnesota 63, Temple 58; St. John's 79, Alabama-Birmingham 71; Texas Tech 80, Georgia Tech 72.
Semifinals: Georgetown 88, Minnesota 74; St. John's 64, Texas Tech 63.
Consolation Game: Texas Tech 71, Minnesota 61.
Championship Game: St. John's 70, Georgetown 67.

2003 NCAA BASKETBALL MEN'S DIVISION I TOURNAMENT

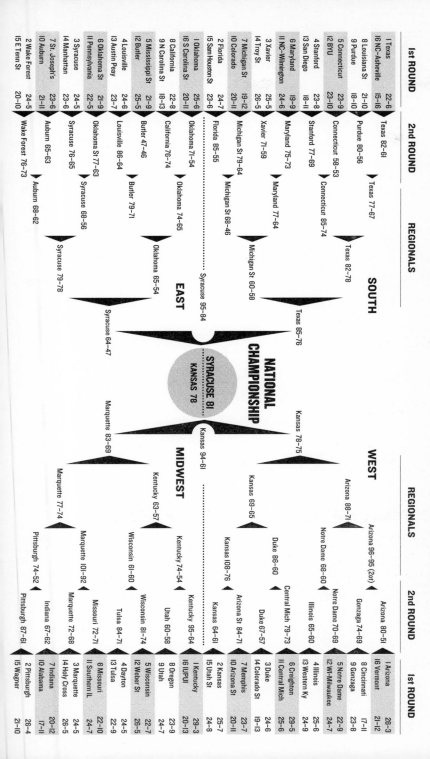

NCAA MEN'S DIVISION I CONFERENCE STANDINGS

AMERICA EAST

	CONFERENCE			ALL GAMES		
	W	L	PCT	W	L	PCT
Boston University	13	3	.813	20	11	.645
†Vermont	11	5	.688	21	12	.636
Hartford	10	6	.625	17	13	.567
Binghamton	9	7	.563	14	13	.519
Northeastern	8	8	.500	16	15	.516
Maine	8	8	.500	14	16	.467
Stony Brook	7	9	.438	13	16	.448
Albany	3	13	.188	7	21	.250
New Hampshire	3	13	.188	5	23	.179

ATLANTIC COAST

	CONFERENCE			ALL GAMES		
	W	L	PCT	W	L	PCT
Wake Forest	13	3	.813	25	6	.806
†Duke	12	5	.706	26	7	.788
Maryland	11	5	.688	21	10	.677
N Carolina St	9	8	.529	18	13	.581
Georgia Tech	7	9	.438	15	15	.500
N Carolina	6	10	.375	19	16	.528
Virginia	6	10	.375	16	15	.516
Clemson	5	11	.313	15	13	.536
Florida St	4	12	.250	14	15	.483

ATLANTIC SUN

	CONFERENCE			ALL GAMES		
	W	L	PCT	W	L	PCT
†Troy St	14	2	.875	26	6	.813
Mercer	14	2	.875	23	6	.793
Central Florida	11	5	.688	21	11	.656
Jacksonville St	10	6	.625	20	9	.690
Samford	9	7	.563	13	15	.464
Georgia St	8	8	.500	14	15	.483
Jacksonville	8	8	.500	13	16	.448
Stetson	4	12	.250	6	20	.231
Florida Atlantic	3	13	.188	7	21	.250
Gardner Webb	2	14	.125	5	24	.172
Campbell	1	15	.063	5	22	.185

ATLANTIC 10

EAST	CONFERENCE			ALL GAMES		
	W	L	PCT	W	L	PCT
St. Joseph's	12	4	.750	23	7	.767
Rhode Island	10	6	.625	20	11	.645
Temple	10	6	.625	18	16	.514
Massachusetts	6	10	.375	12	18	.400
Fordham	3	13	.188	4	24	.143
St. Bonaventure	1	15	.063	7	22	.241
WEST						
Xavier	15	1	.938	26	6	.813
†Dayton	14	2	.875	25	6	.806
Richmond	10	6	.625	16	13	.552
LaSalle	6	10	.375	13	16	.448
George Washington	5	11	.313	12	17	.414
Duquesne	4	12	.250	10	20	.333

BIG EAST

EAST	CONFERENCE			ALL GAMES		
	W	L	PCT	W	L	PCT
Connecticut	10	6	.625	23	10	.697
Boston College	10	6	.625	19	12	.594
Providence	8	8	.500	18	14	.563
Villanova	8	8	.500	15	16	.484
St. John's	7	9	.438	21	13	.600
Miami (FL)	4	12	.250	11	17	.393
Virginia Tech	4	12	.250	11	18	.379
WEST						
Syracuse	13	3	.813	30	5	.857
†Pittsburgh	13	3	.813	28	5	.848
Notre Dame	10	6	.625	24	10	.706
Seton Hall	10	6	.625	17	13	.567
Georgetown	6	10	.375	19	15	.543
W Virginia	5	11	.313	14	15	.483
Rutgers	4	12	.250	12	16	.429

BIG SKY

	CONFERENCE			ALL GAMES		
	W	L	PCT	W	L	PCT
†Weber St	14	0	1.000	26	6	.813
Eastern Washington	9	5	.643	18	13	.581
Idaho St	7	7	.500	15	14	.517
Montana	7	7	.500	13	17	.433
Northern Arizona	6	8	.429	15	13	.517
Sacramento St	5	9	.357	12	17	.414
Montana St	5	9	.357	11	16	.393
Portland St	3	11	.214	5	22	.185

BIG SOUTH

	CONFERENCE			ALL GAMES		
	W	L	PCT	W	L	PCT
Winthrop	11	3	.786	20	10	.667
Charleston Southern	8	6	.571	14	14	.500
Liberty	8	6	.571	14	15	.483
Elon	8	6	.571	12	15	.444
†UNC-Asheville	7	7	.500	15	17	.469
Radford	6	8	.429	10	20	.333
Coastal Carolina	5	9	.357	13	15	.464
High Point	3	11	.214	7	20	.259
Birmingham Southern	0	0	—	19	9	.679

BIG 10

	CONFERENCE			ALL GAMES		
	W	L	PCT	W	L	PCT
Wisconsin	12	4	.750	24	8	.750
†Illinois	11	5	.688	25	7	.781
Purdue	10	6	.625	19	11	.633
Michigan St	10	6	.625	22	13	.629
Michigan	10	6	.625	17	13	.567
Indiana	8	8	.500	21	13	.618
Minnesota	8	8	.500	19	14	.559
Ohio St	7	9	.433	17	15	.531
Iowa	7	9	.438	17	14	.515
Northwestern	3	13	.188	12	17	.414
Penn St	2	14	.125	7	21	.250

† Conference tourney winner.
Note: Standings based on regular-season conference play only; overall records include all tournament play.

NCAA MEN'S DIVISION I CONFERENCE STANDINGS (CONT.)

BIG 12

	CONFERENCE			ALL GAMES		
	W	L	PCT	W	L	PCT
Kansas	14	2	.875	30	8	.789
Texas	13	3	.813	26	7	.788
†Oklahoma	12	4	.750	27	7	.794
Oklahoma St	10	6	.625	22	10	.688
Colorado	9	7	.563	20	12	.625
Missouri	9	7	.563	22	11	.667
Texas Tech	6	10	.375	22	13	.629
Texas A&M	6	10	.375	14	14	.500
Iowa St	5	11	.313	17	14	.531
Baylor	5	11	.313	14	14	.500
Kansas St	4	12	.250	13	17	.433
Nebraska	3	13	.188	11	19	.367

BIG WEST

	CONFERENCE			ALL GAMES		
	W	L	PCT	W	L	PCT
Santa Barbara	14	4	.778	18	14	.563
UC–Irvine	13	5	.722	20	9	.690
†Utah St	12	6	.667	23	9	.719
Cal Poly	10	8	.556	16	13	.552
Idaho	9	9	.500	13	15	.464
Cal St–Northridge	8	10	.444	14	15	.483
Cal St–Fullerton	8	10	.444	10	19	.345
Pacific	7	11	.389	12	16	.429
UC–Riverside	5	13	.278	6	18	.250
Long Beach St	4	14	.222	5	22	.185

COLONIAL

	CONFERENCE			ALL GAMES		
	W	L	PCT	W	L	PCT
†UNC-Wilmington	15	3	.833	24	7	.774
Va. Commonwealth	12	6	.667	18	10	.643
Drexel	12	8	.667	19	12	.613
George Mason	11	7	.611	16	12	.571
Delaware	9	9	.500	15	14	.517
Old Dominion	9	9	.500	12	15	.444
James Madison	8	10	.444	13	17	.433
William & Mary	7	11	.389	12	16	.429
Hofstra	6	12	.333	8	21	.276
Towson	1	17	.056	4	24	.143

CONFERENCE USA

AMERICAN	CONFERENCE			ALL GAMES		
	W	L	PCT	W	L	PCT
Marquette	14	2	.875	27	6	.818
†Louisville	11	5	.688	25	7	.781
Cincinnati	9	7	.563	17	12	.586
St. Louis	9	7	.563	16	14	.533
DePaul	8	8	.500	16	13	.552
Charlotte	8	8	.500	13	16	.448
E Carolina	3	13	.188	12	15	.444

NATIONAL						
Memphis	13	3	.813	23	7	.767
AL-Birmingham	8	8	.500	21	13	.618
Tulane	8	8	.500	16	15	.516
S Florida	7	9	.438	15	14	.517
Houston	6	10	.375	8	20	.286
Southern Miss	5	11	.313	13	16	.448
Texas Christian	3	13	.188	9	19	.321

HORIZON LEAGUE

	CONFERENCE			ALL GAMES		
	W	L	PCT	W	L	PCT
Butler	14	2	.875	27	6	.818
†WI-Milwaukee	13	3	.813	24	8	.750
IL-Chicago	12	4	.750	21	9	.700
Detroit	9	7	.563	18	12	.600
Loyola Chicago	9	7	.563	15	16	.484
Wright St	4	12	.250	10	18	.357
WI–Green Bay	4	12	.250	10	20	.333
Youngstown St	4	12	.250	9	20	.310
Cleveland St	3	13	.188	8	22	.267

IVY LEAGUE

	CONFERENCE			ALL GAMES		
	W	L	PCT	W	L	PCT
Pennsylvania	14	0	1.000	22	6	.786
Brown	12	2	.857	17	12	.586
Princeton	10	4	.714	16	11	.593
Yale	8	6	.571	14	13	.519
Harvard	4	10	.286	12	15	.444
Cornell	4	10	.286	9	18	.333
Dartmouth	4	10	.286	8	19	.296
Columbia	0	14	.000	2	25	.074

METRO ATLANTIC

	CONFERENCE			ALL GAMES		
	W	L	PCT	W	L	PCT
†Manhattan	14	4	.778	23	7	.767
Fairfield	13	5	.722	19	12	.613
Siena	12	6	.667	21	11	.636
Niagara	12	6	.667	17	12	.586
Iona	11	7	.611	17	12	.586
Marist	8	10	.444	13	16	.448
Rider	7	11	.389	12	16	.429
Canisius	6	12	.333	10	18	.357
St. Peter's	6	12	.333	10	19	.345
Loyola (MD)	1	17	.056	4	24	.143

MID-AMERICAN

EAST	CONFERENCE			ALL GAMES		
	W	L	PCT	W	L	PCT
Kent St	12	6	.667	21	10	.677
Miami (OH)	11	7	.611	13	15	.464
Akron	9	9	.500	14	14	.500
Marshall	9	9	.500	14	15	.483
Ohio	8	10	.444	14	16	.467
Buffalo	2	16	.111	5	23	.179

WEST						
†Central Michigan	14	4	.778	25	7	.781
Northern Illinois	11	7	.611	17	14	.548
Western Michigan	10	8	.556	20	11	.625
Eastern Michigan	8	10	.444	14	14	.500
Bowling Green	8	10	.444	13	16	.448
Ball St	8	10	.444	12	17	.414
Toledo	7	11	.389	13	16	.448

SOUTHEASTERN

EAST	CONFERENCE			ALL GAMES		
	W	L	PCT	W	L	PCT
†Kentucky	16	0	1.000	32	4	.889
Florida	12	4	.750	25	8	.758
Georgia	11	5	.688	19	8	.704
Tennessee	9	7	.563	17	12	.586
S Carolina	5	11	.313	12	16	.429
Vanderbilt	3	13	.188	11	18	.379
WEST						
Mississippi St	9	7	.563	21	10	.677
Louisiana St	8	8	.500	21	11	.656
Auburn	8	8	.500	22	12	.647
Alabama	7	9	.438	17	12	.586
Mississippi	4	12	.250	14	15	.483
Arkansas	4	12	.250	9	19	.321

SOUTHERN

NORTH	CONFERENCE			ALL GAMES		
	W	L	PCT	W	L	PCT
Appalachian St	11	5	.688	19	10	.655
†E Tennessee St	11	5	.688	20	11	.645
Davidson	11	5	.688	17	10	.630
Western Carolina	6	10	.375	9	19	.321
Virginia Military	3	13	.188	10	20	.333
UNC–Greensboro	3	13	.188	7	22	.241
SOUTH						
Charleston	13	3	.813	25	8	.758
TN-Chattanooga	11	5	.688	21	9	.700
Georgia Southern	8	8	.500	16	13	.552
Wofford	8	8	.500	14	15	.483
Furman	8	8	.500	14	17	.452
The Citadel	3	13	.188	8	20	.286

SOUTHLAND

	CONFERENCE			ALL GAMES		
	W	L	PCT	W	L	PCT
†Sam Houston St	17	3	.850	23	7	.767
Stephen F. Austin	16	4	.800	21	8	.724
Texas-Arlington	13	7	.650	16	13	.552
SW Texas St	11	9	.550	17	12	.586
McNeese St	10	10	.500	15	14	.517
Lamar	10	10	.500	13	14	.481
Louisiana-Monroe	10	10	.500	12	16	.429
SE Louisiana	9	11	.450	11	16	.407
Texas–San Antonio	7	13	.350	10	17	.370
Northwestern St	6	14	.300	6	21	.222
Nicholls St	1	19	.050	3	25	.107

SOUTHWESTERN ATHLETIC

	CONFERENCE			ALL GAMES		
	W	L	PCT	W	L	PCT
Prairie View	14	4	.778	17	12	.586
Mississippi Valley St	13	5	.722	15	14	.517
†Texas Southern	11	7	.611	18	13	.581
Alabama St	11	7	.611	14	15	.483
Alcorn St	10	8	.556	14	19	.424
Grambling	9	9	.500	12	18	.400
Jackson St	9	9	.500	10	18	.357
Southern	5	13	.278	9	20	.310
Alabama A&M	4	14	.222	8	19	.296
Arkansas–Pine Bluff	4	14	.222	4	24	.143

SUN BELT

EAST	CONFERENCE			ALL GAMES		
	W	L	PCT	W	L	PCT
†Western Kentucky	12	2	.857	24	9	.727
Middle Tennessee St	9	5	.643	16	14	.533
AR–Little Rock	8	6	.571	19	11	.633
Arkansas St	6	8	.429	13	15	.464
Florida International	1	13	.071	8	21	.276
WEST						
Louisiana-Lafayette	12	3	.800	20	10	.667
New Mexico St	9	6	.600	20	9	.690
Denver	7	8	.467	17	15	.531
New Orleans	7	8	.467	15	14	.517
S Alabama	7	8	.467	14	14	.500
N Texas	2	13	.133	7	21	.250

WEST COAST

	CONFERENCE			ALL GAMES		
	W	L	PCT	W	L	PCT
Gonzaga	12	2	.857	24	9	.727
†San Diego	10	4	.714	18	12	.600
San Francisco	9	5	.643	15	14	.517
Pepperdine	7	7	.500	15	13	.536
St. Mary's (CA)	6	8	.429	15	15	.500
Santa Clara	4	10	.286	13	15	.464
Portland	4	10	.286	11	17	.393
Loyola Marymount	4	10	.286	11	20	.355

WESTERN ATHLETIC

	CONFERENCE			ALL GAMES		
	W	L	PCT	W	L	PCT
Fresno St	13	5	.722	20	8	.714
†Tulsa	12	6	.667	23	10	.697
Rice	11	7	.611	19	10	.655
Southern Methodist	11	7	.611	17	13	.567
Nevada	11	7	.611	18	14	.563
Hawaii	9	9	.500	18	13	.563
Louisiana Tech	9	9	.500	12	15	.444
Boise St	7	11	.389	13	16	.448
San Jose St	4	14	.222	7	21	.250
Texas–El Paso	3	15	.167	6	24	.200

INDEPENDENTS

	ALL GAMES		
	W	L	PCT
Centenary	14	14	.500
TX A&M–Corpus Christi	14	15	.483
TX–Pan American	10	20	.333
IU–PU Fort Wayne	9	21	.300
Lipscomb	8	20	.286
Morris Brown	8	20	.286
Savannah St	3	24	.111

†Conference tourney winner.

MID-CONTINENT

	CONFERENCE			ALL GAMES		
	W	L	PCT	W	L	PCT
Valparaiso	12	2	.857	20	11	.645
Oakland	10	4	.714	17	11	.607
†Indiana-Purdue	10	4	.714	20	14	.588
Oral Roberts	9	5	.643	18	10	.643
MO–Kansas City	7	7	.500	9	20	.310
Southern Utah	5	9	.357	11	17	.393
Western Illinois	3	11	.214	7	21	.250
Chicago St	0	14	.000	3	27	.100

MID-EASTERN ATHLETIC

	CONFERENCE			ALL GAMES		
	W	L	PCT	W	L	PCT
†S Carolina St	15	3	.833	20	11	.645
Hampton	13	5	.722	19	11	.633
Delaware St	13	5	.722	15	12	.556
Florida A&M	11	7	.611	17	12	.586
Coppin St	11	7	.611	11	17	.393
Norfolk St	10	8	.556	14	15	.483
Howard	9	9	.500	13	17	.433
Morgan St	6	12	.333	7	22	.241
Bethune Cookman	5	13	.278	8	22	.267
MD-Eastern Shore	5	13	.278	5	23	.179
N Carolina A&T	1	17	.056	1	26	.037

MISSOURI VALLEY

	CONFERENCE			ALL GAMES		
	W	L	PCT	W	L	PCT
Southern Illinois	16	2	.889	24	7	.774
†Creighton	15	3	.833	29	5	.853
Wichita St	12	6	.667	18	12	.600
SW Missouri St	12	6	.667	17	12	.586
Evansville	8	10	.444	12	16	.429
Bradley	8	10	.444	12	18	.400
Northern Iowa	7	11	.389	11	17	.393
Drake	5	13	.278	10	20	.333
Illinois St	5	13	.278	8	21	.276
Indiana St	2	16	.111	7	24	.226

MOUNTAIN WEST

	CONFERENCE			ALL GAMES		
	W	L	PCT	W	L	PCT
Utah	11	3	.786	25	8	.758
Brigham Young	11	3	.786	23	9	.719
Nevada–Las Vegas	8	6	.571	21	11	.656
Wyoming	8	6	.571	21	11	.656
San Diego St	6	8	.429	16	14	.533
†Colorado St	5	9	.357	19	14	.576
New Mexico	4	10	.286	10	18	.357
Air Force	3	11	.214	12	16	.429

NORTHEAST

	CONFERENCE			ALL GAMES		
	W	L	PCT	W	L	PCT
†Wagner	14	4	.778	21	11	.656
Monmouth (NJ)	13	5	.722	15	13	.536
Central Conn	12	6	.667	15	13	.536
Quinnipiac	10	8	.556	17	12	.586
St. Francis (PA)	10	8	.556	14	14	.500
Fairleigh Dickinson	9	9	.500	15	14	.517
St. Francis (NY)	9	9	.500	14	16	.467
Robert Morris	7	11	.389	10	17	.370
LIU–Brooklyn	7	11	.389	9	19	.321
Mt. St. Mary's	6	12	.333	11	16	.407
Sacred Heart	6	12	.333	8	21	.276
MD-Balt County	5	13	.278	7	20	.259

OHIO VALLEY

	CONFERENCE			ALL GAMES		
	W	L	PCT	W	L	PCT
†Austin Peay	13	3	.813	23	8	.742
Morehead St	13	3	.813	20	9	.690
Tennessee Tech	11	5	.688	20	12	.625
Murray St	9	7	.563	17	12	.586
Eastern Illinois	9	7	.563	14	15	.483
Tennessee-Martin	7	9	.438	14	14	.500
Eastern Kentucky	5	11	.313	11	17	.393
SE Missouri St	5	11	.313	11	19	.367
Tennessee St	0	16	.000	2	25	.074

PAC 10

	CONFERENCE			ALL GAMES		
	W	L	PCT	W	L	PCT
Arizona	17	1	.944	28	4	.875
Stanford	14	4	.778	24	9	.727
California	13	5	.722	22	9	.710
Arizona St	11	7	.611	20	12	.625
†Oregon	10	8	.556	23	10	.697
Oregon St	6	12	.333	13	15	.464
Southern California	6	12	.333	13	14	.433
UCLA	6	12	.333	10	19	.345
Washington	5	13	.278	10	17	.370
Washington St	2	16	.111	7	20	.259

PATRIOT LEAGUE

	CONFERENCE			ALL GAMES		
	W	L	PCT	W	L	PCT
†Holy Cross	13	1	.929	26	5	.839
American	9	5	.643	16	14	.533
Colgate	9	5	.643	14	14	.500
Lehigh	8	6	.571	16	12	.571
Bucknell	7	7	.500	14	15	.483
Lafayette	6	8	.429	13	16	.448
Navy	4	10	.286	8	20	.286
Army	0	14	.000	5	22	.185

†Conference tourney winner.

NCAA MEN'S DIVISION I INDIVIDUAL LEADERS*

SCORING

	CLASS	GP	FG	3FG	FT	PTS	AVG
Ruben Douglas, New Mexico	Sr	28	218	94	253	783	28.0
Henry Domercant, Eastern Illinois	Sr	29	252	84	222	810	27.9
Mike Helms, Oakland	Jr	28	241	74	196	752	26.9
Michael Watson, Missouri–Kansas City	Jr	29	247	118	128	740	25.5
Troy Bell, Boston College	Sr	31	224	106	227	781	25.2
Keydren Clark, St. Peter's	Fr	29	231	109	151	722	24.9
Luis Flores, Manhattan	Jr	30	231	56	221	739	24.6
Chris Williams, Ball St	Sr	30	226	64	220	736	24.5
Mike Sweetney, Georgetown	Jr	34	264	0	248	776	22.8
Kevin Martin, Western Carolina	So	24	161	50	174	546	22.8
Willie Green, Detroit	Sr	30	244	37	153	678	22.6
Ricky Minard, Morehead St	Jr	29	225	54	149	653	22.5
Chris Kaman, Central Michigan	Jr	31	244	0	206	694	22.4
Seth Doliboa, Wright St	Jr	28	217	67	124	625	22.3
Marcus Hatten, St. John's (NY)	Sr	34	277	56	146	756	22.2
Carmelo Anthony, Syracuse	Fr	35	277	56	168	778	22.2
Andrew Wisniewski, Centenary (LA)	Jr	28	207	53	150	617	22.0
Andre Emmett, Texas Tech	Jr	34	297	11	136	741	21.8
Ron Williamson, Howard	Sr	30	197	104	152	650	21.7
Julius Jenkins, Georgia Southern	Sr	27	213	74	84	584	21.6
Darshan Luckie, St. Francis (PA)	Fr	28	201	46	157	605	21.6
Dwyane Wade, Marquette	Jr	33	251	14	194	710	21.5
Brandon Hunter, Ohio	Sr	30	217	11	199	644	21.5
Jermaine Hall, Wagner	Sr	32	273	7	133	686	21.4
Marques Green, St. Bonaventure	Jr	27	182	94	116	574	21.3

FIELD-GOAL PERCENTAGE

	CLASS	GP	FG	FGA	PCT
Adam Mark, Belmont	Jr	28	199	297	67.0
Ricky White, Maine	Sr	24	131	198	66.2
Matt Nelson, Colorado St	So	31	205	319	64.3
Armond Williams, IL-Chicago	Jr	30	168	263	63.9
Michael Harris, Rice	So	28	172	276	62.3
Chris Kaman, Central Michigan	Jr	31	244	392	62.2
David Gruber, Northern Iowa	Jr	28	141	231	61.0
Ike Diogu, Arizona St	Fr	32	209	344	60.8
Omar Bartlett, Jacksonville St	Sr	30	178	293	60.8
Jason Keep, San Diego	Sr	30	195	323	60.4

Note: Minimum 5 made per game.

FREE-THROW PERCENTAGE

	CLASS	GP	FT	FTA	PCT
Steve Drabyn, Belmont	Jr	29	78	82	95.1
Matt Logie, Lehigh	Sr	28	91	96	94.8
Hollis Price, Oklahoma	Sr	34	130	140	92.9
Brian Dux, Canisius	Sr	28	115	125	92.0
J.J. Redick, Duke	Fr	33	102	111	91.9
Tim Parker, Chattanooga	Sr	30	78	85	91.8
Dwayne Byfield, Monmouth	So	28	72	79	91.1
Gerry McNamara, Syracuse	Fr	35	90	99	90.9
Kyle Korver, Creighton	Sr	34	109	120	90.8
Jeb Ivey, Portland St	Sr	27	69	76	90.8

Note: Minimum 2.5 made per game.

REBOUNDS

	CLASS	GP	REB	AVG
Brandon Hunter, Ohio	Sr	30	378	12.6
Amien Hicks, Morris Brown	Sr	24	298	12.4
Adam Sonn, Belmont	Sr	29	352	12.1
Chris Kaman, Central Michigan	Jr	31	373	12.0
David West, Xavier	Sr	32	379	11.8
Louis Truscott, Houston	Sr	28	315	11.3
Emeka Okafor, Connecticut	So	33	370	11.2
Kenny Adeleke, Hofstra	So	29	320	11.0
James Singleton, Murray St	Sr	29	320	11.0
James Thomas, Texas	Jr	33	363	11.0

ASSISTS

	CLASS	GP	A	AVG
Martell Bailey, IL-Chicago	Jr	30	244	8.1
Marques Green, St. Bonaventure	Jr	27	216	8.0
T.J. Ford, Texas	So	33	254	7.7
Elliott Prasse-Freeman, Harvard	Sr	28	207	7.7
Antawn Doby, Long Island	Sr	26	193	7.4
Richard Little, VMI	Jr	30	216	7.2
Steve Blake, Maryland	Sr	31	221	7.1
Chris Thomas, Notre Dame	So	34	236	6.9
Raymond Felton, N Carolina	Fr	35	236	6.7
Luke Ridnour, Oregon	Jr	33	218	6.6

*Includes games played in tournaments.

NCAA MEN'S DIVISION I INDIVIDUAL LEADERS* (CONT.)

THREE-POINT FIELD-GOAL PERCENTAGE

	CLASS	GP	FG	FGA	PCT
Jeff Schiffner, Pennsylvania	Jr	28	74	150	49.3
Kyle Korver, Creighton	Sr	34	129	269	48.0
Terrence Woods, Florida A&M	Jr	28	139	304	45.7
Chez Marks, Morehead St	Sr	29	82	180	45.6
Tyson Dorsey, Samford	Jr	27	75	165	45.5
Tim Keller, Air Force	So	28	78	173	45.1
Pat Carroll, St. Joseph's	So	30	76	169	45.0
Dedrick Dye, Wagner	Sr	32	96	217	44.2
Jimmy Boykin, Coppin St	Jr	28	72	163	44.2
Brett Blizzard, UNC-Wilmington	Sr	31	109	247	44.1

Note: Minimum 1.5 made per game.

THREE-POINT FIELD GOALS MADE PER GAME

	CLASS	GP	FG	AVG
Terrence Woods, Florida A&M	Jr	28	139	5.0
Demon Brown, Charlotte	Jr	29	137	4.7
Michael Watson, MO–Kansas City	Jr	29	118	4.1
Brad Boyd, Louisiana-Lafayette	Jr	27	104	3.9
Kyle Korver, Creighton	Sr	34	129	3.8
Keydren Clark, St. Peter's	Fr	29	109	3.8
Shawn Hall, Appalachian St	Sr	28	103	3.7

Five tied with 3.5

BLOCKED SHOTS

	CLASS	GP	BS	AVG
Emeka Okafor, Connecticut	So	33	156	4.7
Nick Billings, Binghamton	So	27	117	4.3
Justin Rowe, Maine	Sr	25	105	4.2
Deng Gai, Fairfield	So	25	96	3.8
Robert Battle, Drexel	Sr	31	116	3.7
Kyle Davis, Auburn	Jr	34	124	3.6
Kendrick Moore, Oral Roberts	Sr	28	94	3.4
David Harrison, Colorado	So	32	106	3.3
Mike Sweetney, Georgetown	Sr	34	109	3.2
Chris Kaman, Central Michigan	Jr	31	98	3.2

STEALS

	CLASS	GP	S	AVG
Alexis McMillan, Stetson	Sr	22	87	4.0
Zakee Wadood, E Tenn St	Jr	29	93	3.2
Jay Heard, Jacksonville St	Sr	30	95	3.2
Eric Bush, Alabama-Birmingham	Sr	34	106	3.1
Marcus Hatten, St. John's	Sr	34	100	2.9
Rawle Marshall, Oakland	So	28	80	2.9
Marcus Banks, UNLV	Sr	32	91	2.8
Tim Pickett, Florida St	Jr	29	82	2.8
Demetrice Williams, S Alabama	Sr	28	76	2.7
Robby Collum, Western Michigan	Sr	31	83	2.7

*Includes games played in tournaments.

GO FIGURE

28 Number of NCAA tournaments Syracuse played in before winning its first national championship. The Orangemen had a record of 40–28 and had reached three Final Fours in their previous 27 tournament appearances.

27 NCAA Tournament appearances for St. John's and Notre Dame, the schools who have now reached the most tournaments without taking home the top prize.

51 Seasons since the NCAA men's scoring leader has come from the national championship team. Clyde Lovellette of Kansas led the nation by averaging 28.4 points per game in 1952, the year the Jayhawks won their first national championship by defeating St. John's 80–63 in the final.

2 Players who have led the nation in both scoring and rebounding during the same season. The first to do so was Wichita State senior forward Xavier McDaniel, who averaged 27.2 points and 14.8 rebounds in 1983. The other was TCU senior forward Kurt Thomas, who averaged 28.9 points and 14.6 rebounds per game in 1995.

.001 Lead in career coaching winning percentage for Connecticut women's basketball coach Geno Auriemma over Tennessee's Pat Summitt. Auriemma, whose Huskies won the 2003 national championship over Summitt's Lady Vols, has a career winning percentage of .835, while his archrival Summitt, the alltime leader with 821 wins, has won at an .834 clip.

SINGLE-GAME HIGHS

POINTS

54	Michael Watson, Missouri–Kansas City, Feb 22 (vs Oral Roberts)
53	Antawn Doby, Long Island, Feb 22 (vs St. Francis)
52	Ron Williamson, Howard, Jan 21 (vs N Carolina A&T)

REBOUNDS

26	Brandon Hunter, Ohio, Jan 8 (vs Akron)
24	Erroyl Bing, E Carolina, Jan 25 (vs S Florida)
24	Brandon Hunter, Ohio, Dec 31 (vs St. Bonaventure)

ASSISTS

17	Antawn Doby, Long Island, Dec 15 (vs St. Francis [NY])
17	Zakee Smith, Cal St–Fullerton, Dec 4 (vs Pepperdine)
16	Malcolm Campbell, Alabama St, Feb 10 (vs Mississippi Valley)
16	Blake Stepp, Gonzaga, Dec 20 (vs Long Beach St)

THREE-POINT FIELD GOALS

12	Terrence Woods, Florida A&M, Mar 1 (vs Coppin St)
11	Terrence Woods, Florida A&M, Feb 1 (vs N Carolina A&T)
11	Ron Williamson, Howard, Jan 21 (vs N Carolina A&T)

STEALS

10	Marcus Hatten, St. John's (NY), Feb 18 (vs Syracuse)
10	Joseph Frazier, Cal St–Northridge, Dec 7 (vs Bethany [CA])
10	Rawle Marshall, Oakland, Dec 2 (vs Texas A&M)

BLOCKED SHOTS

11	David Harrison, Colorado, Mar 8 (vs Nebraska)
11	Jordan Cornette, Notre Dame, Nov 17 (vs Belmont)

Four tied with 10.

☆ INTRAMURAL EXTRAORDINAIRE ☆

[NOTRE DAME]

IT IS CALLED Bookstore Basketball because it began in 1972 on courts behind Notre Dame's bookstore. Now 800-plus student teams go at it every April, and it's all-weather, single-elimination, call-your-own-fouls action until the round of 128. For the final, high school refs blow the whistles, and 6,000 fans watch teams with funny names (Mmm Cheese, Project Mayhem) go at it like Duke and North Carolina. First prize: nothing but bragging rights.

BOB ROSATO

NCAA MEN'S DIVISION I TEAM LEADERS

SCORING OFFENSE

	GP	W	L	PTS	AVG
Arizona	32	28	4	2725	85.2
Appalachian St	29	19	10	2434	83.9
Kansas	38	30	8	3141	82.7
E Tenn St	31	20	11	2543	82.0
Louisville	32	25	7	2612	81.6
Oregon	33	23	10	2689	81.5
Morehead St	29	20	9	2355	81.2
Chattanooga	30	21	9	2435	81.2
Duke	33	26	7	2677	81.1
Davidson	27	17	10	2180	80.7

SCORING DEFENSE

	GP	W	L	PTS	AVG
Air Force	28	12	16	1596	57.0
Miami (OH)	28	13	15	1643	58.7
Holy Cross	31	26	5	1821	58.7
Bucknell	29	14	15	1706	58.8
Pittsburgh	33	28	5	1955	59.2
Wisconsin	32	24	8	1899	59.3
St. Joseph's	30	23	7	1784	59.5
Mississippi St	31	21	10	1852	59.7

Three tied at 60.0.

SCORING MARGIN

	OFF	DEF	MAR
Kansas	82.7	66.9	15.8
Pittsburgh	74.9	59.2	15.7
Arizona	85.2	70.7	14.5
Creighton	79.1	64.8	14.3
Kentucky	77.3	64.1	13.1
Illinois	74.6	61.6	13.1
Maryland	79.7	66.7	13.0
Louisville	81.6	68.7	13.0
Holy Cross	70.3	58.7	11.6

Two tied with 11.5.

FIELD-GOAL PERCENTAGE

	FG	FGA	PCT
Morehead St	854	1674	51.0
Pittsburgh	893	1766	50.6
Colorado St	876	1733	50.5
Central Michigan	864	1714	50.4
Creighton	974	1956	49.8
Kansas	1182	2393	49.4
Stephen F. Austin	753	1534	49.1
Kentucky	1026	2102	48.8
Maine	827	1697	48.7
Akron	761	1562	48.7

FIELD-GOAL PERCENTAGE DEFENSE

	FG	FGA	PCT
St. Joseph's	609	1639	37.2
Illinois	657	1741	37.7
Maryland	704	1864	37.8
Connecticut	817	2157	37.9
Syracuse	878	2253	39.0
Pittsburgh	682	1750	39.0
Florida St	650	1662	39.1
Sam Houston St	676	1727	39.1
Lamar	621	1577	39.4
Oklahoma St	699	1775	39.4

FREE-THROW PERCENTAGE

	FT	FTA	PCT
Manhattan	560	711	78.8
Providence	496	636	77.9
Marist	442	568	77.8
Davidson	413	531	77.8
Oregon	530	685	77.4
Marquette	585	759	77.1
N Carolina St	488	634	77.0
Marshall	468	609	76.8
Eastern Illinois	453	590	76.8
Central Michigan	601	789	76.2

THREE-POINT FIELD GOALS MADE PER GAME

	GP	FG	AVG
Mississippi Valley	29	299	10.3
St. Bonaventure	27	271	10.1
Davidson	27	269	10.0
Troy St	32	312	9.8
Missouri–Kansas City	29	272	9.4
Charleston	33	308	9.3
Samford	28	258	9.2
Baylor	28	254	9.1
Pennsylvania	28	251	9.0
Oregon	33	291	8.8

REBOUNDING MARGIN

	GP	REB	OPP REB	MARGIN/G
Wake Forest	31	1292	993	+9.6
Kansas	38	1589	1288	7.9
Holy Cross	31	1131	887	7.9
Vermont	33	1295	1052	7.4
Utah St	33	1154	923	7.0
Texas	33	1386	1158	6.9
DePaul	29	1075	875	6.9
Davidson	27	1110	926	6.8
Mercer	29	1171	977	6.7
Pittsburgh	33	1203	984	6.6

2003 NCAA BASKETBALL WOMEN'S DIVISION I TOURNAMENT

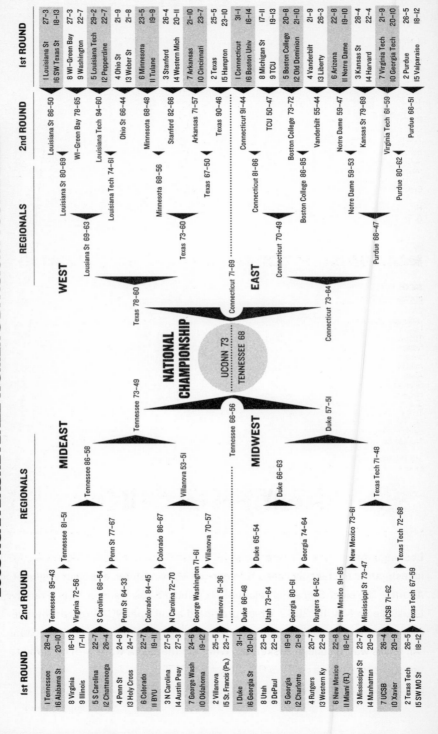

NCAA WOMEN'S CHAMPIONSHIP GAME BOX SCORE

CONNECTICUT 73

CONNECTICUT	MIN	FG M-A	FT M-A	REB O-T	A	PF	TP
Taurasi	37	8-15	8-8	1-4	1	2	28
Conlon	39	3-7	2-4	0-4	6	2	11
Moore	35	2-5	0-0	1-4	3	2	4
Turner	21	5-7	0-0	1-1	1	3	10
Strother	32	6-11	2-2	0-3	3	2	17
Battle	12	0-3	0-0	0-0	1	0	0
Crockett	24	1-1	1-2	2-6	0	5	3
Totals	200	25-49	13-16	5-22	15	16	73

Percentages: FG—.510, FT—.813. 3-pt goals: 10–21, .476 (Taurasi 4–9, Conlon 3–5, Strother 3–7). Team rebounds: 2. Blocked shots: 1 (Taurasi). Turnovers: 11 (Taurasi 3, Moore 3, Turner 2, Strother 1, Battle 1, Crockett 1). Steals: 4 (Conlon 2, Battle 2).

Halftime: Connecticut 35, Tennessee 30.
A: 28,210. Officials: Mattingly, Barlow, Dean.

TENNESSEE 68

TENNESSEE	MIN	FG M-A	FT M-A	REB O-T	A	PF	TP
Butts	17	2-4	0-0	1-1	2	3	4
G. Jackson	35	6-14	3-6	6-9	4	3	15
Lawson	40	5-13	5-5	1-5	5	1	18
Moore	25	2-4	0-0	1-2	1	1	5
Ely	25	3-6	0-0	0-2	0	1	6
Zolman	11	0-0	0-0	1-2	0	2	0
B. Jackson	20	4-10	2-2	1-5	0	3	13
Robinson	17	1-2	1-6	4-8	1	2	3
McDaniel	6	1-3	0-0	1-2	0	2	2
Fluker	4	1-1	0-0	1-1	0	0	2
Totals	200	25-57	11-19	20-40	13	18	68

Percentages: FG—.439, FT—.579. 3-pt goals: 7–18, .389 (G. Jackson 0-2, Lawson 3-8, Moore 1-1, B. Jackson). Team rebounds: 3. Blocked shots: 1 (G. Jackson). Turnovers: 15 (Butts 1, G. Jackson 2, Lawson 3, Moore 1, Ely 2, Zolman 1, B. Jackson 3, Robinson 1, Team 1). Steals: 7 (Butts 1, Lawson 1, Morre 3, Ely 1, Zolman 1).

NCAA WOMEN'S DIVISION I INDIVIDUAL LEADERS

SCORING

PLAYER AND TEAM	CLASS	GP	TFG	3FG	FT	PTS	AVG
Chandi Jones, Houston	Jr	28	275	52	168	770	27.5
Molly Creamer, Bucknell	Sr	28	239	62	219	759	27.1
La Toya Thomas, Mississippi St	Sr	31	297	18	182	794	25.6
Tiffany Webb, Wright St	So	28	246	50	132	674	24.1
Kelly Mazzante, Penn St	Jr	35	292	98	155	837	23.9
Jocelyn Penn, S Carolina	Sr	30	282	14	138	716	23.9
Allison Curtin, Tulsa	Sr	30	231	56	174	692	23.1
Alana Beard, Duke	Jr	37	294	24	201	813	22.0
Shanika Freeman, Jacksonville St	So	29	212	21	184	629	21.7
Hana Peljito, Harvard	Jr	24	178	24	130	510	21.3
Shalayna Johnson, Uof Md Baltimore County	Sr	23	179	72	53	483	21.0
Tamara James, Miami (FL)	Fr	31	238	19	155	650	21.0
Nikki Reddick, Coastal Carolina	Jr	27	171	83	135	560	20.7
Lindsay Whalen, Minnesota	Jr	31	225	34	155	639	20.6
Tamara Bowie, Ball St	Sr	30	237	28	116	618	20.6

 # SORRY, WRONG NUMBER

Looking into wire transfers received by Louisville center Marvin Stone, NCAA investigators mistakenly called 53-year-old Marvin Stone, a project engineer in Atlanta. The elder Stone (no relation) received a $450 transfer from a relative in Lousiville on Nov. 15, 2002, which prompted a call from NCAA representative Deana Garner. "I had a thousand things running through my head," said Stone. "All I do is watch college basketball. What did the NCAA want with me? You're not going to confuse us. He's 6' l0", and I'm 5' 7"."

FIELD-GOAL PERCENTAGE

PLAYER AND TEAM	CLASS	GP	FG	FGA	PCT
Courtney Coleman, Ohio St	Sr	32	184	278	66.2
Janel McCarville, Minnesota	So	30	155	236	65.7
Chantelle Anderson, Vanderbilt	Sr	32	217	341	63.6
Gerlonda Hardin, Austin Peay	Jr	31	198	312	63.5
Jocelyn Penn, S Carolina	Sr	30	282	449	62.8
Beth Swink, St. Francis (PA)	So	31	199	318	62.6
Michelle Smith, UAB	Sr	26	151	242	62.4
Shawntinice Polk, Arizona	Fr	31	218	358	60.9
Liene Jansone, Siena	Jr	33	234	388	60.3
Khara Smith, Depaul	Fr	32	181	301	60.1

Note: Minimum 5 made per game.

REBOUNDS

PLAYER AND TEAM	CLASS	GP	REB	AVG
Jennifer Butler, Massachusetts	Sr	28	412	14.7
Angela Buckner,Wichita St	Jr	28	366	13.1
Cheryl Ford, Louisiana Tech	Sr	34	438	12.9
Ashlee Kelly, Quinnipiac	Jr	28	338	12.1
Tori Talbert, SW Texas St	So	32	385	12.0
Alex Cook, Northern Iowa	So	30	360	12.0
Rosalee Mason, Manhattan	Jr	30	342	11.4
Amie Williams, Jackson St	Jr	29	318	11.0
Jamie Gray, Evansville	Jr	27	296	11.0

Two tied with 10.8

FREE-THROW PERCENTAGE

PLAYER AND TEAM	CLASS	GP	FT	FTA	PCT
Jill Marano, La Salle	So	29	88	93	94.6
Kandi Brown, Morehead St	Jr	28	104	111	93.7
Kim McDonough, St. Peter's	Sr	28	81	88	92.0
Erin Thorn, Brigham Young	Sr	31	87	95	91.6
Carey Sauer, San Francisco	Jr	29	112	123	91.1
Molly McDowell, Southern IL	Sr	27	113	125	90.4
Casey Rost, Western Mich	So	32	121	134	90.3
Jen Perugini, Youngstown St	So	28	81	91	89.0
Katie Houlehan, MO-Kansas City	So	28	72	81	88.9
Jennifer Youngblood, N Illinois	Jr	28	70	79	88.6

Note: Minimum 2.5 made per game.

ASSISTS

PLAYER AND TEAM	CLASS	GP	A	AVG
La'Terrica Dobin, Northwestern St	Jr	28	298	10.6
Latesha Lee, Jackson St	Jr	29	214	7.4
Laura Ingham, Nevada	Sr	29	212	7.3
Ashley McElhiney, Vanderbilt	Sr	30	219	7.3
Ivelina Vrancheva, Florida Int'l	Jr	30	217	7.2
Yolanda Paige, W Virginia	So	28	199	7.1
Jess Cichowicz, James Madison	Sr	28	194	6.9
Sara Nord, Louisville	Jr	29	199	6.9
Cricket Williams, San Jose St	Jr	28	192	6.9
Cristina Ciocan, S Carolina	Jr	31	207	6.7

THREE-POINT FIELD-GOAL PERCENTAGE

PLAYER AND TEAM	CLASS	GP	FG	FGA	PCT
Sinnamonn Garrett, New Mex St	Jr	28	68	137	49.6
Jess Hansen, UCSB	Sr	32	67	142	47.2
Kate Bulger, W Virginia	Jr	28	77	164	47.0
Lindsay Bowen, Michigan St	Fr	29	77	166	46.4
Laura Spanheimer, Creighton	So	33	77	168	45.8
Sara Potts, Kentucky	So	27	74	163	45.4
Caity Matter, Ohio St	So	32	106	235	45.1
Kara Lawson, Tennessee	Sr	38	77	171	45.0
Angela Davidson, NW St	Sr	27	54	123	43.9
Katie Davis, Villanova	Sr	34	104	237	43.9

Note: Minimum 1.5 made per game.

BLOCKED SHOTS

PLAYER AND TEAM	CLASS	GP	BS	AVG
Amie Williams, Jackson St	Jr	29	152	5.2
Sandora Irvin, Texas Christian	So	33	128	3.9
Christen Roper, Hawaii	Jr	30	110	3.7
Amy Collins, Stephen F. Austin	Sr	28	91	3.3
Alyssa Shriver, Tulsa	Sr	30	96	3.2
Sonja Brown, Southern Miss	Sr	28	89	3.2
Ugo Oha, George Washington	Jr	32	93	2.9
Hollie Tyler, Montana	So	30	86	2.9
Teana McKiver, Tulane	Sr	29	80	2.8
Brooke McAfee, IUPUI	Fr	28	75	2.7

NCAA MEN'S DIVISION II INDIVIDUAL LEADERS

SCORING

PLAYER AND TEAM	CLASS	GP	TFG	3FG	FT	PTS	AVG
Ron Christy, Teikyo Post	Jr	29	295	64	134	788	27.2
Alexus Foyle, BYU-Hawaii	Sr	23	261	11	81	614	26.7
Jerome Beasley, N Dakota	Sr	29	293	33	153	772	26.6
Tim Black, Barton	Sr	28	215	63	221	714	25.5
Patrick Pope, St. Augustine's	Sr	27	204	65	212	685	25.4
Ben Dewar, Lake Superior St	Sr	26	190	69	173	622	23.9
Spencer Ross, Queens (NC)	Jr	33	256	56	220	788	23.9
Robbie Ballard, Emporia St	Sr	27	226	95	83	630	23.3
Wykeen Kelly, Salem International	Sr	30	216	91	168	691	23.0
Rod Edwards, Ouachita Baptist	Jr	28	193	91	167	644	23.0

NCAA MEN'S DIVISION II INDIVIDUAL LEADERS (CONT.)

REBOUNDS

PLAYER AND TEAM	CLASS	GP	REB	AVG
Billy McDaniel, AR-Monticello	Fr	27	345	12.8
Gordon James, Bridgeport	Jr	30	379	12.6
Fred Hooks, Humboldt St.	Jr	29	353	12.2
Brian Atkins, Concord	Jr	28	320	11.4
Dwight Windom, Lincoln Memorial	Sr	29	324	11.2
Kenyon Booker, Shaw	Sr	30	333	11.1
Danny Jones, Tarleton St.	Sr	33	364	11.0
Marcus West, Mt. Olive	Jr	28	306	10.9
Ramzee Stanton, West Chester	Sr	30	326	10.9
Jayson Williams, Lane	Jr	28	303	10.8
Jakim Donaldson, Edinboro	So	27	291	10.8

ASSISTS

PLAYER AND TEAM	CLASS	GP	A	AVG
Clayton Smith, Metro St	Sr	33	274	8.3
Wayne Hinton, Johnson Smith	Sr	29	237	8.2
Marlon Parmer, Kentucky Wesleyan	Sr	35	286	8.2
Josh Mueller, S Dakota	So	28	227	8.1
Jamie Holden, St. Joseph's (IN)	Jr	26	207	8.0
Aaron Smith, Columbia Union	Sr	27	194	7.2
Cornelius McMurray, Bowie St	Sr	33	228	6.9
Deshawn Bowman, Columbus St	Jr	31	206	6.6
Joe Bakhoum, Oklahoma PH	Sr	25	164	6.6
Ryan Luckman, Bloomsburg	Sr	26	170	6.5

FIELD-GOAL PERCENTAGE

PLAYER AND TEAM	CLASS	GP	FG	FGA	PCT
Anthony Greenup, Shaw	Jr	30	172	242	71.1
Maxie Stamps, Drury	Jr	23	125	189	66.1
Jon Smith, Bowie St.	Jr	35	201	306	65.7
Ramzee Stanton, West Chester	Sr	30	254	402	63.2
Phil Sellers, St. Rose	Sr	25	208	333	62.5
Josh Buettner, Michigan Tech	So	32	187	302	61.9
Ronald Thompson, Morehouse	Jr	25	125	202	61.9
Paul Tonkovich, Caldwell	Sr	26	159	258	61.6
Jon Shepherd, Northeastern St	Jr	35	201	327	61.5
Demond Perris, Emporia St	Jr	28	150	246	61.0

Note: Minimum 5 made per game.

FREE-THROW PERCENTAGE

PLAYER AND TEAM	CLASS	GP	FT	FTA	PCT
Aaron Farley, Harding	Sr	30	137	146	93.8
Derek Paben, S Dakota	Jr	28	78	85	91.8
Robbie Ballard, Emporia St	Sr	27	83	91	91.2
Drew Carlson, Minnesota St–Mankato	Sr	27	83	91	91.2
Germayne Forbes, W Georgia	Jr	28	82	90	91.1
Rico Grier, Pfeiffer	So	29	80	88	90.9
Kelvin Parker, NW Missouri St	Jr	31	96	106	90.6
Cris Brunson, Southern IN	So	32	105	116	90.5
Jacob Fahl, Southwest St	Jr	28	113	125	90.4
Jamar Love, Incarnate Word	Sr	28	111	123	90.2

Note: Minimum 2.5 made per game.

NCAA WOMEN'S DIVISION II INDIVIDUAL LEADERS

SCORING

PLAYER AND TEAM	CLASS	GP	TFG	3FG	FT	PTS	AVG
Tysell Bozeman, Felician	Fr	27	420	31	145	1016	37.6
Monica Tokoro, Cal St–Los Angeles	So	26	258	22	115	653	25.1
Heather Garay, Cal St–Bakersfield	Sr	30	277	0	173	727	24.2
Dani Thomas, Southampton	Sr	28	210	67	168	655	23.4
Mandy Koupal, S Dakota	Jr	32	262	40	176	740	23.1
Shannon Donnelly, Cal St–Stanislaus	Sr	28	233	1	145	612	21.9
Tara Newnam, Southeastern Oklahoma	Sr	25	199	3	124	525	21.0
Naomi Mobley, Shaw	Sr	31	250	6	144	650	21.0
Melissa McKavish, Slippery Rock	Sr	26	183	38	134	538	20.7
Stephanie Heid, Hillsdale	Sr	29	230	26	108	594	20.5

REBOUNDS

PLAYER AND TEAM	CLASS	GP	REB	AVG
Naomi Mobley, Shaw	Sr	31	454	14.6
Litreece Hurn, Lane	So	26	375	14.4
Ivana Stojkovic, Western New Mex	Jr	25	328	13.1
Georgia Gordon, New York Tech	Sr	27	353	13.1
Germaletta Dyson, Paine	Fr	26	337	13.0
Heather Lawrence, Harding	Sr	27	334	12.4
Cherelle Payne, CW Post	Jr	25	308	12.3
Heather Garay, Cal St–Bakersfield	Sr	30	357	11.9
Shannon Donnelly, Cal St–Stanislaus	Sr	28	333	11.9
Mandy Koupal, S Dakota	Jr	32	380	11.9
Amy Swan, Georgian Court	Sr	27	320	11.9

ASSISTS

PLAYER AND TEAM	CLASS	GP	A	AVG
Kelly West, W Liberty St	Jr	32	302	9.4
Jess Hambley, St. Michael's	Jr	29	222	7.7
Ebony Vincent, Wayne St (MI)	Jr	29	222	7.7
Jamie Blakely, Emporia St	Sr	31	220	7.1
Nickie Randall, Bellarmine	Sr	31	216	7.0
Kim Abts, Cal St–Chico	So	26	176	6.8
Monica Tokoro, Cal St–LA	So	26	170	6.5
Jen Gwin, Gannon	So	26	168	6.5
Liz Leonard, Bentley	Sr	35	226	6.5
Martina McCloud, Tuskegee	Sr	29	186	6.4

NCAA WOMEN'S DIVISION II INDIVIDUAL LEADERS (CONT.)

FIELD-GOAL PERCENTAGE

PLAYER AND TEAM	CLASS	GP	FGA	FG	PCT
Melissa Pater, S Dakota St	Sr	35	267	411	65.0
Lindsey Dietz, Minnesota-Duluth	Fr	30	186	294	63.3
Melanie Carter, Abilene Christian	Jr	29	172	276	62.3
Martha Brinker, St. Mary's (TX)	Jr	29	167	268	62.3
Becky Siembak, California (PA)	Jr	35	257	427	61.6
Helen Young, Pitt-Johnstown	Sr	28	186	304	61.2
Catreia Shaw, Clayton St	Sr	27	166	272	61.0
Jessica Guarneri, Wingate	Sr	28	217	356	61.0
Sarah Wright, Bentley	Sr	36	181	300	60.3
Andriette Roberts, Clark Atlanta	Jr	27	136	226	60.2

Note: Minimum 5 made per game.

FREE-THROW PERCENTAGE

PLAYER AND TEAM	CLASS	GP	FTA	FT	PCT
Mary Kacic, Dowling	Sr	31	118	128	92.2
Amanda Davied, Pittsburg St	Sr	28	113	126	89.7
Renee Gagnier, Concord	Jr	26	102	114	89.5
Nickie Randall, Bellarmine	Sr	31	99	112	88.4
Andrea Patterson, Eckerd	Sr	28	113	129	87.6
Becky Mowen, N Dakota	Sr	32	126	144	87.5
Kristin Creswell, Pitt-Johnstown	Jr	28	112	128	87.5
Lyndsey Hawkins, Ouach. Bapt.	Jr	27	123	141	87.2
Lauren Meyer, Georgian Court	So	28	109	126	86.5
Haley Hobson, Midwestern St.	Fr	30	76	88	86.4
Randi Johnson, Lake Superior St	So	28	76	88	86.4

Note: Minimum 2.5 made per game.

NCAA MEN'S DIVISION III INDIVIDUAL LEADERS

SCORING

PLAYER AND TEAM	CLASS	GP	TFG	3FG	FT	PTS	AVG
Patrick Glover, Johnson St	Sr	26	269	37	188	763	29.3
Rich Melzer, WI-River Falls	Jr	26	284	0	163	731	28.1
Willie Chandler, Misericordia	Sr	28	251	93	135	730	26.1
Derek Reich, Chicago	Sr	25	221	38	156	636	25.4
Adam Turner, Bard	Fr	21	191	35	114	531	25.3
Robert Hennigan, Emerson	Jr	25	184	101	154	623	24.9
Shawn Jones, Westfield St	Sr	25	215	43	141	614	24.6
Rohan Russell, Johnson & Wales	Jr	25	190	92	136	608	24.3
Steve Wood, Grinnell	Jr	25	206	60	136	608	24.3
Ray Robinson, Waynesburg	Sr	25	217	73	95	602	24.1

REBOUNDS

PLAYER AND TEAM	CLASS	GP	REB	AVG
Jed Johnson, Maine Maritime	Sr	25	414	16.6
Joe Corbett, Hobart	Sr	23	331	14.4
Anthony Fitzgerald, Villa Julie	Fr	25	337	13.5
Darren Pugh, Lebanon Valley	Sr	26	324	12.5
Jon Schwadron, Dickinson	Sr	25	303	12.1
Derek Suttles, MacMurray	Jr	24	284	11.8
Craig Coupe, Tufts	So	25	285	11.4
Matt Beacom, Pitt-Bradford	Sr	29	328	11.3
Patrick Glover, Johnson St	Sr	26	294	11.3
Perry Davis, Buffalo St	Jr	27	303	11.2
Kyle McNamar, Curry	Sr	25	280	11.2

ASSISTS

PLAYER AND TEAM	CLASS	GP	A	AVG
Tennyson Whitted, Ramapo	Sr	30	253	8.4
Michael Crotty, Williams	Jr	32	245	7.7
Jesse Farrell, Trinity (CT)	So	24	176	7.3
Cliff Foster, La Roche	Jr	26	173	6.7
Paul Russo, Emory & Henry	Sr	26	171	6.6
Travis Magnusson, ME-Farmington	Fr	25	163	6.5
Evan Fowler, Mary Washington	Jr	29	187	6.4
Labeb Abdullah, Savannah A&D	Sr	26	167	6.4
Trevelle Boyd, E Texas Baptist	Sr	26	163	6.3
Tim Gaspar, UMass-Dartmouth	Sr	27	167	6.2

FIELD-GOAL PERCENTAGE

PLAYER AND TEAM	CLASS	GP	FG	FGA	PCT
Aaron Marshall, St. Lawrence	So	27	206	305	67.5
Gian Paul Gonzalez, Messiah	Fr	22	144	218	66.1
Ryan Hodges, Cal Lutheran	Jr	25	129	197	65.5
Omar Warthen, Neumann	Sr	29	149	229	65.1
John Thomas, Fontbonne	Sr	25	128	198	64.6
Bryan Nelson, Wooster	Sr	31	221	341	64.4
Tim Dworak, WI-Oshkosh	Sr	32	283	446	63.5
Kwesi Liverpool, York (NY)	Fr	24	128	202	63.4
Keith Davis, Savannah A&D	Jr	27	206	327	63.0
Mark Gabriel, Haverford	So	18	141	227	62.1
Andy Larkin, Rochester	Jr	27	139	224	62.1

Note: Minimum 5 made per game.

FREE-THROW PERCENTAGE

PLAYER AND TEAM	CLASS	GP	FT	FTA	PCT
Nick Wilkins, Coe	So	26	66	69	95.7
Matt Larson, Linfield	So	25	99	108	91.7
Sean Fleming, Clark (MA)	Sr	24	109	120	90.8
Aaron Faulkner, St. Norbert	So	23	77	85	90.6
Victor Garcia, Knox	Sr	21	114	126	90.5
Steve King, Fontbonne	Sr	24	81	90	90.0
Nick Bennett, WI-Stevens Pt	So	24	62	69	89.9
B. Constantine, Wm. Paterson	Jr	25	77	86	89.5
Ryan Connor, Salem St	Jr	28	90	101	89.1
Bryan Nelson, Wooster	Sr	31	193	218	88.5

Note: Minimum 2.5 made per game.

NCAA WOMEN'S DIVISION III INDIVIDUAL LEADERS

SCORING

PLAYER AND TEAM	CLASS	GP	TFG	3FG	FT	PTS	AVG
Tiffany Trent, Cazenovia	Jr	23	208	35	165	616	26.8
Amy Campion, Salisbury	Sr	28	241	59	140	681	24.3
Doris Zimmerman, Wilson	Sr	28	256	7	136	65	23.4
Amy Meggers, Buena Vista	Jr	27	232	41	110	615	22.8
Heather Francouer, Oglethorpe	Sr	26	190	23	188	591	22.7
Melody Bongiorno, Chapman	Jr	27	219	23	141	602	22.3
Rebecca Segert, Merchant Marine	Jr	22	144	48	152	488	22.2
Kelly Heil, Ohio Wesleyan	So	28	222	50	110	604	21.6
Tanasha Ellis, E Texas Baptist	Sr	25	195	0	148	538	21.5
Angel Hall, Anderson (IN)	Jr	27	182	103	108	575	21.3

REBOUNDS

PLAYER AND TEAM	CLASS	GP	REB	AVG
Andreen Gilpin, UMass-Boston	Sr	26	408	15.7
Janice Coppolino, Framingham St	Sr	23	360	15.7
Whitney Bull, Wilkes	Sr	24	323	13.5
Siobhan Zerilla, Wilmington (OH)	So	29	381	13.1
Kristin Bhiary, St. Joseph's (LI)	Sr	27	350	13.0
Erica Dabney, Mary Baldwin	Fr	26	337	13.0
Becky Worsham, Trinity (DC)	Fr	26	335	12.9
Cheryl Kulesa, Rutgers-Camden	Sr	28	340	12.1
Kelly Weismuller, Brooklyn	Fr	24	288	12.0
Julia Knights, Maine Maritime	Fr	27	323	12.0
Shelly Ulfig, Alma	Sr	26	311	12.0

FIELD-GOAL PERCENTAGE

PLAYER AND TEAM	CLASS	GP	FG	FGA	PCT
Kelly Weismuller, Brooklyn	Fr	24	205	296	69.3
Alicia Davis, Loras	Jr	29	174	257	67.7
Jessica Justice, Mt. Holyoke	Sr	26	158	244	64.8
Kathy Darling, Johns Hopkins	Sr	28	206	322	64.0
Lindsey Chappell, Earlham	Jr	24	159	250	63.6
Danielle Fitzpatrick, Brandeis	Jr	21	138	217	63.6
Elizabeth Klotz, Fontbonne	Jr	25	178	286	62.2
Olivia Zurek, Bates	So	26	146	251	58.2
Tanasha Ellis, E Texas Baptist	Sr	25	195	338	57.7
Tara Rausch, Wilmington (OH)	Jr	29	232	403	57.6

Note: Minimum 5 made per game.

ASSISTS

PLAYER AND TEAM	CLASS	GP	A	AVG
A. Poppleton, Notre Dame (MD)	Sr	27	226	8.4
Diana Esterkamp, Otterbein	Jr	25	182	7.3
Megan Woodruff, Wilmington (OH)	Sr	29	209	7.2
Maggie Allenn, Mt. St. Vincent	Jr	25	160	6.4
Leslie Livingstone, Misericordia	Sr	28	174	6.2
Bernice Amadeo, New Jersey City	So	25	155	6.2
Diana Olaya, Lehman	Sr	24	148	6.2
Brooke Johnson, Peace	Jr	25	154	6.2
Evita Estevez, Emmanuel (MA)	Fr	30	178	5.9

Four tied with 5.8.

FREE-THROW PERCENTAGE

PLAYER AND TEAM	CLASS	GP	FT	FTA	PCT
Angel Hall, Anderson (IN)	Jr	27	108	118	91.5
Jessica Gates, Muskingum	Sr	26	83	93	89.2
Brandi Cochran, Hollins	So	26	115	129	89.1
M. Woodruff, Wilmington (OH)	Sr	29	137	154	89.0
Katie Robinson, Swarthmore	Jr	27	99	113	87.6
Nikki Bablik, Bethany (WV)	So	26	67	77	87.0
Michelle Bedard, Endicott	Sr	26	75	87	86.2
Abby Pyzik, Lynchburg	Sr	26	68	79	86.1
Melody Bongiorno, Chapman	Jr	27	141	164	86.0
Eleanor Kelley, Colorado College	Sr	23	172	201	85.6

Note: Minimum 2.5 made per game.

 # THE REPLACEMENTS

With several of last season's stellar underclassmen leaving for the NBA, their college teams have big sneakers to fill. Here are the players who are penciled in to try.

TEAM	NBA-BOUND PLAYER	POSITION	REPLACEMENT, '03-'04 CLASS	SKINNY
GEORGIA TECH	Chris Bosh*	F	Theodis Tarver, Soph.	A late bloomer last season, the 6'9"Tarver had 4.2 blocks per 40 minutes.
NOTRE DAME	Chris Thomas*	PG	Chris Quinn, Soph.	The 6'2" Quinn had a superb 3.4 assist-to-turnover ratio in 2002-2003
OREGON	Luke Ridnour	PG	Aaron Brooks, Fr.	Heralded 6-foot recruit from Seattle's Franklin High is billed as T.J. Ford with a jump shot
SYRACUSE	Carmelo Anthony	SF	Josh Pace, Jr.	The opportunistic 6'5" Pace has an ugly shot but can fill out a stat line
TEXAS	T.J. Ford	PG	Royal Ivey, Sr.	Rugged 6'3", All-Big 12 defender needs to get a better handle

*Has not signed with agent; eligible to return to school

NCAA MEN'S DIVISION I CHAMPIONSHIP RESULTS

NCAA FINAL FOUR RESULTS

YEAR	WINNER	SCORE	RUNNER-UP	THIRD PLACE	FOURTH PLACE	WINNING COACH
1939	Oregon	46–33	Ohio St	*Oklahoma	*Villanova	Howard Hobson
1940	Indiana	60–42	Kansas	*Duquesne	*Southern Cal	Branch McCracken
1941	Wisconsin	39–34	Washington St	*Pittsburgh	*Arkansas	Harold Foster
1942	Stanford	53–38	Dartmouth	*Colorado	*Kentucky	Everett Dean
1943	Wyoming	46–34	Georgetown	*Texas	*DePaul	Everett Shelton
1944	Utah	42–40 (OT)	Dartmouth	*Iowa St	*Ohio St	Vadal Peterson
1945	Oklahoma St	49–45	NYU	*Arkansas	*Ohio St	Hank Iba
1946	Oklahoma St	43–40	N Carolina	Ohio St	California	Hank Iba
1947	Holy Cross	58–47	Oklahoma	Texas	CCNY	Alvin Julian
1948	Kentucky	58–42	Baylor	Holy Cross	Kansas St	Adolph Rupp
1949	Kentucky	46–36	Oklahoma St	Illinois	Oregon St	Adolph Rupp
1950	CCNY	71–68	Bradley	N Carolina St	Baylor	Nat Holman
1951	Kentucky	68–58	Kansas St	Illinois	Oklahoma St	Adolph Rupp
1952	Kansas	80–63	St. John's (NY)	Illinois	Santa Clara	Forrest Allen
1953	Indiana	69–68	Kansas	Washington	Louisiana St	Branch McCracken
1954	La Salle	92–76	Bradley	Penn St	Southern Cal	Kenneth Loeffler
1955	San Francisco	77–63	La Salle	Colorado	Iowa	Phil Woolpert
1956	San Francisco	83–71	Iowa	Temple	Southern Meth	Phil Woolpert
1957	N Carolina	54–53 (3OT)	Kansas	San Francisco	Michigan St	Frank McGuire
1958	Kentucky	84–72	Seattle	Temple	Kansas St	Adolph Rupp
1959	California	71–70	W Virginia	Cincinnati	Louisville	Pete Newell
1960	Ohio St	75–55	California	Cincinnati	NYU	Fred Taylor
1961	Cincinnati	70–65 (OT)	Ohio St	Vacated‡	Utah	Edwin Jucker
1962	Cincinnati	71–59	Ohio St	Wake Forest	UCLA	Edwin Jucker
1963	Loyola (IL)	60–58 (OT)	Cincinnati	Duke	Oregon St	George Ireland
1964	UCLA	98–83	Duke	Michigan	Kansas St	John Wooden
1965	UCLA	91–80	Michigan	Princeton	Wichita St	John Wooden
1966	UTEP	72–65	Kentucky	Duke	Utah	Don Haskins
1967	UCLA	79–64	Dayton	Houston	N Carolina	John Wooden
1968	UCLA	78–55	N Carolina	Ohio St	Houston	John Wooden
1969	UCLA	92–72	Purdue	Drake	N Carolina	John Wooden
1970	UCLA	80–69	Jacksonville	New Mexico St	St.Bonaventure	John Wooden
1971	UCLA	68–62	Vacated‡	Vacated‡	Kansas	John Wooden
1972	UCLA	81–76	Florida St	N Carolina	Louisville	John Wooden
1973	UCLA	87–66	Memphis St	Indiana	Providence	John Wooden
1974	N Carolina St	76–64	Marquette	UCLA	Kansas	Norm Sloan
1975	UCLA	92–85	Kentucky	Louisville	Syracuse	John Wooden
1976	Indiana	86–68	Michigan	UCLA	Rutgers	Bob Knight
1977	Marquette	67–59	N Carolina	UNLV	NC-Charlotte	Al McGuire
1978	Kentucky	94–88	Duke	Arkansas	Notre Dame	Joe Hall
1979	Michigan St	75–64	Indiana St	DePaul	Penn	Jud Heathcote
1980	Louisville	59–54	Vacated‡	Purdue	Iowa	Denny Crum
1981	Indiana	63–50	N Carolina	Virginia	Louisiana St	Bob Knight
1982	N Carolina	63–62	Georgetown	*Houston	*Louisville	Dean Smith
1983	N Carolina St	54–52	Houston	*Georgia	*Louisville	Jim Valvano
1984	Georgetown	84–75	Houston	*Kentucky	*Virginia	John Thompson
1985	Villanova	66–64	Georgetown	St. John's (NY)	Vacated‡	Rollie Massimino
1986	Louisville	72–69	Duke	*Kansas	*Louisiana St	Denny Crum
1987	Indiana	74–73	Syracuse	*UNLV	*Providence	Bob Knight
1988	Kansas	83–79	Oklahoma	*Arizona	*Duke	Larry Brown
1989	Michigan	80–79 (OT)	Seton Hall	*Duke	*Illinois	Steve Fisher
1990	UNLV	103–73	Duke	*Arkansas	*Georgia Tech	Jerry Tarkanian
1991	Duke	72–65	Kansas	*UNLV	*N Carolina	Mike Krzyzewski
1992	Duke	71–51	Michigan	*Cincinnati	*Indiana	Mike Krzyzewski
1993	N Carolina	77–71	Michigan	*Kansas	*Kentucky	Dean Smith
1994	Arkansas	76–72	Duke	*Arizona	*Florida	Nolan Richardson

NCAA FINAL FOUR RESULTS (CONT.)

YEAR	WINNER	SCORE	RUNNER-UP	THIRD PLACE	FOURTH PLACE	WINNING COACH
1995	UCLA	89–78	Arkansas	*N Carolina	*Oklahoma St	Jim Harrick
1996	Kentucky	76–67	Syracuse	Vacated‡	Mississippi St	Rick Pitino
1997	Arizona	84–79 (OT)	Kentucky	*Minnesota	*N Carolina	Lute Olson
1998	Kentucky	78–69	Utah	*Stanford	*N Carolina	Tubby Smith
1999	Connecticut	77–74	Duke	*Michigan St	*Ohio St	Jim Calhoun
2000	Michigan St	89–76	Florida	*Wisconsin	*N Carolina	Tom Izzo
2001	Duke	82–72	Arizona	*Maryland	*Michigan St	Mike Krzyzewski
2002	Maryland	64–52	Indiana	*Kansas	*Oklahoma	Gary Williams
2003	Syracuse	81–78	Kansas	*Marquette	*Texas	Jim Boeheim

*Tied for third place. ‡Student-athletes representing St. Joseph's (PA) in 1961, Villanova in 1971, Western Kentucky in 1971, UCLA in 1980, Memphis State in 1985 and Massachusetts in 1996 were declared ineligible subsequent to the tournament. Under NCAA rules, the teams' and ineligible student-athletes' records were deleted, and the teams' places in the standings were vacated.

NCAA FINAL FOUR MVPS

YEAR	WINNER, SCHOOL	GP	FIELD GOALS		3-PT FG		FREE THROWS		REB	A	STL	BS	AVG
			FGM	PCT	FGA	FGM	FTM	PCT					
1939	None selected												
1940	Marv Huffman, Indiana	2	7	—	—	—	4	—	—	—	—	—	9.0
1941	John Kotz, Wisconsin	2	8	—	—	—	6	—	—	—	—	—	11.0
1942	Howard Dallmar, Stanford	2	8	—	—	—	4	66.7	—	—	—	—	10.0
1943	Ken Sailors, Wyoming	2	10	—	—	—	8	72.7	—	—	—	—	14.0
1944	Arnie Ferrin, Utah	2	11	—	—	—	6	—	—	—	—	—	14.0
1945	Bob Kurland, Oklahoma St	2	16	—	—	—	5	—	—	—	—	—	18.5
1946	Bob Kurland, Oklahoma St	2	21	—	—	—	10	66.7	—	—	—	—	26.0
1947	George Kaftan, Holy Cross	2	18	—	—	—	12	70.6	—	—	—	—	24.0
1948	Alex Groza, Kentucky	2	16	—	—	—	5	—	—	—	—	—	18.5
1949	Alex Groza, Kentucky	2	19	—	—	—	14	—	—	—	—	—	26.0
1950	Irwin Dambrot, CCNY	2	12	42.9	—	—	4	50.0	—	—	—	—	14.0
1951	None selected												
1952	Clyde Lovellette, Kansas	2	24	—	—	—	18	—	—	—	—	—	33.0
1953	*B.H. Horn, Kansas	2	17	—	—	—	17	—	—	—	—	—	25.5
1954	Tom Gola, La Salle	2	12	—	—	—	14	—	—	—	—	—	19.0
1955	Bill Russell, San Francisco	2	19	—	—	—	9	—	—	—	—	—	23.5
1956	*Hal Lear, Temple	2	32	—	—	—	16	—	—	—	—	—	40.0
1957	*Wilt Chamberlain, Kansas	2	18	51.4	—	—	19	70.4	25	—	—	—	32.5
1958	*Elgin Baylor, Seattle	2	18	34.0	—	—	12	75.0	41	—	—	—	24.0
1959	*Jerry West, West Virginia	2	22	66.7	—	—	22	68.8	25	—	—	—	33.0
1960	Jerry Lucas, Ohio State	2	16	66.7	—	—	3	100.0	23	—	—	—	17.5
1961	*Jerry Lucas, Ohio State	2	20	71.4	—	—	16	94.1	25	—	—	—	28.0
1962	Paul Hogue, Cincinnati	2	23	63.9	—	—	12	63.2	38	—	—	—	29.0
1963	Art Heyman, Duke	2	18	41.0	—	—	15	68.2	19	—	—	—	25.5
1964	Walt Hazzard, UCLA	2	11	55.0	—	—	8	66.7	10	—	—	—	15.0
1965	*Bill Bradley, Princeton	2	34	63.0	—	—	19	95.0	24	—	—	—	43.5
1966	*Jerry Chambers, Utah	2	25	53.2	—	—	20	83.3	35	—	—	—	35.0
1967	Lew Alcindor, UCLA	2	14	60.9	—	—	11	45.8	38	—	—	—	19.5
1968	Lew Alcindor, UCLA	2	22	62.9	—	—	9	90.0	34	—	—	—	26.5
1969	Lew Alcindor, UCLA	2	23	67.7	—	—	16	64.0	41	—	—	—	31.0
1970	Sidney Wicks, UCLA	2	15	71.4	—	—	9	60.0	34	—	—	—	19.5
1971	*†Howard Porter, Villanova	2	20	48.8	—	—	7	77.8	24	—	—	—	23.5
1972	Bill Walton, UCLA	2	20	69.0	—	—	17	73.9	41	—	—	—	28.5
1973	Bill Walton, UCLA	2	28	82.4	—	—	2	40.0	30	—	—	—	29.0
1974	David Thompson, NC State	2	19	51.4	—	—	11	78.6	17	—	—	—	24.5
1975	Richard Washington, UCLA	2	23	54.8	—	—	8	72.7	20	—	—	—	27.0
1976	Kent Benson, Indiana	2	17	50.0	—	—	7	63.6	18	—	—	—	20.5
1977	Butch Lee, Marquette	2	11	34.4	—	—	8	100.0	6	2	1	1	15.0
1978	Jack Givens, Kentucky	2	28	65.1	—	—	8	66.7	17	4	1	3	32.0
1979	Earvin Johnson, Michigan St	2	17	68.0	—	—	19	86.4	17	3	0	2	26.5
1980	Darrell Griffith, Louisville	2	23	62.2	—	—	11	68.8	7	15	0	2	28.5

NCAA FINAL FOUR MVPS (CONT.)

YEAR	WINNER, SCHOOL	GP	FIELD GOALS		3-PT FG		FREE THROWS		REB	A	STL	BS	AVG
			FGM	PCT	FGA	FGM	FTM	PCT					
1981	Isiah Thomas, Indiana	2	14	56.0	—	—	9	81.8	4	9	3	4	18.5
1982	James Worthy, N Carolina	2	20	74.1	—	—	2	28.6	8	9	0	4	21.0
1983	*Akeem Olajuwon, Houston	2	16	55.2	—	—	9	64.3	40	3	2	5	20.5
1984	Patrick Ewing, Georgetown	2	8	57.1	—	—	2	100.0	18	1	1	15	9.0
1985	Ed Pinckney, Villanova	2	8	57.1	—	—	12	75.0	15	6	3	0	14.0
1986	Pervis Ellison, Louisville	2	15	60.0	—	—	6	75.0	24	2	3	1	18.0
1987	Keith Smart, Indiana	2	14	63.6	1	0	7	77.8	7	7	0	2	17.5
1988	Danny Manning, Kansas	2	25	55.6	1	0	6	66.7	17	4	8	9	28.0
1989	Glen Rice, Michigan	2	24	49.0	16	7	4	100.0	16	1	0	3	29.5
1990	Anderson Hunt, UNLV	2	19	61.3	16	9	2	50.0	4	9	1	1	24.5
1991	Christian Laettner, Duke	2	12	54.5	1	1	21	91.3	17	2	1	2	23.0
1992	Bobby Hurley, Duke	2	10	41.7	12	7	8	80.0	3	11	0	3	17.5
1993	Donald Williams, N Carolina	2	15	65.2	14	10	10	100.0	4	2	2	0	25.0
1994	Corliss Williamson, Arkansas	2	21	50.0	0	0	10	71.4	21	8	4	3	26.0
1995	Ed O'Bannon, UCLA	2	16	45.7	8	3	10	76.9	25	3	7	1	22.5
1996	Tony Delk, Kentucky	2	15	41.7	16	8	6	54.6	9	2	3	2	22.0
1997	Miles Simon, Arizona	2	17	45.9	10	3	17	77.3	8	6	0	1	27.0
1998	Jeff Sheppard, Kentucky	2	16	55.2	10	4	7	77.8	10	7	4	0	21.5
1999	Richard Hamilton, UConn	2	20	51.3	7	3	8	72.7	12	4	2	1	25.5
2000	Mateen Cleaves, Mich St	2	8	44.4	4	3	10	83.3	6	5	2	0	14.5
2001	Shane Battier, Duke	2	13	50.0	12	5	12	70.6	19	8	2	6	21.5
2002	Juan Dixon, Maryland	2	16	59.3	15	7	12	80.0	8	5	7	0	25.5
2003	Carmelo Anthony, Syracuse	2	19	54.3	6	9	9	81.1	24	8	4	0	26.5

*Not a member of the championship-winning team.   †Record later vacated.

BEST NCAA TOURNAMENT
SINGLE-GAME SCORING PERFORMANCES

PLAYER AND TEAM	YEAR	ROUND	FG	3FG	FT	TP
Austin Carr, Notre Dame vs Ohio	1970	1st	25	—	11	61
Bill Bradley, Princeton vs Wichita St	1965	C*	22	—	14	58
Oscar Robertson, Cincinnati vs Arkansas	1958	C	21	—	14	56
Austin Carr, Notre Dame vs Kentucky	1970	2nd	22	—	8	52
Austin Carr, Notre Dame vs Texas Christian	1971	1st	20	—	12	52
David Robinson, Navy vs Michigan	1987	1st	22	0	6	50
Elvin Hayes, Houston vs Loyola (IL)	1968	1st	20	—	9	49
Hal Lear, Temple vs SMU	1956	C*	17	—	14	48
Austin Carr, Notre Dame vs Houston	1971	C	17	—	13	47
Dave Corzine, DePaul vs Louisville	1978	2nd	18	—	10	46

C=regional third place; C*=third-place game.

NIT CHAMPIONSHIP RESULTS

YEAR	WINNER	SCORE	RUNNER-UP	YEAR	WINNER	SCORE	RUNNER-UP
1938	Temple	60–36	Colorado	1971	N Carolina	84–66	Georgia Tech
1939	Long Island U	44–32	Loyola (IL)	1972	Maryland	100–69	Niagara
1940	Colorado	51–40	Duquesne	1973	Virginia Tech	92–91 (OT)	Notre Dame
1941	Long Island U	56–42	Ohio U	1974	Purdue	97–81	Utah
1942	W Virginia	47–45	W Kentucky	1975	Princeton	80–69	Providence
1943	St. John's (NY)	48–27	Toledo	1976	Kentucky	71–67	NC-Charlotte
1944	St. John's (NY)	47–39	DePaul	1977	St. Bonaventure	94–91	Houston
1945	DePaul	71–54	Bowling Green	1978	Texas	101–93	N Carolina St
1946	Kentucky	46–45	Rhode Island	1979	Indiana	53–52	Purdue
1947	Utah	49–45	Kentucky	1980	Virginia	58–55	Minnesota
1948	St. Louis	65–52	NYU	1981	Tulsa	86–84 (OT)	Syracuse
1949	San Francisco	48–47	Loyola (IL)	1982	Bradley	67–58	Purdue
1950	CCNY	69–61	Bradley	1983	Fresno St	69–60	DePaul
1951	BYU	62–43	Dayton	1984	Michigan	83–63	Notre Dame
1952	La Salle	75–64	Dayton	1985	UCLA	65–62	Indiana
1953	Seton Hall	58–46	St. John's (NY)	1986	Ohio St	73–63	Wyoming
1954	Holy Cross	71–62	Duquesne	1987	Southern Miss	84–80	La Salle
1955	Duquesne	70–58	Dayton	1988	Connecticut	72–67	Ohio St
1956	Louisville	93–80	Dayton	1989	St. John's (NY)	73–65	St. Louis
1957	Bradley	84–83	Memphis St	1990	Vanderbilt	74–72	St. Louis
1958	Xavier (OH)	78–74 (OT)	Dayton	1991	Stanford	78–72	Oklahoma
1959	St. John's (NY)	76–71 (OT)	Bradley	1992	Virginia	81–76	Notre Dame
1960	Bradley	88–72	Providence	1993	Minnesota	62–61	Georgetown
1961	Providence	62–59	St. Louis	1994	Villanova	80–73	Vanderbilt
1962	Dayton	73–67	St. John's (NY)	1995	Virginia Tech	65–64 (OT)	Marquette
1963	Providence	81–66	Canisius	1996	Nebraska	60–56	St. Joseph's
1964	Bradley	86–54	New Mexico	1997	Michigan	82–73	Florida St
1965	St. John's (NY)	55–51	Villanova	1998	Minnesota	79–72	Penn St
1966	BYU	97–84	NYU	1999	California	61–60	Clemson
1967	Southern IL	71–56	Marquette	2000	Wake Forest	71–61	Notre Dame
1968	Dayton	61–48	Kansas	2001	Tulsa	79–60	Alabama
1969	Temple	89–76	Boston College	2002	Memphis	72–62	S Carolina
1970	Marquette	65–53	St. John's (NY)	2003	St. John's	70–67	Georgetown

NCAA MEN'S DIVISION I SEASON LEADERS

SCORING AVERAGE

YEAR	PLAYER AND TEAM	HT	CLASS	GP	FG	3FG	FT	PTS	AVG
1948	Murray Wier, Iowa	5-9	Sr	19	152	—	95	399	21.0
1949	Tony Lavelli, Yale	6-3	Sr	30	228	—	215	671	22.4
1950	Paul Arizin, Villanova	6-3	Sr	29	260	—	215	735	25.3
1951	Bill Mlkvy, Temple	6-4	Sr	25	303	—	125	731	29.2
1952	Clyde Lovellette, Kansas	6-9	Sr	28	315	—	165	795	28.4
1953	Frank Selvy, Furman	6-3	Jr	25	272	—	194	738	29.5
1954	Frank Selvy, Furman	6-3	Sr	29	427	—	355	1209	41.7
1955	Darrell Floyd, Furman	6-1	Jr	25	344	—	209	897	35.9
1956	Darrell Floyd, Furman	6-1	Sr	28	339	—	268	946	33.8
1957	Grady Wallace, S Carolina	6-4	Sr	29	336	—	234	906	31.2
1958	Oscar Robertson, Cincinnati	6-5	So	28	352	—	280	984	35.1
1959	Oscar Robertson, Cincinnati	6-5	Jr	30	331	—	316	978	32.6
1960	Oscar Robertson, Cincinnati	6-5	Sr	30	369	—	273	1011	33.7
1961	Frank Burgess, Gonzaga	6-1	Sr	26	304	—	234	842	32.4
1962	Billy McGill, Utah	6-9	Sr	26	394	—	221	1009	38.8
1963	Nick Werkman, Seton Hall	6-3	Jr	22	221	—	208	650	29.5
1964	Howard Komives, Bowling Green	6-1	Sr	23	292	—	260	844	36.7
1965	Rick Barry, Miami (FL)	6-7	Sr	26	340	—	293	973	37.4
1966	Dave Schellhase, Purdue	6-4	Sr	24	284	—	213	781	32.5
1967	Jim Walker, Providence	6-3	Sr	28	323	—	205	851	30.4

NCAA MEN'S DIVISION I SEASON LEADERS (CONT.)

SCORING AVERAGE (CONT.)

YEAR	PLAYER AND TEAM	HT	CLASS	GP	FG	3FG	FT	PTS	AVG
1968	Pete Maravich, Louisiana St	6-5	So	26	432	—	274	1138	43.8
1969	Pete Maravich, Louisiana St	6-5	Jr	26	433	—	282	1148	44.2
1970	Pete Maravich, Louisiana St	6-5	Sr	31	522	—	337	1381	44.5
1971	Johnny Neumann, Mississippi	6-6	So	23	366	—	191	923	40.1
1972	Dwight Lamar, SW Louisiana	6-1	Jr	29	429	—	196	1054	36.3
1973	William Averitt, Pepperdine	6-1	Sr	25	352	—	144	848	33.9
1974	Larry Fogle, Canisius	6-5	So	25	326	—	183	835	33.4
1975	Bob McCurdy, Richmond	6-7	Sr	26	321	—	213	855	32.9
1976	Marshall Rodgers, TX-Pan American	6-2	Sr	25	361	—	197	919	36.8
1977	Freeman Williams, Portland St	6-4	Jr	26	417	—	176	1010	38.8
1978	Freeman Williams, Portland St	6-4	Sr	27	410	—	149	969	35.9
1979	Lawrence Butler, Idaho St	6-3	Sr	27	310	—	192	812	30.1
1980	Tony Murphy, Southern-BR	6-3	Sr	29	377	—	178	932	32.1
1981	Zam Fredrick, S Carolina	6-2	Sr	27	300	—	181	781	28.9
1982	Harry Kelly, Texas Southern	6-7	Jr	29	336	—	190	862	29.7
1983	Harry Kelly, Texas Southern	6-7	Sr	29	333	—	169	835	28.8
1984	Joe Jakubick, Akron	6-5	Sr	27	304	—	206	814	30.1
1985	Xavier McDaniel, Wichita St	6-7	Sr	31	351	—	142	844	27.2
1986	Terrance Bailey, Wagner	6-2	Jr	29	321	—	212	854	29.4
1987	Kevin Houston, Army	5-11	Sr	29	311	63	268	953	32.9
1988	Hersey Hawkins, Bradley	6-3	Sr	31	377	87	284	1125	36.3
1989	Hank Gathers, Loyola Marymount	6-7	Jr	31	419	0	177	1015	32.7
1990	Bo Kimble, Loyola Marymount	6-5	Sr	32	404	92	231	1131	35.3
1991	Kevin Bradshaw, U.S. Int'l	6-6	Sr	28	358	60	278	1054	37.6
1992	Brett Roberts, Morehead St	6-8	Sr	29	278	66	193	815	28.1
1993	Greg Guy, TX-Pan American	6-1	Jr	19	189	67	111	556	29.3
1994	Glenn Robinson, Purdue	6-8	Jr	34	368	79	215	1030	30.3
1995	Kurt Thomas, Texas Christian	6-9	Sr	27	288	3	202	781	28.9
1996	Kevin Granger, Texas Southern	6-3	Sr	24	194	30	230	648	27.0
1997	Charles Jones, LIU-Brooklyn	6-3	Jr	30	338	109	118	903	30.1
1998	Charles Jones, LIU-Brooklyn	6-3	Sr	30	326	116	101	869	29.0
1999	Alvin Young, Niagara	6-3	Sr	29	253	65	157	728	25.1
2000	Courtney Alexander, Fresno St	6-6	Sr	27	252	58	107	669	24.8
2001	Ronnie McCollum, Centenary	6-4	Sr	27	244	85	214	787	29.1
2002	Jason Conley, Virginia Military	6-5	Fr	28	285	79	171	820	29.3
2003	Ruben Douglas, New Mexico	6-5	Sr	28	218	94	253	783	28.0

REBOUNDS

YEAR	PLAYER AND TEAM	HT	CLASS	GP	REB	AVG
1951	Ernie Beck, Pennsylvania	6-4	So	27	556	20.6
1952	Bill Hannon, Army	6-3	So	17	355	20.9
1953	Ed Conlin, Fordham	6-5	So	26	612	23.5
1954	Art Quimby, Connecticut	6-5	Jr	26	588	22.6
1955	Charlie Slack, Marshall	6-5	Jr	21	538	25.6
1956	Joe Holup, George Washington	6-6	Sr	26	604	†.256
1957	Elgin Baylor, Seattle	6-6	Jr	25	508	†.235
1958	Alex Ellis, Niagara	6-5	Sr	25	536	†.262
1959	Leroy Wright, Pacific	6-8	Jr	26	652	†.238
1960	Leroy Wright, Pacific	6-8	Sr	17	380	†.234
1961	Jerry Lucas, Ohio St	6-8	Jr	27	470	†.198
1962	Jerry Lucas, Ohio St	6-8	Sr	28	499	†.211
1963	Paul Silas, Creighton	6-7	Sr	27	557	20.6
1964	Bob Pelkington, Xavier (OH)	6-7	Sr	26	567	21.8
1965	Toby Kimball, Connecticut	6-8	Sr	23	483	21.0
1966	Jim Ware, Oklahoma City	6-8	Sr	29	607	20.9
1967	Dick Cunningham, Murray St	6-10	Jr	22	479	21.8
1968	Neal Walk, Florida	6-10	Jr	25	494	19.8
1969	Spencer Haywood, Detroit	6-8	So	22	472	21.5
1970	Artis Gilmore, Jacksonville	7-2	Jr	28	621	22.2
1971	Artis Gilmore, Jacksonville	7-2	Sr	26	603	23.2

REBOUNDS (CONT.)

YEAR	PLAYER AND TEAM	HT	CLASS	GP	REB	AVG
1972	Kermit Washington, American	6-8	Jr	23	455	19.8
1973	Kermit Washington, American	6-8	Sr	22	439	20.0
1974	Marvin Barnes, Providence	6-9	Sr	32	597	18.7
1975	John Irving, Hofstra	6-9	So	21	323	15.4
1976	Sam Pellom, Buffalo	6-8	So	26	420	16.2
1977	Glenn Mosley, Seton Hall	6-8	Sr	29	473	16.3
1978	Ken Williams, N Texas St	6-7	Sr	28	411	14.7
1979	Monti Davis, Tennessee St	6-7	Jr	26	421	16.2
1980	Larry Smith, Alcorn St	6-8	Sr	26	392	15.1
1981	Darryl Watson, Miss Valley	6-7	Sr	27	379	14.0
1982	LaSalle Thompson, Texas	6-10	Jr	27	365	13.5
1983	Xavier McDaniel, Wichita St	6-7	So	28	403	14.4
1984	Akeem Olajuwon, Houston	7-0	Jr	37	500	13.5
1985	Xavier McDaniel, Wichita St	6-8	Sr	31	460	14.8
1986	David Robinson, Navy	6-11	Jr	35	455	13.0
1987	Jerome Lane, Pittsburgh	6-6	So	33	444	13.5
1988	Kenny Miller, Loyola (IL)	6-9	Fr	29	395	13.6
1989	Hank Gathers, Loyola (CA)	6-7	Jr	31	426	13.7
1990	Anthony Bonner, St. Louis	6-8	Sr	33	456	13.8
1991	Shaquille O'Neal, Louisiana St	7-1	So	28	411	14.7
1992	Popeye Jones, Murray St	6-8	Sr	30	431	14.4
1993	Warren Kidd, Middle Tenn St	6-9	Sr	26	386	14.8
1994	Jerome Lambert, Baylor	6-8	Jr	24	355	14.8
1995	Kurt Thomas, Texas Christian	6-9	Sr	27	393	14.6
1996	Marcus Mann, Mississippi Valley	6-8	Sr	29	394	13.6
1997	Tim Duncan, Wake Forest	6-11	Sr	31	457	14.7
1998	Ryan Perryman, Dayton	6-7	Sr	33	412	12.5
1999	Ian McGinnis, Dartmouth	6-8	So	26	317	12.2
2000	Darren Phillips, Fairfield	6-7	Sr	29	405	14.0
2001	Chris Marcus, Western Kentucky	7-1	Jr	31	374	12.1
2002	Jeremy Bishop, Quinnipiac	6-6	Jr	29	347	12.0
2003	Brandon Hunter, Ohio	6-7	Sr	30	378	12.6

†From 1956–1962, title was based on highest individual recoveries out of total by both teams in all games.

ASSISTS

YEAR	PLAYER AND TEAM	CLASS	GP	A	AVG
1984	Craig Lathen, IL-Chicago	Jr	29	274	9.45
1985	Rob Weingard, Hofstra	Sr	24	228	9.50
1986	Mark Jackson, St. John's (NY)	Jr	36	328	9.11
1987	Avery Johnson, Southern-BR	Jr	31	333	10.74
1988	Avery Johnson, Southern-BR	Sr	30	399	13.30
1989	Glenn Williams, Holy Cross	Sr	28	278	9.93
1990	Todd Lehmann, Drexel	Sr	28	260	9.29
1991	Chris Corchiani, N Carolina St	Sr	31	299	9.65
1992	Van Usher, Tennessee Tech	Sr	29	254	8.76
1993	Sam Crawford, New Mex St	Sr	34	310	9.12
1994	Jason Kidd, California	So	30	272	9.06
1995	Nelson Haggerty, Baylor	Sr	28	284	10.10
1996	Raimonds Miglinieks, UC-Irvine	Sr	27	230	8.52
1997	Kenny Mitchell, Dartmouth	Sr	26	203	7.81
1998	Ahlon Lewis, Arizona St	Sr	32	294	9.19
1999	Doug Gottlieb, Oklahoma St	Jr	34	299	8.79
2000	Mark Dickel, UNLV	Sr	31	280	9.03
2001	Markus Carr, Cal St-Northridge	Jr	32	286	8.94
2002	T.J. Ford, Texas	Fr	33	273	8.27
2003	Martell Bailey, IL-Chicago	Jr	30	244	8.13

NCAA MEN'S DIVISION I SEASON LEADERS (CONT.)

BLOCKED SHOTS

YEAR	PLAYER AND TEAM	CLASS	GP	BS	AVG
1986	David Robinson, Navy	Jr	35	207	5.91
1987	David Robinson, Navy	Sr	32	144	4.50
1988	Rodney Blake, St. Joseph's (PA)	Sr	29	116	4.00
1989	Alonzo Mourning, Georgetown	Fr	34	169	4.97
1990	Kenny Green, Rhode Island	Sr	26	124	4.77
1991	Shawn Bradley, Brigham Young	Fr	34	177	5.21
1992	Shaquille O'Neal, Louisiana St	Jr	30	157	5.23
1993	Theo Ratliff, Wyoming	Jr	28	124	4.43
1994	Grady Livingston, Howard	Jr	26	115	4.42
1995	Keith Closs, Central Conn St	Fr	26	139	5.35
1996	Keith Closs, Central Conn St	So	28	178	6.36
1997	Adonal Foyle, Colgate	Jr	28	180	6.43
1998	Jerome James, Florida A&M	Sr	27	125	4.63
1999	Tarvis Williams, Hampton	Jr	27	135	5.00
2000	Ken Johnson, Ohio St	Sr	30	161	5.37
2001	Tarvis Williams, Hampton	Sr	32	147	4.59
2002	Wojciech Myrda, LA-Monroe	Sr	32	172	5.38
2003	Emeka Okafor, Connecticut	So	33	156	4.73

STEALS

YEAR	PLAYER AND TEAM	CLASS	GP	S	AVG
1986	Darron Brittman, Chicago St	Sr	28	139	4.96
1987	Tony Fairley, Charleston Sou	Sr	28	114	4.07
1988	Aldwin Ware, Florida A&M	Sr	29	142	4.90
1989	Kenny Robertson, Cleveland St	Jr	28	111	3.96
1990	Ronn McMahon, E Washington	Sr	29	130	4.48
1991	Van Usher, Tennessee Tech	Jr	28	104	3.71
1992	Victor Snipes, NE Illinois	So	25	86	3.44
1993	Jason Kidd, California	Fr	29	110	3.80
1994	Shawn Griggs, SW Louisiana	Sr	30	120	4.00
1995	Roderick Anderson, Texas	Sr	30	101	3.37
1996	Pointer Williams, McNeese St	Sr	27	118	4.37
1997	Joel Hoover, MD-Eastern Shore	Fr	28	90	3.21
1998	Bonzi Wells, Ball St	Sr	29	103	3.55
1999	Shawnta Rogers, George Wash	Sr	29	103	3.55
2000	Carl Williams, Liberty	Sr	28	107	3.82
2001	Greedy Daniels, Texas Christian	Jr	25	108	4.32
2002	Desmond Cambridge, AL A&M	Sr	29	160	5.52
2003	Alexis McMillan, Stetson	Sr	22	87	3.95

NCAA MEN'S DIVISION I ALLTIME INDIVIDUAL LEADERS

SINGLE GAME RECORDS

SCORING HIGHS VS NON-DIVISION I OPPONENT

PTS	PLAYER AND TEAM VS OPPONENT	DATE
72	Kevin Bradshaw, U.S. Int'l vs Loyola Marymount	1-5-91
69	Pete Maravich, Louisiana St vs Alabama	2-7-70
68	Calvin Murphy, Niagara vs Syracuse	12-7-68
66	Jay Handlan, Washington & Lee vs Furman	2-17-51
66	Pete Maravich, Louisiana St vs Tulane	2-10-69
66	Anthony Roberts, Oral Roberts vs N Carolina A&T	2-19-77
65	Anthony Roberts, Oral Roberts vs Oregon	3-9-77
65	Scott Haffner, Evansville vs Dayton	2-18-89
64	Pete Maravich, Louisiana St vs Kentucky	2-21-70
63	Johnny Neumann, Mississippi vs Louisiana St	1-30-71
63	Hersey Hawkins, Bradley vs Detroit	2-22-88

SINGLE GAME RECORDS (CONT.)

SCORING HIGHS VS NON-DIVISION I OPPONENT

PTS	PLAYER AND TEAM VS OPPONENT	DATE
100	Frank Selvy, Furman vs Newberry	2-13-54
85	Paul Arizin, Villanova vs Philadelphia NAMC	2-12-49
81	Freeman Williams, Portland St vs Rocky Mountain	2-3-78
73	Bill Mlkvy, Temple vs Wilkes	3-3-51
71	Freeman Williams, Portland St vs Southern Oregon	2-9-77

REBOUNDING HIGHS BEFORE 1973

PTS	PLAYER AND TEAM VS OPPONENT	DATE
51	Bill Chambers, William & Mary vs Virginia	2-14-53
43	Charlie Slack, Marshall vs Morris Harvey	1-12-54
42	Tom Heinsohn, Holy Cross vs Boston College	3-1-55
40	Art Quimby, Connecticut vs Boston U	1-11-55
39	Maurice Stokes, St. Francis (PA) vs John Carroll	1-28-55
39	Dave DeBusschere, Detroit vs Central Michigan	1-30-60
39	Keith Swagerty, Pacific vs UC-Santa Barbara	3-5-65

REBOUNDING HIGHS SINCE 1973

PTS	PLAYER AND TEAM VS OPPONENT	DATE
35	Larry Abney, Fresno St vs Southern Methodist	2-17-00
34	David Vaughn, Oral Roberts vs Brandeis	1-8-73
32	Jervaughn Scales, Southern-BR vs Grambling	2-7-94
32	Durand Macklin, Louisiana St vs Tulane	11-26-76
31	Jim Bradley, Northern Illinois vs WI-Milwaukee	2-19-73
31	Calvin Natt, NE Louisiana vs Georgia Southern	12-29-76

ASSISTS

A	PLAYER AND TEAM VS OPPONENT	DATE
22	Tony Fairley, Baptist vs Armstrong St	2-9-87
22	Avery Johnson, Southern-BR vs Texas Southern	1-25-88
22	Sherman Douglas, Syracuse vs Providence	1-28-89
21	Mark Wade, UNLV vs Navy	12-29-86
21	Kelvin Scarborough, New Mexico vs Hawaii	2-13-87
21	Anthony Manuel, Bradley vs UC-Irvine	12-19-87
21	Avery Johnson, Southern-BR vs Alabama St	1-16-88

STEALS

S	PLAYER AND TEAM VS OPPONENT	DATE
13	Mookie Blaylock, Oklahoma vs Centenary	12-12-87
13	Mookie Blaylock, Oklahoma vs Loyola Marymount	12-17-88
12	Kenny Robertson, Cleveland St vs Wagner	12-3-88
12	Terry Evans, Oklahoma vs Florida A&M	1-27-93
12	Richard Duncan, Middle Tenn St vs Eastern Kentucky	2-20-99
12	Greedy Daniels, Texas Christian vs AR–Pine Bluff	12-30-00
12	Jehiel Lewis, Navy vs Bucknell	1-12-02

BLOCKED SHOTS

BS	PLAYER AND TEAM VS OPPONENT	DATE
14	David Robinson, Navy vs NC–Wilmington	1-4-86
14	Shawn Bradley, Brigham Young vs Eastern Kentucky	12-7-90
14	Roy Rogers, Alabama vs Georgia	2-10-96
14	Loren Woods, Arizona vs Oregon	2-3-00
13	Kevin Roberson, Vermont vs New Hampshire	1-9-92
13	Jim McIlvaine, Marquette vs Northeastern (IL)	12-9-92
13	Keith Closs, Central Conn. St vs St. Francis (PA)	12-21-94
13	D'or Fischer, Northwestern St vs SW Texas St	1-22-01
13	Wojciech Myrda, LA–Monroe vs Texas–San Antonio	1-17-02

SINGLE SEASON RECORDS

POINTS

PLAYER AND TEAM	YEAR	GP	FG	3FG	FT	PTS
Pete Maravich, Louisiana St	1970	31	522	—	337	1381
Elvin Hayes, Houston	1968	33	519	—	176	1214
Frank Selvy, Furman	1954	29	427	—	355	1209
Pete Maravich, Louisiana St	1969	26	433	—	282	1148
Pete Maravich, Louisiana St	1968	26	432	—	274	1138
Bo Kimble, Loyola Marymount	1990	32	404	92	231	1131
Hersey Hawkins, Bradley	1988	31	377	87	284	1125
Austin Carr, Notre Dame	1970	29	444	—	218	1106
Austin Carr, Notre Dame	1971	29	430	—	241	1101
Otis Birdsong, Houston	1977	36	452	—	186	1090

SCORING AVERAGE

PLAYER AND TEAM	YEAR	GP	FG	3FG	FT	PTS
Pete Maravich, Louisiana St	1970	31	522	337	1381	44.5
Pete Maravich, Louisiana St	1969	26	433	282	1148	44.2
Pete Maravich, Louisiana St	1968	26	432	274	1138	43.8
Frank Selvy, Furman	1954	29	427	355	1209	41.7
Johnny Neumann, Mississippi	1971	23	366	191	923	40.1
Freeman Williams, Portland St	1977	26	417	176	1010	38.8
Billy McGill, Utah	1962	26	394	221	1009	38.8
Calvin Murphy, Niagara	1968	24	337	242	916	38.2
Austin Carr, Notre Dame	1970	29	444	218	1106	38.1
Austin Carr, Notre Dame	1971	29	430	241	1101	38.0

REBOUNDS

PLAYER AND TEAM	YEAR	GP	REB	PLAYER AND TEAM	YEAR	GP	REB
Walt Dukes, Seton Hall	1953	33	734	Artis Gilmore, Jacksonville	1970	28	621
Leroy Wright, Pacific	1959	26	652	Tom Gola, La Salle	1955	31	618
Tom Gola, La Salle	1954	30	652	Ed Conlin, Fordham	1953	26	612
Charlie Tyra, Louisville	1956	29	645	Art Quimby, Connecticut	1955	25	611
Paul Silas, Creighton	1964	29	631	Bill Russell, San Francisco	1956	29	609
Elvin Hayes, Houston	1968	33	624	Jim Ware, Oklahoma City	1966	29	607

REBOUND AVERAGE BEFORE 1973

PLAYER AND TEAM	YEAR	GP	REB	AVG
Charlie Slack, Marshall	1955	21	538	25.6
Leroy Wright, Pacific	1959	26	652	25.1
Art Quimby, Connecticut	1955	25	611	24.4
Charlie Slack, Marshall	1956	22	520	23.6
Ed Conlin, Fordham	1953	26	612	23.5

REBOUND AVERAGE SINCE 1973*

PLAYER AND TEAM	YEAR	GP	REB	A
Kermit Washington, Amer.	1973	22	439	20.0
Marvin Barnes, Providence	1973	30	571	19.0
Marvin Barnes, Providence	1974	32	597	18.7
Pete Padgett, NV-Reno	1973	26	462	17.8
Jim Bradley, Northern IL	1973	24	426	17.8

*Freshmen became eligible for varsity play in 1973.

ASSISTS

PLAYER AND TEAM	YEAR	GP	A	PLAYER AND TEAM	YEAR	GP	A
Mark Wade, UNLV	1987	38	406	Sherman Douglas, Syracuse	1989	38	326
Avery Johnson, Southern-BR	1988	30	399	Sam Crawford, New Mex. St	1993	34	310
Anthony Manuel, Bradley	1988	31	373	Greg Anthony, UNLV	1991	35	310
Avery Johnson, Southern-BR	1987	31	333	Reid Gettys, Houston	1984	37	309
Mark Jackson, St. John's (NY)	1986	32	328	Carl Golston, Loyola (IL)	1985	33	305

ASSIST AVERAGE

PLAYER AND TEAM	YEAR	GP	A	A	PLAYER AND TEAM	YEAR	GP	A	A
Avery Johnson, Southern-BR	1988	30	399	13.3	Chris Corchiani, N Carolina St	1991	31	299	9.6
Anthony Manuel, Bradley	1988	31	373	12.0	Tony Fairley, Charleston So.*	1987	28	270	9.6
Avery Johnson, Southern-BR	1987	31	333	10.7	Tyrone Bogues, Wake Forest	1987	29	276	9.5
Mark Wade, UNLV	1987	38	406	10.7	Ron Weingard, Hofstra	1985	24	228	9.5
Nelson Haggerty, Baylor	1995	28	284	10.1	Craig Neal, Georgia Tech	1988	32	303	9.5
Glenn Williams, Holy Cross	1989	28	278	9.9	*Formerly Baptist.				

SINGLE SEASON RECORDS (CONT.)

FIELD-GOAL PERCENTAGE

PLAYER AND TEAM	YEAR	GP	FG	FGA	PCT
Steve Johnson, Oregon St	1981	28	235	315	74.6
Dwayne Davis, Florida	1989	33	179	248	72.2
Keith Walker, Utica	1985	27	154	216	71.3
Steve Johnson, Oregon St	1980	30	211	297	71.0
Adam Mark, Belmont	2002	26	150	212	70.8
Oliver Miller, Arkansas	1991	38	254	361	70.4
Alan Williams, Princeton	1987	25	163	232	70.3
Mark McNamara, California	1982	27	231	329	70.2
Warren Kidd, Middle Tennessee St	1991	30	173	247	70.0
Pete Freeman, Akron	1991	28	175	250	70.0

Based on qualifiers for annual championship.

FREE-THROW PERCENTAGE

PLAYER AND TEAM	YEAR	GP	FT	FTA	PCT
Craig Collins, Penn St	1985	27	94	98	95.9
Steve Drabyn, Belmont	2003	29	78	82	95.1
Rod Foster, UCLA	1982	27	95	100	95.0
Clay McKnight, Pacific	2000	24	74	78	94.9
Matt Logie, Lehigh	2003	28	91	96	94.8
Danny Basile, Marist	1994	27	84	89	94.4
Carlos Gibson, Marshall	1978	28	84	89	94.4
Jim Barton, Dartmouth	1986	26	65	69	94.2
Gary Buchanan, Villanova	2001	31	97	103	94.2
Jack Moore, Nebraska	1982	27	123	131	93.9

Based on qualifiers for annual championship.

THREE-POINT FIELD-GOAL PERCENTAGE

PLAYER AND TEAM	YEAR	GP	3FG	3FGA	PCT
Glenn Tropf, Holy Cross	1988	29	52	82	63.4
Sean Wightman, Western Michigan	1992	30	48	76	63.2
Keith Jennings, E Tennessee St	1991	33	84	142	59.2
Dave Calloway, Monmouth (NJ)	1989	28	48	82	58.5
Steve Kerr, Arizona	1988	38	114	199	57.3
Reginald Jones, Prairie View	1987	28	64	112	57.1
Jim Cantamessa, Siena	1998	29	66	117	56.4
Joel Tribelhorn, Colorado St	1989	33	76	135	56.3
Mike Joseph, Bucknell	1988	28	65	116	56.0
Brian Jackson, Evansville	1995	27	53	95	55.8
Amory Sanders, SE Missouri St	2001	24	53	95	55.8

Based on qualifiers for annual championship.

STEALS

PLAYER AND TEAM	YEAR	GP	S
Desmond Cambridge, Alabama A&M	2002	29	160
Mookie Blaylock, Oklahoma	1988	39	150
Aldwin Ware, Florida A&M	1988	29	142
Darron Brittman, Chicago St	1986	28	139
John Linehan, Providence	2002	31	139

BLOCKED SHOTS

PLAYER AND TEAM	YEAR	GP	BS
David Robinson, Navy	1986	35	207
Adonal Foyle, Colgate	1997	28	180
Keith Closs, Central Conn St	1996	28	178
Shawn Bradley, BYU	1991	34	177
Wojiech Myrda, LA–Monroe	2002	32	172

STEAL AVERAGE

PLAYER AND TEAM	YEAR	GP	S	AVG
D. Cambridge, Alabama A&M	2002	29	160	5.52
Darron Brittman, Chicago St	1986	28	139	4.96
Aldwin Ware, Florida A&M	1988	29	142	4.90
John Linehan, Providence	2002	31	139	4.48
Ronn McMahon, E Washington	1990	29	130	4.48

BLOCKED-SHOT AVERAGE

PLAYER AND TEAM	YEAR	GP	BS	AVG
Adonal Foyle, Colgate	1997	28	180	6.43
Keith Closs, Central Conn St	1996	28	178	6.36
David Robinson, Navy	1986	35	207	5.91
Adonal Foyle, Colgate	1996	29	165	5.69
Wojiech Myrda, LA-Monroe	2002	32	172	5.37

CAREER RECORDS

POINTS

PLAYER AND TEAM	HT	FINAL YEAR	GP	FG	3FG*	FT	PTS
Pete Maravich, Louisiana St.	6-5	1970	83	1387	—	893	3667
Freeman Williams, Portland St.	6-4	1978	106	1369	—	511	3249
Lionel Simmons, La Salle	6-7	1990	131	1244	56	673	3217
Alphonso Ford, Mississippi Valley	6-2	1993	109	1121	333	590	3165
Harry Kelly, Texas Southern	6-7	1983	110	1234	—	598	3066
Hersey Hawkins, Bradley	6-3	1988	125	1100	118	690	3008
Oscar Robertson, Cincinnati	6-5	1960	88	1052	—	869	2973
Danny Manning, Kansas	6-10	1988	147	1216	10	509	2951
Alfredrick Hughes, Loyola (IL)	6-5	1985	120	1226	—	462	2914
Elvin Hayes, Houston	6-8	1968	93	1215	—	454	2884
Larry Bird, Indiana St.	6-9	1979	94	1154	—	542	2850
Otis Birdsong, Houston	6-4	1977	116	1176	—	480	2832
Kevin Bradshaw, Bethune-Cookman, U.S. Int'l.	6-6	1991	111	1027	132	618	2804
Allan Houston, Tennessee	6-6	1993	128	902	346	651	2801
Hank Gathers, Southern Cal, Loyola Marymount	6-7	1990	117	1127	0	469	2723
Reggie Lewis, Northeastern	6-7	1987	122	1043	30 (1)	592	2708
Daren Queenan, Lehigh	6-5	1988	118	1024	29	626	2703
Byron Larkin, Xavier (OH)	6-3	1988	121	1022	51	601	2696
David Robinson, Navy	7-1	1987	127	1032	1	604	2669
Wayman Tisdale, Oklahoma	6-9	1985	104	1077	—	507	2661

*Listed is the number of three-pointers scored since it became the national rule in 1987; the number in the parentheses is number scored prior to 1987—these counted as three points in the game but counted as two-pointers in the national rankings. The three-pointers in the parentheses are not included in total points.

SCORING AVERAGE

PLAYER AND TEAM	FINAL YEAR	GP	FG	FT	PTS	AVG
Pete Maravich, Louisiana St.	1968	83	1387	893	3667	44.2
Austin Carr, Notre Dame	1971	74	1017	526	2560	34.6
Oscar Robertson, Cincinnati	1960	88	1052	869	2973	33.8
Calvin Murphy, Niagara	1970	77	947	654	2548	33.1
Dwight Lamar, Southwestern Louisiana	1973	57	768	326	1862	32.7
Frank Selvy, Furman	1954	78	922	694	2538	32.5
Rick Mount, Purdue	1970	72	910	503	2323	32.3
Darrell Floyd, Furman	1956	71	868	545	2281	32.1
Nick Werkman, Seton Hall	1964	71	812	649	2273	32.0
Willie Humes, Idaho St.	1971	48	565	380	1510	31.5
William Averitt, Pepperdine	1973	49	615	311	1541	31.4
Elgin Baylor, Coll. of Idaho, Seattle	1958	80	956	588	2500	31.3
Elvin Hayes, Houston	1968	93	1215	454	2884	31.0
Freeman Williams, Portland St.	1978	106	1369	511	3249	30.7
Larry Bird, Indiana St.	1979	94	1154	542	2850	30.3

REBOUNDS BEFORE 1973

PLAYER AND TEAM	FINAL YEAR	GP	REB
Tom Gola, La Salle	1955	118	2201
Joe Holup, George Washington	1956	104	2030
Charlie Slack, Marshall	1956	88	1916
Ed Conlin, Fordham	1955	102	1884
Dickie Hemric, Wake Forest	1955	104	1802

CAREER RECORDS (CONT.)

REBOUNDS SINCE 1973*

PLAYER AND TEAM	FINAL YEAR	GP	REB
Tim Duncan, Wake Forest	1997	128	1570
Derrick Coleman, Syracuse	1990	143	1537
Malik Rose, Drexel	1996	120	1514
Ralph Sampson, Virginia	1983	132	1511
Pete Padgett, NV-Reno	1976	104	1464

ASSISTS

PLAYER AND TEAM	FINAL YEAR	GP	REB
Bobby Hurley, Duke	1993	140	1076
Chris Corchiani, N Carolina St	1991	124	1038
Ed Cota, N Carolina	2000	138	1030
Keith Jennings, E Tennessee St	1991	127	983
Sherman Douglas, Syracuse	1989	138	960

FIELD-GOAL PERCENTAGE

PLAYER AND TEAM	FINAL YEAR	FG	FGA	PCT
Steve Johnson, Oregon St	1981	828	1222	67.8
Michael Bradley, Kentucky/Villanova	2001	441	651	67.7
Murray Brown, Florida St	1980	566	847	66.8
Lee Campbell, SW Missouri St	1990	411	618	66.5
Warren Kidd, Middle Tennessee St	1993	496	747	66.4

Note: Minimum 400 field goals and 4 FG made per game.

FREE-THROW PERCENTAGE

PLAYER AND TEAM	FINAL YEAR	FT	FTA	PCT
Greg Starrick, Kentucky; Southern Illinois	1972	341	375	90.9
Jack Moore, Nebraska	1982	446	495	90.1
Steve Henson, Kansas St	1990	361	401	90.0
Steve Alford, Indiana	1987	535	596	89.8
Bob Lloyd, Rutgers	1967	543	605	89.8

Note: Minimum 300 free throws made.

*Freshmen became eligible for varsity play in 1973.

THREE-POINT FIELD GOALS MADE

PLAYER AND TEAM	FINAL YEAR	GP	3FG
Curtis Staples, Virginia	1998	122	413
Keith Veney, Lamar; Marshall	1997	111	409
Doug Day, Radford	1993	117	401
Ronnie Schmitz, MO–Kansas City	1993	112	378
Mark Alberts, Akron	1993	103	375

THREE-POINT FIELD-GOAL PERCENTAGE

PLAYER AND TEAM	FINAL YEAR	3FG	3FGA	PCT
Tony Bennett, WI–Green Bay	1992	290	584	49.7
David Olson, Eastern Illinois	1992	262	562	46.6
Ross Land, Northern Arizona	2000	308	664	46.4
Dan Dickau, Washington/Gonzaga	2002	215	465	46.2
Sean Jackson, Ohio/Princeton	1992	243	528	46.0

Note: Minimum 200 3-point field goals and 2.0 3FG/G.

STEALS

PLAYER AND TEAM	FINAL YEAR	GP	S
John Linehan, Providence	2002	122	385
Eric Murdock, Providence	1991	117	376
Pepe Sanchez, Temple	2000	116	365
Cookie Belcher, Nebraska	2001	131	353
Kevin Braswell, Georgetown	2002	128	349

CAREER RECORDS (CONT.)

BLOCKED SHOTS

PLAYER AND TEAM	FINAL YEAR	GP	BS
Wojciech Myrda, Louisiana-Monroe........2002		115	535
Adonal Foyle, Colgate 1997		87	492
Tim Duncan, Wake Forest.......................1997		128	481
Alonzo Mourning, Georgetown 1992		120	453
Tarvis Williams, Hampton........................2001		114	452

NCAA MEN'S DIVISION I TEAM LEADERS

LONGEST—HOME COURT

TEAM	GAMES	YEARS	TEAM	GAMES	YEARS
Kentucky 129		1943–55	Lamar 80		1978–84
St. Bonaventure 99		1948–61	Long Beach St..............75		1968–74
UCLA............................98		1970–76	UNLV.............................72		1974–78
Cincinnati......................86		1957–64	Arizona 71		1987–92
Marquette 81		1967–73	Cincinnati......................68		1972–78
Arizona 81		1945–51	Western Kentucky.........67		1949–55

NCAA MEN'S DIVISION I WINNING STREAKS

LONGEST—FULL SEASON

TEAM	GAMES	YEARS	ENDED BY
UCLA..88		1971–74	Notre Dame (71–70)
San Francisco.........................60		1955–57	Illinois (62–33)
UCLA..47		1966–68	Houston (71–69)
UNLV.......................................45		1990–91	Duke (79–77)
Texas.......................................44		1913–17	Rice (24–18)
Seton Hall...............................43		1939–41	LIU-Brooklyn (49–26)
LIU-Brooklyn 43		1935–37	Stanford (45–31)
UCLA..41		1968–69	Southern Cal (46–44)
Marquette 39		1970–71	Ohio St (60–59)
Cincinnati 37		1962–63	Wichita St (65–64)
N Carolina...............................37		1957–58	W Virginia (75–64)

LONGEST—REGULAR SEASON

TEAM	GAMES	YEARS	ENDED BY
UCLA..76		1971–74	Notre Dame (71–70)
Indiana....................................57		1975–77	Toledo (59–57)
Marquette 56		1970–72	Detroit (70–49)
Kentucky 54		1952–55	Georgia Tech (59–58)
San Francisco.........................51		1955–57	Illinois (62–33)
Pennsylvania 48		1970–72	Temple (57–52)
Ohio State 47		1960–62	Wisconsin (86–67)
Texas.......................................44		1913–17	Rice (24–18)
UCLA..43		1966–68	Houston (71–69)
LIU-Brooklyn 43		1935–37	Stanford (45–31)
Seton Hall...............................42		1939–41	LIU-Brooklyn (49–26)

DIVISION I TEAM ALLTIME WINS

TEAM	FIRST YEAR	YRS	W	L	T
Kentucky	1903	100	1849	572	1
N Carolina	1911	93	1808	666	0
Kansas	1899	105	1801	753	0
Duke	1906	98	1706	775	0
St. John's (NY)	1908	96	1661	763	0
Temple	1895	107	1607	874	0
Syracuse	1901	102	1602	737	0
Pennsylvania	1897	103	1555	876	2
Indiana	1901	103	1540	825	0
UCLA	1920	84	1520	672	0
Notre Dame	1898	98	1529	838	1
Oregon St	1902	102	1517	1067	0
Utah	1909	95	1492	775	0
Princeton	1901	103	1475	896	0
Washington	1896	101	1444	980	0
Purdue	1897	105	1453	849	0

Note: Minimum of 25 years in Division I.

DIVISION I ALLTIME WINNING PERCENTAGE

TEAM	FIRST YEAR	YRS	W	L	T	PCT
Kentucky	1903	100	1849	572	1	.764
N Carolina	1911	93	1808	666	0	.731
UNLV	1959	45	925	363	0	.718
Kansas	1899	105	1801	753	0	.705
Duke	1906	98	1706	775	0	.688
St. John's (NY)	1908	96	1661	763	0	.685
Syracuse	1901	102	1602	737	0	.685
UCLA	1920	84	1520	672	0	.678
Western Kentucky	1915	84	1466	723	0	.670
Utah	1909	95	1492	775	0	.658
Indiana	1901	103	1540	825	0	.651
Arkansas	1924	80	1377	742	0	.650
Temple	1895	107	1607	874	0	.648
Louisville	1912	89	1431	778	0	.648
Notre Dame	1898	98	1529	838	1	.646

Note: Minimum of 25 years in Division I.

HELP WANTED

Last spring, two of the winningest players in NCAA history interviewed for the vacant head coaching position at Columbia, which had its losingest basketball season ever (2–14, including 0–14 in the Ivy League). After firing coach Armond Hill, Columbia brought in Kareem Abdul-Jabbar (who was 88–2 with three national championships at UCLA) and Bobby Hurley (who was 119–26 with two titles at Duke). The Lions ended up hiring Villanova assistant Joseph Jones .

NCAA MEN'S DIVISION I WINNINGEST COACHES

ACTIVE COACHES

WINS

COACH AND TEAM	W
James Phelan, Mt. St. Mary's (MD)	830
Bob Knight, Texas Tech	809
Lefty Driesell, Georgia St	786
Lou Henson, New Mexico St	762
Eddie Sutton, Oklahoma St	724
John Chaney, Temple	692
Lute Olson, Arizona	690
Mike Krzyzewski, Duke	663
Jim Calhoun, Connecticut	647
Jim Boeheim, Syracuse	653

Note: Includes record at 4-year colleges only.

WINNING PERCENTAGE

COACH AND TEAM	YRS	W	L	PCT
Roy Williams, Kansas	15	418	101	.805
Jim Boeheim, Syracuse	27	653	226	.743
Lute Olson, Arizona	30	690	240	.742
Rick Majerus, Utah	19	407	142	.741
Mike Krzyzewski, Duke	28	663	234	.739
Bob Huggins, Cincinnati	22	517	184	.738
Rick Pitino, Louisville	17	396	144	.733
Bob Knight, Texas Tech	37	809	311	.722
John Chaney, Temple	31	692	269	.720
Tom Izzo, Michigan St	8	189	78	.708

Note: Minimum 5 years as a Division I head coach; includes record at 4-year colleges only.

ALLTIME WINNINGEST MEN'S DIVISION I COACHES

	W
Dean Smith (N Carolina)	879
Adolph Rupp (Kentucky)	876
Jim Phelan (Mt. St. Mary's)	830
Bob Knight (Army, Indiana, Texas Tech)	809
Lefty Driesell (Davidson, Maryland, James Madison, Georgia St)	786
Jerry Tarkanian (Long Beach St, UNLV, Fresno St)	778
Hank Iba (NW Missouri St, Colorado, Oklahoma St)	767
Lou Henson (Hardin-Simmons, New Mexico St, Illinois)	762
Ed Diddle (Western Kentucky)	759
Phog Allen (Baker, Kansas, Haskell, Central Missouri St, Kansas)	746
Norm Stewart (Northern Iowa, Missouri)	731
Eddie Sutton (Creighton, Arkansas, Kentucky, Oklahoma St)	724
Ray Meyer (DePaul)	724
Don Haskins (UTEP)	719
John Chaney (Cheyney St, Temple)	692
Denny Crum (Louisville)	675

WINNING PERCENTAGE

COACH (TEAM, YEARS)	YRS	W	L	PCT
Clair Bee (Rider 29–31, LIU-Brooklyn 32–45, 46–51)	21	412	87	.826
Adolph Rupp (Kentucky 31–72)	41	876	190	.822
Roy Williams (Kansas 89–)	15	418	101	.805
John Wooden (Indiana St 47–48, UCLA 49–75)	29	664	162	.804
John Kresse (Charleston 80–02)	23	560	143	.797
Jerry Tarkanian (Long Beach St 69–73, UNLV 74–92, Fresno St 95–02)	31	778	202	.794
Dean Smith (N Carolina 62–97)	36	879	254	.776
Harry Fisher (Columbia 07–16, Army 22–23, 25)	13	147	44	.770
Frank Keaney (Rhode Island 21–48)	27	387	117	.768
George Keogan (St. Louis 16, Allegheny 19, Valparaiso 20–21, Notre Dame 24–43)	24	385	117	.767
Jack Ramsay (St. Joseph's [PA] 56–66)	11	231	71	.765
Vic Bubas (Duke 60–69)	10	213	67	.761
Charles (Chick) Davies (Duquesne 25–43, 47–48)	21	314	106	.748
Ray Mears (Wittenberg 57–62, Tennessee 63–77)	21	399	135	.747
Jim Boeheim (Syracuse 77–)	27	653	226	.743
Lute Olson (Long Beach St 73–74, Iowa 74–83, Arizona 83–)	30	690	240	.742
Rick Majerus (Marquette 84–86, Ball St 88–89, Utah 90–)	19	407	142	.741
Al McGuire (Belmont Abbey 58–64, Marquette 65–77)	20	405	143	.739
Everett Case (N Carolina St 47–64)	18	376	133	.739
Phog Allen (Baker 06–08, Kansas 08–09, Haskell 09, Cent MO St 13–19, Kansas 20–56)	48	746	264	.739
Mike Krzyzewski (Army 76–80, Duke 81–)	28	663	234	.739

Note: Minimum 10 head coaching seasons in Division I.

NCAA WOMEN'S DIVISION I CHAMPIONSHIP RESULTS

YEAR	WINNER	SCORE	RUNNER-UP	WINNING COACH
1982	Louisiana Tech	76–62	Cheyney	Sonja Hogg
1983	Southern Cal	69–67	Louisiana Tech	Linda Sharp
1984	Southern Cal	72–61	Tennessee	Linda Sharp
1985	Old Dominion	70–65	Georgia	Marianne Stanley
1986	Texas	97–81	Southern Cal	Jody Conradt
1987	Tennessee	67–44	Louisiana Tech	Pat Summitt
1988	Louisiana Tech	56–54	Auburn	Leon Barmore
1989	Tennessee	76–60	Auburn	Pat Summitt
1990	Stanford	88–81	Auburn	Tara VanDerveer
1991	Tennessee	70–67 (OT)	Virginia	Pat Summitt
1992	Stanford	78–62	Western Kentucky	Tara VanDerveer
1993	Texas Tech	84–82	Ohio State	Marsha Sharp
1994	N Carolina	60–59	Louisiana Tech	Sylvia Hatchell
1995	Connecticut	70–64	Tennessee	Geno Auriemma
1996	Tennessee	83–65	Georgia	Pat Summitt
1997	Tennessee	68–59	Old Dominion	Pat Summitt
1998	Tennessee	93–75	Louisiana Tech	Pat Summitt
1999	Purdue	62–45	Duke	Carolyn Peck
2000	Connecticut	71–52	Tennessee	Geno Auriemma
2001	Notre Dame	68–66	Purdue	Muffet McGraw
2002	Connecticut	82–70	Oklahoma	Geno Auriemma
2003	Connecticut	73–68	Tennessee	Geno Auriemma

NCAA WOMEN'S DIVISION I ALLTIME INDIVIDUAL LEADERS

SINGLE-GAME RECORDS

SCORING HIGHS

PTS	PLAYER AND TEAM VS OPPONENT	YEAR
60	Cindy Brown, Long Beach St vs San Jose St	1987
58	Kim Perrot, SW Louisiana vs SE Louisiana	1990
58	Lorri Bauman, Drake vs SW Missouri St	1984
56	Jackie Stiles, SW Missouri St vs Evansville	2000
55	Patricia Hoskins, Mississippi Valley vs Southern-BR	1989
55	Patricia Hoskins, Mississippi Valley vs Alabama St	1989
54	Anjinea Hopson, Grambling vs Jackson St	1994
54	Mary Lowry, Baylor vs Texas	1994
54	Wanda Ford, Drake vs SW Missouri St	1986

Three tied with 53.

REBOUNDS

REB	PLAYER AND TEAM VS OPPONENT	YEAR
40	Deborah Temple, Delta St vs AL-Birmingham	1983
37	Rosina Pearson, Bethune-Cookman vs Florida Memorial	1985
33	Maureen Formico, Pepperdine vs Loyola (CA)	1985
31	Darlene Beale, Howard vs S Carolina St	1987
30	Cindy Bonforte, Wagner vs Queens (NY)	1983
30	Kayone Hankins, New Orleans vs. Nicholls St	1994
30	Wanda Ford, Drake vs Eastern Illinois	1985
30	Jennifer Butler, Massachusetts vs Florida	2003

Three tied with 29.

ASSISTS

A	PLAYER AND TEAM VS OPPONENT	YEAR
23	Michelle Burden, Kent St vs Ball St	1991
22	Shawn Monday, Tennessee Tech vs Morehead St	1988
22	Veronica Pettry, Loyola (IL) vs Detroit	1989
22	Tine Freil, Pacific vs Wichita St	1991
21	Tine Freil, Pacific vs Fresno St	1992
21	Amy Bauer, Wisconsin vs Detroit	1989
21	Neacole Hall, Alabama St vs Southern-BR	1989

Six tied with 20.

SINGLE SEASON RECORDS

POINTS

PLAYER AND TEAM	YEAR	GP	FG	3FG	FT	PTS
Jackie Stiles, SW Missouri St	2001	35	365	65	267	1062
Cindy Brown, Long Beach St	1987	35	362	—	250	974
Genia Miller, Cal St-Fullerton	1991	33	376	0	217	969
Sheryl Swoopes, Texas Tech	1993	34	356	32	211	955
Andrea Congreaves, Mercer	1992	28	353	77	142	925
Wanda Ford, Drake	1986	30	390	—	139	919
Chamique Holdsclaw, Tennessee	1998	39	370	9	166	915
Barbara Kennedy, Clemson	1982	31	392	—	124	908
Patricia Hoskins, Mississippi Valley	1989	27	345	13	205	908
LaTaunya Pollard, Long Beach St	1983	31	376	—	155	907

SCORING AVERAGE

PLAYER AND TEAM	YEAR	GP	FG	3FG	FT	PTS	AVG
Patricia Hoskins, Mississippi Valley	1989	27	345	13	205	908	33.6
Andrea Congreaves, Mercer	1992	28	353	77	142	925	33.0
Deborah Temple, Delta St	1984	28	373	—	127	873	31.2
Andrea Congreaves, Mercer	1993	26	302	51	150	805	31.0
Wanda Ford, Drake	1986	30	390	—	139	919	30.6
Anucha Browne, Northwestern	1985	28	341	—	173	855	30.5
LeChandra LeDay, Grambling	1988	28	334	36	146	850	30.4
Jackie Stiles, SW MIssouri St	2001	35	365	65	267	1062	30.3
Kim Perrot, Southwestern Louisiana	1990	28	308	95	128	839	30.0
Tina Hutchinson, San Diego St	1984	30	383	—	132	898	29.9
Jan Jensen, Drake	1991	30	358	6	166	888	29.6
Genia Miller, Cal St-Fullerton	1991	33	376	0	217	969	29.4
Barbara Kennedy, Clemson	1982	31	392	—	124	908	29.3
LaTaunya Pollard, Long Beach St	1983	31	376	—	155	907	29.3
Lisa McMullen, Alabama St	1991	28	285	126	119	815	29.1

REBOUNDS

PLAYER AND TEAM	YEAR	GP	REB	PLAYER AND TEAM	YEAR	GP	REB
Wanda Ford, Drake	1985	30	534	Rosina Pearson, Beth.-Cookman	1985	26	480
Wanda Ford, Drake	1986	30	506	Patricia Hoskins, Miss Valley	1987	28	476
Anne Donovan, Old Dominion	1983	35	504	Cheryl Miller, Southern Cal	1985	30	474
Darlene Jones, Miss Valley	1983	31	487	Darlene Beale, Howard	1987	29	459
Melanie Simpson, Okla. City	1982	37	481	Olivia Bradley, W Virginia	1985	30	458

REBOUND AVERAGE

PLAYER AND TEAM	YEAR	GP	REB	AVG
Rosina Pearson, Bethune-Cookman	1985	26	480	18.5
Wanda Ford, Drake	1985	30	534	17.8
Katie Beck, E Tennessee St	1988	25	441	17.6
DeShawne Blocker, E Tennessee St	1994	26	450	17.3
Patricia Hoskins, Mississippi Valley	1987	28	476	17.0
Wanda Ford, Drake	1986	30	506	16.9
Patricia Hoskins, Mississippi Valley	1989	27	440	16.3
Joy Kellogg, Oklahoma City	1984	23	373	16.2
Deborah Mitchell, Mississippi Coll.	1983	28	447	16.0
Cheryl Miller, Southern California	1985	30	474	15.8

SINGLE SEASON RECORDS (CONT)

FIELD-GOAL PERCENTAGE

PLAYER AND TEAM	YEAR	GP	FG	FGA	PCT
Myndee Larsen, Southern Utah	1998	28	249	344	72.4
Chantelle Anderson, Vanderbilt	2001	34	292	404	72.3
Deneka Knowles, Southeastern La.	1996	26	199	276	72.1
Barbara Farris, Tulane	1998	27	151	210	71.9
Renay Adams, Tennessee Tech	1991	30	185	258	71.7
Regina Days, Georgia Southern	1986	27	234	332	70.5
Kim Wood, WI-Green Bay	1994	27	188	271	69.4
Kelly Lyons, Old Dominion	1990	31	308	444	69.4
Alisha Hill, Howard	1995	28	194	281	69.0
Ruth Riley, Notre Dame	1999	31	198	290	68.3

Based on qualifiers for annual championship.

FREE-THROW PERCENTAGE

PLAYER AND TEAM	YEAR	GP	FT	FTA	PCT
Ginny Doyle, Richmond	1992	29	96	101	95.0
Jill Marano, La Salle	2003	29	88	93	94.6
Sue Bird, Connecticut	2002	39	98	104	94.2
Paula Corder-King, SE Missouri St	1999	28	111	118	94.1
Kandi Brown, Morehead St	2003	28	104	111	93.7
Linda Cyborski, Delaware	1991	29	74	79	93.7
Kandi Brown, Morehead St	2002	29	74	79	93.7
Paula Corder-King, SE Missouri St	2000	27	69	74	93.2
Jennifer Howard, N Carolina St	1994	27	118	127	92.9
Keely Feeman, Cincinnati	1986	30	76	82	92.7

Based on qualifiers for annual championship.

CAREER RECORDS

POINTS

PLAYER AND TEAM	YRS	GP	PTS
Jackie Stiles, SW Missouri St	1997–01	129	3393
Patricia Hoskins, Mississippi Valley	1985–89	110	3122
Lorri Bauman, Drake	1981–84	120	3115
Chamique Holdsclaw, Tennessee	1995–99	148	3025
Cheryl Miller, Southern Cal	1983–86	128	3018
Cindy Blodgett, Maine	1994–98	118	3005
Valorie Whiteside, Appalachian St.	1984–88	116	2944
Joyce Walker, Louisiana St	1981–84	117	2906
Sandra Hodge, New Orleans	1981–84	107	2860
Andrea Congreaves, Mercer	1989–93	108	2796

SCORING AVERAGE

PLAYER AND TEAM	YRS	GP	FG	3FG	FT	PTS	AVG
Patricia Hoskins, Mississippi Valley	1985–89	110	1196	24	706	3122	28.4
Sandra Hodge, New Orleans	1981–84	107	1194	—	472	2860	26.7
Jackie Stiles, SW Missouri St	1997–01	129	1160	221	852	3393	26.3
Lorri Bauman, Drake	1981–84	120	1104	—	907	3115	26.0
Andrea Congreaves, Mercer	1989–93	108	1107	153	429	2796	25.9
Cindy Blodgett, Maine	1994–98	118	1055	219	676	3005	25.5
Valorie Whiteside, Appalachian St	1984–88	116	1153	0	638	2944	25.4
Joyce Walker, Louisiana St	1981–84	117	1259	—	388	2906	24.8
Tarcha Hollis, Grambling	1988–91	85	904	3	247	2058	24.2
Korie Hlede, Duquesne	1994–98	109	1045	162	379	2631	24.1

NCAA MEN'S DIVISION II CHAMPIONSHIP RESULTS

YEAR	WINNER	SCORE	RUNNER-UP	THIRD PLACE	FOURTH PLACE
1957	Wheaton (IL)	89–65	Kentucky Wesleyan	Mt St Mary's (MD)	Cal St-Los Angeles
1958	S Dakota	75–53	St. Michael's	Evansville	Wheaton (IL)
1959	Evansville	83–67	SW Missouri St	N Carolina A&T	Cal St-Los Angeles
1960	Evansville	90–69	Chapman	Kentucky Wesleyan	Cornell College
1961	Wittenberg	42–38	SE Missouri St	S Dakota St	Mt St Mary's (MD)
1962	Mt St Mary's (MD)	58–57 (OT)	Cal St-Sacramento	Southern Illinois	Nebraska Wesleyan
1963	S Dakota St	44–42	Wittenberg	Oglethorpe	Southern Illinois
1964	Evansville	72–59	Akron	N Carolina A&T	Northern Iowa
1965	Evansville	85–82 (OT)	Southern Illinois	N Dakota	St Michael's
1966	Kentucky Wesleyan	54–51	Southern Illinois	Akron	N Dakota
1967	Winston-Salem	77–74	SW Missouri St	Kentucky Wesleyan	Illinois St
1968	Kentucky Wesleyan	63–52	Indiana St	Trinity (TX)	Ashland
1969	Kentucky Wesleyan	75–71	SW Missouri St	†Vacated	Ashland
1970	Philadelphia Textile	76–65	Tennessee St	UC-Riverside	Buffalo St
1971	Evansville	97–82	Old Dominion	†Vacated	Kentucky Wesleyan
1972	Roanoke	84–72	Akron	Tennessee St	Eastern Mich
1973	Kentucky Wesleyan	78–76 (OT)	Tennessee St	Assumption	Brockport St
1974	Morgan St	67–52	SW Missouri St	Assumption	New Orleans
1975	Old Dominion	76–74	New Orleans	Assumption	TN-Chattanooga
1976	Puget Sound	83–74	TN-Chattanooga	Eastern Illinois	Old Dominion
1977	TN-Chattanooga	71–62	Randolph-Macon	N Alabama	Sacred Heart
1978	Cheyney	47–40	WI-Green Bay	Eastern Illinois	Central Florida
1979	N Alabama	64–50	WI-Green Bay	Cheyney	Bridgeport
1980	Virginia Union	80–74	New York Tech	Florida Southern	N Alabama
1981	Florida Southern	73–68	Mt St Mary's (MD)	Cal Poly-SLO	WI-Green Bay
1982	District of Columbia	73–63	Florida Southern	Kentucky Wesleyan	Cal St-Bakersfield
1983	Wright St	92–73	District of Columbia	*Cal St-Bakersfield	*Morningside
1984	Central Missouri St	81–77	St. Augustine's	*Kentucky Wesleyan	*N Alabama
1985	Jacksonville St	74–73	S Dakota St	*Kentucky Wesleyan	*Mt St. Mary's (MD)
1986	Sacred Heart	93–87	SE Missouri St	*Cheyney	*Florida Southern
1987	Kentucky Wesleyan	92–74	Gannon	*Delta St	*Eastern Montana
1988	Lowell	75–72	AK-Anchorage	Florida Southern	Troy St
1989	N Carolina Central	73–46	SE Missouri St	UC-Riverside	Jacksonville St
1990	Kentucky Wesleyan	93–79	Cal St-Bakersfield	N Dakota	Morehouse
1991	N Alabama	79–72	Bridgeport (CT)	*Cal St-Bakersfield	*Virginia Union
1992	Virginia Union	100–75	Bridgeport (CT)	*Cal St-Bakersfield	*California (PA)
1993	Cal St-Bakersfield	85–72	Troy St (AL)	*New Hampshire Coll	*Wayne St (MI)
1994	Cal St-Bakersfield	92–86	Southern Indiana	*New Hampshire Coll	*Washburn
1995	Southern Indiana	71–63	UC-Riverside	*Norfolk St	*Indiana (PA)
1996	Fort Hays St	70–63	Northern Kentucky	*California (PA)	*Virginia Union
1997	Cal St-Bakersfield	57–56	Northern Kentucky	*Lynn	*Salem-Teikyo
1998	UC-Davis	83–77	Kentucky Wesleyan	*St. Rose	*Virginia Union
1999	Kentucky Wesleyan	75–60	Metropolitan St	*Truman St	*Florida Southern
2000	Metropolitan St	97–79	Kentucky Wesleyan	*Missouri Southern	*Seattle Pacific
2001	Kentucky Wesleyan	72–63	Washburn	*Western Washington	*Tampa
2002	Metropolitan St	80–72	Kentucky Wesleyan	*Shaw	*Indiana (PA)
2003	Northeastern St (OK)	75–64	Kentucky Wesleyan	*Bowie St	*Queens (NC)

*Indicates tied for third. †Student-athletes representing American International in 1969 and Southwestern Louisiana in 1971 were declared ineligible subsequent to the tournament. Under NCAA rules, the teams' and ineligible student-athletes' records were deleted, and the teams' places in the final standings were vacated.

NCAA MEN'S DIVISION II ALLTIME INDIVIDUAL LEADERS

SINGLE-GAME SCORING HIGHS

PTS	PLAYER AND TEAM VS OPPONENT	DATE
113	Bevo Francis, Rio Grande vs Hillsdale	1954
84	Bevo Francis, Rio Grande vs Alliance	1954
82	Bevo Francis, Rio Grande vs Bluffton	1954
80	Paul Crissman, Southern Cal Col vs Pacific Christian	1966
77	William English, Winston-Salem vs Fayetteville St	1968

NCAA MEN'S DIVISION II
ALLTIME INDIVIDUAL LEADERS (CONT.)

SINGLE SEASON RECORDS

SCORING AVERAGE

PLAYER AND TEAM	YEAR	GP	FG	FT	PTS	AVG
Bevo Francis, Rio Grande	1954	27	444	367	1255	46.5
Earl Glass, Mississippi Industrial	1963	19	322	171	815	42.9
Earl Monroe, Winston-Salem	1967	32	509	311	1329	41.5
John Rinka, Kenyon	1970	23	354	234	942	41.0
Willie Shaw, Lane	1964	18	303	121	727	40.4

REBOUND AVERAGE

PLAYER AND TEAM	YEAR	GP	REB	AVG
Tom Hart, Middlebury	1956	21	620	29.5
Tom Hart, Middlebury	1955	22	649	29.5
Frank Stronczek, American Int'l	1966	26	717	27.6
R.C. Owens, College of Idaho	1954	25	677	27.1
Maurice Stokes, St Francis (PA)	1954	26	689	26.5

ASSISTS

PLAYER AND TEAM	YEAR	GP	A
Steve Ray, Bridgeport	1989	32	400
Steve Ray, Bridgeport	1990	33	385
Tony Smith, Pfeiffer	1992	35	349
Jim Ferrer, Bentley	1989	31	309
Rob Paternostro, New Hamp. Coll.	1995	33	309

ASSIST AVERAGE

PLAYER AND TEAM	YEAR	GP	A	AVG
Steve Ray, Bridgeport	1989	32	400	12.5
Steve Ray, Bridgeport	1990	33	385	11.7
Demetri Beekman, Assumption	1993	23	264	11.5
Ernest Jenkins, NM Highlands	1995	27	291	10.8
Brian Gregory, Oakland	1989	28	300	10.7

FIELD-GOAL PERCENTAGE

PLAYER AND TEAM	YEAR	PCT
Todd Linder, Tampa	1987	75.2
Maurice Stafford, N Alabama	1984	75.0
Matthew Cornegay, Tuskegee	1982	74.8
Brian Moten, W Georgia	1992	73.4
Ed Phillips, Alabama A&M	1968	73.3

FREE-THROW PERCENTAGE

PLAYER AND TEAM	YEAR	PCT
Paul Cluxton, N Kentucky	1997	100.0
Tomas Rimkus, Pace	1997	95.6
C.J. Cowgill, Chaminade	2001	95.0
Billy Newton, Morgan St	1976	94.4
Kent Andrews, McNeese St	1968	94.4

CAREER RECORDS

POINTS

PLAYER AND TEAM	YRS	PTS
Travis Grant, Kentucky St	1969–72	4045
Bob Hopkins, Grambling	1953–56	3759
Tony Smith, Pfeiffer	1989–92	3350
Earnest Lee, Clark Atlanta	1984–87	3298
Joe Miller, Alderson-Broaddus	1954–57	3294

CAREER SCORING AVERAGE

PLAYER AND TEAM	YRS	GP	PTS	AVG
Travis Grant, Kentucky St	1969–72	121	4045	33.4
John Rinka, Kenyon	1967–70	99	3251	32.8
Florindo Vieira, Quinnipiac	1954–57	69	2263	32.8
Willie Shaw, Lane	1961–64	76	2379	31.3
Mike Davis, Virginia Union	1966–69	89	2758	31.0

REBOUND AVERAGE

PLAYER AND TEAM	YRS	GP	REB	AVG
Tom Hart, Middlebury	1953, 55–56	63	1738	27.6
Maurice Stokes, St. Francis (PA)	1953–55	72	1812	25.2
Frank Stronczek, American Int'l	1965–67	62	1549	25.0
Bill Thieben, Hofstra	1954–56	76	1837	24.2
Hank Brown, Lowell Tech	1965–67	49	1129	23.0

NCAA MEN'S DIVISION II
ALLTIME INDIVIDUAL LEADERS (CONT.)

CAREER RECORDS (CONT.)

ASSISTS

PLAYER AND TEAM	YRS	A
Demetri Beekman, Assumption 1990–93	1044
Adam Kaufman, Edinboro..............1998–01	936
Rob Paternostro, New Hamp. Coll. ...1992–95	919
Gallagher Driscoll, St. Rose 1989–92	878
Tony Smith, Pfeiffer......................1989–92	828

ASSIST AVERAGE

PLAYER AND TEAM	YRS	GP	A	AVG
Steve Ray, Bridgeport 1989–90	65	785	12.1
Demetri Beekman, Assumption...1990–93	119	1044	8.8
Ernest Jenkins, NM Highlands .1992–95	84	699	8.3
Adam Kaufman, Edinboro........1998–01	116	936	8.1
Mark Benson, Texas A&I.........1989–91	86	674	7.8

Note: Minimum 550 Assists.

FIELD-GOAL PERCENTAGE

PLAYER AND TEAM	YRS	PCT
Todd Linder, Tampa......................1984–87	70.8
Tom Schurfranz, Bellarmine 1989–92	70.2
Chad Scott, California (PA)............1991–94	70.0
Ed Phillips, Alabama, A&M 1968–71	68.9
Ulysses Hackett, SC-Spartanburg ..1990–92	67.9

Note: Minimum 400 FGM.

FREE-THROW PERCENTAGE

PLAYER AND TEAM	YRS	PCT
Paul Cluxton, N Kentucky 1994–97	93.5
Kent Andrews, McNeese St.......1967–69	91.6
Jon Hagen, Mankato St..............1963–65	90.0
Dave Reynolds, Davis & Elkins...1986–89	89.3
Michael Shue, Lock Haven.........1994–97	88.5

Note: Minimum 250 FTM.

NCAA MEN'S DIVISION III
CHAMPIONSHIP RESULTS

YEAR	WINNER	SCORE	RUNNER-UP	THIRD PLACE	FOURTH PLACE
1975	LeMoyne-Owen	57–54	Glassboro St	Augustana (IL)	Brockport St
1976	Scranton	60–57	Wittenberg	Augustana (IL)	Plattsburgh St
1977	Wittenberg	79–66	Oneonta St	Scranton	Hamline
1978	North Park	69–57	Widener	Albion	Stony Brook
1979	North Park	66–62	Potsdam St	Franklin & Marshall	Centre
1980	North Park	83–76	Upsala	Wittenberg	Longwood
1981	Potsdam St	67–65 (OT)	Augustana (IL)	Ursinus	Otterbein
1982	Wabash	83–62	Potsdam St	Brooklyn	Cal St-Stanislaus
1983	Scranton	64–63	Wittenberg	Roanoke	WI–Whitewater
1984	WI–Whitewater	103–86	Clark (MA)	DePauw	Upsala
1985	North Park	72–71	Potsdam St	Nebraska Wesleyan	Widener
1986	Potsdam St	76–73	LeMoyne-Owen	Nebraska Wesleyan	Jersey City St
1987	North Park	106–100	Clark (MA)	Wittenberg	Stockton St
1988	Ohio Wesleyan	92–70	Scranton	Nebraska Wesleyan	Hartwick
1989	WI–Whitewater	94–86	Trenton St	Southern Maine	Centre
1990	Rochester	43–42	DePauw	Washington (MD)	Calvin
1991	WI–Platteville	81–74	Franklin & Marshall	Otterbein	Ramapo (NJ)
1992	Calvin	62–49	Rochester	WI–Platteville	Jersey City St
1993	Ohio Northern	71–68	Augustana	Mass–Dartmouth	Rowan
1994	Lebanon Valley Coll	66–59 (OT)	New York University	Wittenberg	St Thomas (MN)
1995	WI–Platteville	69–55	Manchester	Rowan	Trinity (CT)
1996	Rowan	100–93	Hope (MI)	Illinois Wesleyan	Franklin & Marshall
1997	Illinois Wesleyan	89–86	Nebraska Wesleyan	Williams	Alvernia
1998	WI–Platteville	69–56	Hope (MI)	Williams	Wilkes
1999	WI–Platteville	76–75 (2 OT)	Hampden-Sydney	William Paterson	Connecticut Coll.
2000	Calvin	79–74	WI–Eau Claire	Salem St	Franklin & Marshall
2001	Catholic	76–62	William Paterson	*Illinois Wesleyan	*Ohio Northern
2002	Otterbein	102–83	Elizabethtown	Carthage	Rochester
2003	Williams	67–65	Gustavus Adolphus	Wooster	Hampden Sydney

NCAA MEN'S DIVISION III
ALLTIME INDIVIDUAL LEADERS

SINGLE-GAME SCORING HIGHS

PTS	PLAYER AND TEAM VS OPPONENT	YEAR
77	Jeff Clement, Grinnell vs Illinois College	1998
69	Steve Diekmann, Grinnell vs Simpson	1995
63	Joe DeRoche, Thomas vs St. Joseph's (ME)	1988
62	Shannon Lilly, Bishop vs Southwest Assembly of God	1983
61	Steve Honderd, Calvin vs Kalamazoo	1993
61	Dana Wilson, Husson vs Ricker	1974
61	Joshua Metzger, Wisconsin Lutheran vs Grinnell	2000

SINGLE SEASON RECORDS

SCORING AVERAGE

PLAYER AND TEAM	YEAR	GP	FG	FT	PTS	AVG
Steve Diekmann, Grinnell	1995	20	223	162	745	37.3
Rickey Sutton, Lyndon St	1976	14	207	93	507	36.2
Shannon Lilly, Bishop	1983	26	345	218	908	34.9
Dana Wilson, Husson	1974	20	288	122	698	34.9
Rickey Sutton, Lyndon St	1977	16	223	112	558	34.9

REBOUND AVERAGE

PLAYER AND TEAM	YEAR	GP	REB	AVG
Joe Manley, Bowie St	1976	29	579	20.0
Fred Petty, New Hampshire College	1974	22	436	19.8
Larry Williams, Pratt	1977	24	457	19.0
Charles Greer, Thomas	1977	17	318	18.7
Larry Parker, Plattsburgh St	1975	23	430	18.7

ASSISTS

PLAYER AND TEAM	YEAR	GP	A
Robert James, Kean	1989	29	391
Tennyson Whitted, Ramapo	2002	29	319
Ricky Spicer, WI-Whitewater	1989	31	295
Joe Marcotte, NJ Tech	1995	30	292
Andre Bolton, Chris. Newport	1996	30	289

ASSIST AVERAGE

PLAYER AND TEAM	YEAR	GP	A	AVG
Robert James, Kean	1989	29	391	13.5
Albert Kirchner, Mt. St. Vincent	1990	24	267	11.1
Tennyson Whitted, Ramapo	2002	29	319	11.0
Ron Torgalski, Hamilton	1989	26	275	10.6
Louis Adams, Rust	1989	22	227	10.3

FIELD-GOAL PERCENTAGE

PLAYER AND TEAM	YEAR	PCT
Travis Weiss, St. John's (MN)	1994	76.6
Pete Metzelaars, Wabash	1982	75.3
Tony Rychlec, Mass. Maritime	1981	74.9
Tony Rychlec, Mass. Maritime	1982	73.1
Russ Newnan, Menlo	1991	73.0

FREE-THROW PERCENTAGE

PLAYER AND TEAM	YEAR	PCT
Korey Coon, IL Wesleyan	2000	96.3
Chanse Young, Manchester	1998	95.6
Andy Enfield, Johns Hopkins	1991	95.3
Nick Wilkins, Coe	2003	95.7
Chris Carideo, Widener	1992	95.2
Yudi Teichman, Yeshiva	1989	95.2

CAREER RECORDS

POINTS

PLAYER AND TEAM	YRS	PTS
Andre Foreman, Salisbury St	1989–92	2940
Lamont Strothers, Chris. Newport	1988–91	2709
Matt Hancock, Colby	1987–90	2678
Scott Fitch, Geneseo St	1990–94	2634
Greg Grant, Trenton St	1987–89	2611

CAREER SCORING AVERAGE

PLAYER AND TEAM	YRS	GP	AVG
Dwain Govan, Bishop	1974–75	55	32.8
Dave Russell, Shepherd	1974–75	60	30.6
Rickey Sutton, Lyndon St	1976–79	80	29.7
John Atkins, Knoxville	1976–78	70	28.7
Steve Petnik, Windham	1974–77	76	27.6

REBOUND AVERAGE

PLAYER AND TEAM	YRS	GP	REB	AVG
Larry Parker, Plattsburgh St	1975–78	85	1482	17.4
Charles Greer, Thomas	1975–77	58	926	16.0
Willie Parr, LeMoyne-Owen	1974–76	76	1182	15.6
Michael Smith, Hamilton	1989–92	107	1632	15.2
Dave Kufeld, Yeshiva	1977–80	81	1222	15.1

ASSIST AVERAGE

PLAYER AND TEAM	YRS	AVG
Phil Dixon, Shenandoah	1993–96	8.6
Steve Artis, Chris. Newport	1990–93	8.1
David Genovese, Mt. St. Vincent	1992–95	7.5
Kevin Root, Eureka	1989–91	7.1
Dennis Jacobi, Bowdoin	1989–92	7.1

SI's TOP 50 SPORTS COLLEGES

1	**STANFORD**	22 Top 10 teams, including national champion cross country and water polo; Cardinal won its ninth straight Sears Cup, lost in Finals of 2003 CWS.
2	**TEXAS**	First Div. I-A school to have FB in the Top 10, hoops go to Final Four and baseball advance to the College World Series; basketball player of the year T.J. Ford.
3	**OKLAHOMA**	Basketball made the Elite Eight, while FB finished No. 8; Men's gymnastics repeated as national champs; OU has a top 10 golf course.
4	**FLORIDA**	Twelve Gators teams finished in the top 25, excellent women's programs and rabid student fans; 85% of students are involved in rec and intramural sports.
5	**OHIO STATE**	National FB champs; 10 top 20 teams; students jump in freezing lake for good luck in football against Michigan.
6	**LOUISIANA STATE**	Tigers won women's indoor track; finished No. 3 in women's basketball; few colleges rock harder than Tiger Stadium and Deaf Dome.

7	**SOUTH CAROLINA**	Gamecocks finished No. 3 in women's indoor track; No. 15 in baseball; No. 16 in women's hoops; opened a $48 million rec center in February.
8	**MINNESOTA**	Hockey team defended their NCAA title for its fifth overall championship; eight other teams were in top 25; the "U" has glorious football history.
9	**NORTH CAROLINA**	Tar Heels finished top 20 in 10 sports; women's soccer went to Final Four; basketball was 19-16, but stole Roy Williams from Kansas.
10	**TENNESSEE**	Women's hoops was No. 2 and went to Final Four; men's indoor track No. 5; Vols are so flush with sports riches that they have two Olympic-sized pools.
11	**MICHIGAN**	Wolverines led the nation in football attendance for the 28th time in 29 years; eight teams made the Top 10 and four individuals won national titles.
12	**UCLA**	SI's No. 1 school in '97 had 9 top 10 teams last year, but none in major sports.; softball won the Women's College World Series.
13	**GEORGIA**	Three minor-sports made top 10, FB ranked No. 3; has best rec center (430,000 sq. ft., three pools).
14	**COLORADO**	Cross country runner Jorge Torres won individual national title; top 20 in FB; Boulder the running capital of the U.S.
15	**NOTRE DAME**	Baseball and hoops made NCAAs; resurgent year for Tyrone Willingham and FB; intramurals include full-pads tackle FB.
16	**MIAMI**	Football finished No. 2; hoops couldn't make NCAAs; fun IM arena flag FB; beach 15 minutes away.
17	**NEBRASKA**	Top 15 in baseball and four women's sports, Flag-FB hotbed; one bogey: Johnny Carson's alma mater next to last in Big 12 golf.
18	**ARIZONA**	Three top 10 women's teams; No. 2 in hoops; disabled sports big; Annika Sorenstam, Trevor Hoffman alums.
19	**DUKE**	Top 10 in women's golf, tennis and lax and two top 10 hoops teams; Achilles heel FB (2-10); alums Elton Brand, John Feinstein.

BEST TAILGATING

[OLE MISS]

MIKE MAPLE

ON FOOTBALL Saturdays as many as 25,000 Mississippi supporters gather for pregame food and drink in the Grove, 10 acres of lawn, shaded by stately oaks, in the heart of the university's campus in Oxford. There is no more beautiful spot to tailgate, nor one richer in tradition; the Grove has been the site of pregame picnicking for more than half a century. The fans start arriving by car at 4:00 a.m., many dressed formally, as if they were headed to a wedding. They greet old classmates and friends amid barbeque grills, silver candelabras and plenty of bourbon. Two hours before kickoff they cheer wildly as Rebels players march by on their way to the stadium. After the game, win or lose, many in the crowd return to the Grove to party until midnight. They have one thing in common: They can't wait until the next football Saturday. —*Glenn Kaplan*

20	**SOUTHERN CALIFORNIA**	Women's golf won NCAAs; Carson Palmer was NFL's No. 1 draft pick; No. 4 in FB; has most men's team championships (71).
21	**ILLINOIS**	Men's tennis went undefeated, swept NCAA team, singles and doubles crowns; Orange Krush fans rule; claims to have invented homecoming (1910).
22	**SYRACUSE**	NCAA champ in hoops; men's lacrosse went to its 21st straight Final Four; zip code is 13244 to honor 44 worn by Jim Brown and others.

23	**OREGON**	Pole vaulter Becky Holliday, ranked fourth in the world, broke the collegiate record with her clearance of 14-8; heavenly running trails; best sports-management.
24	**MARYLAND**	Top 20 in hoops and FB; women No. 5 in field hockey, No. 2 in lax and No. 3 in men's soccer; alums Steve Francis, Connie Chung.
25	**ARIZONA STATE**	Alma mater of Barry Bonds, Phil Mickelson; top 20 in baseball, golf, six other sports; fans toss tortillas when FB team scores.
26	**ALABAMA**	No. 2 in gymnastics; top 15 in men's and women's swimming; NFL draftees every year since '71; FB coach Mike Price dismissed.
27	**CLEMSON**	Tigers top 5 in baseball, track; golf won NCAAs; FB won a minor bowl; engineering students won their third national concrete canoe championship.
28	**BRIGHAM YOUNG**	Cougar women won their second consecutive NCAA cross country title, made hoops tournament; 12 of 19 teams competed in the NCAAs.
29	**MICHIGAN STATE**	Hockey team finished ranked 15th; hoops made the Elite Eight; Izzone cheering section good n' rowdy.
30	**FLORIDA STATE**	Politically incorrect Seminoles top 15 in FB, baseball; have $60 million in facilities renovations in the works; IM go-kart racing.
31	**UCONN**	Women's hoops (37-1) defended their national title; men made Sweet 16; FB (6-6) struggling since move up to I-A in '99.
32	**PENN STATE**	Six top 10 teams; FB was 9-4 and tailback Larry Johnson won the Maxwell and Walter Camp Player of the Year Awards.
33	**WASHINGTON**	10 teams in top 20; strong crew program: men No. 2 and women No. 3; FB coach Rick Neuheisel fired after gambling controversy.
34	**AUBURN**	No. 1 in men's and women's swimming, top 20 in seven other sports; hoops made Sweet 16; campus museum has Charles Barkley mannequin.
35	**CAL**	Football had decent 7–5 year; softball was runner-up in the Women's College World Series; swimmer Natalie Coughlin a future Olympic star.

36	**ARKANSAS**	Men's indoor track won its 38th national championship; seven of eight men's teams went to the NCAAs.
37	**RICE**	Won College World Series, top 25 in women's track, swimming; inventive Marching Owl Band (MOB) tooted horns despite a 4–7 football season.
38	**GEORGIA TECH**	Top 15 in baseball and golf and top 25 in volleyball; rec center (which houses '96 Olympic pool) tripled to 300,000 sq. ft.
39	**VIRGINIA**	Four top ten teams; lacrosse won NCAA championship; three alums were on U.S. World Cup squad; 94% of students use A+ rec facilities.
40	**WAKE FOREST**	Field hockey won the national title; men's golf ranked No. 3.; championship year for alum Tim Duncan.
41	**HARVARD**	Most varsity teams of any school (41); men's hockey finished No. 10; women's hockey NCAA runner-up; FB went 6-1; women's crew won national championship.
42	**INDIANA**	Hoops exited in second round of NCAA tournament; men's soccer won seventh straight Big 10 title; 50 club sports; Little 500 bike race a gem.
43	**WISCONSIN**	Top 10 in X-C, men's hoops made NCAAs; FB won the Alamo Bowl; invented hockey's "sieve!" chant.
44	**KENTUCKY**	Top 10 in riflery; men's hoops made it to the Elite Eight and women to the Sweet 16; FB was 7–5 but still has one more year of NCAA probation.
45	**TEXAS A&M**	Top 10 in three sports and Top 20 in six; made Sweet 16 in v-ball; 20,000-plus fans go to Midnight Yell Practice for football games; superb rec center.
46	**PURDUE**	Alma mater of 22 astronauts launched six sports into the Top 20, including women's hoops; two campus golf courses; IM home run derby.
47	**KANSAS**	National finalist in basketball; unsurpassed at Midnight Madness; Wilt's alma mater; James Naismith buried five miles from campus.
48	**PEPPERDINE**	Amazing success for school of 3,000; four Top 10 teams; female golfer of the year Katherine Hull; Malibu campus overlooks Pacific.

| 49 | **OKLAHOMA ST.** | Wrestling won national championship under coach of the year John Smith; five Top 20 teams; Cowboys have ice hockey club. |
| 50 | **KANSAS ST.** | Women were ranked No. 8 in hoops and tennis went to Sweet 16; FB finished No. 6; Harleys circle stadium before annual biker-tribute FB game. |

QUIZ TIME!

Alumni Matchup

1) George Steinbrenner

2) Arnold Palmer

3) Dick Vitale

4) Ted Turner

5) Bill Parcells

6) John Madden

A) Cal Poly–San Luis Obispo

B) Wichita State

C) Brown

D) Seton Hall

E) Wake Forest

F) Williams

Who Did What?

1) Orville Redenbacher

2) Tommy Lee Jones

3) Strom Thurmond

4) Dean Cain

5) ESPN's Robin Roberts

6) Andrew Shue

A) Played basketball at Southeastern Louisiana

B) Ran track at Purdue

C) Was All-Ivy football player at Harvard

D) Ran cross-country at Clemson

E) Was All-Ivy soccer player at Dartmouth

F) Was All-America football player at Princeton

ANSWERS: Alumni Matchup 1-F, 2-E, 3-D, 4-C, 5-B, 6-A
Who did what? 1-B, 2-C, 3-D, 4-F, 5-A, 6-E

Golden
AGE

Returning last year's roster nearly intact, the Minnesota Golden Gophers eye a third straight NCAA title

I N 2000, Grant Potulny of Grand Forks, N.D., just across the Red River from Minnesota, became the first non-Minnesotan to play ice hockey for the fabled Golden Gophers program since 1987. From 1971 to '81 Minnesota had done just fine, thank you, relying almost exclusively on home grown talent: The team reached six NCAA title games and won three. Coaches saw no reason to look beyond the Land of 10,000 (usually frozen) Lakes for players.

But after the Gophers failed to win a national title in the 1980s and '90s, new coach Don Lucia decided to risk offending Minnesota's rabid fans by recruiting outside the state. Granted, he didn't go far, but folks took time to adjust to this "foreigner" Potulny in their midst.

But by the time he was a sophomore and had scored the game-winning goal in overtime of the 2001–02 NCAA title game against Maine, why, Minnesota fans embraced Potulny as one of their own. Emboldened by the success of his experiment, coach Lucia cast his recruiting net even farther afield in 2002, bringing in Thomas Vanek, a 6'2", 207-pound forward from Graz, Austria.

Once again, the move paid rich dividends, as Vanek scored 31 goals, including two in the national semis against Michigan, and the game-winner in Minnesota's 5–1 win over New Hampshire for the 2002–03 NCAA hockey title.

FAVORITES

Minnesota's victory over UNH made the Gophers the first team since Boston University in 1971 and '72 to repeat as NCAA champs. And before the final whistle blew at Buffalo's HSBC Arena last April, there was talk on the Minnesota bench of a threepeat, a feat not

MINNESOTA

The most outstanding player of last season's Frozen Four, Vanek scored the game-winner in both the semis and the final. He finished the year with 31 goals and 31 assists.

accomplished since Michigan did it from 1951 to '53. It was not idle chatter, either: Minnesota lost just one player, senior Matt DeMarchi, from the 2002–03 championship team. As DeMarchi himself said, "The future of this team is pretty much unstoppable."

Unless he opts for the NHL draft, in which he would probably be a Top 3 pick, if not No. 1, final four MVP Vanek will be back for his sophomore season. At press time, his plans were to return to Minnesota. Potulny, now the captain, will be back as well, and hopefully healthy—he played in just 23 of the Gophers' 45 games last season, producing 15 goals and eight assists. Goalie Travis Weber, who made 26 saves in the championship game, will once again backstop the D, and the Gophers will welcome another stellar recruiting class, including Ryan Potulny, Grant's brother, who led the USHL (a Tier 1 junior league) in scoring last season.

If you're searching for a team that might derail Minnesota's drive for a third straight championship, look no further than the Gophers' opponent in last year's title tilt, **New Hampshire**. Long a bridesmaid but never a bride, the Wildcats have reached the national semis in four of the past six years,

Ayers and the Wildcats hope to go one win further than last season. A second team All-America last year, the UNH goalie produced a .926 save percentage and a 2.18 goals-against average.

playing in the championship game in 1999 as well as last season. Will 2003–04 be the year they finally break through? Mike Ayers, the 2003 USA Hockey College Player of the Year, certainly hopes so, as he returns to mind the UNH net for his senior season. Ayers produced a 2.18 goals-against average and a .926 save percentage last season, when he was a second team all-America. Forwards Steve Saviano (39 points last season) and Patrick Foley return and will captain the Wildcats in 2003–04. The Wildcats top defenseman, Mike Lubesnick, will be back and coach Dick Umile landed 10 quality recruits, including 6'4", 215-pound defenseman John Doherty. New Hampshire will be loaded with experience and youth, a combination they hope will take them one win farther.

Michigan, which fell to Minnesota in overtime in the national semifinals last season, lost five seniors to graduation, including the team's second and third leading scorers, but the Wolverine should bounce back nicely. Jeff Tambellini should be back for his sophomore season, when he hopes to top his team-high 26 goals and 19 assists of last season. Forwards Dwight Helminen (17 goals, 16 assists in 2002–03) and David Moss (14 g, 17 a) should combine with Tambellini to give the Wolverines plenty of scoring punch. Junior defenseman Andy Burnes will once again anchor the Wolverines' rearguard. Having been to the final four in each of the past three seasons, Michigan, like New Hampshire, hopes to break break through in 2003–04 and restore glory to its storied program, which has won nine NCAA titles but none since 1998.

Led by Cornell and Harvard, the Ivy League staged a comeback of sorts in 2002–03. Harvard finished 22-10-2 and qualified for the NCAA tournament, where it fell in the first round to Boston University. **Cornell** went 30-5-1 and advanced to the final four for the first time since 1980. The Big Red rode the terrific goaltending of first-team all-America Dave LeNeveu, who set an NCAA record with his 1.20 goals-against average. LeNeveu also had nine shutouts, a school record. His return alone should make the Big Red the Big Dogs again in the ECAC, and maybe on the national scene.

But Cornell did lose seven seniors, including two-time first team all-America defenseman Doug Murray, and if those losses prove too heavy, the Big Red's spot in the final four could be taken by **Boston College**, the team Cornell defeated in double overtime to advance to the semis last season. A perennial power, the Eagles won it all in 2000–01. They had an uneven campaign last year, dropping out of the national rankings in midseason, but

As a freshman last season, Tambellini led the Wolverines with 45 points on 26 goals and 15 assists. He was named CCHA Rookie of the Year.

come tournament time, the Eagles were ready. They blanked Ohio State 1–0 to advance to their meeting with Cornell. Securing that shutout was sophomore goalie Matti Kaltiainen, a player who has improved steadily every season. He will return next year along with captain Ben Eaves, a Hobey Baker Award finalist (18 goals and 39 assists) in 2002–03. J.D. Forrest (31 points in 34 games) and defenseman Peter Harrold, who became a fixture on the Eagles' power play during his freshman year.

Though it lost Hobey Baker award winner Peter Sejna to the NHL, tiny **Colorado College** is a good bet to stay among the national elite. Sejna jumped to the St. Louis Blues after his junior year (he scored against Avalanche goalie Patrick Roy in his debut), and the Tigers, who sent two other players

to the NHL following last season, will surely miss his NCAA-best 36 goals and 46 assists. But look for Brett Sterling (27 goals, 11 assists as a freshman) and Marty Sertich (9 g, 20 a) to fill the considerable void. Sterling scored four goals in a 6–2 Tigers triumph over Minnesota last February. Defenseman Andrew Canzanella (26 assists) will be back, shoring up the Tigers' defense with goalie Curtis McElhinney (2.37 goals-against average).

Last year's women's season ended with an electrifying 4–3 double overtime win by Minnesota Duluth over Harvard, and those two teams stand an excellent chance of returning to the championship game in 2004. Though **Minnesota Duluth** graduated a talented crop of seniors, who won three consecutive NCAA titles, the Bulldogs will still have Jenny Potter and Caroline Ouellette, who finished

Now a sophomore, Chu hopes to top her sensational freshman year, when she finished second in the nation in scoring.

who had 24 goals and 35 assists as a sophomore, and Greg Rallo, who produced 15 goals and 14 assists in his impressive freshman season. Picked by some wags to finish ninth in the Central Collegiate Hockey Association last season, the Bulldogs won the conference with a 22-5-1 record. That triumph earned Ferris State its first NCAA tourney berth and it did not disappoint, knocking off North Dakota before running into eventual champion Minnesota. Ferris State coach Bob Daniels was named coach of the year by *Inside College Hockey* after guiding his team to 31-10-1 record, the best in school history. The Bulldogs have reason to be optimistic about next season as well, but they won't be sneaking up on anyone this time around.

Ohio State made just the third NCAA tournament appearance in school history last season, going 25-13-5 to qualify for the postseason, where it lost a squeaker to Boston College, 1–0. With Hobey Baker award finalist R.J. Umberger (26 g, 27 a) leading the way, the Buckeyes hope to top that performance. OSU also boasts talented forward Ryan Kesler, who racked up 11 goals and 20 assists as a freshman.

third and fifth in the nation in scoring, respectively, to terrorize opposing defenses. **Harvard** will say goodbye to superstar Jennifer Botterill (47 goals, 65 assists, tops in the country), but should not miss a beat with deadly forwards Julie Chu (42 g, 51 a) and Angela Ruggiero (29 g, 54 a) still in the mix.

Challenges to Harvard's and Minnesota Duluth's dominance could come from the Ivy League, where **Dartmouth**'s program is on the rise, or from the state of Minnesota, where the Bulldogs' in-state rival **Minnesota** has been making strides. Dartmouth and Minnesota both reached the final four last year, meeting in the third-place game, which Dartmouth won 4–2.

DARKHORSES

One of last season's biggest surprises, **Ferris State**, graduated six seniors from its roster but still retains four of its top seven scorers, including Jeff Legue,

Colorado College's Tom Preissing (above left) departed for the NHL, but potent forward Sterling (right) will be back.

The University of **Maine** said goodbye to leading scorer Martin Kariya, brother of NHL superstar Paul, along with a trio of talented seniors, but the Black Bears should still contend in Hockey East and beyond with the likes of Francis Nault (10 g, 26 a), Colin Shields (14 g, 13 a) and Todd Jackson remaining in Orono.

Darkhorses in the women's game, which first staged a national championship in 2001, include **Wisconsin**, **Providence**, **New Hampshire** and **Princeton**—all programs being lifted by the rising tide of NCAA women's hockey.

SIDELINES

While NCAA sports like basketball and soccer are seeing their flow of talent largely siphoned off by the pros, college hockey continues to attract many of the best young players, who see the NCAA game as a legitimate route to the NHL, whether after two, three or four years in school. And this despite the fact that ice hockey, like baseball has long had a minor league system to supply its professional ranks. Hobey Baker award winner Sejna came from Slovakia to play for Colorado College, where he scored 91 goals and had 99 assists in three seasons before making the jump to the NHL. "Hopefully," he said, "this is going to help more European players think that this is the right way to go—through college hockey."

Sejna is not alone. The 2002–03 final four MVP, Vanek of Minnesota, came from Austria to play NCAA hockey, and hundreds of Canadian players come south of the border every fall to suit up for U.S. college teams. The quality of play and the number of games are comparable to minor league hockey, and with an education thrown into the bargain as well, top talents will continue to pursue college hockey as a viable option.

NCAA MEN'S DIVISION I CHAMPIONSHIP GAME BOX SCORE

New Hampshire   1   0   0   —1
Minnesota   1   0   4   —5
Scoring: First Period: 1, Minnesota, Matt DeMarchi (Garrett Smaagaar), 10:58; 2, New Hampshire, Sean Collins, PP (Nathan Martz, Justin Aikins), 19:41. Second Period: None. Third Period: 3, Minnesota, Thomas Vanek (Matt Koalska), 8:14; 4, Minnesota, Jon Waibel (Thomas Vanek), 11:25; 5, Minnesota, Barry Tallackson, PP (Gino Guyer, Chris Harrington), 13:34; 6, Minnesota, Barry Tallackson, EN (Grant Potulny), 18:31.
Shots on Goal: New Hampshire: 7-9-11—27; Minnesota: 16-14-15—45

NCAA MEN'S DIVISION I INDIVIDUAL LEADERS

GOALS

PLAYER AND TEAM	CLASS	GP	G	AVG
Peter Sejna, Colorado College	Jr	42	36	0.86
Chris Kunitz, Ferris St	Sr	42	35	0.83
Brandon Bochenski, N Dakota	So	43	35	0.81
Joe Tallari, Niagara	Jr	34	26	0.76
Brett Sterling, Colorado College	Fr	36	27	0.75
Christopher Higgins, Yale	So	28	20	0.71
Grant Stevenson, Minn St–Mankato	So	38	27	0.71
Shane Joseph, Minn St–Mankato	Jr	41	29	0.71
Dominic Moore, Harvard	Sr	34	24	0.71
Thomas Vanek, Minnesota	Fr	45	31	0.69

ASSISTS

PLAYER AND TEAM	CLASS	GP	A	AVG
Noah Clarke, Colorado College	Sr	42	49	1.17
Peter Sejna, Colorado College	Jr	42	46	1.10
Ben Eaves, Boston College	Jr	36	39	1.08
Chris Kunitz, Ferris St	Sr	42	44	1.05
Brian Herbert, Quinnipiac	Sr	30	29	0.97
Grant Stevenson, Minn St–Mankato	So	38	36	0.95
Martin Kariya, Maine	Sr	39	36	0.92
Stephen Baby, Cornell	Sr	36	33	0.92
Brad Fast, Michigan St	Sr	39	35	0.90
Zach Parise, N Dakota	Fr	39	35	0.90

POINTS

PLAYER AND TEAM	CLASS	GP	G	A	PTS	PTS/G
Peter Sejna, Colorado College	Jr	42	36	46	82	1.95
Chris Kunitz, Ferris St	Sr	42	35	44	79	1.88
Noah Clarke, Colorado College	Sr	42	21	49	70	1.67
Grant Stevenson, Minn St–Mankato	So	38	27	36	63	1.66
Joe Tallari, Niagara	Jr	34	26	29	55	1.62
Shane Joseph, Minn St–Mankato	Jr	41	29	36	65	1.59
Ben Eaves, Boston College	Jr	36	18	39	57	1.58
Zach Parise, N Dakota	Fr	39	26	35	61	1.56
Dominic Moore, Harvard	Sr	34	24	27	51	1.50
Christopher Higgins, Yale	So	28	20	21	41	1.46

NCAA MEN'S DIVISION I INDIVIDUAL LEADERS (CONT.)

GOALS-AGAINST AVERAGE

PLAYER AND TEAM	CLASS	MIN	G	GAA
Dave LeNeveu, Cornell	So	1946	39	1.20
Frank Doyle, Maine	So	1180	42	2.14
Mike Ayers, New Hampshire	Jr	2499	91	2.18
Matti Kaltiainen, Boston College	So	1843	68	2.21
Mike Betz, Ohio St	Jr	2140	80	2.24
Eddy Ferhi, Sacred Heart	Sr	1769	67	2.27
Adam Berkhoel, Denver	Jr	1436	55	2.30
Yann Danis, Brown	Jr	2069	80	2.32
Al Montoya, Michigan	Fr	2547	99	2.33
Mike Brown, Ferris St	So	2404	94	2.35

SAVE PERCENTAGE

PLAYER AND TEAM	CLASS	GA	SAVES	SV%
Dave LeNeveu, Cornell	So	39	607	.940
Yann Danis, Brown	Jr	80	1043	.929
Mike Brown, Ferris St	So	94	1206	.928
Mike Ayers, New Hampshire	Jr	91	1139	.926
Dov Grumet-Morris, Harvard	So	69	847	.925
Bobby Goepfert, Providence	Fr	30	365	.924
Eddy Ferhi, Sacred Heart	Sr	67	808	.923
Jamie Holden, Quinnipiac	So	53	613	.920
Scott Munroe, Alabama-Huntsville	Fr	49	542	.917
Josh Gartner, Yale	Fr	47	517	.917

NCAA WOMEN'S DIVISION I CHAMPIONSHIP GAME BOX SCORE

Harvard	0	3	0	0	0—3
Minnesota-Duluth	2	1	0	0	1—4

Scoring: First Period: 1, MN-Duluth, Caroline Ouellette (Jenny Potter), 5:17; 2, MN-Duluth, Hanne Sikio (unassisted), 12:30. Second Period: 3, Harvard, Jennifer Botterill (unassisted), 00:21; 4, Harvard, Lauren McAuliffe (Nicole Corriero, Jamie Hagerman), 00:44; 5, Harvard, Nicole Corriero (Jamie Hagerman, Ashley Banfield), 14:46; 6, MN-Duluth, Hanne Sikio (Joanne Eustace), 17:34. Third Period: None. First Overtime: None. Second Overtime: 7, Nora Tallus (Erika Holst, Joanne Eustace), 4:19.

Shots on Goal: Harvard: 5-11-12-14-2—44; Minnesota-Duluth: 5-13-10-10-3—41

NCAA WOMEN'S DIVISION I INDIVIDUAL LEADERS

GOALS

PLAYER AND TEAM	CLASS	GP	G	AVG
Jennifer Botterill, Harvard	Sr	32	47	1.47
Julie Chu, Harvard	Fr	34	42	1.24
Erika Holst, MN-Duluth	Sr	32	34	1.06
Kolt Bloxson, Holy Cross	Fr	25	26	1.04
Natalie Darwitz, Minnesota	Fr	33	33	1.00

ASSISTS

PLAYER AND TEAM	CLASS	GP	A	AVG
Jennifer Botterill, Harvard	Sr	32	65	2.03
Angela Ruggiero, Harvard	Jr	34	54	1.59
Jenny Potter, MN-Duluth	Jr	36	57	1.58
Julie Chu, Harvard	Fr	34	51	1.50
Caroline Ouellette, MN-Duluth	Fr	32	42	1.31

NCAA WOMEN'S DIVISION I INDIVIDUAL LEADERS (CONT.)

POINTS

PLAYER AND TEAM	CLASS	GP	G	A	PTS	PTS/G
Jennifer Botterill, Harvard	Sr	32	47	65	112	3.50
Julie Chu, Harvard	Fr	34	42	51	93	2.74
Jenny Potter, MN-Duluth	Jr	36	31	57	88	2.44
Angela Ruggiero, Harvard	Jr	34	29	54	83	2.44
Caroline Ouellette, MN-Duluth	Fr	32	31	42	73	2.28

GOALS-AGAINST AVERAGE

PLAYER AND TEAM	CLASS	MIN	G	GAA
Tiffany Ribble, Mercyhurst	Sr	1340	33	1.48
Jen Huggon, New Hampshire	Sr	2086	53	1.52
Jessica Ruddock, Harvard	Jr	1679	43	1.54
Desirae Clark, Mercyhurst	So	694	19	1.64
Dawn Froats, Maine	Sr	784	22	1.68

SAVE PERCENTAGE

PLAYER AND TEAM	CLASS	GA	SAVES	SV%
Tiffany Ribble, Mercyhurst	Sr	33	449	.932
Jen Huggon, New Hampshire	Sr	53	705	.930
Chanda Gunn, Northeastern	Jr	57	739	.928
Desirae Clark, Mercyhurst	So	19	246	.928
Anna VanderMarliere, Wayne St (MI)	Jr	51	653	.928

NCAA MEN'S DIVISION III CHAMPIONSHIP GAME BOX SCORE

Oswego St	0	1	0	—1
Norwich	0	0	2	—2

Scoring: First Period: None. Second Period: 1, Oswego St, John Hirliman, PP (Mark Strzoda, Rob Smith), 18:04. Third Period: 2, Norwich, Aaron Lee (Marshall Lee, Chris Petracco), 5:50; 3, Toza Crnilovic (Phil Aucoin), 7:01.

Shots on Goal: Oswego St: 8-7-7—22; Norwich: 8-15-13—36

NCAA MEN'S DIVISION III INDIVIDUAL LEADERS

GOALS

PLAYER AND TEAM	CLASS	GP	G	AVG
Nick Cote, Mass Liberal Arts	Jr	23	33	1.43
Brian Yingling, Lebanon Valley	Sr	27	36	1.33
Travis Banga, New England Coll	Jr	25	29	1.16
Scott Goodman, Suffolk	Sr	21	21	1.00
Mike Lukajic, Oswego St	Jr	33	33	1.00

ASSISTS

PLAYER AND TEAM	CLASS	GP	A	AVG
Sean Pero, Curry	So	25	35	1.40
Don Patrick, Oswego St	Jr	33	41	1.24
Brian Doherty, Curry	So	27	32	1.19
Mike Bournazakis, RIT	Sr	24	28	1.17
Ryan Francke, RIT	Jr	23	26	1.13

NCAA MEN'S DIVISION III INDIVIDUAL LEADERS (CONT.)

POINTS

PLAYER AND TEAM	CLASS	GP	G	A	PTS	PTS/G
Brian Yingling, Lebanon Valley	Sr	27	36	29	65	2.41
Sean Pero, Curry	So	25	23	35	58	2.32
Nick Cote, Mass Liberal Arts	Jr	23	33	16	49	2.13
Brian Doherty, Curry	So	27	24	32	56	2.07
Manu Mau'u, Johnson & Wales	So	25	23	28	51	2.04

GOALS-AGAINST AVERAGE

PLAYER AND TEAM	CLASS	MIN	G	GAA
J.D. Hadiaris, Colby	Sr	842	22	1.57
Jamie Vanek, Wentworth Inst	Sr	974	27	1.66
Dan Meneghin, WI–River Falls	Fr	839	24	1.72
Zack Sikich, St. Thomas (MN)	So	725	23	1.90
Bob Berg, Marian (WI)	So	604	20	1.99
Jacques Vezina, WI–River Falls	Sr	1023	34	1.99

SAVE PERCENTAGE

PLAYER AND TEAM	CLASS	GA	SAVES	SV%
Jamie Vanek, Wentworth Inst	Sr	27	428	.941
Cody Brown, Lake Forest	So	39	532	.932
Zack Sikich, St. Thomas (MN)	So	23	305	.930
Dan Meneghin, WI–River Falls	Fr	24	307	.927
J.D. Hadiaris, Colby	Sr	22	270	.925

GO FIGURE

82 Points by Peter Sejna of Colorado College, the most in the nation in 2003. His 36 goals also led Division I and were enough to earn him the Hobey Baker Award as the best collegiate hockey player. Sejna, a native of Slovakia, became the first European-born player to be so honored.

31 Years between Minnesota's back-to-back national championships in 2002 and 2003, and the last time a team repeated as NCAA champion. In 1972, Boston University, which beat Minnesota for the title in '71, downed Cornell for a second straight title.

1.14 Goals-against average in 2003 for Cornell sophomore goalie Dave LeNeveu, the lowest in college hockey history. LeNeveu also led the nation in shutouts (nine), winning percentage (.919), and save percentage (.942).

419 Career victories for Vermont head coach Mike Gilligan, the most among active Division I head coaches and 15th all time. The alltime leader in coaching wins is Ron Mason, who retired from Michigan State in 2002 with 924 career wins.

4 Hobey Baker Award winners who have had their names engraved on the Stanley Cup as players, through the 2003 NHL season. Minnesota's Neal Broten, Tom Kurvers of Minnesota-Duluth, Tony Hrkac of North Dakota and Boston University's Chris Drury all won college hockey's top award before they were part of an NHL championship team.

NCAA MEN'S DIVISION I

YEAR	CHAMPION	COACH	SCORE	RUNNER-UP	MOST OUTSTANDING PLAYER
1948	Michigan	Vic Heyliger	8–4	Dartmouth	Joe Riley, Dartmouth, F
1949	Boston College	John Kelley	4–3	Dartmouth	Dick Desmond, Dartmouth, G
1950	Colorado College	Cheddy Thompson	13–4	Boston University	Ralph Bevins, Boston University, G
1951	Michigan	Vic Heyliger	7–1	Brown	Ed Whiston, Brown, G
1952	Michigan	Vic Heyliger	4–1	Colorado College	Kenneth Kinsley, Colorado College, G
1953	Michigan	Vic Heyliger	7–3	Minnesota	John Matchefts, Michigan, F
1954	Rensselaer	Ned Harkness	5–4 (OT)	Minnesota	Abbie Moore, Rensselaer, F
1955	Michigan	Vic Heyliger	5–3	Colorado College	Philip Hilton, Colorado College, D
1956	Michigan	Vic Heyliger	7–5	Michigan Tech	Lorne Howes, Michigan, G
1957	Colorado College	Thomas Bedecki	13–6	Michigan	Bob McCusker, Colorado Coll, F
1958	Denver	Murray Armstrong	6–2	N Dakota	Murray Massier, Denver, F
1959	N Dakota	Bob May	4–3 (OT)	Michigan St	Reg Morelli, N Dakota, F
1960	Denver	Murray Armstrong	5–3	Michigan Tech	Bob Marquis, Boston University, F
1961	Denver	Murray Armstrong	12–2	St. Lawrence	Barry Urbanski, Boston Univ, G
1962	Michigan Tech	John MacInnes	7–1	Clarkson	Louis Angotti, Michigan Tech, F
1963	N Dakota	Barney Thorndycraft	6–5	Denver	Al McLean, N Dakota, F
1964	Michigan	Allen Renfrew	6–3	Denver	Bob Gray, Michigan, G
1965	Michigan Tech	John MacInnes	8–2	Boston College	Gary Milroy, Michigan Tech, F
1966	Michigan St	Amo Bessone	6–1	Clarkson	Gaye Cooley, Michigan St, G
1967	Cornell	Ned Harkness	4–1	Boston University	Walt Stanowski, Cornell, D
1968	Denver	Murray Armstrong	4–0	N Dakota	Gerry Powers, Denver, G
1969	Denver	Murray Armstrong	4–3	Cornell	Keith Magnuson, Denver, D
1970	Cornell	Ned Harkness	6–4	Clarkson	Daniel Lodboa, Cornell, D
1971	Boston Univ	Jack Kelley	4–2	Minnesota	Dan Brady, Boston Univ, G
1972	Boston Univ	Jack Kelley	4–0	Cornell	Tim Regan, Boston Univ, G
1973	Wisconsin	Bob Johnson	4–2	Vacated	Dean Talafous, Wisconsin, F
1974	Minnesota	Herb Brooks	4–2	Michigan Tech	Brad Shelstad, Minnesota, G
1975	Michigan Tech	John MacInnes	6–1	Minnesota	Jim Warden, Michigan Tech, G
1976	Minnesota	Herb Brooks	6–4	Michigan Tech	Tom Vanelli, Minnesota, F
1977	Wisconsin	Bob Johnson	6–5 (OT)	Michigan	Julian Baretta, Wisconsin, G
1978	Boston Univ	Jack Parker	5–3	Boston College	Jack O'Callahan, Boston Univ, D
1979	Minnesota	Herb Brooks	4–3	N Dakota	Steve Janaszak, Minnesota, G
1980	N Dakota	John Gasparini	5–2	Northern Michigan	Doug Smail, N Dakota, F
1981	Wisconsin	Bob Johnson	6–3	Minnesota	Marc Behrend, Wisconsin, G
1982	N Dakota	John Gasparini	5–2	Wisconsin	Phil Sykes, N Dakota, F
1983	Wisconsin	Jeff Sauer	6–2	Harvard	Marc Behrend, Wisconsin, G
1984	Bowling Green	Jerry York	5–4 (OT)	MN–Duluth	Gary Kruzich, Bowling Green, G
1985	Rensselaer	Mike Addesa	2–1	Providence	Chris Terreri, Providence, G
1986	Michigan St	Ron Mason	6–5	Harvard	Mike Donnelly, Michigan St, F
1987	N Dakota	John Gasparini	5–3	Michigan St	Tony Hrkac, N Dakota, F
1988	Lake Superior St	Frank Anzalone	4–3 (OT)	St. Lawrence	Bruce Hoffort, Lake Superior St, G

NCAA MEN'S DIVISION I (CONT.)

YEAR	CHAMPION	COACH	SCORE	RUNNER-UP	MOST OUTSTANDING PLAYER
1989	Harvard	Bill Cleary	4–3 (OT)	Minnesota	Ted Donato, Harvard, F
1990	Wisconsin	Jeff Sauer	7–3	Colgate	Chris Tancill, Wisconsin, F
1991	N Michigan	Rick Comley	8–7 (3OT)	Boston Univ	Scott Beattie, N Michigan, F
1992	Lake Superior St	Jeff Jackson	4–2	Wisconsin	Paul Constantin, Lake Superior St, F
1993	Maine	Shawn Walsh	5–4	Lake Superior St	Jim Montgomery, Maine, F
1994	Lake Superior St	Jeff Jackson	9–1	Boston Univ	Sean Tallaire, Lake Superior St, F
1995	Boston Univ	Jack Parker	6–2	Maine	Chris O'Sullivan, Boston Univ, F
1996	Michigan	Red Berenson	3–2 (OT)	Colorado College	Brendan Morrison, Michigan, F
1997	N Dakota	Dean Blais	6–4	Boston Univ	Matt Henderson, N Dakota, F
1998	Michigan	Red Berenson	3–2 (OT)	Boston Coll	Marty Turco, Michigan, G
1999	Maine	Shawn Walsh	3–2 (OT)	New Hampshire	Alfie Michaud, Maine, G
2000	N Dakota	Dean Blais	4–2	Boston College	Lee Goren, N Dakota, F
2001	Boston College	Jerry York	3–2 (OT)	N Dakota	Chuck Kobasew, Boston College, F
2002	Minnesota	Don Lucia	4–3 (OT)	Maine	Grant Potulny, Minnesota, F
2003	Minnesota	Don Lucia	5–1	New Hampshire	Thomas Vanek, Minnesota, F

NCAA MEN'S DIVISION III

YEAR	CHAMPION	COACH	SCORE	RUNNER-UP
1984	Babson	Bob Riley	8–0	Union (NY)
1985	RIT	Bruce Delventhal	5–1	Bemidji St
1986	Bemidji St	R.H. (Bob) Peters	8–5	Vacated
1987	Vacated			Oswego St
1988	WI–River Falls	Rick Kozuback	7–1, 3–5, 3–0	Elmira
1989	WI–Stevens Point	Mark Mazzoleni	3–3, 3–2	RIT
1990	WI–Stevens Point	Mark Mazzoleni	10–1, 3–6, 1–0	Plattsburgh St
1991	WI–Stevens Point	Mark Mazzoleni	6–2	Mankato St
1992	Plattsburgh St	Bob Emery	7–3	WI–Stevens Point
1993	WI–Stevens Point	Joe Baldarotta	4–3	WI–River Falls
1994	WI–River Falls	Dean Talafous	6–4	WI–Superior
1995	Middlebury	Bill Beaney	1–0	Fredonia St
1996	Middlebury	Bill Beaney	3–2	RIT
1997	Middlebury	Bill Beaney	3–2	WI–Superior
1998	Middlebury	Bill Beaney	2–1	WI–Stevens Point
1999	Middlebury	Bill Beaney	5–0	WI–Superior
2000	Norwich	Michael McShane	2–1	St. Thomas (MN)
2001	Plattsburgh	Bob Emery	6–2	RIT
2002	WI–Superior	Dan Stauber	3–2	Norwich
2003	Norwich	Michael McShane	2–1	Oswego St

NCAA WOMEN'S DIVISION I

YEAR	CHAMPION	COACH	SCORE	RUNNER-UP
2001	Minnesota-Duluth	Shannon Miller	4–2	St. Lawrence
2002	Minnesota-Duluth	Shannon Miller	3–2	Brown
2003	Minnesota-Duluth	Shannon Miller	4–3 (2OT)	Harvard

OK State
CORRAL

With talented returnees in seven of 10 weight classes, Oklahoma State hopes to rope in a second straight title

T HERE'S NEVER BEEN any doubt where the heart of American wrestling beats most fiercely: on an axis running straight from the cornfields of Iowa down to the prairies of Oklahoma. Schools from those two states have dominated college wrestling for so long now, it almost makes you wonder if those original toga-ed Olympic wrestlers weren't farmboy ringers, competing on forged passports for Sparta or Troy. Of 73 collegiate wrestling championships dating back to 1928, all but seven have gone to schools from Iowa or Oklahoma.

FAVORITES

Last year, in Kansas City, **Oklahoma State** easily outscored runner up Minnesota, 143 points to 104.5, to run its record total of national titles to 31. No one will be the least bit surprised if Coach John Smith's team wins again in March 2004 at the Savvis Center in St. Louis. Not only were those 143 points the most any Oklahoma State team had ever scored at nationals, but in the 10 weight classes the Cowboys

return seven wrestlers, including their two champions, sensational sophomore Jake Rosholt, who was seeded 10th before winning the title at 184 pounds, and senior Johnny Thompson at 133. It doesn't hurt that Smith has recruited well the past few years—even if he somehow failed to land his own nephew, Mark Perry, who pulled the collegiate wrestling equivalent of a Kennedy turning Republican by matriculating at archrival Iowa, where he is expected to redshirt.

Things will have to break just about perfectly for any school planning to dethrone Oklahoma State next season. **Minnesota**, which won national titles in 2000 and 2001, lost a lot to graduation. According to *InterMat*, the Gophers had the best recruiting class of any school, and though underclassmen are having a greater impact these days than ever before—eight of 20 finalists at last year's nationals were freshmen or sophomores, and five won titles—it's still hard to imagine those young Gophers offsetting Oklahoma State's experience and talent.

ED ZURGAAP

Spearheading Oklahoma State's bid to repeat will be two-time NCAA champ Thompson (top), whose 133-pound division could be the most exciting weight class at this year's NCAAs.

Still, nothing is going to affect college wrestling more in 2003–04 than the fact that it's an Olympic waiver year. For a handful of the very best wrestlers, that may mean sitting out the college season in order to pursue their dreams of wrestling in Athens. Brandon Paulson of Minnesota began the trend in 1996, when he successfully petitioned the NCAA to grant him an extra year of eligibility; he went on to win a silver medal in Greco Roman. This year, who wrestles and who sits out may decide whether or not Oklahoma State gets any real competition in St. Louis.

Topping the list of talent not current-ly enrolled at Oklahoma State is Iowa heavyweight Steve Mocco, who, last year, as a sophomore, won the national title to highlight an undefeated season. A lot would seem to be riding on Mocco's broad shoulders this year—even, per-haps, the fate of his coach Jim Zalesky, whose job is rumored to ride on how well **Iowa** performs in 2003–04. The Hawkeyes, who won an astounding 20 of 26 championships from 1975 to 2000, finished eighth in 2002–03, and their rabid fans won't tolerate that for long. A message posted on the "Hawk Nest" message board on the final day of nationals captured the discontent in wrestling-mad Iowa: "This could be the worst year of wrestling in 30 years . . . we have been so used to finishing one, two or three (rarely) that this seems like a downer. We were in 6th place heading into the finals. Is it time to seek a new

Coming off an undefeated season, heavyweight Mocco (right) is crucial to Iowa's hopes of reclaiming glory: the 20-time champion Hawkeyes have not won the NCAAs since 2000.

coach?" Rumors have Dan Gable returning, or one of the fiery Brands brothers, Tom or Terry, taking over if Zalesky's team doesn't move way, way up this year.

One team that has ascended precipitiously in recent years is **Lehigh**, which has spearheaded a welcome resurgence in Eastern wrestling. Last year the Mountain Hawks finished fourth in the NCAAs, and have been ranked as high as second for next year. Lehigh has a quartet of terrific sophomores, led by Troy Letters, who enters the season ranked first at 165 pounds. But Lehigh's chance of challenging Oklahoma State depends on one wrestler, 197-pounder Jon Trenge, twice a national runner-up. Trenge may opt to exercise the Olympic waiver, and without the big points he

would surely grab, it's hard to picture Lehigh in the hunt.

"There's no way Iowa's going to win without Mocco and no way Lehigh's going to win without Trenge," says Ron Good, editor of *Amateur Wrestling News*. "Let's put it this way: Those two guys redshirt and OSU's got a cakewalk."

DARKHORSES

Iowa State, runner up as recently as 2002—with unbeaten Cael Sanderson providing not only points but also inspiration—finished a shocking 19th in 2003. The Cyclones are young but talented and should rebound well next season. **Oklahoma** certainly ought to vie for the Top 5, while resurgent **Missouri** stands a good chance of finishing in the Top 10, provided it qualifies enough wrestlers in the tough Big 12 tournament. For depth, the Big 10 just might challenge the Big 12. Last year **Michigan** got its first national champion in a long

time in Ryan Bertin, who could push the Wolverines higher than last year's seventh place finish. **Illinois**, led by Alex Tirapelle at 157, figures to be tough too.

Farther down the list are **Hofstra** and the Ivy league teams, which, only five years ago, seemed to be doomed but are now flourishing. Besides **Cornell**, which finished 10th in the nation last year, largely on the strength of Travis Lee's win at 125 pounds, **Penn**, **Harvard** and **Columbia** all have strong programs. Two-time All America Jesse Jantzen of Harvard is ranked first at 149 pounds.

ONES TO WATCH
One of the best battles of the 2003–04 wrestling season will come at 133 pounds, where Cornell's Travis Lee is stepping up a weight class and could end up facing Oklahoma State's Johnny Thompson, who already has two titles in the weight class. Lee is an unusual champion not only because he wrestles

for Cornell but also because he is from Hawaii, which produces championship wrestlers about as often as it does snow. Throw in 2003 third-place finisher Josh Moore of Penn State and you have probably the most competitive class in the tournament.

Other probable standouts include sophomore Teyon Ware of Oklahoma, who last year, as a true freshman, traded his redshirt for a singlet and won the national title at 141 pounds. And if Mocco does sit out the year, the heavyweight division will be wide open. The favorite in that case would be Ohio State senior Tommy Rowlands, who beat Mocco several times during Mocco's freshman year before being plagued by injuries in 2003.

DIVISION I INDIVIDUAL CHAMPIONS

	CHAMPION	RUNNER-UP
125 lb	Travis Lee, Cornell	Chris Fleeger, Purdue
133 lb	Johnny Thompson, Oklahoma St	Ryan Lewis, Minnesota
141 lb	Teyon Ware, Oklahoma	Dylan Long, Northern Iowa
149 lb	Eric Larkin, Arizona St	Jared Lawrence, Minnesota
157 lb	Ryan Bertin, Michigan	Alex Tirapelle, Illinois
165 lb	Matt Lackey, Illinois	Troy Letters, Lehigh
174 lb	Robbie Waller, Oklahoma	Carl Fronhofer, Pittsburgh
184 lb	Jake Rosholt, Oklahoma St	Scott Barker, Missouri
197 lb	Damion Hahn, Minnesota	Jon Trenge, Lehigh
HWT	Steve Mocco, Iowa	Kevin Hoy, Air Force

DIVISION II INDIVIDUAL CHAMPIONS

	CHAMPION	RUNNER-UP
125 lb	Mark Dodgen, Central Oklahoma	Jared Haberman, Western St
133 lb	Cole Province, Central Oklahoma	Mitch Waite, Nebraska-Omaha
141 lb	Shane Barnes, Adams St	Merrick Meyer, Truman St
149 lb	Waylon Lowe, Findlay	Brandon Pfizenmaier, Nebraska-Kearney
157 lb	Paul Carlson, N Dakota St	Brody Olson, Northern Colorado
165 lb	Shawn Silvis, Central Oklahoma	Jake Emerick, Minnesota St–Mankato
174 lb	Frank Kuchera, Nebraska-Kearney	Jon Duncombe, St. Cloud St
184 lb	Mauricio Wright, San Francisco St	Tyler Jones, S Dakota St
197 lb	Chad Wallace, Nebraska-Omaha	Brian Kraemer, N Dakota St
285 lb	Les Sigmund, Nebraska-Omaha	Dustin Darveaux, St. Cloud St

DIVISION III INDIVIDUAL CHAMPIONS

	CHAMPION	RUNNER-UP
125 lb	Heath Ropp, Wartburg	Mitchell Marcks, Kings College
133 lb	Dave Ilaria, College of NJ	Ozzie Saxon, Wartburg
141 lb	Wil Kelly, Wartburg	Jim Morgan, Kings College
149 lb	Rami Ratel, Montclair St	Garrett Kurth, Luther
157 lb	Marcus LeVesseur, Augsburg	Kevin Bratland, Wartburg
165 lb	Jesse Reyerson, Luther	Pat North, RIT
174 lb	Cody Koenig, WI–Stevens Point	Eduard Aliakseyenka, Montclair St
184 lb	Bradley Marten, WI–Stevens Point	Sonny Alvarez, Wartburg
197 lb	Brent Meyers, Upper Iowa	Yan White, WI–Stevens Point
285 lb	Leroy Gardner, Wartburg	Ryan Allen, WI-LaCrosse

DIVISION I TEAM CHAMPIONS

YEAR	CHAMPION	PTS	COACH	RUNNER-UP-	PTS	MOST OUTSTANDING WRESTLER
1928	Oklahoma St*		E.C. Gallagher			
1929	Oklahoma St	26	E.C. Gallagher	Michigan	18	
1930	Oklahoma St*	27	E.C. Gallagher	Illinois	14	
1931	Oklahoma St*		E.C. Gallagher	Michigan		
1932	Indiana*		W.H. Thom	Oklahoma St		Edwin Belshaw, Indiana
1933	OK St*/Iowa St*		E. Gallagher/ H. Otopalik			A. Kelley, OK St/ P. Johnson, Harv
1934	Oklahoma St	29	E.C. Gallagher	Indiana	19	Ben Bishop, Lehigh
1935	Oklahoma St	36	E.C. Gallagher	Oklahoma	18	Ross Flood, Oklahoma St
1936	Oklahoma	14	Paul Keen	Central St/ OK St	10	Wayne Martin, Oklahoma
1937	Oklahoma St	31	E.C. Gallagher	Oklahoma	13	Stanley Henson, Oklahoma St
1938	Oklahoma St	19	E.C. Gallagher	Illinois	15	Joe McDaniels, Oklahoma St
1939	Oklahoma St	33	E.C. Gallagher	Lehigh	12	Dale Hanson, Minnesota
1940	Oklahoma St	24	E.C. Gallagher	Indiana	14	Don Nichols, Michigan
1941	Oklahoma St	37	Art Griffith	Michigan St	26	Al Whitehurst, Oklahoma St
1942	Oklahoma St	31	Art Griffith	Michigan St	26	David Arndt, Oklahoma St
1946	Oklahoma St	25	Art Griffith	Northern Iowa Northern Iowa	24	Gerald Leeman,
1947	Cornell	32	Paul Scott	Northern Iowa	19	William Koll, Northern Iowa
1948	Oklahoma St	33	Art Griffith	Michigan St	28	William Koll, Northern Iowa
1949	Oklahoma St	32	Art Griffith	Northern Iowa	27	Charles Hetrick, Oklahoma St
1950	Northern Iowa	30	David McCuskey	Purdue	16	Anthony Gizoni, Waynesburg
1951	Oklahoma	24	Port Robertson	Oklahoma St	23	Walter Romanowski, Cornell
1952	Oklahoma	22	Port Robertson	Northern Iowa	21	Tommy Evans, Oklahoma
1953	Penn St	21	Charles Speidel	Oklahoma	15	Frank Bettucci, Cornell
1954	Oklahoma St	32	Art Griffith	Pittsburgh	17	Tommy Evans, Oklahoma
1955	Oklahoma St	40	Art Griffith	Penn St	31	Edward Eichelberger, Lehigh
1956	Oklahoma St	65	Art Griffith	Oklahoma	62	Dan Hodge, Oklahoma
1957	Oklahoma	73	Port Robertson	Pittsburgh	66	Dan Hodge, Oklahoma
1958	Oklahoma St	77	Myron Roderick	Iowa St	62	Dick Delgado, Oklahoma
1959	Oklahoma St	73	Myron Roderick	Iowa St	51	Ron Gray, Iowa St
1960	Oklahoma	59	Thomas Evans	Iowa St	40	Dave Auble, Cornell
1961	Oklahoma St	82	Myron Roderick	Oklahoma	63	E. Gray Simons, Lock Haven
1962	Oklahoma St	82	Myron Roderick	Oklahoma	45	E. Gray Simons, Lock Haven
1963	Oklahoma	48	Thomas Evans	Iowa St	45	Mickey Martin, Oklahoma
1964	Oklahoma St	87	Myron Roderick	Oklahoma	58	Dean Lahr, Colorado
1965	Iowa St	87	Harold Nichols	Oklahoma St	86	Yojiro Uetake, Oklahoma St
1966	Oklahoma St	79	Myron Roderick	Iowa St	70	Yojiro Uetake, Oklahoma St
1967	Michigan St	74	Grady Peninger	Michigan	63	Rich Sanders, Portland St
1968	Oklahoma St	81	Myron Roderick	Iowa St	78	Dwayne Keller, Oklahoma St
1969	Iowa St	104	Harold Nichols	Oklahoma	69	Dan Gable, Iowa St
1970	Iowa St	99	Harold Nichols	Michigan St	84	Larry Owings, Washington
1971	Oklahoma St	94	Tommy Chesbro	Iowa St	66	Darrell Keller, Oklahoma St
1972	Iowa St	103	Harold Nichols	Michigan St	72½	Wade Schalles, Clarion
1973	Iowa St	85	Harold Nichols	Oregon St	72½	Greg Strobel, Oregon St
1974	Oklahoma	69½	Stan Abel	Michigan	67	Floyd Hitchcock, Bloomsburg
1975	Iowa	102	Gary Kurdelmeier	Oklahoma	77	Mike Frick, Lehigh
1976	Iowa	123½	Gary Kurdelmeier	Iowa St	85¾	Chuck Yagla, Iowa
1977	Iowa St	95½	Harold Nichols	Oklahoma St	88¾	Nick Gallo, Hofstra

*Unofficial champions.

DIVISION I TEAM CHAMPIONS (CONT.)

YEAR	CHAMPION	PTS	COACH	RUNNER-UP-	PTS	MOST OUTSTANDING WRESTLER
1978	...Iowa	94½	Dan Gable	Iowa St	94	Mark Churella, Michigan
1979	...Iowa	122½	Dan Gable	Iowa St	88	Bruce Kinseth, Iowa
1980	...Iowa	110¾	Dan Gable	Oklahoma St	87	Howard Harris, Oregon St
1981	...Iowa	129¾	Dan Gable	Oklahoma	100¼	Gene Mills, Syracuse
1982	...Iowa	131¾	Dan Gable	Iowa St	111	Mark Schultz, Oklahoma
1983	...Iowa	155	Dan Gable	Oklahoma St	102	Mike Sheets, Oklahoma St
1984	...Iowa	123¾	Dan Gable	Oklahoma St	98	Jim Zalesky, Iowa
1985	...Iowa	145¼	Dan Gable	Oklahoma	98½	Barry Davis, Iowa
1986	...Iowa	158	Dan Gable	Oklahoma	84¼	Marty Kistler, Iowa
1987	...Iowa St	133	Jim Gibbons	Iowa	108	John Smith, Oklahoma St
1988	...Arizona St	93	Bobby Douglas	Iowa	85½	Scott Turner, N Carolina St
1989	...Oklahoma St	91¼	Joe Seay	Arizona St	70½	Tim Krieger, Iowa St
1990	...Oklahoma St	117¾	Joe Seay	Arizona St	104¾	Chris Barnes, Oklahoma St
1991	...Iowa /	157	Dan Gable	Oklahoma St	108¾	Jeff Prescott, Penn St
1992	...Iowa	149	Dan Gable	Oklahoma St	100½	Tom Brands, Iowa
1993	...Iowa	123¾	Dan Gable	Penn St	87½	Terry Steiner, Iowa
1994	...Oklahoma St	94¾	John Smith	Iowa	76½	Pat Smith, Oklahoma St
1995	...Iowa	134	Dan Gable	Oregon St	77½	T.J. Jaworsky, N Carolina
1996	...Iowa	122½	Dan Gable	Iowa St	78½	Les Gutches, Oregon St
1997	...Iowa	170	Dan Gable	Oklahoma St	113½	Lincoln McIlravy, Iowa
1998	...Iowa	115	Jim Zalesky	Minnesota	102	Joe Williams, Iowa
1999	...Iowa	100½	Jim Zalesky	Minnesota	98½	Cael Sanderson, Iowa St
2000	...Iowa	116	Jim Zalesky	Iowa St	109½	Cael Sanderson, Iowa St
2001	...Minnesota	138½	J Robinson	Iowa	125½	Cael Sanderson, Iowa St
2002	...Minnesota	126½	J Robinson	Iowa St	104	Cael Sanderson, Iowa St
2003	...Oklahoma St	143	John Smith	Minnesota	104½	Eric Larkin, Arizona St

GO FIGURE

31 NCAA wrestling titles for the Oklahoma State Cowboys, the most team championships by any school in any sport in NCAA history. No. 31 came in 2003. It was the school's first wrestling crown since 1994.

159 Wins without a loss in the career of Iowa State's Cael Sanderson, a four-time NCAA champion. Three of Sanderson's titles came in the 184-pound class; the fourth came at 197 pounds.

1 Four-time NCAA champion besides Sanderson. Pat Smith of Oklahoma State won the 158-pound title in 1990, '91, '92 and '94. Thirty-eight other Division I wrestlers from an assortment of weight classes have won as many as three career NCAA championships.

13 Consecutive seasons that the Big Ten conference has sent a team to the Division I wrestling finals. Iowa (10 appearances, nine titles in that span), Minnesota (four appearances, two titles) and Penn State (one appearance) have all reached the finals.

9 Seconds it took at the 1983 championships for Louisiana State's Clarence Richardson to record a fall against Portland State's Scott Mansur in the 177-pound weight class, the fastest pin in NCAA history under collegiate rules.

DIVISION II TEAM CHAMPIONS

YEAR	CHAMPION	YEAR	CHAMPION
1963	Western St (CO)	1984	SIU–Edwardsville
1964	Western St (CO)	1985	SIU–Edwardsville
1965	Mankato St	1986	SIU–Edwardsville
1966	Cal Poly–SLO	1987	Cal St–Bakersfield
1967	Portland St	1988	N Dakota St
1968	Cal Poly–SLO	1989	Portland St
1969	Cal Poly–SLO	1990	Portland St
1970	Cal Poly–SLO	1991	NE–Omaha
1971	Cal Poly–SLO	1992	Central Oklahoma
1972	Cal Poly–SLO	1993	Central Oklahoma
1973	Cal Poly–SLO	1994	Central Oklahoma
1974	Cal Poly–SLO	1995	Central Oklahoma
1975	Northern Iowa	1996	Pittsburgh–Johnstown
1976	Cal St–Bakersfield	1997	San Francisco St
1977	Cal St–Bakersfield	1998	N Dakota St
1978	Northern Iowa	1999	Pittsburgh–Johnstown
1979	Cal St–Bakersfield	2000	N Dakota St
1980	Cal St–Bakersfield	2001	N Dakota St
1981	Cal St–Bakersfield	2002	Central Oklahoma
1982	Cal St–Bakersfield	2003	Central Oklahoma
1983	Cal St–Bakersfield		

DIVISION III TEAM CHAMPIONS

YEAR	CHAMPION	YEAR	CHAMPION
1974	Wilkes	1989	Ithaca
1975	John Carroll	1990	Ithaca
1976	Montclair St	1991	Augsburg
1977	Brockport St	1992	Brockport
1978	Buffalo	1993	Augsburg
1979	Trenton St	1994	Ithaca
1980	Brockport St	1995	Augsburg
1981	Trenton St	1996	Wartburg
1982	Brockport St	1997	Augsburg
1983	Brockport St	1998	Augsburg
1984	Trenton St	1999	Wartburg
1985	Trenton St	2000	Augsburg
1986	Montclair St	2001	Augsburg
1987	Trenton St	2002	Augsburg
1988	St. Lawrence	2003	Wartburg

TIGERS, TIGERS, Burning Bright

The Auburn men and women won NCAA titles last season, and no one doubts that they can do it again

A CONSTANT CACOPHONY of quirky sounds accompanies every NCAA swim meet. The pool reverberates with team chants and cheers, electronic starting beeps and whistles designed to keep breaststrokers on rhythm. There is an innocent enthusiasm which, at other events, would probably seem corny. Maybe it's all those swim parents letting off a little steam after a lifetime of ferrying kids to pre-dawn practices. Maybe it's the swimmers themselves relishing the chance to prove—to themselves as much as to anyone—that all those two-a-days have actually been worth it. Whatever the reason, if you go to an NCAA swim meet, bring some ear plugs.

FAVORITES

Last year no team cheered more wildly than **Auburn**, and no one had better reason to. In an awesome display of depth and balance, the Tiger men and women both won national championships in 2003; it was the first time that both win-

ning teams were coached by the same person. In Auburn's case that's Dave Marsh, ably assisted by co-women's head coach Kim Brackin. First, the Tiger women handily defended their team title before a rabid crowd at their home pool, scoring 536 points to runnerup Georgia's 373. One week later, the Auburn men traveled to Austin and shocked everyone by racking up 609.5 points, the second highest total in meet history, to beat both the host Longhorns (413) and favored Stanford (374). "A-U-B. . .U-R-N!" chanted the Auburn swimmers (who obviously devote far more time to working out than to working out clever cheers). "It's great to be an Auburn Tiger!" went another cheer, which, by the looks of things, ought to be the case this year, too.

"I can't see how, barring something totally unforeseen, they won't repeat," said Phil Whitten, editor of both *Swimming World* magazine and the SwimInfo website. "Both teams have almost every-

body back, plus the coaching staff has done some major recruiting."

Auburn's strength will again be its depth and balance. In last year's men's championship meet, the Tigers scored in every single event, and every one of the 17 swimmers they brought to the meet produced points. "They have a bunch of no-name people who somehow manage to beat all the name people," said Whitten, who ascribed the team's success not only to the wonderfully modest Marsh but also to the "competence and sense of team you encounter from the coaching staff to the athletes and all the way down to the secretaries." When Marsh first arrived at Auburn 14 years ago, it cannot have been easy luring top athletes to a small southern town—"a suburb of Opelika," cracks Whitten—where football is always going to be king. For the foreseeable future, the college swimming world had best get used to Marsh Madness.

One of the big guns returning for Auburn will be sprinter Fred Bousquet, a

Hansen capped each of his first three years at Texas with national titles in the 100 and 200 breaststrokes, setting records in both events last year.

Frenchman. "Freddy Bisquits," as he is known in one of his team's better cheers, arrived in January 2003, only a few months before contributing mightily to the Tiger championship cause by defeating Cal's Anthony Ervin, the Olympic co–gold medalist, in the 50 freestyle, and anchoring three Tiger relays that finished second. Indeed, in a meet with four relays, it is going to be hard to beat Auburn: The Tigers placed four swimmers in the championship final of both the 50 free and the 100 breast, and five of those eight finalists are returning in 2004.

The other top Tiger coming back to school is George Bovell, a 6'5" engineering student from Trinidad and Tobago. Bovell, whose dad was a collegiate swimmer and whose mom was an Olympic track and field athlete for Barbados, set

an NCAA record when he won the 200 individual medley at the 2003 nationals in 1:42.66. "This kid could medal at the Olympics," said Whitten. "He's extremely versatile."

Auburn is so deep it even has national-caliber divers—and divers who are deep: Check out Cesar Garcia, co-champion in the 10-meter platform. He happens to be a mechanical engineer with a 3.97 GPA.

The Auburn women lost top scorer Maggie Bowen to graduation, but they return plenty of stars, including Kirsty Coventry, a junior from Harare, Zimbabwe, who was runnerup in both the 100 and 200 backstrokes last year. She'll look to go one better in 2004. Margaret Hoelzer, from nearby Huntsville, Ala., will be back, and should score points in the two butterflys and relays. Becky Short and Eileen

At the 2003 NCAAs, Peirsol, then a freshman, became the first American to break 1:40.00 in the 200 back.

Coparropa went 2-3 in both the 50 and 100 freestyles last year, and will make the Tiger relays tough to beat.

DARKHORSES

If anyone has a chance to beat Auburn, it's **Georgia** on the women's side, and **Texas**, **Stanford** and **Cal** on the men's. But most objective observers consider that chance slim at best. The Georgia women are led by sophomore Mary DeScenza, a pre-veterinary medicine major who last year gave the Bulldogs a shot of adrenalin by winning the 200 butterfly and finishing second to Cal's Natalie Coughlin in the 100 fly.

As usual, the Texas men have depth; they also have two returning superstars in backstroker Aaron Peirsol and breast-stroker Brendan Hansen. Stanford, led by 100 back champ Peter Marshall, has the talent to challenge Texas but probably not Auburn. Cal returns 100 free champ Duje Drangaja and 50 free runner-up Mike Cavic, but after those two stars, the Bears are relatively thin.

ONES TO WATCH

Texas backstroker Peirsol is the relatively rare NCAA swimmer who also happens to be the world record holder in his speciality, the 200. At last year's NCAA meet he swam 1:39.16 to become the first backstroker to break 1:40 for the 200, a barrier that's even more notable because no less a giant than Mark Spitz was the first swimmer to break it—and he was swimming freestyle. Peirsol's teammate Hansen joins Tara (Captain) Kirk of Stanford in attempting to win both the 100 and 200 breaststokes for the fourth straight year,

a feat that has never been accomplished in any stroke.

Still, the best swimmer at the 2004 NCAAs probably will be the astoundingly versatile Coughlin, whom rival coach Richard Quick of Stanford compares to the legendary Spitz. Now a senior at Cal, Coughlin, a 5'8" psychology major from Concord, Calif., was named World Swimmer of the Year for 2002, an *annus mirabilis* in which she became the first woman to break one minute for the 100 back, clocking 59.58 at the U.S. National Championships in August of that year. At nationals in 2003, she won every event she entered—both backstrokes and the 100 Fly—and swam on three relays, to win the swimmer of the meet award for the second straight year. Don't be surprised when she does it again next year.

Coughlin has found glory for the U.S. and for California, which welcomes her back for her senior season.

2003 NATIONAL CHAMPIONS

MEN

	CHAMPION	TIME/PTS	RUNNER-UP	TIME/PTS
50-yd freestyle	Fred Bousquet, Auburn	19.31	Mike Cavic, California	19.37
100-yd freestyle	Duje Draganja, California	42.02	Anthony Ervin, California	42.11
200-yd freestyle	Simon Burnett, Arizona	1:33.69	Chris Kemp, Texas	1:34.40
500-yd freestyle	Erik Vendt, Southern Cal	4:13.63	Robert Margalis, Georgia	4:14.24
1650-yd freestyle	Erik Vendt, Southern Cal	14:29.85	Peter Vanderkaay, Mich	14:43.73
100-yd backstroke	Peter Marshall, Stanford	45.57	Aaron Peirsol, Texas	45.71
200-yd backstroke	Aaron Peirsol, Texas	1:39.16*#	Markus Rogan, Stanford	1:41.37
100-yd breaststroke	Brendan Hansen, Texas	51.96	Patrick Calhoun, Auburn	53.03
200-yd breaststroke	Brendan Hansen, Texas	1:52.62*#	Vladislav Polyakov, Alabama	1:55.38
100-yd butterfly	Ian Crocker, Texas	45.67	Luis Rojas, Arizona	46.01
200-yd butterfly	Stefan Gherghel, Alabama	1:42.35	Juan Veloz, Arizona	1:42.62
200-yd IM	George Bovell, Auburn	1:42.66*#	Joe Bruckhart, California	1:44.30
400-yd IM	Robert Margalis, Georgia	3:39.92	Erik Vendt, Southern Cal	3:39.95
1-meter diving	Joona Puhakka, Arizona St	395.80	Andy Bradley, S Carolina	359.00
3-meter diving	Phil Jones, Tennessee	649.70	Clayton Moss, Kentucky	646.75
Platform	Caesar Garcia, Auburn	575.80		
	Jason Coben, Michigan			

*NCAA record. #American record.

WOMEN

	CHAMPION	TIME	RUNNER-UP	TIME
50-yd freestyle	Maritza Correia, Georgia	21.83	Becky Short, Auburn	22.11
100-yd freestyle	Maritza Correia, Georgia	47.29*	Becky Short, Auburn	48.53
200-yd freestyle	Jessi Perruquet, N Carolina	1:45.01		
	Heather Kemp, Auburn			
500-yd freestyle	Flavia Rigamonti, SMU	4:37.72	Kaitlin Sandeno, USC	4:39.31
1650-yd freestyle	Flavia Rigamonti, SMU	15:43.90	Cara Lane, Virginia	15:53.49
100-yd backstroke	Natalie Coughlin, California	50.92	Kirsty Coventry, Auburn	53.01
200-yd backstroke	Natalie Coughlin, California	1:50.86	Kirsty Coventry, Auburn	1:53.17
100-yd breaststroke	Tara Kirk, Stanford	58.62	Maggie Bowen, Auburn	59.86
200-yd breaststroke	Tara Kirk, Stanford	2:08.79	Ann Poleska, Alabama	2:09.13
100-yd butterfly	Natalie Coughlin, California	50.62	Mary DeScenza, Georgia	51.93
200-yd butterfly	Mary DeScenza, Georgia	1:53.51	Emily Mason, Arizona	1:54.25
200-yd IM	Maggie Bowen, Auburn	1:55.33	Alenka Kejzar, SMU	1:57.28
			Kirsty Coventry, Auburn	
400-yd IM	Maggie Bowen, Auburn	4:06.15	Emily Mason, Arizona	4:07.07
1-meter diving	Yulia Pakhalina, Houston	339.70	Jamie Sanger, Tennessee	329.90
3-meter diving	Yulia Pakhalina, Houston	657.30	Blythe Hartley, USC	585.15
Platform	Natalia Diea, Ohio St	476.65	Blythe Hartley, USC	456.90

*NCAA record. #American record.

CHAMPIONSHIP RESULTS
MEN
DIVISION I

YEAR	CHAMPION	COACH	PTS	RUNNER-UP	PTS
1937	Michigan	Matt Mann	75	Ohio St	39
1938	Michigan	Matt Mann	46	Ohio St	45
1939	Michigan	Matt Mann	65	Ohio St	58
1940	Michigan	Matt Mann	45	Yale	42
1941	Michigan	Matt Mann	61	Yale	58
1942	Yale	Robert J.H. Kiphuth	71	Michigan	39
1943	Ohio St	Mike Peppe	81	Michigan	47
1944	Yale	Robert J.H. Kiphuth	39	Michigan	38
1945	Ohio St	Mike Peppe	56	Michigan	48
1946	Ohio St	Mike Peppe	61	Michigan	37
1947	Ohio St	MIke Peppe	66	Michigan	39
1948	Michigan	Matt Mann	44	Ohio St	41
1949	Ohio St	Mike Peppe	49	Iowa	35
1950	Ohio St	Mike Peppe	64	Yale	43
1951	Yale	Robert J.H. Kiphuth	81	Michigan St	60
1952	Ohio St	Mike Peppe	94	Yale	81
1953	Yale	Robert J.H. Kiphuth	96½	Ohio St	73½
1954	Ohio St	Mike Peppe	94	Michigan	67
1955	Ohio St	Mike Peppe	90	Yale/ Michigan	51
1956	Ohio St	Mike Peppe	68	Yale	54
1957	Michigan	Gus Stager	69	Yale	61
1958	Michigan	Gus Stager	72	Yale	63
1959	Michigan	Gus Stager	137½	Ohio St	44
1960	Southern Cal	Peter Daland	87	Michigan	73
1961	Michigan	Gus Stager	85	Southern Cal	62
1962	Ohio St	Mike Peppe	92	Southern Cal	46
1963	Southern Cal	Peter Daland	81	Yale	77
1964	Southern Cal	Peter Daland	96	Indiana	91
1965	Southern Cal	Peter Daland	285	Indiana	278½
1966	Southern Cal	Peter Daland	302	Indiana	286
1967	Stanford	Jim Gaughran	275	Southern Cal	260
1968	Indiana	James Counsilman	346	Yale	253
1969	Indiana	James Counsilman	427	Southern Cal	306
1970	Indiana	James Counsilman	332	Southern Cal	235
1971	Indiana	James Counsilman	351	Southern Cal	260
1972	Indiana	James Counsilman	390	Southern Cal	371
1973	Indiana	James Counsilman	358	Tennessee	294
1974	Southern Cal	Peter Daland	339	Indiana	338
1975	Southern Cal	Peter Daland	344	Indiana	274
1976	Southern Cal	Peter Daland	398	Tennessee	237
1977	Southern Cal	Peter Daland	385	Alabama	204
1978	Tennessee	Ray Bussard	307	Auburn	185
1979	California	Nort Thornton	287	Southern Cal	227
1980	California	Nort Thornton	234	Texas	220
1981	Texas	Eddie Reese	259	UCLA	189
1982	UCLA	Ron Ballatore	219	Texas	210
1983	Florida	Randy Reese	238	Southern Meth	227
1984	Florida	Randy Reese	287½	Texas	277
1985	Stanford	Skip Kenney	403½	Florida	302
1986	Stanford	Skip Kenney	404	California	335
1987	Stanford	Skip Kenney	374	Southern Cal	296
1988	Texas	Eddie Reese	424	Southern Cal	369½
1989	Texas	Eddie Reese	475	Stanford	396
1990	Texas	Eddie Reese	506	Southern Cal	423
1991	Texas	Eddie Reese	476	Stanford	420
1992	Stanford	Skip Kenney	632	Texas	356

CHAMPIONSHIP RESULTS (CONT.)

MEN

DIVISION I (CONT.)

YEAR	CHAMPION	COACH	PTS	RUNNER-UP	PTS
1993	Stanford	Skip Kenney	520½	Michigan	396
1994	Stanford	Skip Kenney	566½	Texas	445
1995	Michigan	Jon Urbanchek	561	Stanford	475
1996	Texas	Eddie Reese	479	Auburn	443½
1997	Auburn	David Marsh	496½	Stanford	340
1998	Stanford	Skip Kenney	594	Auburn	394½
1999	Auburn	David Marsh	467½	Stanford	414½
2000	Texas	Eddie Reese	538	Auburn	385
2001	Texas	Eddie Reese	597½	Stanford	457½
2002	Texas	Eddie Reese	512	Stanford	501
2003	Auburn	David Marsh	609½	Texas	413

MEN

DIVISION II

YEAR	CHAMPION	YEAR	CHAMPION
1963	SW Missouri St	1984	Cal St–Northridge
1964	Bucknell	1985	Cal St–Northridge
1965	San Diego St	1986	Cal St–Bakersfield
1966	San Diego St	1987	Cal St–Bakersfield
1967	UC–Santa Barbara	1988	Cal St–Bakersfield
1968	Long Beach St	1989	Cal St–Bakersfield
1969	UC–Irvine	1990	Cal St–Bakersfield
1970	UC–Irvine	1991	Cal St–Bakersfield
1971	UC–Irvine	1992	Cal St–Bakersfield
1972	Eastern Michigan	1993	Cal St–Bakersfield
1973	Cal St–Chico	1994	Oakland (MI)
1974	Cal St–Chico	1995	Oakland (MI)
1975	Cal St–Northridge	1996	Oakland (MI)
1976	Cal St–Chico	1997	Oakland (MI)
1977	Cal St–Northridge	1998	Cal St–Bakersfield
1978	Cal St–Northridge	1999	Drury
1979	Cal St–Northridge	2000	Cal St–Bakersfield
1980	Oakland (MI)	2001	Cal St–Bakersfield
1981	Cal St–Northridge	2002	Cal St–Bakersfield
1982	Cal St–Northridge	2003	Drury
1983	Cal St–Northridge		

MEN

DIVISION III

YEAR	CHAMPION	YEAR	CHAMPION
1975	Cal St–Chico	1990	Kenyon
1976	St. Lawrence	1991	Kenyon
1977	Johns Hopkins	1992	Kenyon
1978	Johns Hopkins	1993	Kenyon
1979	Johns Hopkins	1994	Kenyon
1980	Kenyon	1995	Kenyon
1981	Kenyon	1996	Kenyon
1982	Kenyon	1997	Kenyon
1983	Kenyon	1998	Kenyon
1984	Kenyon	1999	Kenyon
1985	Kenyon	2000	Kenyon
1986	Kenyon	2001	Kenyon
1987	Kenyon	2002	Kenyon
1988	Kenyon	2003	Kenyon
1989	Kenyon		

THE SIX FASTEST POOLS

1. INDIANA U–PURDUE U AT INDIANAPOLIS
As of 2002, 10 world and 88 U.S. records have been set in the IUPUI pool, which had hosted 16 NCAA championships and four U.S. Olympic Swim trials.

2. TEXAS
High filtration rate and oversized lane lines reduce wave action; can't argue with Longhorns' 18 national titles; has underwater speakers and spectators' viewing windows.

3. AUBURN
Excellent gutter system absorbs waves rather than letting them rebound into swimmers.

4. TEXAS A&M
Site of the 2001 men's NCAAs, at which nine U.S. records fell and the Aggie's won their first team title.

5. STANFORD
Avery Aquatic Center boasts three 50-meter pools, including the country's fastest outdoor one.

PETER H. BICK

6. CLEVELAND STATE
Fastest older pool (built in 1973), it's deeper at one end; home to annual underwater jigsaw puzzle assembly contest.

—Brian Cazeneuve

A Jewel of a Pool: swimmers have produced 10 world and 88 American records in the eight-lane stunner at IUPU in Indianapolis.

CHAMPIONSHIP RESULTS (CONT.)

WOMEN
DIVISION I

YEAR	CHAMPION	COACH	PTS	RUNNER-UP	PTS
1982	Florida	Randy Reese	505	Stanford	383
1983	Stanford	George Haines	418½	Florida	389½
1984	Texas	Richard Quick	392	Stanford	324
1985	Texas	Richard Quick	643	Florida	400
1986	Texas	Richard Quick	633	Florida	586
1987	Texas	Richard Quick	648½	Stanford	631½
1988	Texas	Richard Quick	661	Florida	542½
1989	Stanford	Richard Quick	610½	Texas	547
1990	Texas	Mark Schubert	632	Stanford	622½
1991	Texas	Mark Schubert	746	Stanford	653
1992	Stanford	Richard Quick	735½	Texas	651
1993	Stanford	Richard Quick	649½	Florida	421
1994	Stanford	Richard Quick	512	Texas	421
1995	Stanford	Richard Quick	497½	Michigan	478½
1996	Stanford	Richard Quick	478	SMU	397
1997	Southern Cal	Mark Schubert	406	Stanford	395
1998	Stanford	Richard Quick	422	Arizona	378
1999	Georgia	Jack Bauerle	504½	Stanford	441
2000	Georgia	Jack Bauerle	490½	Arizona	472
2001	Georgia	Jack Bauerle	389	Stanford	387½
2002	Auburn	David Marsh	474	Georgia	386
2003	Auburn	David Marsh	536	Georgia	373

WOMEN
DIVISION II

YEAR	CHAMPION	YEAR	CHAMPION
1982	Cal St–Northridge	1993	Oakland (MI)
1983	Clarion	1994	Oakland (MI)
1984	Clarion	1995	Air Force
1985	S Florida	1996	Air Force
1986	Clarion	1997	Drury
1987	Cal St–Northridge	1998	Drury
1988	Cal St–Northridge	1999	Drury
1989	Cal St–Northridge	2000	Drury
1990	Oakland (MI)	2001	Truman St
1991	Oakland (MI)	2002	Truman St
1992	Oakland (MI)	2003	Truman St

WOMEN
DIVISION III

YEAR	CHAMPION	YEAR	CHAMPION
1982	Williams	1993	Kenyon
1983	Williams	1994	Kenyon
1984	Kenyon	1995	Kenyon
1985	Kenyon	1996	Kenyon
1986	Kenyon	1997	Kenyon
1987	Kenyon	1998	Kenyon
1988	Kenyon	1999	Kenyon
1989	Kenyon	2000	Kenyon
1990	Kenyon	2001	Denison
1991	Kenyon	2002	Kenyon
1992	Kenyon	2003	Kenyon

INDIVIDUAL CHAMPIONSHIP RECORDS

MEN

EVENT	TIME	RECORD HOLDER	DATE
50-yard freestyle	19.08	Neil Walker, Texas	3-27-97
100-yard freestyle	41.62	Anthony Ervin, California	3-20-02
200-yard freestyle	1:33.03	Matt Biondi, California	4-3-87
500-yard freestyle	4:08.75	Tom Dolan, Michigan	3-23-95
1,650-yard freestyle	14:26.62	Chris Thompson, Michigan	3-24-01
100-yard backstroke	45.25	Neil Walker, Texas	3-28-97
200-yard backstroke	1:39.16	Aaron Peirsol, Texas	3-29-03
100-yard breaststroke	51.96	Brendan Hansen, Texas	3-28-03
200-yard breaststroke	1:52.62	Brendan Hansen, Texas	3-29-03
100-yard butterfly	45.44	Ian Crocker, Texas	3-29-02
200-yard butterfly	1:41.78	Melvin Stewart, Tennessee	3-30-91
200-yard individual medley	1:42.66	George Bovell, Auburn	3-29-03
400-yard individual medley	3:38.18	Tom Dolan, Michigan	3-24-95

WOMEN

EVENT	TIME	RECORD HOLDER	DATE
50-yard freestyle	21.69	Maritza Correia, Georgia	3-21-02
100-yard freestyle	47.29	Maritza Correia, Georgia	3-22-03
200-yard freestyle	1:43.08	Martina Moravcova, Southern Methodist	3-28-97
500-yard freestyle	4:34.39	Janet Evans, Stanford	3-15-90
1,650-yard freestyle	15:39.14	Janet Evans, Stanford	3-17-90
100-yard backstroke	49.97	Natalie Coughlin, California	3-22-02
200-yard backstroke	1:49.52	Natalie Coughlin, California	3-22-02
100-yard breaststroke	58.62	Tara Kirk, Stanford	3-21-03
200-yard breaststroke	2:07.36	Tara Kirk, Stanford	3-22-02
100-yard butterfly	50.01	Natalie Coughlin, California	3-22-02
200-yard butterfly	1:53.36	Limin Liu, Nevada	3-20-99
200-yard individual medley	1:53.91	Maggie Bowen, Auburn	3-21-02
400-yard individual medley	4:02.28	Summer Sanders, Stanford	3-20-92

GO FIGURE

11 Team swimming and diving championships for both Michigan and Ohio State, the most among all Division I men's teams. USC is next on the list with nine.

11 Individual career NCAA titles won by Stanford's Pablo Morales, the most by any man or woman. Morales, the two time Olympic gold medalist at Barcelona and current coach of the Nebraska women's swimming and diving team, won the the 100-meter butterfly four times (1984 to '87), the 200-meter butterfly four times (1984 to '87), and the 200-meter individual medley three times (1985 to '87). On top of all that, Morales was also part of three championship relay teams.

1 Coach in NCAA history to guide both the men's and women's national championship teams. David Marsh's Auburn men's team won a third national crown in 2003 a week after the Auburn women's team took their second straight national title.

24 Consecutive Division III men's swimming and diving championships for Kenyon College, the longest championship streak for any school in any sport in any division.

47.29 NCAA-record time in the 100-yard freestyle by Georgia's Maritza Correia at the 2003 NCAA championships.

The Usual
SUSPECTS

A handful of teams rule the college lacrosse nation, with few signs of overthrow on the horizon

IT WAS FITTING that in 2003 the men's lacrosse final returned to Baltimore for the first time since 1975. The Baltimore area has long been a hotbed for the sport and has produced many of the nation's top collegiate players. Baltimore is also home to Johns Hopkins University, a perennial powerhouse as synonymous with lacrosse as Duke is with men's basketball.

The Blue Jays routinely ascend to the top of the national rankings, but in recent years the NCAA championship has eluded them. After practically owning the sport from 1978 to '87—a span in which Hopkins won five national championships and finished second three times—the Blue Jays have been competitive, but not dominant. And despite being ranked No. 1 for most of the 2003 season and enjoying a home-field advantage for the Final Four (a record 37,944 fans attended the final), Hopkins extended its titleless streak to 16 years

with a 9–7 championship-game loss to Virginia. (The Cavaliers nearly won the women's title as well, falling 9–8 in overtime to Princeton).

"We'll continue to build because we already have the foundation," said Hopkins coach Dave Pietramala. "Each year, we've taken another step. Hey, we don't lose a lot of games around here. Were we happy just to be in the championship game? No. This is where we should be. We'll be back."

FAVORITES
This section includes plenty of familiar faces, for there are few sports as regional, even tribal, as lacrosse—which, incidentally, was invented by Native Americans.

Though **Johns Hopkins** will need to replace All-America midfielder Adam Doneger and goalie Robert Scherr, the Blue Jays have an excellent chance to make good on coach Pietramala's promise that they will return to the title

Johns Hopkins and Barrie, who scored this acrobatic goal against Syracuse in the semifinals last year, return with one goal in mind: the NCAA title.

game. Junior All-America attackman Kyle Barrie (37 goals, 20 assists) is coming off a breakout year and enters the season with an NCAA-leading streak of 26 games with at least one point. Barrie will be supported by two outstanding midfielders—junior Kyle Harrison, who scored 22 goals, dished out 14 assists and scooped up a team-high 83 ground balls; and senior Kevin Boland (21 g, 25 a). Freshman Scott Smith is the early favorite to replace Scherr in goal.

With an array of impressive returning talent, including All-America goalie Tillman Johnson, defending champion **Virginia** should be back, too. Though the Cavaliers must replace All-America midfielder Chris Totelli (26 g, 23 a), they retain a trio of big-time scorers in juniors John Christmas (36 g, 12 a), Joe Yevoli (23 g, 26 a) and sophomore Matt Ward (26 g, 20 a).

Coming off a down year by its standards, **Syracuse** showed signs of life at the end of the season before getting drilled by Hopkins in the national semifinal. The Orangemen have some holes to fill on defense, but they will have plenty of scoring punch with seniors Michael Powell (31 g, 33 a), Brian Nee (24 g, 6 a), Sean Lindsay (29 g, 7 a) and sophomore Brian Crockett (20 g, 10 a).

The team the Orangemen eliminated from the NCAAs, six-time NCAA champ **Princeton**, packs plenty of firepower with senior attackman Ryan Boyle, who led the nation in points per game (4.5) in 2003, scoring 10 goals and making 49 assists. Also look for big things from the Tigers' sophomore attackman Jason Doneger (41 g, 3 a), whose older brother Adam starred at Hopkins last season.

Rounding out the men's favorites is

Powell (22), who scored 31 goals last season, has played in two NCAA title games in three years at Syracuse.

1997 and '98 runner-up **Maryland**, which will once again field one of the nation's top teams. The Terps have a pair of potential difference-makers in sophomore attackman Joe Walters (33 g, 13 a) and senior defenseman Chris Passavia.

On the women's side, defending champion **Princeton** lost player of the year Rachael Becker to graduation, but has some big guns returning to the fold, including senior midfielder Theresa Sherry (46 g, 6 a), junior midfielder Elizabeth Pillion (34 g, 11 a) and senior defenseman Kate Norbury.

In 2002, the Tigers broke **Maryland**'s seven-year stranglehold on the women's title, and have now won two in a row, but Maryland is by no means out of the championship picture. The Terps remain a potent threat behind scoring machine Kelly Coppedge, a senior who scored a whopping 73 goals in 2003. Another proficient scorer, junior Amy Appelt (58 g, 25 a), makes **Virginia** dangerous, and **Loyola** (MD) is always strong, and will be difficult to score on

with interchangeably solid goalies Cindy Nicolaus and Kim Lawton.

DARKHORSES

With a solid recruiting base on lacrosse-mad Long Island, the **Hofstra** men are always competitive. The Pride will be particularly strong in the back with senior All-America defenseman Brian Zuchelli. Another New York team, **Cornell**, must replace four-time All-America defenseman Ryan McClay, but with senior Andrew Collins (20 g, 39 a) and junior Sean Greenhalgh (37 g, 9 a) the Big Red should give Princeton a run in the Ivy League, as should **Dartmouth**, which made its first NCAA appearance in 2003.

High-scoring senior attackman Jeff Zywicki (41 g, 21 a) and junior defenseman Matt Garcia make **Massachusetts** worth watching, and **Georgetown**, with

Now a senior, Sherry delivered a second consecutive NCAA title to Princeton last season, scoring in overtime of the final against Virginia.

Walid Hajj (23 goals last season), has been a program on the rise in recent seasons.

Towson is another team with a plethora of budding talent. Though they lost their top three scorers, the Tigers, who finished second in the 1991 national tournament, are looking for senior midfielder Drew Pfarr (16 g, 5 a), among others, to help restore the program to the nation's elite.

Another team looking to reclaim past glory is **North Carolina**, which dominated the 1980s along with Johns Hopkins. The Tar Heels have a star in junior goalie Paul Spellman, who became the first Tar Heel netminder to lead the team in ground balls since 1982.

ONES TO WATCH

Princeton's Boyle is the early favorite for 2004 player of the year, but several proficient goal scorers could give Boyle a run for his money. Lehigh's Tony Lowe (43 goals), Duke's Matt Rewkowski (36), Delaware's Matt Alrich (35) and Notre Dame's Dan Berger (32) are all blessed with the ability to put the ball in the net, and Mike Powell, descended from a long line of accomplished Powells at Syracuse, is considered by many to be the best player in the country.

On the women's side, nobody can fill the net like Maryland's senior Coppedge, whose 73 goals led the nation last season. But keep an eye on Duke senior Suzanne Wosczyna (45 g, 32 a), Central Connecticut State sophomore Tracy Uellendahl (49 g, 13 a), Boston University senior Alyssa Trudel (44 g, 42 a) and Denver senior Patience Baldwin (52 goals). Their teams may not compete for the national title, but they could be in the hunt for the player of the year award.

Finally, no list of NCAA lacrosse personalities would be complete without including Virginia goalie Tillman Johnson. The first time veteran Cavs coach Dom Starsia laid eyes on Johnson was at a summer camp before Johnson's senior year at St. Mary's High in Annapolis, Md. Starsia watched the young goalie complete one workout and offered him a scholarship on the spot. It didn't take long for Johnson to make his mark. He started as a freshman and has been a steadying force in the Cavaliers net ever since. "He's the best goalie I've ever had," says Starsia. And no one will be surprised if he backstops another national title in 2004.

MEN'S DIVISION I
CHAMPIONSHIP GAME BOX SCORE

	1	2	3	4
Virginia	4	2	2	1—9
Johns Hopkins	0	4	1	2—7

Virgina scoring: A.J. Shannon 4, John Christmas 2, Chris Rotelli 1, Billy Glading 1, Matt Ward 1.
Hopkins scoring: Adam Doneger 2, Kyle Barrie 1, Bobby Benson 1, Joe McDermott 1 Greg Peyser 1, Corey Harned 1.

NCAA MEN'S DIVISION I INDIVIDUAL LEADERS

GOALS

PLAYER AND TEAM	CLASS	GP	G	AVG
Tony Lowe, Lehigh	Jr	14	43	3.07
Sean Hartofilis, Princeton	Sr	14	41	2.93
Sean Greenhalgh, Cornell	So	13	37	2.85
Jason Doneger, Princeton	Fr	15	41	2.73
Bobby Benson, Johns Hopkins	Sr	16	41	2.56
Jeff Zywicki, Massachusetts	Jr	16	41	2.56
John Bogosian, Hobart	Sr	13	33	2.54
Jon Thompson, Brown	Sr	14	35	2.50
Travis Eckler, Hartford	Sr	17	42	2.47
Kyle Barrie, Johns Hopkins	So	15	37	2.47

ASSISTS

PLAYER AND TEAM	CLASS	GP	A	AVG
Ryan Boyle, Princeton	Jr	13	49	3.77
Andrew Collins, Cornell	Jr	13	39	3.00
Brian Marks, Villanova	Sr	15	43	2.87
Jeff Bryan, Army	Jr	16	45	2.81
Chris Cara, Bucknell	So	13	30	2.31
Patrick Walsh, Notre Dame	Fr	14	32	2.29
Luke Daquino, Albany	So	16	35	2.19
Michael Powell, Syracuse	Jr	16	33	2.06
Brendan Morgan, Drexel	Jr	12	23	1.92
Mark Miyashita, Canisius	Sr	14	26	1.86

POINTS

PLAYER AND TEAM	CLASS	GP	G	A	PTS	PTS/G
Ryan Boyle Princeton	Jr	13	10	49	59	4.54
Andrew Collins, Cornell	Jr	13	20	39	59	4.54
Brian Marks, Villanova	Sr	15	24	43	67	4.47
Michael Powell, Syracuse	Jr	16	31	33	64	4.00
Ryan Ward, Butler	Sr	13	27	24	51	3.92
Jeff Zywicki, Massachusetts	Jr	16	41	21	62	3.88
Kyle Barrie, Johns Hopkins	So	15	37	20	57	3.80
Curtis Smith, Ohio St	Sr	14	33	20	53	3.79
Chris Cara, Bucknell	So	13	19	30	49	3.77
Travis Eckler, Hartford	Sr	17	42	22	64	3.76

NCAA MEN'S DIVISION I INDIVIDUAL LEADERS (CONT.)

GOALS AGAINST AVERAGE

PLAYER AND TEAM	CLASS	G	MIN	GAA
Joseph Canuso, Villanova	Fr	15	900	6.07
Mike Gabel, Vermont	So	13	773	6.13
Justin Sussman, Bucknell	Sr	13	741	6.88
Andrew McMinn, Providence	So	14	894	6.91
Andrew Goldstein, Dartmouth	So	14	819	7.10
Rob Scherr, Johns Hopkins	Sr	16	919	7.12
Dan McCormick, Maryland	Sr	16	913	7.23
Rich D'Andrea, Georgetown	So	14	825	7.27
Tillman Johsnon, Virginia	Jr	17	972	7.28
Andrew Jarolimek, Colgate	Fr	15	881	7.49
Stewart Crosland, Notre Dame	Jr	14	737	7.49

WOMEN'S DIVISION I CHAMPIONSHIP GAME BOX SCORE

	1	2	OT	
Princeton	3	4	1	—8
Virginia	4	3	0	—7

Princeton scoring: Theresa Sherry 3, Lindsey Biles 2, Elizabeth Pillion 2, Whitney Miller 1
Virginia scoring: Cary Chasney 3, Amy Appelt 1, Caitlin Banks 1, Morgan Thalenberg 1 Courtney Young 1.

NCAA WOMEN'S DIVISION I INDIVIDUAL LEADERS

GOALS

PLAYER AND TEAM	CLASS	GP	G	AVG
Tracy Uellendahl, Central Conn St	Fr	13	49	3.77
Suzanne Wosczyna, Old Dominion	Jr	12	45	3.75
Patience Baldwin, Denver	Jr	14	52	3.71
Kathleen Mikowski, Hofstra	Sr	16	57	3.56
Jill Toomey, George Mason	Sr	17	59	3.47

ASSISTS

PLAYER AND TEAM	CLASS	GP	A	AVG
Melissa Ellers, Georgetown	Jr	17	56	3.29
Emily Rice, Davidson	Sr	16	49	3.06
Danielle Werner, Stony Brook	Fr	17	51	3.00
Regina Oliver, Ohio St	So	18	53	2.94
Rachael Becker, Princeton	Sr	20	56	2.80

POINTS

PLAYER AND TEAM	CLASS	GP	G	A	PTS	PTS/G
Suzanne Wosczyna, Old Dominion	Jr	12	45	32	77	6.42
Tracy Uellendahl, Central Conn St	Fr	13	49	13	62	4.77
Lauren Aumiller, Virginia	Sr	22	64	36	100	4.55
Alyssa Trudel, Boston University	So	19	44	42	86	4.53
Kathleen Mikowski, Hofstra	Sr	16	57	14	71	4.44

GOALS AGAINST AVERAGE

PLAYER AND TEAM	CLASS	G	MIN	GAA
Kim Lawton, Loyola (MD)	Jr	19	570	5.37
Sarah Kolodner, Princeton	So	20	1102	6.42
Alexis Benechanos, Maryland	Sr	20	1097	6.62
Megan Huether, Duke	Fr	18	1036	6.95
Anne Sheridan, Boston University	So	19	914	7.02

MEN'S DIVISION II
CHAMPIONSHIP GAME BOX SCORE

	1	2	3	4
New York Tech	2	2	2	3—9
Limestone	1	0	0	3—4

New York Tech scoring: Tom Zummo 2, Joe Gabrysiak 2, Paul Montali 2, Sean Meagher 2, Joseph Vasold 1.
Limestone scoring: Devan Spiker 2, Robert Woody 2.

NCAA MEN'S DIVISION II INDIVIDUAL LEADERS

GOALS

PLAYER AND TEAM	CLASS	GP	G	AVG
Jeremy Jablonski, Pace	Fr	14	61	4.36
Dan Naglieri, Dowling	Fr	11	44	4.00
Paul Mantali, New York Tech	So	13	47	3.62
Jon Yuengling, Bryant	Jr	17	60	3.53
Joe Ourelio, Dominican (NY)	So	8	26	3.25

ASSISTS

PLAYER AND TEAM	CLASS	GP	A	AVG
Jeremy Johnson, Wheeling Jesuit	Sr	12	39	3.25
Ryan Spillett, Le Moyne	Sr	14	43	3.07
Ryan Knope, Bryant	Sr	17	47	2.76
Sal Betty, Dominican (NY)	So	8	22	2.75
Brian Boyle, New York Tech	Jr	14	38	2.71

POINTS

PLAYER AND TEAM	CLASS	GP	G	A	PTS	PTS/G
Jeremy Johnson, Wheeling Jesuit	Sr	12	30	39	69	5.75
Dan Naglieri, Dowling	Fr	11	44	14	58	5.27
Jeremy Jablonski, Pace	Fr	14	61	12	73	5.21
Devan Spiker, Limestone	Sr	16	42	39	81	5.06
Jon Yuengling, Bryant	Jr	17	60	26	86	5.06

GOALS AGAINST AVERAGE

PLAYER AND TEAM	CLASS	G	MIN	GAA
Matt Malloy, Limestone	Sr	16	881	6.40
Tom Kimble, Le Moyne	Sr	12	469	7.16
Greg Horowitz, Bryant	Sr	14	548	7.67
Matt Hunter, New York Tech	Sr	14	711	7.07
Mark Miller, Adelphi	Sr	10	559	8.48

HEARD ON CAMPUS

"At Virginia Commonwealth we don't have a football team so we
wear T-shirts that say VCU FOOTBALL: UNDEFEATED."

MEN'S DIVISION III CHAMPIONSHIP GAME BOX SCORE

	1	2	3	4	OT
Middlebury	3	1	4	5	0—13
Salisbury	3	7	1	2	1—14

Middlebury scoring: Greg Bastis 3, Charley Howe 2, Mike Frissora 2, Andrew Giordano 2, Jonathan Sisto 2, Mike Saraceni 1, Ben Tobey 1.
Salisbury scoring: Josh Bergey 4, Chris Phillips 3, Joe Tamberrino 2, Andy Arnold 2, Scott Simmons 1, Justin Smith 1, Kevin Gemmell 1.

NCAA MEN'S DIVISION III INDIVIDUAL LEADERS

GOALS

PLAYER AND TEAM	CLASS	GP	G	AVG
P.J. Matthews, Mt. Ida	Fr	12	56	4.67
Kenny Seitles, Roger Williams	Jr	14	61	4.36
Brian Manion, Widener	Jr	16	65	4.06
Matt Silverio, Hamilton	Sr	18	72	4.00
Andy Bonasera, Roanoke	Sr	14	52	3.71

ASSISTS

PLAYER AND TEAM	CLASS	GP	A	AVG
Louis Lucchetti, Lasell	So	15	52	3.47
Rob Weaver, McDaniel	So	13	43	3.31
Kevin Lally, Endicott	Fr	18	58	3.22
Kris Davis, Roanoke	Jr	16	50	3.13
Jamie Lockard, Widener	Sr	16	48	3.00

POINTS

PLAYER AND TEAM	CLASS	GP	G	A	PTS	PTS/G
P.J. Matthews, Mt. Ida	Fr	12	56	17	73	6.08
Reese Baillie, Centenary (NJ)	So	15	48	43	91	6.07
Josh Bergey, Salisbury	Sr	20	72	48	120	6.00
Kenny Seitles, Roger Williams	Jr	14	61	21	82	5.86
Steve Littlewood, Widener	Sr	16	53	39	92	5.75

GOALS AGAINST AVERAGE

PLAYER AND TEAM	CLASS	G	MIN	GAA
Joe Zebrowski, Clarkson	So	13	723	5.89
Ansel Sanders, Washington & Lee	Jr	14	815	5.89
Steve Feltmann, Cortland St	Sr	20	1030	5.94
Reeves Craig, Goucher	So	16	978	5.95
Mike Taylor, Salisbury	So	16	357	6.05

MEN'S DIVISION I

YEAR	CHAMPION	COACH	SCORE	RUNNER-UP
1971	Cornell	Richie Moran	12–6	Maryland
1972	Virginia	Glenn Thiel	13–12	Johns Hopkins
1973	Maryland	Bud Beardmore	10–9 (2 OT)	Johns Hopkins
1974	Johns Hopkins	Bob Scott	17–12	Maryland
1975	Maryland	Bud Beardmore	20–13	Navy
1976	Cornell	Richie Moran	16–13 (OT)	Maryland
1977	Cornell	Richie Moran	16–8	Johns Hopkins
1978	Johns Hopkins	Henry Ciccarone	13–8	Cornell
1979	Johns Hopkins	Henry Ciccarone	15–9	Maryland
1980	Johns Hopkins	Henry Ciccarone	9–8 (2 OT)	Virginia
1981	N Carolina	Willie Scroggs	14–13	Johns Hopkins
1982	N Carolina	Willie Scroggs	7–5	Johns Hopkins
1983	Syracuse	Roy Simmons Jr	17–16	Johns Hopkins
1984	Johns Hopkins	Don Zimmerman	13–10	Syracuse
1985	Johns Hopkins	Don Zimmerman	11–4	Syracuse
1986	N Carolina	Willie Scroggs	10–9 (OT)	Virginia
1987	Johns Hopkins	Don Zimmerman	11–10	Cornell
1988	Syracuse	Roy Simmons Jr	13–8	Cornell
1989	Syracuse	Roy Simmons Jr	13–12	Johns Hopkins
1990	Syracuse	Roy Simmons Jr	21–9	Loyola (MD)
1991	N Carolina	Dave Klarmann	18–13	Towson St
1992	Princeton	Bill Tierney	10–9	Syracuse
1993	Syracuse	Roy Simmons Jr	13–12	N Carolina
1994	Princeton	Bill Tierney	9–8 (OT)	Virginia
1995	Syracuse	Roy Simmons Jr	13–9	Maryland
1996	Princeton	Bill Tierney	13–12 (OT)	Virginia
1997	Princeton	Bill Tierney	19–7	Maryland
1998	Princeton	Bill Tierney	15–5	Maryland
1999	Virginia	Dom Starsia	12–10	Syracuse
2000	Syracuse	John Desko	13–7	Princeton
2001	Princeton	Bill Tierney	10–9 (OT)	Syracuse
2002	Syracuse	John Desko	13–12	Princeton
2003	Virginia	Dom Starsia	9–7	Johns Hopkins

MEN'S DIVISION II (DISCONTINUED, THEN RENEWED)

YEAR	CHAMPION	COACH	SCORE	RUNNER-UP
1974	Towson St	Carl Runk	18–17 (OT)	Hobart
1975	Cortland St	Chuck Winters	12–11	Hobart
1976	Hobart	Jerry Schmidt	18–9	Adelphi
1977	Hobart	Jerry Schmidt	23–13	Washington (MD)
1978	Roanoke	Paul Griffin	14–13	Hobart
1979	Adelphi	Paul Doherty	17–12	MD–Baltimore County
1980	MD–Baltimore County	Dick Watts	23–14	Adelphi
1981	Adelphi	Paul Doherty	17–14	Loyola (MD)
1993	Adelphi	Kevin Sheehan	11–7	LIU–C.W. Post
1994	Springfield	Keith Bugbee	15–12	New York Tech
1995	Adelphi	Sandy Kapatos	12–10	Springfield
1996	LIU–C.W. Post	Tom Postel	15–10	Adelphi
1997	New York Tech	Jack Kaley	18–11	Adelphi
1998	Adelphi	Sandy Kapatos	18–6	LIU–C.W. Post
1999	Adelphi	Sandy Kapatos	11–8	LIU–C.W. Post
2000	Limestone	Mike Cerino	10–9	LIU–C.W. Post
2001	Adelphi	Sandy Kapatos	14–10	Limestone
2002	Limestone	T.W. Johnson	11–9	New York Tech
2003	New York Tech	Jack Kaley	9–4	Limestone

MEN'S DIVISION III

Year	Champion	Coach	Score	Runner-Up
1980	Hobart	Dave Urick	11–8	Cortland St
1981	Hobart	Dave Urick	10–8	Cortland St
1982	Hobart	Dave Urick	9–8 (OT)	Washington (MD)
1983	Hobart	Dave Urick	13–9	Roanoke
1984	Hobart	Dave Urick	12–5	Washington (MD)
1985	Hobart	Dave Urick	15–8	Washington (MD)
1986	Hobart	Dave Urick	13–10	Washington (MD)
1987	Hobart	Dave Urick	9–5	Ohio Wesleyan
1988	Hobart	Dave Urick	18–9	Ohio Wesleyan
1989	Hobart	Dave Urick	11–8	Ohio Wesleyan
1990	Hobart	B.J. O'Hara	18–6	Washington (MD)
1991	Hobart	B.J. O'Hara	12–11	Salisbury St
1992	Nazareth (NY)	Scott Nelson	13–12	Hobart
1993	Hobart	B.J. O'Hara	16–10	Ohio Wesleyan
1994	Salisbury St	Jim Berkman	15–9	Hobart
1995	Salisbury St	Jim Berkman	22–13	Nazareth
1996	Nazareth	Scott Nelson	11–10 (OT)	Washington (MD)
1997	Nazareth	Scott Nelson	15–14 (OT)	Washington (MD)
1998	Washington (MD)	John Haus	16–10	Nazareth
1999	Salisbury St	Jim Berkman	13–6	Middlebury
2000	Middlebury	Erin Quinn	16–12	Salisbury St
2001	Middlebury	Erin Quinn	15–10	Gettysburg
2002	Middlebury	Erin Quinn	14–9	Gettysburg
2003	Salisbury	Jim Berkman	14–13 (OT)	Middlebury

 # GOLDEN GOALS

In spite of a terminal illness, Loyola lacrosse coach Diane Geppi-Aikens went two for two in attaining the goals she set for herself last spring. In the April 28, 2003, edition of Sports Illustrated, Geppi-Aikens wrote about having late-stage brain cancer, which confined her to a wheelchair. "I have two goals: getting to the Final Four and to my son Michael's graduation," she wrote. The top-ranked Greyhounds reached the semis with a win over Yale, then lost 5–3 to Princeton. With their season over, the team gathered in a circle in the locker room. "We talked about the adversity we overcame all year," said Geppi-Aikens. "I told them I was proud of them. There were a lot of tears and laughter." Nineteen days later, on May 31, Geppi-Aikens attended Michael's high school graduation. She passed away on June 29.

WOMEN'S DIVISION I*

YEAR	CHAMPION	COACH	SCORE	RUNNER-UP
2001 ....Maryland		Cindy Timchal	14–13 (OT)	Georgetown
2002 ....Princeton		Chris Sailer	12–7	Georgetown
2003 ....Princeton		Chris Sailer	8–7 (OT)	Virginia

WOMEN'S DIVISION II*

YEAR	CHAMPION	COACH	SCORE	RUNNER-UP
2001	LIU–C.W. Post	Karen MacCrate	13–9	W Chester
2002	Westchester	Ginny Martino	11–6	Stonehill
2003	Stonehill	Michael Daly	9–8	Longwood

WOMEN'S DIVISION I AND II*

YEAR	CHAMPION	COACH	SCORE	RUNNER-UP
1982	Massachusetts	Pamela Hixon	9–6	Trenton St
1983	Delaware	Janet Smith	10–7	Temple
1984	Temple	Tina Sloan Green	6–4	Maryland
1985	New Hampshire	Marisa Didio	6–5	Maryland
1986	Maryland	Sue Tyler	11–10	Penn St
1987	Penn St	Susan Scheetz	7–6	Temple
1988	Temple	Tina Sloan Green	15–7	Penn St
1989	Penn St	Susan Scheetz	7–6	Harvard
1990	Harvard	Carole Kleinfelder	8–7	Maryland
1991	Virginia	Jane Miller	8–6	Maryland
1992	Maryland	Cindy Timchal	11–10	Harvard
1993	Virginia	Jane Miller	8–6 (OT)	Princeton
1994	Princeton	Chris Sailer	10–7	Virginia
1995	Maryland	Cindy Timchal	13–5	Princeton
1996	Maryland	Cindy Timchal	10–5	Virginia
1997	Maryland	Cindy Timchal	8–7	Loyola (MD)
1998	Maryland	Cindy Timchal	11–5	Virginia
1999	Maryland	Cindy Timchal	16–6	Virginia
2000	Maryland	Cindy Timchal	16–8	Princeton

*Divisions I and II competed for a single championship until 2001.

WOMEN'S DIVISION III

YEAR	CHAMPION	SCORE	RUNNER-UP
1985	Trenton St	7–4	Ursinus
1986	Ursinus	12–10	Trenton St
1987	Trenton St	8–7 (OT)	Ursinus
1988	Trenton St	14–11	William Smith
1989	Ursinus	8–6	Trenton St
1990	Ursinus	7–6	St. Lawrence
1991	Trenton St	7–6	Ursinus
1992	Trenton St	5–3	William Smith
1993	Trenton St	10–9	William Smith
1994	Trenton St	29–11	William Smith
1995	Trenton St	14–13	William Smith
1996	Trenton St	15–8	Middlebury
1997	Middlebury	14–9	College of NJ*
1998	Coll of NJ	14–9	Williams
1999	Middlebury	10–9	Amherst
2000	Coll of NJ	14–8	Williams
2001	Middlebury	11–10	Amherst
2002	Middlebury	12–6	College of NJ*
2003	Amherst	11–9	Middlebury

*Formerly Trenton St

GO FIGURE

4 — Number of the 214 institutions with Division I, II or III men's lacrosse teams that are located west of the Mississippi River. They are: the U.S. Air Force Academy, the University of Denver, Colorado College and Whittier College, and they're all located in Colorado.

32 — Consecutive Division I NCAA lacrosse tournament appearances by 2003 finalist Johns Hopkins. The only tournament the Blue Jays didn't appear in was the first, in 1971.

21 — Consecutive seasons in which Syracuse has made it to the Men's Division I Final Four. During that span the Orangemen won the title eight times, although the school's 1990 title was stripped by the NCAA Committee on Infractions because of a questionable car loan made to a player.

1 — School that has won both the men's and women's Division I championship in the same season. In 1994, the Princeton men defeated Virginia in overtime to win their title while the Lady Tigers beat Maryland 10–7 in the women's final.

108,790 — Spectators at the three-day 2003 men's lacrosse Final Four at M&T Bank Stadium in Baltimore. That total set a new record, shattering the previous one of 73,983 set in 1997 at Byrd Stadium on the campus of the University of Maryland, in College Park.

AFTER A SKEIN of near misses during the past two decades, Clemson finally landed its first NCAA golf championship, taking the 2003 title at Oklahoma State's Karsten Creek course. The Stillwater course's degree of difficulty—it's an unforgiving, 7,215-yard, par 72—made the championship all the sweeter for the Tigers and coach Larry Penley.

Sure, the Tigers were ranked No. 1 all season, but as the NCAAs began, coach Penley was being referred to as the Phil Mickelson of college golf—good enough to contend but lacking the *je ne sais quoi* to win the big one. With nine Top 10 finishes, including two runner-ups since 1984, Penley could hardly argue with that assessment, but last year he silenced it once and for all as his Tigers edged Oklahoma State by two strokes.

"I had been obsessed with the darn thing," said Penley. "It drove me nuts for a while. I just finally got to the point where I had to let it go. If it happened, it happened and if it didn't I was OK with that."

But Penley's star golfer, All-America D.J. Trahan, was determined to make it happen: He decided to return for his senior season instead of turning pro so he could help Clemson win a national championship. Of course, Trahan would need help to deliver a title to Penley, and

If at First...

The Clemson Tigers taught college golf a lesson in perseverance last season; can they do it again in 2004?

he got it with terrific play at Karsten Creek from teammates Jack Ferguson, Matt Hendrix, Ben Duncan and Gregg Jones, all of whom, in addition to Trahan, are native-born South Carolinians.

"We've had good teams, teams that have won tournaments, big tournaments during the course of the year," said Penley. "But we never could figure it out [at the NCAAs]. Maybe it took a ridiculously hard golf course for us to win."

While the Tigers battled Oklahoma State to the wire at Karsten Creek, USC ran away with the 2003 women's title, winning by 15 strokes over Pepperdine.

FAVORITES

Don't expect **Clemson** to fall too far. Trahan was the only senior on the Tigers' 2003 roster, and senior Hendrix and junior Ferguson will be two of the top golfers in the nation in 2004. And among Penley's incoming freshmen are South Carolina's last two high school Class 4A champions. That title drought has ended, and could give way to a championship deluge.

Florida, which tied for fourth at Karsten Creek, may have something to say about that. The Gators are led by three-time All-America Camillo Villegas, a native of Colombia who will be a favorite for player of the year. Florida also has a pair of rising young stars in sophomores Matt Every, James Vargas and Brett Stegmaier. Every finished tied for 12th in the individual competition at last year's nationals.

Watch out for **UCLA** as well. The Bruins

Cho, who finished third at last year's NCAAs, will try to lead the Trojans back to the national championship.

Williams, the national runner-up in his junior year, returns for Auburn and should help the Tigers contend in the SEC, if not beyond.

eligibility and turn pro, coach Mike Holder produces All-Americas like General Motors puts out trucks. This year should be no different as Oklahoma State will have plenty of talent and experience, including the appropriately named senior, Par Nilsson, junior Alex Noren and sophomores Zack Robinson and Chris Clarke.

Coming off a banner year, complete with a runaway victory at the NCAAs and an individual national champion in Mikaela Parmlid, the **USC** women are looking for more of the same in 2004. They lost Parmlid and Becky Lundi, but the Women of Troy still have to be considered the team to beat with sophomore Irene Cho (third at last year's NCAAs), junior Anna Rawson (tied for 11th) and sophomore Tanya Dergal.

Last season's national runner-up, **Pepperdine**, welcomes back Carolina Llano (tied for 19th at the nationals), Courtney Clark and Rachel Kyono. **Texas** has established itself as one of the most consistent programs in women's golf, and should be in the mix again with senior Janice Olivencia and juniors Perry Swenson and Lisa Ferrero. **Duke** entered last year's championships as the favorite before stumbling to a 10th place finish. Expect the Blue Devils to climb back to the top of the rankings with seniors Leigh Anne Hardin and Virada Nirapathpongporn (tied for 11th in the 2003 NCAAs).

DARKHORSES

Auburn should give Florida a run for the men's SEC title and has a star in senior All-America Lee Williams, who finished second to surprise winner Alejandro

return the entire roster from the team that finished third in last year's NCAAs, including a foursome of seasoned seniors, John Merrick, Travis Johnson, Steve Conway and Roy Moon, who should be near the top of the national rankings all season long.

Georgia Tech, which tied Washington for 11th at Karsten Creek, should be a contender in 2004. The Yellow Jackets lost All-America Troy Matteson but have budding talents in juniors Nicholas Thompson and Chad Wongluekiet and sophomore Thomas Jordan.

No list of favorites would be complete without the inclusion of perennial power **Oklahoma State**, which has won nine national titles and finished runner-up last season. Though the Cowboys lost two-time golfer of the year Hunter Mahan, who decided to give up his final year of

Canizares of Arizona State (see sidelines) in last year's NCAA individual championships. With senior Jason Hartwick and sophomore Matthew Rosenfeld, **Texas** has a chance to improve upon its ninth-place finish at the 2003 nationals, and although graduation will hurt **Wake Forest**, which tied Florida for fourth last season, the Demon Deacons bring back their top golfer, two-time All-America Bill Haas. The fairway strollin' Rebels of **UNLV**, who finished 13th at Karsten Creek, have two of the nation's best in All-America Ryan Moore and Travis Whisman.

On the women's side, don't look past **Arizona**, which boasts one of the nation's top golfers in sophomore Erica Blasberg, or **Ohio State**, which is coming off its best year ever (fourth at the 2003 NCAAs) and brings back junior Kristen White and senior Allison Hanna. **UCLA** has a pair of up-and-comers in senior Hana Kim and junior Charlotte Mayorkas. Kim finished only four strokes off the pace at Purdue last year, and the Bruins came in fifth as a team.

SIDELINES

While hosting a member of the Spanish national team in the fall of 2002, Arizona State coach Randy Lein learned of a promising young Spanish golfer named Alejandro Canizares. The national-team player put Lein in touch with Canizares, and, as Lein described it, "We started emailing, and that was that. Easiest recruiting job I've ever had." And most fruitful: As a freshman, Canizares won the 2003 NCAA individual title.

While most college golf stars are domestic products, they are scattered from sea to shining sea—from Washington's Brock Mackenzie, who averaged 71.63 per round last season, to Justin Smith of Minnesota, who gives the 2002 NCAA champs a chance in any match, to North Carolina's Dustin Bray, a candidate for All-America in 2004. Other potential All-Americas include Arkansas' Andrew Dahl, Tulsa's David Inglis and Arizona's Chris Nallan.

Topping his spectacular freshman year will be a challenge for Arizona State's Canizares, the defending NCAA individual champion.

NCAA CHAMPIONSHIPS

MEN'S DIVISION I—TEAM
KARSTEN CREEK, STILLWATER, OK
(PAR 72; 7,095 YDS) MAY 27–30

TEAM	SCORES				TOTAL	OVER/UNDER PAR
Clemson	299	302	287	303	1191	+39
Oklahoma St	299	300	290	304	1193	+41
UCLA	303	295	301	298	1197	+45
Florida	302	300	297	299	1198	+46
Wake Forest	304	306	290	298	1198	+46
Arizona St	306	308	297	291	1202	+50
Augusta St	311	306	294	302	1213	+61
Auburn	299	303	301	312	1215	+63
N Carolina	308	308	299	301	1216	+64
Texas	306	314	299	297	1216	+64
Georgia Tech	310	306	302	300	1218	+66
Washington	314	300	301	303	1218	+66
UNLV	313	300	295	312	1220	+68
Southern Cal	300	311	298	312	1221	+69
N Carolina St	299	317	296	312	1224	+72
Georgia	315	306	297	308	1226	+74
Arizona	307	308	303	311	1229	+77
Wichita St	308	309	299	316	1232	+80

MEN'S DIVISION I—INDIVIDUAL

INDIVIDUAL, SCHOOL	SCORES				TOTAL	OVER/UNDER PAR
Alejandro Canizares, Arizona St	77	70	71	69	287	-1
Lee Williams, Auburn	69	72	71	77	289	+1
Chris Stroud, Lamar	70	77	70	73	290	+2
Matthew Rosenfeld, Texas	71	76	71	72	290	+2
Brock Mackenzie, Washington	77	71	72	71	291	+3
Jason Hartwick, Texas	77	70	72	73	292	+4
Ricky Barnes, Arizona	75	74	70	73	292	+4
Hunter Mahan, Oklahoma St	73	71	73	76	293	+5
Chez Reavie, Arizona St	74	77	70	73	294	+6
Andrew Dahl, Arkansas	73	81	70	71	295	+7
Jason Moon, N Carolina St	72	73	75	75	295	+7

MEN'S DIVISION II—TEAM
CROSSWATER GC, SUNRIVER, OR
(PAR 72; 7,296 YDS) MAY 20–23

TEAM	SCORES				TOTAL	OVER/UNDER PAR
Francis Marion	284	286	285	294	1149	−3
Rollins	303	286	288	286	1163	+11
CSU-Stanislaus	292	288	294	297	1171	+19
CSU-Bakersfield	295	287	296	294	1172	+20
CSU-Chico	296	282	304	292	1174	+22

MEN'S DIVISION II—INDIVIDUAL

INDIVIDUAL, SCHOOL	SCORES				TOTAL	+/- PAR
Andrew McArthur, Pfeiffer	72	69	69	69	279	-9
Scott Usher, South Carolina-Aiken	71	65	72	73	281	-7
Tommy Medina, Grand Canyon	72	67	73	70	282	-6
Bill Noon, CSU-Bakersfield	72	72	69	71	284	-4
Fredrik Ohlsson, Francis Marion	70	72	69	74	285	-3

NCAA CHAMPIONSHIPS (CONT.)

MEN'S DIVISION III—TEAM
**DORNOCH GC, DELAWARE, OH
(PAR 71; 6,613 YDS) MAY 12-15**

TEAM	SCORES				TOTAL	OVER/UNDER PAR
Averett	303	291	296	285	1175	+39
Wesley	292	302	287	299	1180	+44
Ohio Wesleyan	310	301	286	287	1184	+48
St. John's (MN)	307	299	285	293	1184	+48
Methodist	310	296	286	296	1188	+52

MEN'S DIVISION III—INDIVIDUAL

INDIVIDUAL, SCHOOL	SCORES				TOTAL	OVER/UNDER PAR
Janne Mommo, Averett	75	65	69	72	281	-3
Nathan Proshek, St. John's (MN)	74	69	69	72	284	even
Toni Karjalainen, Averett	71	73	72	72	288	+4
Adam Horton, Methodist	73	71	72	73	289	+5
Neil Johnson, Gustavus Adolphus	74	76	69	70	289	+5
Zac Oakley, Wesley	75	70	72	72	289	+5

WOMEN'S DIVISION I—TEAM
**KAMPEN C, WEST LAFAYETTE, IN
PAR 72; 6,225 YDS) MAY 20-23**

TEAM	SCORES				TOTAL	+/- PAR
Southern Cal	305	303	293	296	1197	+45
Pepperdine	315	298	295	304	1212	+60
Texas	317	310	290	296	1213	+61
Ohio St	309	307	305	293	1214	+62
Oklahoma St	309	302	301	304	1216	+64
UCLA	314	314	296	292	1216	+64
Arizona	318	314	295	290	1217	+65
Florida	313	307	298	303	1221	+69
Auburn	317	303	300	304	1224	+72
Duke	318	314	294	299	1225	+73

WOMEN'S DIVISION I—INDIVIDUAL

INDIVIDUAL, SCHOOL	SCORES				TOTAL	+/- PAR
Mikaela Parmlid, Southern Cal	72	73	70	72	287	-1
Andrea Vander Lende, Florida	77	74	69	77	297	+9
Erica Blasberg, Arizona	78	81	70	69	298	+10
Irene Cho, Southern Cal	74	79	73	72	298	+10
Kim Welch, Washington St	76	72	77	74	299	+11
Danielle Downey, Auburn	76	73	77	74	300	+12
Janice Olivencia, Texas	80	77	70	73	300	+12
Kristen White, Ohio St	76	77	74	73	300	+12
Linda Wessberg, Oklahoma St	80	76	71	73	300	+12
Lindsey Wright, Pepperdine	78	73	73	76	300	+12

NCAA CHAMPIONSHIPS SEASON (CONT.)

WOMEN'S DIVISION II—TEAM
MISSION INN GC, HOWYINHILLS, FL
(PAR 73; 5,982 YDS) MAY 14–17

TEAM	SCORES				TOTAL	+/- PAR
Rollins	315	307	310	305	1237	+69
Florida Southern	325	326	313	312	1276	+108
Northen Colorado	322	339	331	320	1312	+144
Grand Valley St	332	332	332	325	1321	+153
Longwood	336	343	318	327	1324	+156

WOMEN'S DIVISION II—INDIVIDUAL

INDIVIDUAL, SCHOOL	SCORES				TOTAL	+/- PAR
Charlotte Campbell, Rollins	78	74	76	71	299	+7
Pamela Feggans, Florida Southern	80	76	71	76	303	+11
Emily Russell, Northern Colorado	76	79	78	74	307	+15
Freddie Seeholzer, Rollins	78	74	75	80	307	+15
Kim Keyer-Scott, Northern Kentucky	74	77	79	80	310	+18

WOMEN'S DIVISION III—TEAM
THE GC OF LAWSONIA, GREEN LAKE, WI
(PAR 73; 5,846 YDS) MAY 13–16

TEAM	SCORES				TOTAL	+/- PAR
Methodist	316	329	329	321	1295	+127
Mary Hardin-Baylor	333	350	338	327	1348	+180
De Pauw	335	353	330	331	1349	+181
St. Mary's (IN)	345	355	331	322	1353	+185
Wisconsin-Oshkosh	343	344	333	341	1361	+193

WOMEN'S DIVISION III—INDIVIDUAL

INDIVIDUAL, SCHOOL	SCORES				TOTAL	+/- PAR
Stefanie Simmerman, St. Mary's (IN)	76	82	77	80	315	+23
Jessie Hunter, Methodist	77	82	78	82	319	+27
Jennifer Prock, Wisconsin-Eau Claire	85	77	82	79	323	+31
Michelle Meadows, Methodist	79	79	83	82	323	+31
Kristy Schaaf, Macalester	86	83	78	79	326	+34

MEN'S DIVISION I

RESULTS, 1897–1938

TEAM	SCORE	OVER/UNDER PAR	INDIVIDUAL CHAMPION
1897	Yale	Ardsley Casino	Louis Bayard Jr, Princeton
1898	Harvard (spring)		John Reid Jr, Yale
1898	Yale (fall)		James Curtis, Harvard
1899	Harvard		Percy Pyne, Princeton
1900	No tournament		
1901	Harvard	Atlantic City	H. Lindsley, Harvard
1902	Yale (spring)	Garden City	Charles Hitchcock Jr, Yale
1902	Harvard (fall)	Morris County	Chandler Egan, Harvard
1903	Harvard	Garden City	F.O. Reinhart, Princeton
1904	Harvard	Myopia	A.L. White, Harvard
1905	Yale	Garden City	Robert Abbott, Yale
1906	Yale	Garden City	W.E. Clow Jr, Yale
1907	Yale	Nassau	Ellis Knowles, Yale
1908	Yale	Brae Burn	H.H. Wilder, Harvard
1909	Yale	Apawamis	Albert Seckel, Princeton
1910	Yale	Essex County	Robert Hunter, Yale
1911	Yale	Baltusrol	George Stanley, Yale
1912	Yale	Ekwanok	F.C. Davison, Harvard
1913	Yale	Huntingdon Valley	Nathaniel Wheeler, Yale
1914	Princeton	Garden City	Edward Allis, Harvard
1915	Yale	Greenwich	Francis Blossom, Yale
1916	Princeton	Oakmont	J.W. Hubbell, Harvard
1917–18	No tournament		
1919	Princeton	Merion	A.L. Walker Jr, Columbia
1920	Princeton	Nassau	Jess Sweetster, Yale
1921	Dartmouth	Greenwich	Simpson Dean, Princeton
1922	Princeton	Garden City	Pollack Boyd, Dartmouth
1923	Princeton	Siwanoy	Dexter Cummings, Yale
1924	Yale	Greenwich	Dexter Cummings, Yale
1925	Yale	Montclair	Fred Lamprecht, Tulane
1926	Yale	Merion	Fred Lamprecht, Tulane
1927	Princeton	Garden City	Watts Gunn, Georgia Tech
1928	Princeton	Apawamis	Maurice McCarthy, Georgetown
1929	Princeton	Hollywood	Tom Aycock, Yale
1930	Princeton	Oakmont	G.T. Dunlap Jr, Princeton
1931	Yale	Olympia Fields	G.T. Dunlap Jr, Princeton
1932	Yale	Hot Springs	J.W. Fischer, Michigan
1933	Yale	Buffalo	Walter Emery, Oklahoma
1934	Michigan	Cleveland	Charles Yates, Georgia Tech
1935	Michigan	Congressional	Ed White, Texas
1936	Yale	North Shore	Charles Kocsis, Michigan
1937	Princeton	Oakmont	Fred Haas Jr, Louisiana St
1938	Stanford	Louisville	John Burke, Georgetown

RESULTS, 1939-2003

YEAR	CHAMPION (SCORE)	COACH	RUNNER-UP (SCORE)	HOST OR SITE	INDIVIDUAL CHAMPION
1939	Stanford (612)	Eddie Twiggs	Northwestern (614) Princeton (614)	Wakonda	Vincent D'Antoni, Tulane
1940	Princeton (601) Louisiana St (601)	Walter Bourne Mike Donahue		Ekwanok	Dixon Brooke, Virginia
1941	Stanford (580)	Eddie Twiggs	Louisiana St (599)	Ohio St	Earl Stewart, Louisiana St
1942	Louisiana St (590) Stanford (590)	Mike Donahue Eddie Twiggs		Notre Dame	Frank Tatum Jr, Stanford
1943	Yale (614)	William Neale Jr	Michigan (618)	Olympia Fields	Wallace Ulrich, Carleton
1944	Notre Dame (311)	George Holderith	Minnesota (312)	Inverness	Louis Lick, Minnesota
1945	Ohio St (602)	Robert Kepler	Northwestern (621)	Ohio St	John Lorms, Ohio St
1946	Stanford (619)	Eddie Twiggs	Michigan (624)	Princeton	George Hamer, Georgia
1947	Louisiana St (606)	T.P. Heard	Duke (614)	Michigan	Dave Barclay, Michigan
1948	San Jose St (579)	Wilbur Hubbard	Louisiana St (588)	Stanford	Bob Harris, San Jose St
1949	N Texas (590)	Fred Cobb	Purdue (600) Texas (600)	Iowa St	Harvie Ward, N Carolina
1950	N Texas (573)	Fred Cobb	Purdue (577)	New Mexico	Fred Wampler, Purdue
1951	N Texas (588)	Fred Cobb	Ohio St (589)	Ohio St	Tom Nieporte, Ohio St
1952	N Texas (587)	Fred Cobb	Michigan (593)	Purdue	Jim Vickers, Oklahoma
1953	Stanford (578)	Charles Finger	N Carolina (580)	Broadmoor	Earl Moeller, Oklahoma St
1954	SMU (572)	Graham Ross	N Texas (573)	Houston	Hillman Robbins, Memphis St
1955	Louisiana St (574)	Mike Barbato	N Texas (583)	Tennessee	Joe Campbell, Purdue
1956	Houston (601)	Dave Williams	N Texas (602) Purdue (602)	Ohio St	Rick Jones, Ohio St
1957	Houston (602)	Dave Williams	Stanford (603)	Broadmoor	Rex Baxter Jr., Houston
1958	Houston (570)	Dave Williams	Oklahoma St (582)	Williams	Phil Rodgers, Houston
1959	Houston (561)	Dave Williams	Purdue (571)	Oregon	Dick Crawford, Houston
1960	Houston (603)	Dave Williams	Purdue (607) Oklahoma St (607)	Broadmoor	Dick Crawford, Houston
1961	Purdue (584)	Sam Voinoff	Arizona St (595)	Lafayette	Jack Nicklaus, Ohio St
1962	Houston (588)	Dave Williams	Oklahoma St (598)	Duke	Kermit Zarley, Houston
1963	Oklahoma St (581)	Labron Harris	Houston (582)	Wichita St	R.H. Sikes, Arkansas
1964	Houston (580)	Dave Williams	Oklahoma St (587)	Broadmoor	Terry Small, San Jose St
1965	Houston (577)	Dave Williams	Cal St–LA (587)	Tennessee	Marty Fleckman, Houston
1966	Houston (582)	Dave Williams	San Jose St (586)	Stanford	Bob Murphy, Florida
1967	Houston (585)	Dave Williams	Florida (588)	Shawnee, PA	Hale Irwin, Colorado
1968	Florida (1154)	Buster Bishop	Houston (1156)	New Mexico St	Grier Jones, Oklahoma St
1969	Houston (1223)	Dave Williams	Wake Forest (1232)	Broadmoor	Bob Clark, Cal St–LA
1970	Houston (1172)	Dave Williams	Wake Forest (1182)	Ohio St	John Mahaffey, Houston
1971	Texas (1144)	George Hannon	Houston (1151)	Arizona	Ben Crenshaw, Texas
1972	Texas (1146)	George Hannon	Houston (1159)	Cape Coral	Ben Crenshaw, Texas Tom Kite, Texas
1973	Florida (1149)	Buster Bishop	Oklahoma St (1159)	Oklahoma St	Ben Crenshaw, Texas
1974	Wake Forest (1158)	Jess Haddock	Florida (1160)	San Diego St	Curtis Strange, Wake Forest
1975	Wake Forest (1156)	Jess Haddock	Oklahoma St (1189)	Ohio St	Jay Haas, Wake Forest
1976	Oklahoma St (1166)	Mike Holder	Brigham Young (1173)	New Mexico	Scott Simpson, USC
1977	Houston (1197)	Dave Williams	Oklahoma St (1205)	Colgate	Scott Simpson, USC
1978	Oklahoma St (1140)	Mike Holder	Georgia (1157)	Oregon	David Edwards, Oklahoma St
1979	Ohio St (1189)	James Brown	Oklahoma St (1191)	Wake Forest	Gary Hallberg, Wake Forest
1980	Oklahoma St (1173)	Mike Holder	Brigham Young (1177)	Ohio St	Jay Don Blake, Utah St
1981	BYU (1161)	Karl Tucker	Oral Roberts (1163)	Stanford	Ron Commans, USC
1982	Houston (1141)	Dave Williams	Oklahoma St (1151)	Pinehurst	Billy Ray Brown, Houston
1983	Oklahoma St (1161)	Mike Holder	Texas (1168)	Fresno St	Jim Carter, Arizona St
1984	Houston (1145)	Dave Williams	Oklahoma St (1146)	Houston	John Inman, N Carolina
1985	Houston (1172)	Dave Williams	Oklahoma St (1175)	Florida	Clark Burroughs, Ohio St
1986	Wake Forest (1156)	Jess Haddock	Oklahoma St (1160)	Wake Forest	Scott Verplank, Oklahoma St
1987	Oklahoma St (1160)	Mike Holder	Wake Forest (1176)	Ohio St	Brian Watts, Oklahoma St
1988	UCLA (1176)	Eddie Merrins	UTEP (1179) Oklahoma (1179) Oklahoma St (1179)	Southern Cal	E.J. Pfister, Oklahoma St
1989	Oklahoma (1139)	Gregg Grost	Texas (1158)	Oklahoma Oklahoma St	Phil Mickelson, Arizona St

MEN'S DIVISION I (CONT.)

RESULTS, 1939–2003 (CONT.)

YEAR	CHAMPION (SCORE)	COACH	RUNNER-UP (SCORE)	HOST OR SITE	INDIVIDUAL CHAMPION
1990	Arizona St (1155)	Steve Loy	Florida (1157)	Florida	Phil Mickelson, Arizona St
1991	Oklahoma St (1161)	Mike Holder	N Carolina (1168)	San Jose St	Warren Schutte, UNLV
1992	Arizona (1129)	Rick LaRose	Arizona St (1136)	New Mexico	Phil Mickelson, Arizona St
1993	Florida (1145)	Buddy Alexander	Georgia Tech (1146)	Kentucky	Todd Demsey, Arizona St
1994	Stanford (1129)	Wally Goodwin	Texas (1133)	McKinney, TX	Justin Leonard, Texas
1995	Oklahoma St* (1156)	Mike Holder	Stanford (1156)	Ohio St	Chip Spratlin, Auburn
1996	Arizona St (1186)	Randy Lein	UNLV (1189)	Chattanooga	Tiger Woods, Stanford
1997	Pepperdine (1148)	John Geiberger	Wake Forest (1151)	Evanston, IL	Charles Warren, Clemson
1998	UNLV (1118)	Dwaine Knight	Clemson (1121)	Albuquerque	James McLean, Minnesota
1999	Georgia (1180)	Chris Haack	Oklahoma St (1183)	Chaska, MN	Donald Luke, Northwestern
2000	Oklahoma St* (1116)	Mike Holder	Georgia Tech (1116)	Opelika, AL	Charles Howell, Oklahoma St
2001	Florida (1126)	Buddy Alexander	Clemson (1144)	Durham, NC	Nick Gilliam, Florida
2002	Minnesota (1134)	Brad James	Georgia Tech	Ohio St	Troy Matteson, Ga. Tech
2003	Clemson (1191)	Larry Penley	Oklahoma St (1193)	Oklahoma St	Alejandro Canizares, Ariz St

*Won sudden death playoff. Notes: Match play, 1897–1964; par-70 tournaments held in 1969, 1973 and 1989; par-71 tournaments held in 1968, 1981 and 1988; all other championships par-72 tournaments. Scores are based on 4 rounds instead of 2 after 1967.

GO FIGURE

57 Consecutive appearances in the NCAA men's golf championships for Oklahoma State, a streak that is still active. In those tournaments the Cowboys won nine team titles and were runners up 14 times.

21 NCAA golf titles for Yale, the most by any school in the sport's history. Yale's last championship came in 1943.

8 Collegiate tournaments won by former Stanford player Tiger Woods, including the last four he entered. During the two seasons he spent as a member of the Cardinal golf team, Woods won an NCAA individual title, led the nation in scoring average and set a Pac-10 record by shooting an 11-under 61 in the first round of the 1996 conference tournament.

62 Record-low score by Stanford's Notah Begay in the second round of the 1994 NCAA individual tournament. While Begay's single round performance was historic, it was not enough to defeat Justin Leonard of Texas, who shot a 271 for four rounds to take the NCAA individual title.

15 Strokes, the USC women's team's margin of victory over Pepperdine at the 2003 NCAA Division I golf championships. As impressive as USC's triumph was, it fell well short of the NCAA record for margin of victory, which Tulsa set in the first women's tournament, in 1982, downing TCU by 36 strokes.

MEN'S DIVISION II

YEAR	CHAMPION	YEAR	CHAMPION
1963	SW Missouri St	1984	Troy St
1964	Southern Illinois	1985	Florida Southern
1965	Middle Tennessee St	1986	Florida Southern
1966	Cal St–Chico	1987	Tampa
1967	Lamar	1988	Tampa
1968	Lamar	1989	Columbus St
1969	Cal St–Northridge	1990	Florida Southern
1970	Rollins	1991	Florida Southern
1971	New Orleans	1992	Columbus St
1972	New Orleans	1993	Abilene Christian
1973	Cal St–Northridge	1994	Columbus St
1974	Cal St–Northridge	1995	Florida Southern
1975	UC–Irvine	1996	Florida Southern
1976	Troy St	1997	Columbus St
1977	Troy St	1998	Florida Southern
1978	Columbus St	1999	Florida Southern
1979	UC–Davis	2000	Florida Southern
1980	Columbus St	2001	W Florida
1981	Florida Southern	2002	Rollins
1982	Florida Southern	2003	Francis Marion
1983	SW Texas St		

Note: Par-71 tournaments held in 1967, 1970, 1976–78, 1985, 1988 and 2001; par-70 tournament held in 1996; all other championships par-72 tournaments.

MEN'S DIVISION III

YEAR	CHAMPION	YEAR	CHAMPION
1975	Wooster	1990	Methodist (NC)
1976	Cal St–Stanislaus	1991	Methodist (NC)
1977	Cal St–Stanislaus	1992	Methodist (NC)
1978	Cal St–Stanislaus	1993	UC–San Diego
1979	Cal St–Stanislaus	1994	Methodist (NC)
1980	Cal St–Stanislaus	1995	Methodist (NC)
1981	Cal St–Stanislaus	1996	Methodist (NC)
1982	Ramapo	1997	Methodist (NC)
1983	Allegheny	1998	Methodist (NC)
1984	Cal St–Stanislaus	1999	Methodist (NC)
1985	Cal St–Stanislaus	2000	Greensboro
1986	Cal St–Stanislaus	2001	WI–Eau Claire
1987	Cal St–Stanislaus	2002	Guilford
1988	Cal St–Stanislaus	2003	Averett
1989	Cal St–Stanislaus		

FUND FACT

Wisconsin–Green Bay raises funds for athletics by charging admission to a 15-acre corn maze near its campus.

WOMEN'S DIVISION I

YEAR	CHAMPION	COACH	SCORE	RUNNER-UP	SCORE	INDIVIDUAL CHAMPION
1982	Tulsa	Dale McNamara	1191	Texas Christian	1227	Kathy Baker, Tulsa
1983	Texas Christian	Fred Warren	1193	Tulsa	1196	Penny Hammel, Miami (FL)
1984	Miami (FL)	Lela Cannon	1214	Arizona St	1221	Cindy Schreyer, Georgia
1985	Florida	Mimi Ryan	1218	Tulsa	1233	Danielle Ammaccapane, Arizona St
1986	Florida	Mimi Ryan	1180	Miami (FL)	1188	Page Dunlap, Florida
1987	San Jose St	Mark Gale	1187	Furman	1188	Caroline Keggi, New Mexico
1988	Tulsa	Dale McNamara	1175	Georgia	1182	Melissa McNamara, Tulsa
				Arizona	1182	
1989	San Jose St	Mark Gale	1208	Tulsa	1209	Pat Hurst, San Jose St
1990	Arizona St	Linda Vollstedt	1206	UCLA	1222	Susan Slaughter, Arizona
1991	UCLA*	Jackie Steinmann	1197	San Jose St	1197	Annika Sorenstam, Arizona
1992	San Jose St	Mark Gale	1171	Arizona	1175	Vicki Goetze, Georgia
1993	Arizona St	Linda Vollstedt	1187	Texas	1189	Charlotta Sorenstam, Texas
1994	Arizona St	Linda Vollstedt	1189	Southern Cal	1205	Emilee Klein, Arizona St
1995	Arizona St	Linda Vollstedt	1155	San Jose St	1181	Kristel Mourgue d'Algue, Arizona St
1996	Arizona*	Rick LaRose	1240	San Jose St	1240	Marisa Baena, Arizona
1997	Arizona St	Linda Vollstedt	1178	San Jose St	1180	Heather Bowie, Texas
1998	Arizona St	Linda Vollstedt	1155	Florida	1173	Jennifer Rosales, USC
1999	Duke	Dan Brooks	895	Arizona St/Georgia	903	Grace Park, Arizona St
2000	Arizona	Todd McCorkle	1175	Stanford	1196	Jenna Daniels, Arizona
2001	Georgia	Todd McCorkle	1176	Duke	1179	Candy Hannemann, Duke
2002	Duke	Dan Brooks	1164	Arizona/Auburn/ Texas	1160	Virada Nirapathpongporn, Duke
2003	Southern Cal	Andrea Gaston	1197	Pepperdine	1212	Mikaela Parmlid, USC

*Won sudden death playoff. Note: Par-74 tournaments held in 1983 and 1988; par-72 tournament held in 1990, 2000 and 2001; all other championships par-73 tournaments.

WOMEN'S DIVISION II

YEAR	CHAMPION
2000	Florida Southern
2001	Florida Southern
2002	Florida Southern
2003	Rollins

WOMEN'S DIVISION III

YEAR	CHAMPION
1996	Methodist (NC)
1997	Lynn
1998	Methodist (NC)
1999	Methodist (NC)
2000	Methodist (NC)
2001	Methodist (NC)
2002	Methodist (NC)
2003	Methodist (NC)

HOLDING Serve

The champions in men's and women's tennis will be difficult to unseat as they return most of their stars

C RAIG TILEY came to Illinois in 1992 to begin work on a graduate degree. To earn some spending money while he was in school, he started teaching tennis lessons in his spare time. Word spread quickly that Tiley was a pretty good teacher, and the following year he was asked to lead the moribund Illinois tennis program back to respectability. It was an uphill battle: The Illini went 0–10 and finished last in the Big Ten in Tiley's first year. Undeterred, he stuck with it, and in less than a decade—in what has to be one of the best coaching jobs in any sport in recent memory—built one of the top programs in the nation.

To say that Tiley started from scratch would be an understatement. In addition to having no history of success, the Illini faced the daunting fact that no

Delic won the NCAA individual crown, helping the Illini, who went 0–10 just 10 years earlier, to the national title.

team outside of California or Georgia had won the NCAA men's team title since 1972, and a team from a cold weather climate hadn't won since 1958. So Tiley's upstarts broke several barriers in 2003, going 32–0 to win the team title, and taking the championships in singles and doubles play as well.

"Craig has all these visions and things constantly created in his mind," said junior Amer Delic, who beat Baylor's Benedikt Dorsch to win the NCAA singles title. "He's the only person who could have done it here. I'm just glad he did it and I'm a part of it."

FAVORITES

The Illini will be the hunted in 2004, but they will be hard to track down. They lose only one senior from their 32–0 team and bring back defending singles champion Amer Delic and doubles titlists Brian Wilson and Rajeev Ram. **Illinois** also has a potential star in junior Chris Martin, who helped the

As a freshman, Liu of Stanford defeated Tennessee's Vilmarie Castellvi 7–6 (5), 6–2 for the NCAA individual championship.

replace All-Americas Scott Lipsky and David Martin. The team will be in the capable hands of sophomore All-America K.C. Corkery, junior Sam Warbug and senior James Pade, who will look to emulate the Cardinal women's team, which finished runner-up to Florida in 2003.

The **Florida** men appear poised to make a run themselves, boasting two of the nation's most talented players in junior Hamid Mirzadeh and sophomore Janne Holmia.

Illini clinch the title with the decisive singles victory.

Vanderbilt, which narrowly lost to Illinois in the 2003 NCAA final, should give the Illini a run again this season. The Commodores bring back the experience and talent of seniors Bobby Reynolds and Chad Harris and junior Matt Lockin. Reynolds and junior Scott Brown will also be a formidable doubles team.

With national singles runner-up Dorsch returning, **Baylor** should again be a force. The Bears, who also have junior Benjamin Becker and senior Matias Marin, have proven they can play with the big boys, going 55-4 over the last two seasons.

Stanford, which lost to Illinois in the national semifinals last season, is to tennis what North Carolina is to women's soccer: always dominant no matter what the year. This season should be no different, even though the Cardinal must

The defending champion **Florida** women return all of their top players, including juniors Alexis Gordon and Zerene Reyes, sophomore Jennifer Magley and senior Julie Rotondi. The **Stanford** women hope to return to the championship match, welcoming back NCAA singles champ Amber Liu, senior Lauren Barnikow and sophomore Alice Barnes. Finally, none of this year's favorites will overlook **Duke**, which will again challenge for the title behind All-Americas Amanda Johnson and Kelly McCain.

DARKHORSES

Still reeling from a second-round exit in last year's men's nationals, **UCLA** should have a better showing with juniors Marcin Matkowski, Chris Lam and Tobias Clemens. The Bruins' Pac-10 rival **Cal** has plenty of talent in juniors Conor Niland, Patrick Nriaud and Mik Ledvonova, and—remember that California-

GARY BOGDON (BOTH)

Florida returns all of its top players, including Rotondi, who celebrated her win over Stanford's Lauren Barnikow, which clinched the 2003 team title for the Gators.

Georgia run of dominance—the **Georgia** Bulldogs suit up one of the nation's top players in senior Bo Hodge.

The **Cal** women have long been a power in doubles, claiming last year's NCAA doubles title with Raquel Kops-Jones and Christina Fusano. Fusano graduated, but the Bears will still be a team to reckon with in the Pac-10. Watch out as well for **Washington**, which is led by All-Americas Dea Sumantri and Claire Carter, and **USC**, which must replace all-everything Jewel Peterson, but still has promising junior Luana Magnani.

SIDELINES

The battle for the 2004 men's singles title figures to be as compelling as any in recent memory. Defending champ Delic of Illinois returns as does his opponent in the 2003 final, Dorsch of Baylor. Pushing those two will be Vanderbilt's Reynolds, Hodge of Georgia, UCLA's Clemens, Washington's Alex Vlaski and Auburn's Rameez Junaid.

It appears as if defending women's singles champion Liu of Stanford—only a sophomore—will be on top for a while, but she could be challenged by teammate Alice Barnes, Agata Cioroch of Georgia, Duke's Kelly McCain and Cristelle Grier of Northwestern.

Finally, tennis fans—especially college tennis fans—will never be confused with the Cameron Crazies. But at Illinois, one enthusiastic student section is taking school spirit to another level. The group, known as the Net Nuts, may not be asked to come to Wimbledon any time soon, but it is giving home-court advantage a new meaning in college tennis. Clad in bright orange t-shirts, numbering more than 150, the boisterous Net Nuts have little regard for gentility. They treat Illini tennis matches like Big Ten football games, cheering wildly for Illinois players and emphatically voicing their opinions when they disagree with a judge's call. "I think it's made it more fun for the players to play and for the people to come out and watch a great team," said former Illinois senior Alex Voss said.

It certainly hasn't hurt the Illini.

MEN

INDIVIDUAL CHAMPIONS 1883-1945

YEAR	CHAMPION	YEAR	CHAMPION
1883	Joseph Clark, Harvard (spring)	1914	George Church, Princeton
1883	Howard Taylor, Harvard (fall)	1915	Richard Williams II, Harvard
1884	W.P. Knapp, Yale	1916	G. Colket Caner, Harvard
1885	W.P. Knapp, Yale	1917–18	No tournament
1886	G.M. Brinley, Trinity (CT)	1919	Charles Garland, Yale
1887	P.S. Sears, Harvard	1920	Lascelles Banks, Yale
1888	P.S. Sears, Harvard	1921	Philip Neer, Stanford
1889	R.P. Huntington Jr, Yale	1922	Lucien Williams, Yale
1890	Fred Hovey, Harvard	1923	Carl Fischer, Philadelphia Osteo
1891	Fred Hovey, Harvard	1924	Wallace Scott, Washington
1892	William Larned, Cornell	1925	Edward Chandler, California
1893	Malcolm Chace, Brown	1926	Edward Chandler, California
1894	Malcolm Chace, Yale	1927	Wilmer Allison, Texas
1895	Malcolm Chace, Yale	1928	Julius Seligson, Lehigh
1896	Malcolm Whitman, Harvard	1929	Berkeley Bell, Texas
1897	S.G. Thompson, Princeton	1930	Clifford Sutter, Tulane
1898	Leo Ware, Harvard	1931	Keith Gledhill, Stanford
1899	Dwight Davis, Harvard	1932	Clifford Sutter, Tulane
1900	Raymond Little, Princeton	1933	Jack Tidball, UCLA
1901	Fred Alexander, Princeton	1934	Gene Mako, Southern Cal
1902	William Clothier, Harvard	1935	Wilbur Hess, Rice
1903	E.B. Dewhurst, Pennsylvania	1936	Ernest Sutter, Tulane
1904	Robert LeRoy, Columbia	1937	Ernest Sutter, Tulane
1905	E.B. Dewhurst, Pennsylvania	1938	Frank Guernsey, Rice
1906	Robert LeRoy, Columbia	1939	Frank Guernsey, Rice
1907	G. Peabody Gardner Jr, Harvard	1940	Donald McNeil, Kenyon
1908	Nat Niles, Harvard	1941	Joseph Hunt, Navy
1909	Wallace Johnson, Pennsylvania	1942	Frederick Schroeder Jr, Stanford
1910	R.A. Holden Jr, Yale	1943	Pancho Segura, Miami (FL)
1911	E.H. Whitney, Harvard	1944	Pancho Segura, Miami (FL)
1912	George Church, Princeton	1945	Pancho Segura, Miami (FL)
1913	Richard Williams II, Harvard		

MEN'S DIVISION I

TEAM AND INDIVIDUAL CHAMPIONS 1946–2003

YEAR	CHAMPION	COACH	PTS	RUNNER-UP	PTS	INDIVIDUAL CHAMPION
1946	Southern Cal	William Moyle	9	William & Mary	6	Robert Falkenburg, Southern Cal
1947	William & Mary	Sharvey G. Umbeck	10	Rice	4	Gardner Larned, William & Mary
1948	William & Mary	Sharvey G. Umbeck	6	San Francisco	5	Harry Likas, San Francisco
1949	San Francisco	Norman Brooks	7	Rollins/Tulane/ Washington	4	Jack Tuero, Tulane
1950	UCLA	William Ackerman	11	California/ Southern Cal	5 5	Herbert Flam, UCLA
1951	Southern Cal	Louis Wheeler	9	Cincinnati	7	Tony Trabert, Cincinnati
1952	UCLA	J.D. Morgan	11	California	5	Hugh Stewart, Southern Cal
				Southern Cal	5	
1953	UCLA	J.D. Morgan	11	California	6	Hamilton Richardson, Tulane
1954	UCLA	J.D. Morgan	15	Southern Cal	10	Hamilton Richardson, Tulane
1955	Southern Cal	George Toley	12	Texas	7	Jose Aguero, Tulane
1956	UCLA	J.D. Morgan	15	Southern Cal	14	Alejandro Olmedo, Southern Cal
1957	Michigan	William Murphy	10	Tulane	9	Barry MacKay, Michigan
1958	Southern Cal	George Toley	13	Stanford	9	Alejandro Olmedo, Southern Cal
1959	Notre Dame/ Tulane Emmet Pare	Thomas Fallon	8 8		8	Whitney Reed, San Jose St
1960	UCLA	J.D. Morgan	18	Southern Cal	8	Larry Nagler, UCLA
1961	UCLA	J.D. Morgan	17	Southern Cal	16	Allen Fox, UCLA
1962	Southern Cal	George Toley	22	UCLA	12	Rafael Osuna, Southern Cal
1963	Southern Cal	George Toley	27	UCLA	19	Dennis Ralston, Southern Cal
1964	Southern Cal	George Toley	26	UCLA	25	Dennis Ralston, Southern Cal
1965	UCLA	J.D. Morgan	31	Miami (FL)	13	Arthur Ashe, UCLA
1966	Southern Cal	George Toley	27	UCLA	23	Charles Pasarell, UCLA
1967	Southern Cal	George Toley	28	UCLA	23	Bob Lutz, Southern Cal
1968	Southern Cal	George Toley	31	Rice	23	Stan Smith, Southern Cal
1969	Southern Cal	George Toley	35	UCLA	23	Joaquin Loyo-Mayo, Southern Cal
1970	UCLA	Glenn Bassett	26	Trinity (TX) Rice	22 22	Jeff Borowiak, UCLA
1971	UCLA	Glenn Bassett	35	Trinity (TX)	27	Jimmy Connors, UCLA
1972	Trinity (TX)	Clarence Mabry	36	Stanford	30	Dick Stockton, Trinity (TX)
1973	Stanford	Dick Gould	33	Southern Cal	28	Alex Mayer, Stanford
1974	Stanford	Dick Gould	30	Southern Cal	25	John Whitlinger, Stanford
1975	UCLA	Glenn Bassett	27	Miami (FL)	20	Bill Martin, UCLA
1976	Southern Cal UCLA	George Toley Glenn Bassett	21 21			Bill Scanlon, Trinity (TX)
1977	Stanford	Dick Gould		Trinity (TX)		Matt Mitchell, Stanford
1978	Stanford	Dick Gould		UCLA		John McEnroe, Stanford
1979	UCLA	Glenn Bassett		Trinity (TX)		Kevin Curren, Texas

MEN'S DIVISION I (CONT.)

TEAM AND INDIVIDUAL CHAMPIONS 1946–2003 (CONT.)

YEAR	CHAMPION	COACH	PTS	RUNNER-UP	PTS	INDIVIDUAL CHAMPION
1980 .....Stanford	Dick Gould		California		Robert Van't Hof, Southern Cal
1981 .....Stanford	Dick Gould		UCLA		Tim Mayotte, Stanford
1982 .....UCLA	Glenn Bassett		Pepperdine		Mike Leach, Michigan
1983 .....Stanford	Dick Gould		SMU		Greg Holmes, Utah
1984 .....UCLA	Glenn Bassett		Stanford		Mikael Pernfors, Georgia
1985 .....Georgia	Dan Magill		UCLA		Mikael Pernfors, Georgia
1986 .....Stanford	Dick Gould		Pepperdine		Dan Goldie, Stanford
1987 .....Georgia	Dan Magill		UCLA		Andrew Burrow, Miami (FL)
1988 .....Stanford	Dick Gould		Louisiana St		Robby Weiss, Pepperdine
1989 .....Stanford	Dick Gould		Georgia		Donni Leaycraft, Louisiana St
1990 .....Stanford	Dick Gould		Tennessee		Steve Bryan, Texas
1991 .....Southern Cal	Dick Leach		Georgia		Jared Palmer, Stanford
1992 .....Stanford	Dick Gould		Notre Dame		Alex O'Brien, Stanford
1993 .....Southern Cal	Dick Leach		Georgia		Chris Woodruff, Tennessee
1994 .....Southern Cal	Dick Leach		Stanford		Mark Merklein, Florida
1995 .....Stanford	Dick Gould		Mississippi		Sargis Sargsian, Arizona St
1996 .....Stanford	Dick Gould		UCLA		Cecil Mamiit, Southern Cal
1997 .....Stanford	Dick Gould		Georgia		Luke Smith, UNLV
1998 .....Stanford	Dick Gould		Georgia		Bob Bryan, Stanford
1999 .....Georgia	Manuel Diaz		UCLA		Jeff Morrison, Florida
2000 .....Stanford	Dick Gould		VA–Commonwealth		Alex Kim, Stanford
2001 .....Georgia	Manuel Diaz		Tennessee		Matias Boeker, Georgia
2002 .....Southern Cal	Dick Leach		Georgia		Matias Boeker, Georgia
2003 .....Illinois	Craig Tiley		Vanderbilt		Amer Delic, Illinois

Note: Prior to 1977, individual wins counted in the team's total points. In 1977, a dual-match single-elimination team championship was initiated, eliminating the point system.

MEN'S DIVISION II TEAM CHAMPIONS

YEAR	CHAMPION	YEAR	CHAMPION
1963 ....Cal St–LA		1984 ....SIU–Edwardsville	
1964 ....Cal St–LA/S Illinois		1985 ....Chapman	
1965 ....Cal St–LA		1986 ....Cal Poly–SLO	
1966 ....Rollins		1987 ....Chapman	
1967 ....Long Beach St		1988 ....Chapman	
1968 ....Fresno St		1989 ....Hampton	
1969 ....Cal St–Northridge		1990 ....Cal Poly–SLO	
1970 ....UC–Irvine		1991 ....Rollins	
1971 ....UC–Irvine		1992 ....UC–Davis	
1972 ....UC–Irvine/ Rollins		1993 ....Lander	
1973 ....UC–Irvine		1994 ....Lander	
1974 ....San Diego		1995 ....Lander	
1975 ....UC–Irvine/San Diego		1996 ....Lander	
1976 ....Hampton		1997 ....Lander	
1977 ....UC–Irvine		1998 ....Lander	
1978 ....SIU–Edwardsville		1999 ....Lander	
1979 ....SIU–Edwardsville		2000 ....Lander	
1980 ....SIU–Edwardsville		2001 ....Rollins	
1981 ....SIU–Edwardsville		2002 ....BYU–Hawaii	
1982 ....SIU–Edwardsville		2003 ....BYU–Hawaii	
1983 ....SIU–Edwardsville			

MEN'S DIVISION III TEAM CHAMPIONS

YEAR	CHAMPION	YEAR	CHAMPION
1976	Kalamazoo	1990	Swarthmore
1977	Swarthmore	1991	Kalamazoo
1978	Kalamazoo	1992	Kalamazoo
1979	Redlands	1993	Kalamazoo
1980	Gustavus Adolphus	1994	Washington (MD)
1981	Claremont-M-S/ Swarthmore	1995	UC–Santa Cruz
1982	Gustavus Adolphus	1996	UC–Santa Cruz
1983	Redlands	1997	Washington (MD)
1984	Redlands	1998	UC–Santa Cruz
1985	Swarthmore	1999	Williams
1986	Kalamazoo	2000	Trinity (TX)
1987	Kalamazoo	2001	Williams
1988	Washington & Lee	2002	Williams
1989	UC–Santa Cruz	2003	Emory

★ ANYONE FOR FISHING? ★

[PENN STATE]

CHUCK SOLOMON

FISHING CLUBS and classes are popular at many colleges, including Purdue and Montana. But Penn State's three-course fly-fishing series—first taught by angling legend George Harvey in 1947—is the perfect mix of fun and education. "Fly fishing is a science: You have to know entomology, geology and hydrology," says instructor Mark Belden, who teaches all of those things, plus casting and fly tying. Some 250 students a year take Belden's courses, which make use of the half-dozen blue-ribbon fishing streams within 30 miles of campus. The students throw back the brown trout they catch but take home a lifelong passion. Says Belden, "If these kids are still dreaming about fly-fishing when at their big-city jobs, I've succeeded."

WOMEN'S DIVISION I

TEAM AND INDIVIDUAL CHAMPIONS

YEAR	CHAMPION	COACH	RUNNER-UP	INDIVIDUAL CHAMPION
1982	Stanford	Frank Brennan	UCLA	Alycia Moulton, Stanford
1983	Southern Cal	Dave Borelli	Trinity (TX)	Beth Herr, Southern Cal
1984	Stanford	Frank Brennan	Southern Cal	Lisa Spain, Georgia
1985	Southern Cal	Dave Borelli	Miami (FL)	Linda Gates, Stanford
1986	Stanford	Frank Brennan	Southern Cal	Patty Fendick, Stanford
1987	Stanford	Frank Brennan	Georgia	Patty Fendick, Stanford
1988	Stanford	Frank Brennan	Florida	Shaun Stafford, Florida
1989	Stanford	Frank Brennan	UCLA	Sandra Birch, Stanford
1990	Stanford	Frank Brennan	Florida	Debbie Graham, Stanford
1991	Stanford	Frank Brennan	UCLA	Sandra Birch, Stanford
1992	Florida	Andy Brandi	Texas	Lisa Raymond, Florida
1993	Texas	Jeff Moore	Stanford	Lisa Raymond, Florida
1994	Georgia	Jeff Wallace	Stanford	Angela Lettiere, Georgia
1995	Texas	Jeff Moore	Florida	Keri Phebus, UCLA
1996	Florida	Andy Brandi	Stanford	Jill Craybas, Florida
1997	Stanford	Frank Brennan	Florida	Lilia Osterloh, Stanford
1998	Florida	Andy Brandi	Duke	Vanessa Webb, Duke
1999	Stanford	Frank Brennan	Florida	Zuzana Lesenarova, UC–SD
2000	Georgia	Jeff Wallace	Stanford	Laura Granville, Stanford
2001	Stanford	Lele Forood	Vanderbilt	Laura Granville, Stanford
2002	Stanford	Lele Forood	Florida	Bea Bielek, Wake Forest
2003	Florida	Roland Thornqvist	Stanford	Amber Liu, Stanford

GO FIGURE

241 Consecutive Michigan Intercollegiate Athletic Association conference wins for Division III Kalamazoo's tennis team before a loss to Hope College. Kalamazoo's impressive streak began after its last conference loss, on April 22, 1962, when it fell 4–3 to, coincidentally enough, Hope.

5 The number of teams who have divided the 27 Division I men's tennis national championships since the single-elimination team title format was initiated in 1977. Stanford has won 15 titles, USC and Georgia four each, UCLA three and Illinois won its first title in 2003.

50% Portion of the alltime NCAA women's Division I singles championships that have been won by players from Stanford. In the 22-year history of the tournament, a Stanford woman has won 11 times, including in 2003, when the Cardinal's Amber Liu took the title. Florida ranks second all time with four women's singles champions.

0 Number of Grand Slam singles titles won by NCAA women's singles champions since the NCAA tournament was established in 1982.

20 Number of Grand Slam titles won by NCAA men's singles champions in the open era (since 1968). Four previous NCAA singles champs, Arthur Ashe, Jimmy Connors, John McEnroe, and Stan Smith, combined to win 11 U.S. Opens, seven Wimbledons and two Australian Opens but were shut out at the French Open.

WOMEN'S DIVISION II TEAM CHAMPIONS

YEAR	CHAMPION	YEAR	CHAMPION
1982	Cal St–Northridge	1993	UC–Davis
1983	TN–Chattanooga	1994	N Florida
1984	TN–Chattanooga	1995	Armstrong St
1985	TN–Chattanooga	1996	Armstrong St
1986	SIU–Edwardsville	1997	Lynn
1987	SIU–Edwardsville	1998	Lynn
1988	SIU–Edwardsville	1999	BYU–Hawaii
1989	SIU–Edwardsville	2000	BYU–Hawaii
1990	UC–Davis	2001	Lynn
1991	Cal Poly–Pomona	2002	BYU–Hawaii
1992	Cal Poly–Pomona	2003	BYU–Hawaii

WOMEN'S DIVISION III TEAM CHAMPIONS

YEAR	CHAMPION	YEAR	CHAMPION
1982	Occidental	1993	Kenyon
1983	Principia	1994	UC–San Diego
1984	Davidson	1995	Kenyon
1985	UC–San Diego	1996	Emory
1986	Trenton St	1997	Kenyon
1987	UC–San Diego	1998	Kenyon
1988	Mary Washington	1999	Amherst
1989	UC–San Diego	2000	Trinity (TX)
1990	Gustavus Adolphus	2001	Williams
1991	Mary Washington	2002	Williams
1992	Pomona-Pitzer	2003	Emory

DYNASTIC
Duo

Having dominated recent track history, the Arkansas men and LSU women show few signs of slowing down

LAST YEAR the NCAA made the first major change in years in the qualifying process for its track and field championship. Previously athletes qualified by meeting either an automatic "A" standard, or a provisional "B" standard (filling out the field in order of performance). Now, athletes qualify by finishing among the top five at one of four regional qualifying meets weeks before the championship or by being awarded one of about a half dozen remaining "wild-card" spots. How well this new system works is a matter of debate. But a couple of things are certain, at least for now: First, top-level international athletes continue to flock to the U.S. for both the education and adventure available to them in the U.S. college system; last year 15 of 38 individual champions were foreigners. Second, no matter how

diverse a Babel the NCAA championships becomes, you can count on two programs, the Arkansas men and the LSU women, figuring near the top of the mix.

FAVORITES

John McDonnell, the revered head men's coach at **Arkansas**, has an interesting résumé. It includes a stint, soon after his arrival from his native Ireland, as a cameraman on *The Soupy Sales Show*. No laughing matter to rival coaches is the rest of his résumé, which includes an NCAA-record 39 titles in cross country, indoor track and outdoor track. Last June, in Sacramento, Arkansas won its 10th outdoor title, scoring 59 points to beat underrated Auburn, which had 50 and USC, which finished third with 41.5. Like every other McDonnell team, Arkansas scored big in the distances, with all but three of the team's points coming in the 800, 1500, steeple, 5,000 and 10,000, the last three of which they

A pillar in Arkansas's solid corps of distance runners, Cragg (626) won the 5,000 at last year's NCAAs.

won. The Razorbacks have lost big points with the graduation of Dan Lincoln, winner of the 3000-meter steeplechase each of the last three years and of the 10,000 last year, but they still have senior Alistair Cragg, the South-African-born, Irish-passport-carrying 5,000 champ. The Razorbacks also return four other runners who've run the metric equivalent of a four-minute mile, including last year's 1500 runnerup Chris Mulvaney.

The Razorbacks know how extremely fortunate they were that Auburn discus thrower Gabor Maté, the collegiate record holder, failed to qualify for the final, costing the Tigers a projected 10 points. Helping to ensure **Auburn**'s second-place finish was Leevan Sands, from the Bahamas, who won the long jump in 26' 5" and finished second in the triple jump. Sands, now a senior, should provide big points again this year, though Auburn's chances are hurt by losing its 1-3 punch in the 400 hurdles.

If McDonnell has an equal on the women's side, it's **Louisiana State**'s Pat Henry, who has won a total of 25 team titles, including last year's championship. Louisiana State will be led once more by senior sprinter Muna Lee, who anchored the Tigers' winning 4 x 100 team and finished runner-up to Aleen Bailey of South Carolina in the 100 and 200. Indoors, Lee won both the 60 and 200. Hurdler Lolo Jones and triple jumper Nicole Toney, pre-meet favorites in 2003 before finishing fifth and fourth, respectively, are also back to make the Tigers team favorites.

DARKHORSES

The **Louisiana State** men, fourth last year with 36 points, should challenge Arkansas and Auburn. The Tigers won both relays

A triple threat in the sprints, Louisiana State's Lee will be back for her senior year, when she hopes to lead the Tigers to their second straight title and 26th overall.

in Sacramento with the same four runners, all of whom return, including 400-meter hurdler Bennie Brazell, who has now anchored Louisiana State to the last two 4 x 100 titles. That's a good start towards the team title, but the Tigers may need more versatility to win. **Stanford**, led by Don Sage and Grant Robison, the NCAA 1500 champs in 2002 and '03, respectively, will contend with Arkansas in the distances, but are thin elsewhere.

On the women's side, **Texas** drew inspiration last year from the example of beloved coach Bev Kearney, who battled back from a horrific car accident that nearly took her life and left her in a wheelchair. The Longhorns got a great boost

Harris (547) will be back for the Gators, and if his form returns with him, the 400 could be the marquee event at the 2004 NCAAs.

from Sanya Richards, who won the 400 in an American junior record of 50.58 and also anchored the Longhorns' 4 x 400 relay, which placed first in Sacramento. Two members of that Texas relay team graduated, whereas the entire foursomes for both runner-up LSU and third-place **South Carolina** return this year. Indeed, the Gamecocks might well have won the relay, and perhaps the meet, had they not lost superstar Lashinda Demus to an "in-school suspension," for reasons coach Curtis Frye chose not to specify. Return Demus to a team spilling over with sprint, hurdles and jump talent, and South Carolina surely is a threat to regain the title it won in 2002.

ONES TO WATCH

At last year's meet, the biggest star, in every sense, was Carl Myerscough, a 6'10" Englishman majoring in art at the University of Nebraska. Derailed by injuries in 2002, Myerscough found himself needing a personal best on his last throw to win the shot put in 2003. "I wanted to commit my whole life to that throw," he said, and did, scoring an Olympic medal-caliber 71' 11". He will be favored to win the shot next year, while the discus favorite will be defending champion Hannes Hopley, an SMU junior from South Africa.

Perhaps the biggest surprise last year came in the men's 400, where unheralded Adam Steele won a race so close you almost couldn't replicate it if you were trying. Steele's winning time was .017—that's 17 thousandths of a second!—better than his teammate, Mitch Potter, who finished third. In that almost imaginary space between them came runner-up Otis Harris of South Carolina. All three athletes return this year, as does Rickey Harris of Florida, who finished second in the 400 in 2002. Should Harris return to form, the 400 will be the most anticipated event in the meet.

Among the women, Tiffany Williams, a junior from Mississippi State, will be defending the 1500 title she won easily in Sacramento, while the Nilsson sisters, Lena and Ida, Swedes who attend Northern Arizona, should have a shot in the distances. Shalane Flanagan of North Carolina, the indoor 3000 champ in 2003 and runnerup in 5000 at the outdoor meet, will make it tough. In the throws Becky Breisch of Nebraska returns as defending champ in the shot and bronze medalist in the discus, though in the shot she'll get a battle from fellow junior Laura Gerraughty of North Carolina.

Indoor Track and Field

2003 INDIVIDUAL NATIONAL CHAMPIONS

MEN

	CHAMPION	TIME/MARK	RUNNER-UP	TIME/MARK
60-meter dash	Julien Dunkley, E Carolina	6.54	Pierre Browne, Mississippi St	6.60
60-meter hurdles	Jabari Greer, Tennessee	7.55	Shamar Sands, Auburn	7.59
200-meter dash	Leo Bookman, Kansas	20.53	Marquis Davis, Mississippi St	20.70
400-meter dash	Gary Kikaya, Tennessee	45.71	Obra Hogans, Seton Hall	45.82
800-meter run	Nate Brannen, Michigan	1:47.79	Fred Sharpe, Auburn	1:48.16
Mile run	Chris Mulvaney, Arkansas	4:05.70	John Jefferson, Indiana	4:06.46
3,000-meter run	Alistair Cragg, Arkansas	7:55.68	Adrian Blincoe, Villanova	7:56.66
5,000-meter run	Alistair Cragg, Arkansas	13:28.93	Boaz Cheboiywo, Eastern Mich	13:29.26
High jump	Jerrick Holmes, Northridge	7 ft 3¾ in	Adam Shunk, N Carolina	7 ft 2½ in
Pole vault	Brad Walker, Washington	19 ft ¼ in	Eric Eshbach, Nebraska	18 ft 3¾ in
Long jump	Brian Johnson, Southern	27 ft 2 in	Frank Tolen, Nebraska	26 ft 6¼ in
Triple jump	Allen Simms, Southern Cal	56 ft 7½ in	Aarik Wilson, Indiana	55 ft 9 in
Shot put	Carl Myerscough, Nebraska	70 ft 6¼ in	Dan Taylor, Ohio St	69 ft 11¾ in
35-pound wt throw	Thomas Freeman, Manhattan	71 ft 2½ in	Drew Loftin, Colorado St	71 ft 1½ in

WOMEN

	CHAMPION	TIME/MARK	RUNNER-UP	TIME/MARK
60-meter dash	Muna Lee, Louisiana St	7.17	Elva Goulbourne, Auburn	7.24
60-meter hurdles	Lolo Jones, Louisiana St	8.00	Danielle Carruthers, Indiana	8.01
200-meter dash	Muna Lee, Louisiana St	22.61	Sanya Richards, Texas	22.90
400-meter dash	LeShinda Demus, S Carolina	51.79	Sanya Richards, Texas	51.87
800-meter run	Lena Nilsson, UCLA	2:05.13	Nicole Cook, Tennessee	2:05.19
Mile run	Johanna Nilsson, Northern Ariz	4:32.49	Tiffany McWilliams, Mississippi St	4:36.51
3,000-meter run	Shalane Flanagan, N Carolina	9:01.05	Lauren Fleshman, Stanford	9:01.58
5,000-meter run	Sara Gorton, Colorado Northern Ariz	15:39.25	Kate O'Neill, Yale	15:40.88
High jump	Nevena Lendel, SMU Northern Ariz	6 ft 2 ¼ in	Alexandra Church, Kent St	6 ft 1½ in
Pole vault	Lacy Janson, Florida St	14 ft 7¼ in	Becky Holliday, Oregon	14 ft 3¼ in
Long jump	Elva Goulbourne, Auburn	22 ft 4¼ in	Rose Richmond, Indiana	21 ft 2 in
Triple jump	Elva Gouldourne, Auburn	45 ft 2 ½ in	Nicole Toney, Louisiana St	45 ft 2¼ in
Shot put	Laura Gerraughty, N Carolina	59 ft 3 in	Jillian Camarena, Stanford	57 ft 2¾ in
20-pound wt throw	Erin Gilreath, Florida	72 ft 3¾ in	Jukina Dickerson, Florida	67 ft 10¾ in

Championship Results

MEN'S DIVISION I

YEAR	CHAMPION	COACH	PTS	RUNNER-UP	PTS
1965	Missouri	Tom Botts	14	Oklahoma St	12
1966	Kansas	Bob Timmons	14	Southern Cal	13
1967	Southern Cal	Vern Wolfe	26	Oklahoma	17
1968	Villanova	Jim Elliott	35	Southern Cal	25
1969	Kansas	Bob Timmons	41½	Villanova	33
1970	Kansas	Bob Timmons	27½	Villanova	26
1971	Villanova	Jim Elliott	22	UTEP	19¾
1972	Southern Cal	Vern Wolfe	19	Bowling Green/ Mich St	18
1973	Manhattan	Fred Dwyer	18	Kansas/Kent St/UTEP	12
1974	UTEP	Ted Banks	19	Colorado	18
1975	UTEP	Ted Banks	36	Kansas	17½
1976	UTEP	Ted Banks	23	Villanova	15
1977	Washington St	John Chaplin	25½	UTEP	25
1978	UTEP	Ted Banks	44	Auburn	38
1979	Villanova	Jim Elliott	52	UTEP	51
1980	UTEP	Ted Banks	76	Villanova	42
1981	UTEP	Ted Banks	76	SMU	51
1982	UTEP	John Wedel	67	Arkansas	30
1983	SMU	Ted McLaughlin	43	Villanova	32
1984	Arkansas	John McDonnell	38	Washington St	28
1985	Arkansas	John McDonnell	70	Tennessee	29
1986	Arkansas	John McDonnell	49	Villanova	22
1987	Arkansas	John McDonnell	39	SMU	31
1988	Arkansas	John McDonnell	34	Illinois	29
1989	Arkansas	John McDonnell	34	Florida	31
1990	Arkansas	John McDonnell	44	Texas A&M	36
1991	Arkansas	John McDonnell	34	Georgetown	27
1992	Arkansas	John McDonnell	53	Clemson	46
1993	Arkansas	John McDonnell	66	Clemson	30
1994	Arkansas	John McDonnell	83	UTEP	45
1995	Arkansas	John McDonnell	59	GMU/Tennessee	26
1996	George Mason	John Cook	39	Nebraska	31½
1997	Arkansas	John McDonnell	59	Auburn	27
1998	Arkansas	John McDonnell	56	Stanford	36½
1999	Arkansas	John McDonnell	65	Stanford	42½
2000	Arkansas	John McDonnell	69½	Stanford	52
2001	Louisiana St	Pat Henry	34	Texas Christian	33
2002	Tennessee	Bill Webb	62½	Louisiana St	44
2003	Arkansas	John McDonnell	52	Auburn	28

MEN'S DIVISION II

YEAR	CHAMPION	YEAR	CHAMPION
1985	SE Missouri St	1994	Abilene Christian
1986	Not held	1995	St. Augustine's
1987	St. Augustine's	1996	Abilene Christian
1988	Abil. Christian/ St. Augustine's	1997	Abilene Christian
		1998	Abilene Christian
1989	St. Augustine's	1999	Abilene Christian
1990	St. Augustine's	2000	Abilene Christian
1991	St. Augustine's	2001	St. Augustine's
1992	St. Augustine's	2002	Abilene Christian
1993	Abilene Christian	2003	Abilene Christian

MEN'S DIVISION III

YEAR	CHAMPION	YEAR	CHAMPION
1985	St. Thomas (MN)	1995	Lincoln (PA)
1986	Frostburg St	1996	Lincoln (PA)
1987	WI–La Crosse	1997	WI–La Crosse
1988	WI–La Crosse	1998	Lincoln (PA)
1989	N Central	1999	Lincoln (PA)
1990	Lincoln (PA)	2000	Lincoln (PA)
1991	WI–La Crosse	2001	WI–La Crosse
1992	WI–La Crosse	2002	WI–La Crosse
1993	WI–La Crosse	2003	WI–La Crosse
1994	WI–La Crosse		

WOMEN'S DIVISION I

YEAR	CHAMPION	COACH	PTS	RUNNER-UP	PTS
1983	Nebraska	Gary Pepin	47	Tennessee	44
1984	Nebraska	Gary Pepin	59	Tennessee	48
1985	Florida St	Gary Winckler	34	Texas	32
1986	Texas	Terry Crawford	31	Southern Cal	26
1987	Louisiana St	Loren Seagrave	49	Tennessee	30
1988	Texas	Terry Crawford	71	Villanova	52
1989	Louisiana St	Pat Henry	61	Villanova	34
1990	Texas	Terry Crawford	50	Wisconsin	26
1991	Louisiana St	Pat Henry	48	Texas	39
1992	Florida	Bev Kearney	50	Stanford	26
1993	Louisiana St	Pat Henry	49	Wisconsin	44
1994	Louisiana St	Pat Henry	48	Alabama	29
1995	Louisiana St	Pat Henry	40	UCLA	37
1996	Louisiana St	Pat Henry	52	Georgia	34
1997	Louisiana St	Pat Henry	49	Texas/Wisconsin	39
1998	Texas	Bev Kearney	60	Louisiana St	30
1999	Texas	Bev Kearney	61	Louisiana St	57
2000	UCLA	Jeanette Bolden	51	S Carolina	41
2001	UCLA	Jeanette Bolden	53½	S Carolina	40
2002	Louisiana St	Pat Henry	57	Florida	35
2003	Louisiana St	Pat Henry	62	S Carolina/Florida	44

WOMEN'S DIVISION II

YEAR	CHAMPION	YEAR	CHAMPION
1985	St. Augustine's	1995	Abilene Christian
1986	Not held	1996	Abilene Christian
1987	St. Augustine's	1997	Abilene Christian
1988	Abilene Christian	1998	Abilene Christian
1989	Abilene Christian	1999	Abilene Christian
1990	Abilene Christian	2000	Abilene Christian
1991	Abilene Christian	2001	St. Augustine's
1992	Alabama A&M	2002	N Dakota St
1993	Abilene Christian	2003	St. Augustine's
1994	Abilene Christian		

WOMEN'S DIVISION III

YEAR	CHAMPION	YEAR	CHAMPION
1985	MA–Boston	1995	WI–Oshkosh
1986	MA–Boston	1996	WI–Oshkosh
1987	MA–Boston	1997	Christopher Newport
1988	Christopher Newport	1998	Christopher Newport
1989	Christopher Newport	1999	Wheaton (MA)
1990	Christopher Newport	2000	Wheaton (MA)
1991	Cortland St	2001	Wheaton (MA)
1992	Christopher Newport	2002	Wheaton (MA)
1993	Lincoln (PA)	2003	Wheaton (MA)
1994	WI–Oshkosh		

INDIVIDUAL CHAMPIONSHIP RECORDS

MEN

EVENT	MARK	RECORD HOLDER	DATE
55-meter dash	6.00	Lee McRae, Pittsburgh	3-14-86
55-meter hurdles	7.07	Allen Johnson, N Carolina	3-13-92
200-meter dash	20.26	Shawn Crawford, Clemson	3-10-00
400-meter dash	45.60	Brandon Couts, Baylor	3-10-00
800-meter run	1:45.33	Patrick Nduwimana, Arizona	3-10-01
Mile run	3:55.33	Kevin Sullivan, Michigan	3-11-95
3,000-meter run	7:46.03	Adam Goucher, Colorado	3-14-98
5,000-meter run	13:36.64	Jonah Koech, Iowa St	3-8-91
High jump	7 ft 9¼ in	Hollis Conway, SW Louisiana	3-11-89
Pole vault	19 ft 2¼ in	Jacob Davis, Texas	3-6-99
Long jump	27 ft 10 in	Carl Lewis, Houston	3-13-81
Triple jump	56 ft 9½ in	Keith Connor, Southern Methodist	3-13-81
Shot put	70 ft 1 in	Janus Robberts, Southern Methodist	3-10-01
35-pound weight throw	80 ft 11¼ in	Scott Russell, Kansas	3-9-02

WOMEN

EVENT	MARK	RECORD HOLDER	DATE
55-meter dash	6.56	Gwen Torrence, Georgia	3-14-87
55-meter hurdles	7.39	Tiffany Lott, BYU	3-7-97
200-meter dash	22.83	Peta-Gaye Dowdie, Louisiana St	3-6-99
400-meter dash	51.05	Maicel Malone, Arizona St	3-9-91
800-meter run	2:01.77	Hazel Clark, Florida	3-5-99
Mile run	4:30.63	Suzy Favor, Wisconsin	3-11-89
3,000-meter run	8:54.98	Stephanie Herbst, Wisconsin	3-15-86
5,000-meter run	15:39.75	Amy Skieresz, Arizona	3-7-97
High jump	6 ft 5½ in	Amy Acuff, UCLA	3-11-95
Pole vault	14 ft 10 ¼ in	Amy Linnen, Arizona	3-13-02
Long jump	22 ft 1 in	Daphne Saunders, Louisiana St	3-12-94
Triple jump	46 ft 9 in	Suzette Lee, Louisiana St	3-8-97
Shot put	60 ft 5¼ in	Teri Tunks, Southern Methodist	3-14-98
35-pound weight throw	71 ft 8¾ in	Dawn Ellerbe, S Carolina	3-7-97

GO FIGURE

1:30:07 — Record time in the 4x200 relay for LSU's quartet of Nadia Davy, Monique Hall, Stephanie Durst and Muna Lee, set on April 5, 2003. The time broke the NCAA record of 1:30:73 set by South Carolina's Erica Whipple, Miki Barber, Lashinda Demus and Aleen Bailey two weeks earlier.

8 — Career individual titles for Ohio State's Jesse Owens, still the most by any man in college history. Owens, the star of the 1936 Berlin Olympics, won the 100-yard dash, 220-yard dash, 220-yard low hurdles and the long jump in 1935, and the 100-meter dash, 200-meter dash, 220-yard low hurdles and long jump in 1936. His four individual titles in a season is also an NCAA record.

12 — The Division I record for consecutive national championships in all sports, set by the Arkansas Razorbacks indoor track and field team from 1984 to 1995. The longest streak of consecutive championships in outdoor track history is nine, set by USC from 1935 to 1943.

.01 — Margin of victory, in seconds, for USC's Angela Williams in the finals of the 2002 NCAA 100-meter dash, over her teammate Natasha Mayers. The win was the fourth consecutive 100-meter title for Williams making her the first sprinter, male or female, to win the same event at the NCAAs for four years in a row.

9.98 — Seconds, Auburn sprinter Coby Miller's time in the 100-meter dash at Durham, N.C., on June 2, 2000, the fastest time ever run by an U.S.-born college sprinter. The alltime NCAA record is held by UCLA's Ato Boldon ,a native of Trinidad, who clocked 9.92 seconds as a college student. Tim Montgomery holds the world record of 9.72 seconds.

Outdoor Track and Field

2003 INDIVIDUAL NATIONAL CHAMPIONS

MEN

	CHAMPION	MARK	RUNNER-UP	MARK
100-meter dash	Mardy Scales, Middle Tenn St	10.25	Pierre Browne, Mississippi St	10.34
200-meter dash	Leo Bookman, Kansas	20.47	Jerome Mathis, Hampton	20.48
400-meter dash	Adam Steele, Minnesota	44.57	Otis Harris, S Carolina	44.57
800-meter run	Sam Burley, Pennsylvania	1:46.50	Jonathan Johnson, Texas Tech	1:46.51
1,500-meter run	Grant Robinson, Stanford	3:40.39	Chris Mulvaney, Arkansas	3:40.44
5,000-meter run	Alistair Cragg, Arkansas	13:47.87	Louis Luchini, Stanford	13:49.81
10,000-meter run	Patrick Gildea, Tennessee	29:12.18	Adam Wallace, Wisconsin	29:15.21
110-meter hurdles	Ryan Wilson, Southern Cal	13.35	Chris Pinnock, Texas A&M	13.40
400-meter hurdles	Dean Griffiths, Auburn	48.55	Rickey Harris, Florida	48.83
3,000-m steeple	Dan Lincoln, Arkansas	8:26.65	Jordan Desilets, Eastern Mich	8:29.44
High jump	David Jaworski, Southern Cal	7 ft 5¾ in	Shaun Kologinczak, Nebraska	7 ft 5¾ in
Pole vault	Eric Eshbach, Nebraska	17 ft 10½ in	Trent Powell, Brigham Young	17 ft 10½ in
Long jump	Leevan Sands, Auburn	26 ft 5 in	Tony Allmond, S Carolina	26 ft 3¾ in
Triple jump	Julien Kapek, Southern Cal	56 ft 2 in	Leevan Sands, Auburn	55 ft 6¼ in
Shot put	Carl Myerscough, Nebraska	71 ft 11 in	Christian Cantwell, Missouri	70 ft 9 in
Discus throw	Hannes Hopley, SMU	200 ft 11 in	Josh Ralston, Texas A&M	198 ft 3 in
Hammer throw	Lucais MacKay, Georgia	230 ft 3 in	Drew Loftin, Colorado St	222 ft 6 in
Javelin throw	Brian Chaput, Pennsylvania	258 ft 2 in	Rob Minnitti, Boise St	246 ft 3 in
Decathlon	Stephen Harris, Tennessee	8061 pts	Will Thomas, Connecticut	7894 pts

WOMEN

	CHAMPION	MARK	RUNNER-UP	MARK
100-meter dash	Aleen Bailey, S Carolina	11.18	Muna Lee, Louisiana St	11.22
200-meter dash	Aleen Bailey, S Carolina	22.65	Muna Lee, Louisiana St	22.76
400-meter dash	Sanya Richards, Texas	50.58	Dee Dee Trotter, Tennessee	50.66
800-meter run	Alice Schmidt, N Carolina	2:01.16	Neisha Bernard-Thomas, LSU	2:01.75
1,500-meter run	Tiffany McWilliams, Mississippi St	4:06.75	Lena Nilsson, UCLA	4:09.86
5,000-meter run	Lauren Fleshman, Stanford	15:24.06	Shalane Flanagan, N Carolina	15:30.60
10,000-meter run	Alicia Craig, Stanford	32:40.03	Kate O'Neill, Yale	32:47.07
100-meter hurdles	Perdita Felicien, Illinois	12.74	Danielle Carruthers, Indiana	12.89
400-meter hurdles	Sheena Johnson, UCLA	54.24	Raasin McIntosh, Texas	55.02
3,000-m steeple	Kassi Andersen, Brigham Young	9:44.95	Ida Nilsson, Northern Arizona	9:46.74
High jump	Whitney Evans, Washington St	6 ft 1¼ in	Jessica Johnson, Arkansas	6 ft 1¼ in
Pole vault	Becky Holliday, Oregon	14 ft 5½ in	Connie Jerz, Arizona	14 ft 1¼ in
Long jump	Elva Goulbourne, Auburn	22 ft 2¼ in	Viktoriya Rybalko, Maine	21 ft 5¼ in
Triple jump	Ineta Radovica, Nebraska	45 ft 8½ in	Shani Marks, Minnesota	45 ft ½ in
Shot put	Becky Breisch, Nebraska	58 ft 3¼ in	Laura Gerraughty, N Carolina	57 ft 10¼ in
Discus throw	Deshaya Williams, Penn St	181 ft 9 in	Stephanie Brown, Cal Poly	181 ft 5 in
Hammer throw	Candice Scott, Florida	229 ft	Julianna Tudja, Southern Cal	218 ft 9 in
Javelin throw	Irina Kharun, Indiana	202 ft 10 in	Inga Stasiulionyte, Southern Cal	171 ft 5 in
Heptathlon	Hyleas Fountain, Georgia	5999 pts	Ellannee Richardson, Washington St	5839 pts

Championship Results

MEN'S DIVISION I

YEAR	CHAMPION	COACH	PTS	RUNNER-UP	PTS
1921	Illinois	Harry Gill	20†	Notre Dame	16†
1922	California	Walter Christie	28†	Penn St	19†
1923	Michigan	Stephen Farrell	29†	Mississippi St	16
1924	No meet				
1925	Stanford*	R.L. Templeton	31†		
1926	Southern Cal*	Dean Cromwell	27†		
1927	Illinois*	Harry Gill	35†		
1928	Stanford	R.L. Templeton	72	Ohio St	31
1929	Ohio St	Frank Castleman	50	Washington	42
1930	Southern Cal	Dean Cromwell	55†	Washington	40
1931	Southern Cal	Dean Cromwell	77†	Ohio St	31†
1932	Indiana	Billy Hayes	56	Ohio St	49†
1933	Louisiana St	Bernie Moore	58	Southern Cal	54
1934	Stanford	R.L. Templeton	63	Southern Cal	54†
1935	Southern Cal	Dean Cromwell	74†	Ohio St	40†
1936	Southern Cal	Dean Cromwell	103†	Ohio St	73
1937	Southern Cal	Dean Cromwell	62	Stanford	50
1938	Southern Cal	Dean Cromwell	67†	Stanford	38
1939	Southern Cal	Dean Cromwell	86	Stanford	44†
1940	Southern Cal	Dean Cromwell	47	Stanford	28†
1941	Southern Cal	Dean Cromwell	81†	Indiana	50
1942	Southern Cal	Dean Cromwell	85†	Ohio St	44†
1943	Southern Cal	Dean Cromwell	46	California	39
1944	Illinois	Leo Johnson	79	Notre Dame	43
1945	Navy	E.J. Thomson	62	Illinois	48†
1946	Illinois	Leo Johnson	78	Southern Cal	42†
1947	Illinois	Leo Johnson	59†	Southern Cal	34†
1948	Minnesota	James Kelly	46	Southern Cal	41†
1949	Southern Cal	Jess Hill	55†	UCLA	31
1950	Southern Cal	Jess Hill	49†	Stanford	28
1951	Southern Cal	Jess Mortenson	56	Cornell	40
1952	Southern Cal	Jess Mortenson	66†	San Jose St	24†
1953	Southern Cal	Jess Mortenson	80	Illinois	41
1954	Southern Cal	Jess Mortenson	66†	Illinois	31†
1955	Southern Cal	Jess Mortenson	42	UCLA	34
1956	UCLA	Elvin Drake	55†	Kansas	51
1957	Villanova	James Elliott	47	California	32
1958	Southern Cal	Jess Mortenson	48†	Kansas	40†
1959	Kansas	Bill Easton	73	San Jose St	48
1960	Kansas	Bill Easton	50	Southern Cal	37
1961	Southern Cal	Jess Mortenson	65	Oregon	47
1962	Oregon	William Bowerman	85	Villanova	40†
1963	Southern Cal	Vern Wolfe	61	Stanford	42
1964	Oregon	William Bowerman	70	San Jose St	40
1965	Oregon	William Bowerman	32		
	Southern Cal	Vern Wolfe	32		
1966	UCLA	Jim Bush	81	Brigham Young	33
1967	Southern Cal	Vern Wolfe	86	Oregon	40
1968	Southern Cal	Vern Wolfe	58	Washington St	57
1969	San Jose St	Bud Winter	48	Kansas	45
1970	Brigham Young	Clarence Robison	35		
	Kansas	Bob Timmons	35		
	Oregon	William Bowerman	35		
1971	UCLA	Jim Bush	52	Southern Cal	41
1972	UCLA	Jim Bush	82	Southern Cal	49
1973	UCLA	Jim Bush	56	Oregon	31

MEN'S DIVISION I (CONT.)

YEAR	CHAMPION	COACH	PTS	RUNNER-UP	PTS
1974	Tennessee	Stan Huntsman	60	UCLA	56
1975	UTEP	Ted Banks	55	UCLA	42
1976	Southern Cal	Vern Wolfe	64	UTEP	44
1977	Arizona St	Senon Castillo	64	UTEP	50
1978	UCLA/UTEP	Jim Bush/Ted Banks	50		
1979	UTEP	Ted Banks	64	Villanova	48
1980	UTEP	Ted Banks	69	UCLA	46
1981	UTEP	Ted Banks	70	SMU	57
1982	UTEP	John Wedel	105	Tennessee	94
1983	SMU	Ted McLaughlin	104	Tennessee	102
1984	Oregon	Bill Dellinger	113	Washington St	94½
1985	Arkansas	John McDonnell	61	Washington St	46
1986	SMU	Ted McLaughlin	53	Washington St	52
1987	UCLA	Bob Larsen	81	Texas	28
1988	UCLA	Bob Larsen	82	Texas	41
1989	Louisiana St	Pat Henry	53	Texas A&M	51
1990	Louisiana St	Pat Henry	44	Arkansas	36
1991	Tennessee	Doug Brown	51	Washington St	42
1992	Arkansas	John McDonnell	60	Tennessee	46½
1993	Arkansas	John McDonnell	69	LSU/Ohio St	45
1994	Arkansas	John McDonnell	83	UTEP	45
1995	Arkansas	John McDonnell	61½	UCLA	55
1996	Arkansas	John McDonnell	55	George Mason	40
1997	Arkansas	John McDonnell	55	Texas	42½
1998	Arkansas	John McDonnell	58½	Stanford	51
1999	Arkansas	John McDonnell	59	Stanford	52
2000	Stanford	Vin Lananna	72	Arkansas	59
2001	Tennessee	Bill Webb	50	Texas Christian	49
2002	Louisiana St	Pat Henry	64	Tennessee	57
2003	Arkansas	John McDonnell	59	Auburn	50

*Unofficial championship. †Fraction of a point.

MEN'S DIVISION II

YEAR	CHAMPION	YEAR	CHAMPION	YEAR	CHAMPION
1963	MD–Eastern Shore	1976	UC–Irvine	1990	St. Augustine's
1964	Fresno St	1977	Cal St–Hayward	1991	St. Augustine's
1965	San Diego St	1978	Cal St–LA	1992	St. Augustine's
1966	San Diego St	1979	Cal Poly–SLO	1993	St. Augustine's
1967	Long Beach St	1980	Cal Poly–SLO	1994	St. Augustine's
1968	Cal Poly–SLO	1981	Cal Poly–SLO	1995	St. Augustine's
1969	Cal Poly–SLO	1982	Abilene Christian	1996	Abilene Christian
1970	Cal Poly–SLO	1983	Abilene Christian	1997	Abilene Christian
1971	Kentucky St	1984	Abilene Christian	1998	St. Augustine's
1972	Eastern Michigan	1985	Abilene Christian	1999	Abilene Christian
1973	Norfolk St	1986	Abilene Christian	2000	Abilene Christian
1974	Eastern Illinois	1987	Abilene Christian	2001	St. Augustine's
	Norfolk St	1988	Abilene Christian	2002	Abilene Christian
1975	Cal St–Northridge	1989	St. Augustine's	2003	Abilene Christian

MEN'S DIVISION III

YEAR	CHAMPION	YEAR	CHAMPION	YEAR	CHAMPION
1974	Ashland	1984	Glassboro St	1994	N Central
1975	Southern–N Orleans	1985	Lincoln (PA)	1995	Lincoln (PA)
1976	Southern–N Orleans	1986	Frostburg St	1996	Lincoln (PA)
1977	Southern–N Orleans	1987	Frostburg St	1997	WI–La Crosse
1978	Occidental	1988	WI–La Crosse	1998	N Central
1979	Slippery Rock	1989	N Central	1999	Lincoln (PA)
1980	Glassboro St	1990	Lincoln (PA)	2000	Nebraska Wesleyan
1981	Glassboro St	1991	WI–La Crosse	2001	WI–La Crosse
1982	Glassboro St	1992	WI–La Crosse	2002	WI–La Crosse
1983	Glassboro St	1993	WI–La Crosse	2003	WI–La Crosse

[Maryland/N.C.]

FITNESS IS crucial to track and field athletes, but some students with a yen to stay in shape find plain old running a bit tedious. A number of colleges are providing ingenious options, none of them more impressive than Maryland's seven-sided, five-story climbing tower known as the Beast. For a facility that promotes fitness as well as feats of derring-do, the two-and-a-half year-old Beast can't be beat: It has 9,000 square feet of surface area, and offers students thousands of climbing routes. Here are four other schools that are also big on adventure sports.

- **WISCONSIN** offers sports ranging from hang gliding to scuba diving through its 72-year-old Hoofers outdoors club, which has about 4,000 members.

- **COLORADO** has a world-class outdoors program that includes rock climbing and skiing in the Rockies.

- **MINNESOTA** has an extensive ice-climbing program. Students sometimes travel south to Iowa to scale old silos that have been iced over for climbers.

- **MIAMI (OHIO)** sends study groups to the South Pacific and around the U.S. to combine environmental classes with activities like sea kayaking and ice climbing.

—Cara O'Reilly

BILL FRAKES

The University of North Carolina also offers its students a taste of adventure sports with the nation's longest zipline (above), a 1,200-foot cable on which students can reach speeds of up to 25 mph while dangling as high as 50 feet off the ground.

WOMEN'S DIVISION I

YEAR	CHAMPION	COACH	PTS	RUNNER-UP	PTS
1982	UCLA	Scott Chisam	153	Tennessee	126
1983	UCLA	Scott Chisam	116½	Florida St	108
1984	Florida St	Gary Winckler	145	Tennessee	124
1985	Oregon	Tom Heinonen	52	Florida St/LSU	46
1986	Texas	Terry Crawford	65	Alabama	55
1987	Louisiana St	Loren Seagrave	62	Alabama	53
1988	Louisiana St	Loren Seagrave	61	UCLA	58
1989	Louisiana St	Pat Henry	86	UCLA	47
1990	Louisiana St	Pat Henry	53	UCLA	46
1991	Louisiana St	Pat Henry	78	Texas	67
1992	Louisiana St	Pat Henry	87	Florida	81
1993	Louisiana St	Pat Henry	93	Wisconsin	44
1994	Louisiana St	Pat Henry	86	Texas	43
1995	Louisiana St	Pat Henry	69	UCLA	58
1996	Louisiana St	Pat Henry	81	Texas	52
1997	Louisiana St	Pat Henry	63	Texas	62
1998	Texas	Bev Kearney	60	UCLA	55
1999	Texas	Bev Kearney	62	UCLA	60
2000	Louisiana St	Pat Henry	59	Southern Cal	56
2001	Southern Cal	Ron Allice	64	UCLA	55
2002	South Carolina	Curtis Frye	82	UCLA	72
2003	Louisiana St	Pat Henry	64	Texas	50

WOMEN'S DIVISION II

YEAR	CHAMPION	YEAR	CHAMPION
1982	Cal Poly–SLO	1993	Alabama A&M
1983	Cal Poly–SLO	1994	Alabama A&M
1984	Cal Poly–SLO	1995	Abilene Christian
1985	Abilene Christian	1996	Abilene Christian
1986	Abilene Christian	1997	St. Augustine's
1987	Abilene Christian	1998	Abilene Christian
1988	Abilene Christian	1999	Abilene Christian
1989	Cal Poly–SLO	2000	St. Augustine's
1990	Cal Poly–SLO	2001	St. Augustine's
1991	Cal Poly–SLO	2002	St. Augustine's
1992	Alabama A&M	2003	Lincoln

WOMEN'S DIVISION III

YEAR	CHAMPION	YEAR	CHAMPION
1982	Central (IA)	1993	Lincoln (PA)
1983	WI–La Crosse	1994	Chris. Newport
1984	WI–La Crosse	1995	WI–Oshkosh
1985	Cortland State	1996	WI–Oshkosh
1986	MA–Boston	1997	WI–Oshkosh
1987	Chris. Newport	1998	Chris. Newport
1988	Chris. Newport	1999	Lincoln (PA)
1989	Chris. Newport	2000	Lincoln (PA)
1990	WI–Oshkosh	2001	Wheaton (MA)
1991	WI–Oshkosh	2002	Wheaton (MA)
1992	Chris. Newport	2003	Wheaton (MA)

INDIVIDUAL CHAMPIONSHIP RECORDS

MEN

EVENT	MARK	RECORD HOLDER	DATE
100-meter dash	9.92	Ato Bolden, UCLA	6-1-96
200-meter dash	19.87	Lorenzo Daniel, Mississippi St	6-3-88
		John Capel, Florida	6-5-99
400-meter dash	44.00	Quincy Watts, Southern Cal	6-6-92
800-meter run	1:44.70	Mark Everett, Florida	6-1-90
1,500-meter run	3:35.30	Sydney Maree, Villanova	6-6-81
3,000-meter steeplechase	8:12.39	Henry Rono, Washington St	6-1-78
5,000-meter run	13:20.63	Sydney Maree, Villanova	6-2-79
10,000-meter run	28:01.30	Suleiman Nyambui, Texas–El Paso	6-1-79
110-meter high hurdles	13.22	Greg Foster, UCLA	6-2-78
400-meter intermediate hurdles	47.85	Kevin Young, UCLA	6-3-88
High jump	7 ft 9¾ in	Hollis Conway, SW Louisiana	6-3-89
Pole vault	19 ft 1 in	Lawrence Johnson, Tennessee	5-29-96
Long jump	28 ft	Erick Walder, Arkansas	6-3-93
Triple jump	57 ft 7¾ in	Keith Connor, Southern Methodist	6-5-82
Shot put	72 ft 2¼ in	John Godina, UCLA	6-3-95
Discus throw	220 ft	Kamy Keshmiri, Nevada	6-5-92
Hammer throw	265 ft 3 in	Balazs Kiss, Southern Cal	5-31-96
Javelin throw (new javelin)	268 ft 7 in	Esko Mikkola, Arizona	6-3-98
Decathlon	8279 pts	Tito Steiner, Brigham Young	6-2/3-81

WOMEN

EVENT	MARK	RECORD HOLDER	DATE
100-meter dash	10.78	Dawn Sowell, Louisiana St	6-3-89
200-meter dash	22.04	Dawn Sowell, Louisiana St	6-2-89
400-meter dash	50.18	Pauline Davis, Alabama	6-3-89
800-meter run	1:59.11	Suzy Favor, Wisconsin	6-1-90
1,500-meter run	4:08.26	Suzy Favor, Wisconsin	6-2-90
3,000-meter run	8:47.35	Vicki Huber, Villanova	6-3-88
5,000-meter run	15:37.77	Amy Skieresz, Arizona	6-5-98
10,000-meter run	32:28.57	Sylvia Mosqueda, Cal St–Los Angeles	6-1-88
100-meter hurdles	12.68	Perdita Felicien, Illinois	6-12-03
400-meter hurdles	54.54	Ryan Tolbert, Vanderbilt	6-6-97
High jump	6 ft 5 in	Amy Acuff, UCLA	6-3-95
Pole vault	14 ft 5¼ in	Tracy O'Hara, UCLA	6-2-00
Long jump	22 ft 9¼ in	Sheila Echols, Louisiana St	6-5-87
Triple jump	46 ft ¾ in	Sheila Hudson, California	6-2-90
Shot put	61 ft 2¼ in	Tressa Thompson, Nebraska	6-4-98
Discus throw	210 ft 10 in	Seilala Sua, UCLA	6-6-99
Hammer throw	220 ft 6 in	Jamine Moton, Clemson	5-29-02
Javelin throw (new javelin)	197 ft 8 in	Angeliki Tsiolakoudi, Texas–El Paso	6-3-00
Heptathlon	6527 pts	Diane Guthrie-Gresham, George Mason	6-2/3-95

Owls' NEST

If its crack pitching staff returns to school, 2003 champ Rice could settle in for an extended title run

WARMING UP BEFORE the decisive Game 3 of last season's College World Series, Rice pitcher Philip Humber was scaring his catcher, Justin Ruchti, just a little bit. Humber not only lacked his best stuff, he also kept bouncing his curve ball in the bullpen dirt. Not the beginning either player had hoped for as they prepared for the biggest game of their careers, a matchup for the national title with hard-hitting Stanford, which had belted 11 homers in the CWS so far—more than double the home run total of any other team in tournament. "When I watched them take batting practice," Owls coach Wayne Graham said of Stanford, "I wanted to hide."

The 6′ 8″ Niemann was the most dominating pitcher in Division I last season, going 17–0 with a 1.70 ERA for the NCAA champion Owls.

Imagine how Ruchti and Humber felt after their game of catch in the pen. But however jangled his nerves were during warmup, Humber settled down once the game started. He retired the Cardinal in order in the top of the first, and when the Owls scored three in the bottom half of the inning, Humber was on his way. Rice scored a CWS–record seven runs in the sixth to break it open and went on to a 14–2 victory. Humber, a 6′4″ righthander, had helped deliver tiny Rice (enrollment: 2,700) its first national title in any sport in school history.

FAVORITES

Rice could very well win its second one next year, and here's why: Humber, the big, talented righty who went 11–3 with a 3.30 ERA last season, was only a sophomore, and he was the *No. 3* starter on the Owls staff. The two guys ahead of him, Jeff Niemann (17–0, 1.70 ERA) and

With shortstop Braun leading a phalanx of young talent returning to Miami, the Hurricanes should be a threat in the 2004 CWS.

Wade Townsend (11–2, 2.20), All-Americas both, were also sophomores. Niemann stands 6' 8" and has excellent command to go with his velocity, and Townsend is a 6' 6" pure power pitcher. Unless they decide to go pro, the Owls will once again have the nation's top staff in 2004. But their title run last season was not all about pitching; Rice's offense was extremely effective, if overlooked at times. Led by sparkplug outfielder Chris Kolkhorst, who hit .355 with 43 RBIs during the regular season, the Owls had a speedy, productive attack. Kolkhorst returns to Houston this season, along with first baseman Vince Sinisi, a junior who batted .355 with nine homers last year, and third baseman Craig Stansberry, a senior who hit .307. Indeed, the Owls were a young team on the rise last season; they could be a veteran team that thoroughly dominates this year.

Then again, it's difficult to repeat as champion in college baseball—only five teams in NCAA history have done it. Just ask **Texas**: The Longhorns came to Omaha in 2003 as the defending champions with an experienced and talented squad, only to be bounced out in the semis by in-state rivals Rice. But Texas should contend again this year, as they return Omar Quintanilla, who batted .351 as a junior, Tim Moss (.327 with 27 stolen bases) and 2002 CWS most outstanding player Huston Street, who played third base in addition to going 8–0 with 14 saves and a 1.38 ERA as a relief pitcher last year. The Longhorns also have the winningest coach in college baseball history in Augie Garrido. Count on them to be in the mix this year.

The same should be said for snakebitten **Stanford**, which has reached three of the past four CWS finals, losing all three. The Cardinal will welcome back senior righthander John Hudgins, who went 3–0 in Omaha last season and became only the fourth player from a losing team to win the most outstanding player award. They'll also have sophomore lefty Mark Romanczuk, who lost the CWS final to Rice, but went 12–0 with a 3.39 ERA during the regular season as a freshman. With outfielders Danny Putnam (who hit .355 with 14 homers and 57 RBIs as a sophomore), Carlos Quentin (.398, 10 HRs, 56 RBIs) and Sam Fuld (.327, with 32 RBIs) leading the offense, and a solid young bullpen, the Cardinal could finally break through in Omaha this season.

One obstacle to Stanford's quest will almost certainly be the extremely talented **Miami** team. Champions in 1982, '85, '99 and 2001, the Hurricanes made a strong postseason run last year and are positively loaded with young talent, including shortstop Ryan Braun, who batted .374 and belted 17 homers as a freshman. He also drove in 74 runs. Rejoining Braun are junior outfielder Danny Figueroa (.328-3-28), senior third baseman Adam Ricks (.329-4-55), and infielder Gaby Sanchez, who hit .329 with seven homers and 56 RBIs as a freshman last year. Senior lefthander

J.D. Cockroft, coming off an 11–2 season with a 2.56 ERA, will anchor the 'Canes pitching staff, which, while not as potent as its corps of hitters, combines with a solid defense to make Miami a bona fide contender.

While Miami's pitching lags slightly behind its hitting, **Cal State Fullerton** has it the other way around. The Titans, who reached the final four in last year's CWS, return a deep and solid pitching staff, including Chad Cordero, arguably the best closer in the country. They can also send to the mound senior righthander John Windsor (10–2 with a 1.82 ERA last season), sophomore righty Dustin Miller (9–2, 3.03) and

senior righthander Wes Littleton, who was a third-team All-America in 2002, but was edged out of the rotation last season—a testament to the Titans' bounty of quality arms. Which is not to say that Fullerton's offensive cupboard is bare: the Titans return senior outfielders Shane Costa (.372-4-54) and Kyle Boyer (.332-6-49), their most effective batters last season, along with Richie Burgos (.324-4-49), Danny Dorn (.366-7-54) and Ronnie Prettyman, who heated up down the stretch last year to

In 2003, the Cardinal's Hudgins became only the fourth player on a losing team to win the CWS outstanding player award.

finish with a .346 batting average.

Another team that can swing the lumber—er, aluminum—is 2000 champion **Louisiana State**. They no longer have legendary coach Skip Bertman in the dugout, but his successor, longtime assistant Smoke Laval, ingratiated himself with the Tiger faithful by getting his team to the 2003 CWS despite a rash of injuries to his pitching staff. That unit featured two freshmen, Justin Maier (8–3, 2.83) and Jason Determann (7–0, 2.67), who will be back, and should make the Tigers even stronger this year. On offense, LSU returns senior shortstop Aaron Hill (.366-9-67), junior outfielders Ryan Patterson (.350-15-49) and Jon Zeringue (.333-14-44). That trio will combine with junior first baseman Clay Harris (.333-15-60) and junior infielder Blake Gill (.304-5-54), to give LSU one of the best offenses in the nation.

DARKHORSES

"Darkhorses" is something of a misnomer here, as most of the teams in this section are known quantities on the

The versatile Street (25) added third base to his relief pitching duties last year; he hopes to lead the Longhorns back to Omaha this season.

national scene, but for one reason or another, they rank slightly below the teams in our Favorites section. The always competitive **South Carolina**, for example, lost a potent chunk of its offense with the departures of third baseman Brian Buscher (.390-14-64) and shortstop Justin Harris (.358-3-32), both seniors last season. The Gamecocks also lost workhorse righthander Chris Hernandez. On the other hand, senior catcher Landon Powell (.338-10-59) and pitching ace David Marchbanks (15–2, 2.39) will both be back in Columbia this season, along with junior second baseman Kevin Melillo, who smacked 11 home runs last season.

Arizona State returns All-Americas Dustin Pedroia (.404-4-52), Jeff Larish (.372-18-95) and Jeremy West (.381-17-71) from a team that went 54–14 last season and came within a game of advancing to the CWS, but the Sun Devils lost

Costa (touching base) and his .372 batting average will be back for the Titans, who lost to Stanford in the CWS semifinals last season.

four pitchers from last year's team, including Ben Thurmond, who went 8–0 with a 2.73 ERA. Still, Erik Averill (8–2 as a freshman) and Ryan Schroyer (1.53 ERA) return to Tempe, and with their firepower on offense, the Sun Devils could make some noise.

Another team that came close to the CWS last year was **Florida State**, which finished 54-13-1 and returns four heavy hitters in Eddy Martinez-Esteve (.371-9-43), Tony Richie (.366-12-78), Stephen Drew (.327-11-59), and Tony McQuade (.324-13-56). But like ASU, the Seminoles lost quality pitching, saying goodbye to seniors Daniel Davidson (10–0, 2.63 ERA) and Matt Lynch (13–4, 3.53).

Finally, **Long Beach State**, whose team is affectionately nicknamed the Dirtbags by its fans, lost ace Abe Alvarez (11–2, 2.35 ERA) to the Boston Red Sox, but returns his fellow All-America Jered Weaver (14–4, 1.96) to a team that went 41–20 last season.

SIDELINES

The smallest school in Division I won its first NCAA title last year largely because of its smallest player. Outfielder Chris Kolkhorst, now a senior, stood much taller than his 5'9" frame during the 2003 CWS. He dived into the leftfield wall to make a game-saving catch in Game 1, and, nursing a sore knee suffered in Game 2, he reached base in his first five at-bats in Game 3, walking twice, hitting two doubles and a single. He scored three runs and drove in two, as the Owls won 14–2 to take the title. But there was one more bit of business: When he arrived at Rice earlier in the year, the scrappy Kolkhorst had asked his teammates to call him the Gritman. They balked, saying he had to earn the nickname. With his relentless hustle at the CWS, it seems he did. During the celebratory pileup behind the pitcher's mound, his teammates made it official. "There's no question any more," said Kolkhorst. "I am the Gritman."

NCAA MEN'S DIVISION I
CHAMPIONSHIP GAME BOX SCORE

Game 1: Rice 4, Stanford 3
Game 2: Stanford 8, Rice 3

GAME 3

Stanford	0	0	0	0	0	0	1	1	0	**2**	**5**	**2**
Rice	3	1	0	0	0	7	0	3	x	**14**	**14**	**0**

W—Humber. **L**—Romanczuk. **SV**—none.
LOB—Stanford 4, Rice 11. **2B**—Rice: Kolkhorst 2, Janish; Stanford: Garko, Hall . **3B**—none. **HR**—none.
S—Rice: Stansberry. **SB**—none. **CS**—Stanford: Carter. **HBP**—Rice: Janish. **DP**—Stanford 1. **T**—2:57.
A—18, 494.

DIVISION I INDIVIDUAL LEADERS

Through 06/08/2003.

BATTING AVERAGE

Minimum 75 at-bats. Minimum 2.5 at-bats per game.

NAME, TEAM	CL	POS	G	AB	H	BA
Rickie Weeks, Southern U.	Jr.	2B	51	163	78	0.479
Mitch Maier, Toledo	Jr.	C	51	194	87	0.448
Josh Anderson, Eastern Ky.	Jr.	OF	53	237	106	0.447
Kelly Hunt, Bowling Green	Sr.	1B	45	171	75	0.439
Adrian Brown, Mississippi Val.	Sr.	OF	50	167	71	0.425
Tim D'Aquila, Central Conn. St.	Jr.	C	50	186	79	0.425
Michael Brown, William & Mary	Sr.	OF	51	201	85	0.423
Ryan Roberts, Texas-Arlington	Sr.	3B	62	230	97	0.422
Jaime Landin, Tex. A&M-Corp. Chris	So.	2B	50	202	85	0.421
Keith Brachold, Marist	So.	OF	54	214	90	0.421
John Gragg, Bethune-Cookman	Sr.	OF	57	214	90	0.421

VICTORIES

Minimum 10.

NAME, TEAM	CL	POS	APP	IP	W	L	PCT
Jeff Niemann, Rice	So.	SP	20	121.3	16	0	1.000
David Marchbanks, South Carolina	Jr.	SP	20	132.0	15	2	0.882
Tim Alvarez, Southeast Mo. St.	Sr.	SP	21	108.3	14	3	0.824
Jered Weaver, Long Beach St.	So.	SP	19	133.3	14	4	0.778
Randy Beam, FL Atlantic	Jr.	SP/RP	17	101.7	13	2	0.867
Matt Lynch, Florida St.	Sr.	SP	19	112.3	13	4	0.765
Mark Romanczuk, Stanford	Fr.	SP	20	103.7	12	0	1.000
Brad Ziegler, Southwest Mo. St.	Sr.	SP	16	100.7	12	1	0.923
Zac Cline, West Virginia	So.	SP	16	125.7	12	3	0.800
Michael Rogers, N Carolina St.	Fr.	SP	17	125.0	12	3	0.800

DIVISION I INDIVIDUAL LEADERS (CONT.)

HOME RUNS PER GAME

Minimum 15 & .30 per game.

NAME, TEAM	CL	POS	G	HR	PG
Billy Becher, New Mexico St.	Jr.	1B	61	32	0.52
Chris Alexander, New Mexico	Sr.	1B	58	25	0.43
Humberto Aguilar, Tex. A&M-Corp. Chris	Sr.	1B	48	20	0.42
Jamie D'Antona, Wake Forest	Jr.	INF	53	21	0.40
Michael Brown, William & Mary	Sr.	OF	51	20	0.39
Chad Boudon, Washington	Jr.	OF	57	22	0.39
Jeff Clement, Southern Cal	Fr.	C	56	21	0.38
Jeff Cook, Southern Miss.	Sr.	OF	63	23	0.37
Clint King, Southern Miss.	So.	OF	63	23	0.37
Matt Hopper, Nebraska	Sr.	1B	62	22	0.35

RUNS BATTED IN PER GAME

Minimum 50 & 1.15 per game.

NAME, TEAM	CL	POS	G	RBI	PG
Billy Becher, New Mexico St.	Jr.	1B	61	118	1.93
Neil Sellers, Eastern Ky.	Jr.	3B	53	85	1.60
Chris Alexander, New Mexico	Sr.	1B	58	93	1.60
Jamie D'Antona, Wake Forest	Jr.	INF	53	82	1.55
Humberto Aguilar, Tex. A&M-Corp. Chris	Sr.	1B	48	74	1.54
Jeff Larish, Arizona St.	So.	1B	65	95	1.46
Ryan Garko, Stanford	Sr.	C	61	88	1.44
Kelly Hunt, Bowling Green	Sr.	1B	45	61	1.36
Beau Hearod, Alabama	Sr.	INF	62	82	1.32
Kevin Vital, Southern U.	Sr.	1B	50	66	1.32

EARNED RUN AVERAGE

Minimum 50 IP & 2.60 ERA.
Pitchers must have 1 IP for every game played by team.

NAME, TEAM	CL	POS	APP	IP	R	ER	ERA
Tom Mastny, Furman	Sr.	SP	16	124.0	23	15	1.09
Cla Meredith, Va. Commonwealth	So.	RP	29	60.3	8	8	1.19
Carlos Fernandez, Louisville	Sr.	SP/RP	32	59.3	10	8	1.21
Huston Street, Texas	So.	RP	37	71.7	12	11	1.38
Aaron Sims, Alabama A&M	Sr.	SP	8	51.0	14	8	1.41
Thomas Pauly, Princeton	Jr.	SP/RP	19	55.3	12	9	1.46
Jamie Merchant, Vermont	Sr.	SP	11	75.0	21	13	1.56
Chuck Bechtel, Marist	Sr.	SP/RP	13	85.0	29	15	1.59
Scott Lewis, Ohio St.	So.	SP	12	83.7	23	15	1.61
Jeff Niemann, Rice	So.	SP	20	121.3	27	22	1.63

STOLEN BASES

Minimum 25 & .45 per game.

NAME, TEAM	CL	POS	G	SB	PG
Josh Anderson, Eastern Ky.	Jr.	OF	53	57	1.08
Sebastien Boucher, Bethune-Cookman	So.	OF	56	48	0.86
Jonny Kaplan, Tulane	Sr.	OF	62	48	0.77
Carl Loadenthal, Rider	Sr.	OF	48	35	0.73
Ryan McGraw, Coastal Caro.	Jr.	OF	63	45	0.71
Graig Badger, Rutgers	Jr.	2B	59	41	0.69
Kenji Williams, Jackson St.	So.	1B	39	27	0.69
Ryan Hubbard, Wake Forest	Sr.	OF	51	35	0.69
Reggie Willits, Oklahoma	Sr.	OF	54	37	0.69
Danny Figueroa, Miami (Fla.)	So.	OF	60	40	0.67

DIVISION I INDIVIDUAL LEADERS (CONT.)

STRIKEOUTS PER NINE INNINGS

Pitchers must have 1 IP for every game played by team.
Minimum 50 IP & 10 K/9.

NAME, TEAM	CL	POS	APP	IP	SO	K/9
Ryan Wagner, Houston	So.	SP/RP	38	79.3	148	16.8
Scott Lewis, Ohio St.	So.	SP	12	83.7	127	13.7
Wade Townsend, Rice	So.	SP/RP	27	104.0	150	13.0
Chris Schutt, Cornell	Jr.	SP	10	62.0	89	12.9
Steve Schmoll, Maryland	Sr.	SP	18	87.7	124	12.7
Thomas Diamond, New Orleans	So.	SP/RP	21	69.0	96	12.5
Casey Abrams, Wright St.	Jr.	SP/RP	19	114.3	158	12.4
Thomas Pauly, Princeton	Jr.	SP/RP	19	55.3	74	12.0
Brad Cherry, Ark.-Little Rock	Jr.	SP/RP	18	82.3	108	11.8
Tim Stauffer, Richmond	Jr.	SP	15	114.0	146	11.5

SAVES

RANK	NAME, TEAM	CL	POS	APP	IP	SV
	Steven Register, Auburn	So.	RP	33	52.0	16
	Ryan Wagner, Houston	So.	SP/RP	38	79.3	15
	Mike Dennison, Wichita St.	Sr.	RP	27	40.7	14
	Mark Badgley, Northern Ill.	Fr.	RP	28	34.0	14
	Matt Dalton, Virginia Tech	Sr.	RP	29	35.7	14
	Matt Davis, Ohio St.	So.	RP	33	38.7	14
	Joey Devine, North Carolina St.	Fr.	RP	36	65.7	14
	Huston Street, Texas	So.	RP	37	71.7	14
	Stephen Head, Mississippi	Fr.	1B	20	57.7	13
	Shaun Marcum, Southwest Mo. St.	Jr.	INF	23	43.0	13
	Scott Beerer, Texas A&M	Jr.	OF	27	49.3	13
	J.P. Gagne, Notre Dame	Sr.	RP	30	60.0	13
	Tony Perez, San Diego	Sr.	OF	30	48.0	13
	Blake Cross, UNC Wilmington	Jr.	SP/RP	35	53.0	13
	Joey Livingston, South Fla.	Sr.	RP	39	54.7	13

NCAA MEN'S DIVISION II CHAMPIONSHIP GAME BOX SCORE

```
Central MO St   2 1 0  0 0 2  1 5 0   11 18  2
Tampa           0 0 0  4 0 0  0 0 0    4  7  0
```

W—Powers. **L**—Beattie. **SV**—none.
LOB—Central Missouri St 10; Tampa 5. **2B**—Central Missouri St: Berry, Downey. **3B**—none. **HR**—Central Missouri St: Norman, Strada, Bryant; Tampa: Duff, Hyland, Castellvy. **S**—none. **SB**—Central Missouri St: Downey, Murphy; Tampa: Monzon, Taylor. **CS**—Central Missouri St: Downey; Tampa: Quigg. **HBP**—Central Missouri St: Berry, Guidry 2. **DP**—Central Missouri St 1, Tampa 1. **T**—2:36. **A**—2,616.

DIVISION II INDIVIDUAL LEADERS

BATTING AVERAGE

Minimum 75 at-bats. Minimum 2.5 at-bats per game.

NAME, TEAM	CL	POS	G	AB	H	BA
Mike Aviles, Concordia (N.Y.)	Sr.	SS	45	190	95	0.500
T.J. Shimizu, Salem Int'l	Jr.	C	44	144	72	0.500
Ashley Farr, S.C.-Aiken	Jr.	OF	54	207	100	0.483
Greg Annino, C.W. Post	Sr.	OF	31	135	65	0.481
Brian Foy, Wayne St. (Neb.)	Sr.	3B	39	143	68	0.476
Milton Redd, Shaw	Sr.	INF	35	121	56	0.463
Hasani Whitfield, Caldwell	So.	OF	35	119	55	0.462
William Sanders, Shaw	So.	OF	33	120	55	0.458
Tim Battaglia, Minn.-Duluth	Jr.	OF	47	156	71	0.455
Joe Cantone, New Haven	Jr.	3B	39	156	71	0.455

RUNS BATTED IN PER GAME

Minimum 45.

NAME, TEAM	CL	POS	G	RBI	PG
Milton Redd, Shaw	Sr.	INF	35	61	1.74
Mike Clohessy, St. Thomas Aquinas	Sr.	1B	45	78	1.73
Dennis Champagne, Virginia St.	Jr.	OF	36	58	1.61
Zach Norman, Central Mo. St.	Jr.	3B	56	87	1.55
Tim O'Sullivan, C.W. Post	Jr.	1B	31	48	1.55
Carlos Abreu, Concordia (N.Y.)	Sr.	INF	45	67	1.49
Joe Strada, Central Mo. St.	Jr.	OF	58	84	1.45
Mike Aviles, Concordia (N.Y.)	Sr.	SS	45	65	1.44
Pat Parker, Fairmont St.	Sr.	OF	33	46	1.39
Brian Foy, Wayne St. (Neb.)	Sr.	3B	39	54	1.38

DIVISION II INDIVIDUAL LEADERS (CONT.)

EARNED RUN AVERAGE

Minimum 50 innings.
Pitchers must have 1 IP for every game played by team.

NAME, TEAM	CL	POS	APP	IP	R	ER	ERA
Brandon DeJaynes, Quincy	Sr.	SP	15	88.3	9	7	0.71
Anthony Zambotti, Indiana (Pa.)	Sr.	SP	11	64.3	14	8	1.12
Mike Sikorski, Slippery Rock	Sr.	SP/RP	12	77.3	24	13	1.51
Tony Watkins, Columbia Union	Sr.	SP	11	67.0	29	12	1.61
Billy Sittig, Stonehill	Fr.	SP/RP	20	52.3	15	10	1.72
Chris Wright, St. Rose	Sr.	SP	9	57.3	16	11	1.73
Matthew Vanfleet, Florida Tech	So.	RP	33	65.3	18	13	1.79
Steve Norris, Slippery Rock	Jr.	SP	12	74.7	18	15	1.81
Justin Olson, Western Ore.	Sr.	RP	25	59.0	21	12	1.83
Greg Tucker, Pfeiffer	So.	RP	11	63.0	25	13	1.86

STOLEN BASES

Minimum 25.

NAME, TEAM	CL	POS	G	SB	PG
Doug Vroman, New Haven	Sr.	OF	38	50	1.32
T.J. Shimizu, Salem Int'l	Jr.	C	44	47	1.07
Dylan Hetzel, Fairmont St.	Sr.	SS	31	33	1.06
Warren Tyson, Shaw	Jr.	INF	31	33	1.06
Jermaine McDougald, St. Augustine's	Fr.	SP/RP	33	35	1.06
Antoine Tucker, Elizabeth City St.	Jr.	OF	29	29	1.00
Clint Keown, S.C.-Aiken	Sr.	OF	53	52	0.98
Godfrey Burnside, St. Augustine's	Fr.	SP/RP	30	26	0.87
Bobby Pentino, Southern Conn. St.	Jr.	OF	37	30	0.81
Jeff Runyon, Fort Hays St.	Jr.	2B	60	46	0.77

STRIKEOUTS PER NINE INNINGS

Minimum 50 innings
Pitchers must have 1 IP for every game played by team.

RANK	NAME, TEAM	CL	POS	APP	IP	SO	K/9
	Tyrell Moore, Albany St. (Ga.)	So.	SP	15	85.3	126	13.3
	Brandon DeJaynes, Quincy	Sr.	SP	15	88.3	126	12.8
	Dusty Hughes, Delta St.	Jr.	SP/RP	15	67.7	93	12.4
	Steve Strohm, Mercyhurst	Sr.	SP/RP	12	56.3	77	12.3
	Corey Phillips, Assumption	Sr.	SP	11	69.0	94	12.3
	Anthony Zambotti, Indiana (Pa.)	Sr.	SP	11	64.3	81	11.3
	Jeff Wigdahl, St. Mary's (Tex.)	Jr.	SP/RP	17	79.0	99	11.3
	Brian Keating, SIU Edwardsville	Jr.	SP	11	56.3	68	10.9
	Casey Mckenzie, Tampa	Jr.	SP	17	93.7	113	10.9
	Steve Bray, New Haven	Sr.	SP/RP	17	96.3	116	10.8

DIVISION II INDIVIDUAL LEADERS (CONT.)

VICTORIES

NAME, TEAM	CL	POS	APP	IP	W	L	PCT
Eric Beattie, Tampa	So.	SP	20	134.3	15	3	0.833
Kyle Ruwe, Nova Southeastern	So.	SP/RP	18	132.0	13	2	0.867
Skip Weast, Central Okla.	Sr.	SP/RP	16	79.0	12	1	0.923
Jon Dobyns, Armstrong Atlantic	Jr.	SP	16	105.7	12	2	0.857
Travis Osborn, Lynn	So.	SP	15	103.0	12	2	0.857
Adam Bass, Ala.-Huntsville	Jr.	SP	17	86.0	11	2	0.846
Josh Sawyer, West Fla.	Fr.	SP/RP	17	93.3	11	2	0.846
Ryan Thompson, Fla. Southern	Jr.	SP/RP	18	118.0	11	2	0.846
Matt McAlpin, Delta St.	Jr.	SP	15	89.3	11	3	0.786
Tyrell Moore, Albany St. (Ga.)	So.	SP	15	85.3	11	3	0.786

SAVES

NAME, TEAM	CL	POS	APP	IP	SV
Don Clement, Southern Colo.	Jr.	SP/RP	28	47.7	13
Nick Wates, Anderson (S.C.)	Sr.	RP	30	48.3	12
Clark Johnson, Cal St. Chico	Sr.	SP/RP	20	38.7	11
Nate McCabe, Neb.-Omaha	Sr.	SP/RP	22	30.0	11
John Schulz, Lynn	Jr.	RP	20	25.7	10
Philip Springman, Cal St. L.A.	Fr.	RP	21	21.3	10
Michael Laniak, St. Edward's	Jr.	RP	23	27.7	10
Justin Cerrato, North Fla.	Jr.	SP/RP	25	44.0	10
Jeremy Noegel, West Fla.	Sr.	RP	25	47.0	10
Dave Ouellette, Mass.-Lowell	Sr.	RP	17	19.7	9
Matthew Vanfleet, Florida Tech	So.	RP	33	65.3	9

SLUGGING PERCENTAGE

Min. 75 at-bats & 2.5 at-bats per game.

NAME, TEAM	CL	POS	G	AB	TB	SLG PCT
Mike Aviles, Concordia (N.Y.)	Sr.	SS	45	190	193	1.016
Eric Jones, Benedict	Sr.	SP/RP	25	77	69	0.896
Chris Leaf, Northeastern St.	Sr.	1B	47	141	125	0.887
Chad Fox, Southeastern Okla.	Sr.	1B	53	171	151	0.883
Milton Redd, Shaw	Sr.	INF	35	121	106	0.876
Antonio Rutledge, Miles	Sr.	OF	32	103	89	0.864
Dennis Champagne, Virginia St.	Jr.	OF	36	113	96	0.850
Guy O'Connell, Tusculum	Jr.	3B	55	206	175	0.850
Brian Foy, Wayne St. (Neb.)	Sr.	3B	39	143	121	0.846
William Brown, Benedict	Jr.	OF	29	97	82	0.845

WALKS

Minimum 30 bases on balls.

NAME, TEAM	CL	POS	G	BB	PG
Warren Tyson, Shaw	Jr.	INF	31	34	1.10
Carlos Abreu, Concordia (N.Y.)	Sr.	INF	45	47	1.04
Darryl Dixon, Shaw	Sr.	INF	34	33	0.97
Dan Jones, Saginaw Valley	Jr.	INF	42	40	0.95
Travis Anderson, Concordia-St. Paul	Jr.	1B	33	31	0.94
Tim Donnelly, Calif. (Pa.)	Jr.	1B	49	46	0.94
Joe Carola, St. Thomas Aquinas	Sr.	INF	43	40	0.93
Trevor Allen, Northern Colo.	Jr.	OF	55	50	0.91
Mike Sharpe, St. Thomas Aquinas	So.	OF	41	37	0.90
Chris Scott, Barton	Sr.	SP	49	43	0.88

NCAA MEN'S DIVISION III CHAMPIONSHIP GAME BOX SCORE

Game 1: Chapman 15, Christopher Newport 2.

GAME 2

Chapman	0	0 4	2 2	1	5 1	0	**15 24 4**
Chris. Newport	1	1 3	0 2	0	0 0	0	**7 9 0**

W—Akamine. **L**—Bruner. **SV**—none.
LOB—Chapman 10; Chris. Newport 13. **2B**—Chapman: Taylor, Graves, Sanders, Levering; Chris. Newport: Moody. **3B**—Chapman: Van Camp. **HR**—Chapman: Graves; Chris. Newport: Turner. **S**—Chapman: Van Camp 3; Chris. Newport: George. **SB**—Chris. Newport: Elliott 5, Moody. **CS**—none. **HBP**—Chapman: Castillo; Chris. Newport: Turner. **DP**—Chris Newport 4. **T**—3:01. **A**—1,484.

DIVISION III INDIVIDUAL LEADERS

BATTING AVERAGE

Minimum 2.5 at-bats per game. Minimum 75 at-bats.

NAME, TEAM	CL	POS	G	AB	H	BA
Nick Johnson, Ripon	Sr.	OF	38	145	79	0.545
Miguel Jaquez, John Jay	So.	OF	35	124	66	0.532
Kurt Piantek, Trinity (Conn.)	Sr.	2B	39	138	71	0.514
Mark Roth, Delaware Valley	Jr.	INF	33	111	56	0.505
Adam Best, Penn St.-Behrend	Jr.	OF	40	144	71	0.493
Luke Wilson, Fontbonne	Jr.	C	32	123	60	0.488
Matt Moore, Rose-Hulman	Jr.	OF	38	130	63	0.485
Chad Cambra, Bridgewater St.	Sr.	SS	39	151	73	0.483
Geoff Neese, Dickinson	Jr.	SP/RP	25	86	41	0.477
Adam Mandel, Denison	Jr.	OF	43	152	72	0.474

HOME RUNS PER GAME

Minimum 8 home runs.

NAME, TEAM	CL	POS	G	HR	PG
Jose Cortez, Pomona-Pitzer	Sr.	C	39	20	0.51
Kurt Piantek, Trinity (Conn.)	Sr.	2B	39	18	0.46
Aaron Giza, Benedictine (Ill.)	Jr.	INF	46	19	0.41
Josh Ross, LeTourneau	Fr.	SP/RP	39	16	0.41
Daryl Murtha, Salve Regina	Jr.	1B	28	11	0.39
Eric Bell, George Fox	Sr.	1B	44	17	0.39
Vince Mancuso, Wis.-Oshkosh	Sr.	OF	44	17	0.39
Kyle Alberson, Bluffton	Jr.	1B	27	10	0.37
Nick Johnson, Ripon	Sr.	OF	38	14	0.37
Joe Marzano, Hiram	Jr.	OF	30	11	0.37

EARNED RUN AVERAGE

Pitchers must have 1 IP for every game played by team.
Minimum 40 innings pitched.

NAME, TEAM	CL	POS	APP	IP	R	ER	ERA
Chad Cosby, Worcester St.	Sr.	SP	8	56.0	16	6	0.96
Mike Luzim, St. Joseph's (L.I.)	Jr.	SP	10	60.7	16	7	1.04
Derrick Rawlings, Va. Wesleyan	Jr.	SP/RP	9	52.0	14	6	1.04
Joey Serfass, Eastern Conn. St.	Jr.	INF	15	66.7	11	8	1.08
Matt DeSalvo, Marietta	Sr.	SP/RP	18	96.0	20	14	1.31
Paul Basdekis, Mt. St. Mary (N.Y.)	Sr.	SP	15	81.0	24	12	1.33
Jason Jarrett, Va. Wesleyan	Jr.	SP/RP	11	80.0	30	12	1.35
Dan Grybash, Carthage	Jr.	SP	10	65.7	18	10	1.37
Ryan France, Chapman	Sr.	INF	16	110.7	25	17	1.38
Corey Brown, Rowan	Jr.	SP/RP	12	43.3	11	7	1.45

DIVISION III INDIVIDUAL LEADERS (CONT.)

STOLEN BASES

Minimum 20 stolen bases.

NAME, TEAM	CL	POS	G	SB	PG
Carlos Hardaway, Rust..................Fr.		INF	33	50	1.52
James Hymon, Rust ....Sr.		SS	33	43	1.30
Jeremy Elliott, Chris. Newport.......Sr.		OF	44	54	1.23
Brad Henry, Hendrix.......................Sr.		INF	37	44	1.19
Tim Reinhardt, Vassar ....Jr.		OF	33	39	1.18
Justin Graf, Muhlenberg ....Sr.		OF	35	41	1.17
Angel Melendez, Old Westbury.....Jr.		INF	37	42	1.14
Nick Hagler, Chowan ....So.		OF	39	42	1.08
Miguel Jaquez, John Jay...............So.		OF	35	35	1.00
Jason Arraiol, Bridgewater St. ....Jr.		2B	38	37	0.97

STRIKEOUTS PER NINE INNINGS

Pitchers must have 1 IP for every game played by team.
Minimum 40 innings pitched.

NAME, TEAM	CL	POS	APP	IP	SO	K/9
Matt DeSalvo, Marietta..Sr.		SP/RP	18	96.0	157	14.7
Luke Deihl, Penn St.-Altoona ....Sr.		SP	9	56.3	81	12.9
Carl Rivers, Western Conn. St. ....Sr.		SP	20	69.7	100	12.9
Steve Plucinski, Lakeland.....................................So.		SP/RP	13	77.7	111	12.9
Nick Secchini, Staten Island ....So.		SP	10	62.7	88	12.6
Cory Schultz, Loras ....Sr.		SP/RP	16	69.3	95	12.3
Forrest Martin, Southwestern (Tex.)....................Sr.		SP	13	76.3	104	12.3
Josh Sharpless, Allegheny ....Sr.		SP/RP	10	63.7	84	11.9
Dustin Jones, Bridgewater (Va.)...........................Jr.		SP/RP	17	77.3	101	11.8
Jason Hirsh, Cal Lutheran ....Jr.		SP	15	100.3	126	11.3

JOY IN MUDVILLE

DAVID BERGMAN

[UCONN]

With 100 Teams, a deejay and an official T-shirt for alll participants, UConn's spring coed "oozeball" tournament is a daylong blast— and an escape from the sad realization that the Huskies' basketball season is over.

DIVISION III INDIVIDUAL LEADERS (CONT.)

VICTORIES

NAME, TEAM	CL	POS	APP	IP	W	L	PCT
Matt DeSalvo, Marietta	Sr.	SP/RP	18	96.0	13	2	0.867
Tyler Mott, Ohio Wesleyan	Jr.	SP/RP	15	91.3	12	1	0.923
Jordan Timm, Wis.-Oshkosh	Jr.	SP	15	77.3	11	0	1.000
Scott Hyde, George Fox	So.	SP	15	100.7	11	1	0.917
David Reece, Methodist	Sr.	SP	25	86.7	11	1	0.917
Paul Basdekis, Mt. St. Mary (N.Y.)	Sr.	SP	15	81.0	11	2	0.846
Mike Beck, George Fox	Jr.	SP	14	87.0	10	0	1.000
Will Carr, Emory	So.	SP/RP	24	65.7	10	0	1.000
Josh Schwartz, Rowan	So.	SP	15	90.7	10	0	1.000
Kevin Tomasiewicz, Wis.-Whitewater	So.	SP/RP	12	70.3	10	0	1.000
Ryan DiPietro, Eastern Conn. St.	Fr.	SP/RP	12	75.0	10	1	0.909
Ryan France, Chapman	Sr.	INF	16	110.7	10	1	0.909
Chema Chavez, Concordia-Austin	Jr.	SP/RP	13	78.7	10	2	0.833
Joey Matis, Hanover	Sr.	SP/RP	15	98.7	10	3	0.769
Greg Cauble, Anderson (Ind.)	Sr.	SP/RP	19	111.0	10	4	0.714

SAVES

NAME, TEAM	CL	POS	APP	IP	SV
Teddy Grothe, Augustana (Ill.)	Sr.	RP	23	27.3	12
Matt Slivinski, Albright	Sr.	OF	12	12.0	11
Ryan Adams, Southern Me.	Sr.	SP	24	39.7	11
Derek Dormanen, Concordia-M'head	Sr.	SS	22	40.3	10
Brandon Manuel, Chowan	Jr.	SP/RP	24	48.3	9
Michael Idol, Guilford	Jr.	RP	25	36.7	9
Ben Thorpe, Heidelberg	Fr.	SP/RP	27	50.3	9
Jason Brown, Chris. Newport	So.	SP/RP	21	41.0	8
Alan Engelhardt, Greenville	Sr.	SP/RP	23	87.7	8
Clint Williams, Anderson (Ind.)	Fr.	SP/RP	24	47.7	8

SLUGGING PERCENTAGE

Min. 75 at-bats & 2.5 at-bats per game.

RANK	NAME, TEAM	CL	POS	G	AB	TB	SLG PCT
	Kurt Piantek, Trinity (Conn.)	Sr.	2B	39	138	135	0.978
	Nick Johnson, Ripon	Sr.	OF	38	145	141	0.972
	Jose Cortez, Pomona-Pitzer	Sr.	C	39	141	132	0.936
	Vince Mancuso, WI-Oshkosh	Sr.	OF	44	155	144	0.929
	Miguel Jaquez, John Jay	So.	OF	35	124	115	0.927
	Nigel Archibald, Centenary (N.J.)	So.	OF	24	81	75	0.926
	Mark Roth, Delaware Valley	Jr.	INF	33	111	101	0.910
	Ryan Carr, Manchester	Jr.	1B	42	135	122	0.904
	Geoff Neese, Dickinson	Jr.	SP/RP	25	86	77	0.895
	Bear Dunn, Worcester St.	Jr.	INF	34	109	95	0.872

CHAMPIONSHIP RESULTS

DIVISION I

YEAR	CHAMPION	COACH	SCORE	RUNNER-UP	MOST OUTSTANDING PLAYER
1947	California*	Clint Evans	8–7	Yale	No award
1948	Southern Cal	Sam Barry	9–2	Yale	No award
1949	Texas*	Bibb Falk	10–3	Wake Forest	Charles Teague, Wake Forest, 2B
1950	Texas	Bibb Falk	3–0	Washington St	Ray VanCleef, Rutgers, CF
1951	Oklahoma*	Jack Baer	3–2	Tennnessee	Sidney Hatfield, Tennessee, P-1B
1952	Holy Cross	Jack Barry	8–4	Missouri	James O'Neill, Holy Cross, P
1953	Michigan	Ray Fisher	7–5	Texas	J.L. Smith, Texas, P
1954	Missouri	John (Hi) Simmons	4–1	Rollins	Tom Yewcic, Michigan St, C
1955	Wake Forest	Taylor Sanford	7–6	Western Michigan	Tom Borland, Oklahoma St, P
1956	Minnesota	Dick Siebert	12–1	Arizona	Jerry Thomas, Minnesota, P
1957	California*	George Wolfman	1–0	Penn St	Cal Emery, Penn St, P-1B
1958	Southern Cal	Rod Dedeaux	8–7†	Missouri	Bill Thom, Southern Cal, P
1959	Oklahoma St	Toby Greene	5–3	Arizona	Jim Dobson, Oklahoma St, 3B
1960	Minnesota	Dick Siebert	2–1‡	Southern Cal	John Erickson, Minnesota, 2B
1961	Southern Cal*	Rod Dedeaux	1–0	Oklahoma St	Littleton Fowler, Oklahoma St, P
1962	Michigan	Don Lund	5–4	Santa Clara	Bob Garibaldi, Santa Clara, P
1963	Southern Cal	Rod Dedeaux	5–2	Arizona	Bud Hollowell, Southern Cal, C
1964	Minnesota	Dick Siebert	5–1	Missouri	Joe Ferris, Maine, P
1965	Arizona St	Bobby Winkles	2–1#	Ohio St	Sal Bando, Arizona St, 3B
1966	Ohio St	Marty Karow	8–2	Oklahoma St	Steve Arlin, Ohio St, P
1967	Arizona St	Bobby Winkles	11–2	Houston	Ron Davini, Arizona St, C
1968	Southern Cal*	Rod Dedeaux	4–3	Southern Illinois	Bill Seinsoth, Southern Cal, 1B
1969	Arizona St	Bobby Winkles	10–1	Tulsa	John Dolinsek, Arizona St, LF
1970	Southern Cal	Rod Dedeaux	2–1	Florida St	Gene Ammann, Florida St, P
1971	Southern Cal	Rod Dedeaux	7–2	Southern Illinois	Jerry Tabb, Tulsa, 1B
1972	Southern Cal	Rod Dedeaux	1–0	Arizona St	Russ McQueen, Southern Cal, P
1973	Southern Cal*	Rod Dedeaux	4–3	Arizona St	Dave Winfield, Minnesota, P-OF
1974	Southern Cal	Rod Dedeaux	7–3	Miami (FL)	George Milke, Southern Cal, P
1975	Texas	Cliff Gustafson	5–1	S Carolina	Mickey Reichenbach, Texas, 1B
1976	Arizona	Jerry Kindall	7–1	Eastern Michigan	Steve Powers, Arizona, P-DH
1977	Arizona St	Jim Brock	2–1	S Carolina	Bob Horner, Arizona St, 3B
1978	Southern Cal*	Rod Dedeaux	10–3	Arizona St	Rod Boxberger, Southern Cal, P
1979	Cal St–Fullerton	Augie Garrido	2–1	Arkansas	Tony Hudson, Cal St–Fullerton, P
1980	Arizona	Jerry Kindall	5–3	Hawaii	Terry Francona, Arizona, LF
1981	Arizona St	Jim Brock	7–4	Oklahoma St	Stan Holmes, Arizona St, LF
1982	Miami (FL)*	Ron Fraser	9–3	Wichita St	Dan Smith, Miami (FL), P
1983	Texas*	Cliff Gustafson	4–3	Alabama	Calvin Schiraldi, Texas, P
1984	Cal St–Fullerton	Augie Garrido	3–1	Texas	John Fishel, Cal St–Fullerton, LF
1985	Miami (FL)	Ron Fraser	10–6	Texas	Greg Ellena, Miami (FL), DH
1986	Arizona	Jerry Kindall	10–2	Florida St	Mike Senne, Arizona, LF
1987	Stanford	Mark Marquess	9–5	Oklahoma St	Paul Carey, Stanford, RF
1988	Stanford	Mark Marquess	9–4	Arizona St	Lee Plemel, Stanford, P
1989	Wichita St	Gene Stephenson	5–3	Texas	Greg Brummett, Wichita St, P
1990	Georgia	Steve Webber	2–1	Oklahoma St	Mike Rebhan, Georgia, P
1991	Louisiana St	Skip Bertman	6–3	Wichita St	Gary Hymel, Louisiana St, C
1992	Pepperdine	Andy Lopez	3–2	Cal St–Fullerton	Phil Nevin, Cal St–Fullerton, 3B

CHAMPIONSHIP RESULTS (CONT.)

DIVISION I (CONT.)

YEAR	CHAMPION	COACH	SCORE	RUNNER-UP	MOST OUTSTANDING PLAYER
1993	Louisiana St	Skip Bertman	8–0	Wichita St	Todd Walker, Louisiana St, 2B
1994	Oklahoma	Larry Cochell	13–5	Georgia Tech	Chip Glass, Oklahoma, CF
1995	Cal St–Fullerton*	Augie Garrido	11–5	Southern Cal	Mark Kotsay, Cal St–Fullerton, CF-P
1996	Louisiana St*	Skip Bertman	9–8	Miami (FL)	Pat Burrell, Miami (FL), 3B
1997	Louisiana St*	Skip Bertman	13–6	Alabama	Brandon Larson, Louisiana St, SS
1998	Southern Cal	Mike Gillespie	21–14	Arizona St	Wes Rachels, Southern Cal, 2B
1999	Miami (FL)	Jim Morris	6–5	Florida St	Marshall McDougall, FSU 3B/2B
2000	Louisiana St*	Skip Bertman	6–5	Stanford	Trey Hodges, Louisiana St, P
2001	Miami (FL)*	Jim Morris	12–1	Stanford	Charlton Jimerson, Miami (FL), OF
2002	Texas	Augie Garrido	12–6	S Carolina	Huston Street, Texas, P
2003	Rice	Wayne Graham	2–1●	Stanford	John Hudgins, Stanford, P

*Undefeated teams in College World Series play. †12 innings. ‡10 innings. #15 innings ●Score in games of three-game series.

GO FIGURE

58 Consecutive games with a hit by Oklahoma State sophomore Robin Ventura in 1987, the longest hitting streak in the history of Division I baseball.

60 Consecutive games with a hit by Damian Costantino of Division III Salve Regina (Newport, R.I.) in 2003, the longest streak in the history of college baseball. Shortly after his streak ended, Costantino met with and was congratulated by Ventura, now a member of the New York Yankees, at New York's spring training camp in Tampa.

30 Trips to the College World Series by the University of Texas Longhorns, more than any other school. Only two other programs, USC (21) and Miami (20), have made as many as 20 trips to the championship tournament.

23 Number of winners of the Golden Spikes Award, given annually to the best player in College Baseball, that have reached the Major Leagues. The award has been bestowed 25 times—the two winners who never made it to the big leagues are 1982 winner Augie Schmidt of the University of New Orleans, and 2000 winner Kip Bougknight of South Carolina, who is still playing in the minor leagues.

.495 Batting average in 2002 for Southern University's Rickie Weeks, the highest single-season average in college baseball since 1991, when Ron Dziezgowski of Duquesne hit .500. Weeks was selected second overall in the 2003 major league amateur draft by the Milwaukee Brewers.

CHAMPIONSHIP RESULTS (CONT.)

DIVISION II

YEAR	CHAMPION
1968	Chapman*
1969	Illinois St*
1970	Cal St-Northridge
1971	Florida Southern
1972	Florida Southern
1973	UC-Irvine*
1974	UC-Irvine
1975	Florida Southern
1976	Cal Poly-Pomona
1977	UC-Riverside
1978	Florida Southern
1979	Valdosta St
1980	Cal Poly-Pomona*
1981	Florida Southern*
1982	UC-Riverside*
1983	Cal Poly-Pomona*
1984	Cal St-Northridge
1985	Florida Southern*

YEAR	CHAMPION
1986	Troy St
1987	Troy St*
1988	Florida Southern*
1989	Cal Poly-SLO
1990	Jacksonville St
1991	Jacksonville St
1992	Tampa*
1993	Tampa
1994	Central Missouri St
1995	Florida Southern*
1996	Kennesaw St*
1997	Cal St-Chico*
1998	Tampa*
1999	Cal St-Chico
2000	SE Oklahoma St
2001	St. Mary's (TX)
2002	Columbus St

DIVISION III

YEAR	CHAMPION
1976	Cal St-Stanislaus
1977	Cal St-Stanislaus
1978	Glassboro St
1979	Glassboro St
1980	Ithaca
1981	Marietta
1982	Eastern Connecticut St
1983	Marietta
1984	Ramapo
1985	WI-Oshkosh
1986	Marietta
1987	Montclair St
1988	Ithaca
1989	NC Wesleyan

YEAR	CHAMPION
1990	Eastern Connecticut St
1991	Southern Maine
1992	William Paterson
1993	Montclair St
1994	WI-Oshkosh
1995	La Verne
1996	William Paterson
1997	Southern Maine
1998	Eastern Connecticut St
1999	N Carolina Wesleyan
2000	Montclair St
2001	St. Thomas (MN)
2002	Eastern Connecticut St

*Undefeated teams in final series.

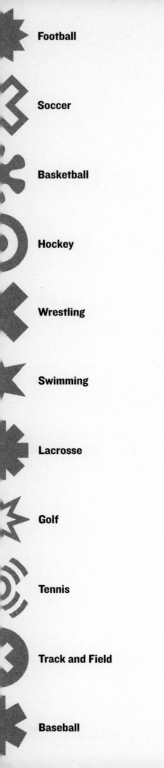

Football

Soccer

Basketball

Hockey

Wrestling

Swimming

Lacrosse

Golf

Tennis

Track and Field

Baseball